Foundations of Kierkegaard's Vision of Community

Foundations of Kierkegaard's Vision of Community

RELIGION, ETHICS, AND POLITICS IN KIERKEGAARD

Edited by
GEORGE B. CONNELL
and
C. STEPHEN EVANS

Humanities Press
New Jersey ▼ London

First published 1992 by Humanities Press International, Inc.
Atlantic Highlands, New Jersey 07716, and
3 Henrietta Street, Covent Garden, London WC2E 8LU

©This collection 1992 by Humanities Press International, Inc.
©1992 by the individual authors

Library of Congress Cataloging-in-Publication Data
Foundations of Kierkegaard's vision of community : religion, ethics,
  and politics in Kierkegaard / edited by George B. Connell and C.
  Stephen Evans.
       p.   cm.
  Includes bibliographical references and index.
  ISBN 0-391-03724-2
  1. Kierkegaard, Søren, 1813–1855—Ethics. 2. Kierkegaard, Søren,
1813–1855—Political and social views. 3. Self (Philosophy).
4. Philosophy and religion. 5. Political science—Philosophy.
6. Ethics, Modern—19th century. I. Connell, George, 1957–
II. Evans, C. Stephen.
B4378.E8F68 1992
198.9—dc20   91-9137
                                                 CIP

A catalog record for this book is available from the British Library.

All rights reserved. No part of this book may be reproduced
or transmitted, in any form or by any means, without written
permission from the publisher.

Printed in the United States of America

Contents

Introduction   vii

PART I   THE RELIGIOUS VISION

1. Kierkegaard the Theologian: The Roots of His Theology in *Works of Love*   2
   Michael Plekon

2. Who Sets the Task? Kierkegaard on Authority   18
   Stephen N. Dunning

3. Ordeal and Repetition in Kierkegaard's Treatment of Abraham and Job   33
   Mark Lloyd Taylor

PART II   ETHICS

4. Judge William's Theonomous Ethics   56
   George B. Connell

5. Getting Isaac Back: Ordeals and Reconciliations in *Fear and Trembling*   71
   Edward Mooney

6. Subjectivity and World in *Works of Love*   96
   Louise Carroll Keeley

PART III   SOCIAL AND POLITICAL THOUGHT

7. Kierkegaard's Teleological Suspension of Religiousness B   110
   Merold Westphal

8. Don Quixote and Kierkegaard's Understanding of the Single   130
   Individual in Society
   Eric J. Ziolkowski

9. *The Sickness unto Death*: A Social Interpretation   144
   Stephen Crites

10. Call Me Ishmael—Call Everybody Ishmael: Kierkegaard on the 161
    Coming-of-Age Crisis of Modern Times
    Bruce Kirmmse

11. Politics and Religion in Kierkegaard's Thought: Secularization 183
    and the Martyr
    Michele Nicoletti

12. Finally Forgiveness: Kierkegaard as a "Springboard" for a   196
    Feminist Theology of Reform
    Wanda Warren Berry

13. Toward a Kierkegaardian Understanding of Hitler, Stalin,
    and the Cold War   218
    Charles Bellinger

Index   231

About the Authors   245

Introduction

> With all his thought and soul, to the last drop of blood, [Hamann] is concentrated in a single word, the passionate protest of a highly gifted genius against an existential system. But the System is hospitable; poor Hamann, you have been reduced to a paragraph by Michelet. . . . Poor Jacobi! Whether anyone visits your grave I do not know, but I know that the paragraph machine plows all your eloquence, all your inwardness under, while a scant few words are registered in the System as your significance.
> Kierkegaard, *Concluding Unscientific Postscript*
> translated by David F. Swenson and Walter Lowrie

Kierkegaard undoubtedly anticipated that, in time, he, like those unfortunates, Hamann and Jacobi, would also be plowed under by the "paragraph machine." That is, he both feared and expected that his challenges to the speculative, systematic philosophical stance of Hegelianism and the corollary social and religious phenomenon of Christendom would shortly be acknowledged as "relatively valid" and so duly entered as paragraphs in a new and improved version of the system.

History has borne him out. Since his emergence in this century as a major philosophical and theological voice, Kierkegaard has routinely been categorized as the quintessential proponent of irrationality and individualism. For decades one could consistently find such a picture of Kierkegaard in everything from undergraduate compendia to specialized monographs.[1] In recent years, however, both of these labels have come under challenge as misleadingly partial and undialectical. As regards the charge of irrationality, recent scholarship has allowed more nuanced appreciations of his view of faith and reason by calling into question the assumption that by "paradox" Kierkegaard means a logical contradiction.[2] But however his notion of it is finally construed, Kierkegaard's use of paradox as a central category in his account of Christian faith makes no sense apart from a deep and abiding commitment to rationality; only in tension with such a commitment can the Paradox generate in the believer the passion Kierkegaard describes as essential to true faith.

While charges of Kierkegaard's irrationalism have come uniformly from the unsympathetic, many of those deeply drawn to his thought have been troubled by what is widely taken to be his asocial individualism.[3] Martin

Buber's essay, "The Question of the Single One," is probably the most poignant expression of such ambivalence. Buber embraces enthusiastically Kierkegaard's notion that God calls "the single one" (*hiin Enkelte*) out from absorption in the crowd, the "we" that is really a self-absolutizing and other-denying "Group-I." But Buber protests what he sees as Kierkegaard's construal of the God-relationship as exclusive and incompatible with real relations to earthly others.

> This relation [to God] is an exclusive one, the exclusive one, and this, according to Kierkegaard, means that it is the excluding relation, excluding all others; more precisely, that it is the relation which in virtue of its unique, essential life drives all other relations into the realm of the inessential.[4]

Drawing almost exclusively on Kierkegaard's journal entries on his broken engagement to Regine Olsen and on the two notes concerning "The Individual" appended to *The Point of View for My Work as an Author*, Buber raises the charge of acosmism (either a refusal to believe in the reality of the world or, as in Buber's use, an absence of concern for and involvement with the world).

Robert Perkins has spoken usefully to the immediate sources of Buber's reading of Kierkegaard as an acosmic individualist,[5] but many readers have reached essentially the same conclusion as Buber on the basis of a much broader survey of Kierkegaard's writings. Of these, Mark C. Taylor is one of the best known and most persistent. First in *Kierkegaard's Pseudonymous Authorship* and later in *Journeys to Selfhood*, Taylor takes Kierkegaard to task precisely on the grounds of excessive emphasis on separate individuality.

> Kierkegaard is convinced that when spirit is so conceived, the journey to selfhood cannot culminate in spiritual community but must be a solitary sojourn that separates self from other. . . . [He] asserts that "to become spirit means to become the single individual [*den Enkelte*]; isolation is a conditio sine qua non, an indispensable condition. Since identity does not arise from internal relation with otherness, but is a function of contrast with or opposition to otherness, "spirit is exactly this: not to be like others." The Kierkegaardian "formula for authentic selfhood" constantly is: "individual in opposition to the others." Rather than forming concrete selfhood, social relations abrogate unique individuality. . . . Kierkegaard argues that "this precisely is spirit, that everyone is an individual before God, that 'community' [*Fælledsskab*] is a lower category than 'the single individual,' which everyone can and should be.[6]

Buber, Taylor, and the many others who share their view of Kierkegaard as a radical individualist call not for the simple rejection of Kierkegaard but instead for a correction of his correction of his age. Buber speaks for them all when he writes, "We have much to learn from [Kierkegaard], but not the final lesson."[7] Opinions as to the source of the finalizing correction vary. Buber points repeatedly to Luther (who married his Katharina) and even to Kierkegaard's own creation, Judge William. Hellmut Toftdahl expresses a widespread Danish view of Kierkegaard and N. F. S. Grundtvig as personal symbols of individualism and communalism, respectively, when he writes that while "the way to the Grundtvigian lies through Kierkegaard's process of individuation," to stop with Kierkegaard is to fall prey to the "close reserve" (*Indesluttethed*) that Kierkegaard himself described as demonic and despairing.[8] Surely, however, most writers who propose communal correctives to Kierkegaard's individualism join Taylor in looking to Hegel for a thoroughly developed articulation of human sociability.[9]

Just as Kierkegaard has not been without defenders against the charge of irrationality, a number of writers have recently challenged the pervasive construal of Kierkegaard as a proponent of asocial individualism. John Elrod's *Kierkegaard and Christendom* undertakes to read Kierkegaard's "second authorship" (the series of primarily religious works written after 1846 under his own name) specifically as a response to the modernization of Denmark. Merold Westphal's *Kierkegaard's Critique of Reason and Society* uncovers a politically pointed ideology critique in the pseudonymous authorship as well as in later works. The breadth of this new sensitivity to the social and political aspects of Kierkegaard's thought is, however, best indicated by the many articles in the *International Kierkegaard Commentary* series that take such a tack.[10] The depth of our sense of how involved Kierkegaard was with his social and political context has, in turn, been markedly improved by the publication of Bruce Kirmmse's *Kierkegaard in Golden Age Denmark*. Kirmmse's detailed account and analysis of that context allow us to appreciate dimensions of Kierkegaard's thought that have hitherto been the special province of Danish scholars.

And, in fact, Danes have made some of the most important contributions to the recent rediscovery of the social and political side of Kierkegaard. Especially noteworthy are Kresten Nordentoft's *Hvad Siger Brand Majoren? Kierkegaard's Opgør med sin Samtid*, and Johannes Sløk's *Da Kierkegaard Tav: Fra Forfatterskab til Kirkestorm*. Sløk writes:

> The point of departure for Kierkegaard is that there exists an at once primary and dialectical relationship between the individual and society. It is meaningless to discuss the individual without reference to the society of which he or she is a member. And it is meaningless to discuss society in a purely abstract way by failing to recognize that society only exists in the ways its constituent individual members live their lives. As formal concepts, individual and society belong inextricably together. This means that the individual receives his or her content as individual from that society to which he or she has belonged since birth. Conversely, society

receives its content from the individuals that make it up. The point of departure for Kierkegaard's thought is in other words a primary, tension-filled reality to which we can well refer as individual/society. . . .

People have thought in terms of a tension between one content, the individual, and another content, the society, and have understood Kierkegaard's thought as an attempt to rescue the individual out of society's smothering grasp, as an individualized, subjective philosophy's proclamation that the existential task for the individual is to isolate oneself from the "social," to become "that single individual," to realize oneself, to choose oneself, to pull oneself back into the inner regions of the soul where one can be oneself unmolested by anything external. And there to cultivate a relation with God. In eternal solitude.

This reading of Kierkegaard is just as fundamentally as it is fatally mistaken.[11]

This is not the place to rehearse Sløk's argument for this claim. Instead, as a complementary effort to dispel simplistic misreadings and to identify the social, communal, and political dimensions of Kierkegaard's thought, we offer the following essays originally delivered at a gathering of philosophers, theologians, biblical scholars, literary critics, sociologists, and historians sponsored by the Howard V. and Edna H. Hong Kierkegaard Library at St. Olaf College in June 1988. Although the conference title was "Kierkegaard as Religious Thinker," the themes of community, ethics, and politics quickly and clearly emerged as central to many of the offerings. This shared concern is especially striking given that the essays focus on a wide variety of Kierkegaardian texts and employ quite different methodologies. While not all of the essays directly state an intention to correct asocial (or even acosmic) readings of Kierkegaard, each brings to light some dimension of the neglected social and communal aspects of his thought as well as addressing in detail a specific aspect of the authorship. It is our hope that together they constitute an even more effective correction to previous misinterpretations than they would severally.

Within the broad sensitivity to the communal dimension of Kierkegaard's thoughts shared by all the essays, several more specific groupings emerged. Accordingly, we have divided the collection into three sections: "The Religious Vision," "Ethics," and "Social and Political Thought," respectively.

By beginning with three articles directly addressing Kierkegaard as a religious thinker, we affirm that Kierkegaard's thoughts about community, as most of his thoughts, are fundamentally grounded in and shaped by his religious commitments. Establishing the profoundly communal character of those convictions is precisely the project undertaken in the collection's first essay, Michael Plekon's "Kierkegaard the Theologian: The Roots of

His Theology in *Works of Love*." There is a double appropriateness to opening this collection with Plekon's contribution. First, over the last decade, Plekon has authored numerous articles challenging the accepted view of Kierkegaard as an asocial and apolitical individualist.[12] Second, and more fundamental, Kierkegaard himself names *Works of Love* as the text best suited to correcting simplistic asocial readings of his works:

> In spite of everything men ought to have learned about my maieutic carefulness, in addition to proceeding slowly and continually letting it seem as if I knew nothing more, not the next thing—now on the occasion of my new Edifying Discourses they will presumably bawl out that I do not know what comes next, that I know nothing about sociality. The fools! Yet on the other hand I owe it to myself to confess before God that in a certain sense there is some truth in it, only not as men understand it, namely that always when I have first presented one aspect sharply and clearly, then I affirm the validity of the other even more strongly. Now I have the theme of the next book. It will be called *Works of Love*.[13]

Though Plekon asserts that a positive communal vision is to be found in all of the late religious writings, even the attack on the church, he agrees with Kierkegaard that *Works of Love* serves as a corrective in bringing to the center themes that are relatively less emphasized or even dialectically marginalized elsewhere. Furthermore, Plekon argues that the theological vision expressed in *Works of Love* shows Kierkegaard himself as standing squarely within the Christian tradition and community of faith rather than hovering in splendid isolation as some sort of "superprotestant." While we find ourselves wondering whether he doesn't overstate his case by making Kierkegaard sound more irenic and Catholic than he really is, Plekon represents an important corrective to the widespread tendency to divorce Kierkegaard's critical pronouncements from their positive theological background and basis. Plekon succeeds in showing that Kierkegaard's thoughts about community grow directly out of a positive religious vision that is rooted in the fundamental doctrinal affirmations of the Church: the goodness of creation, the triune character of God, and the significance of the sacraments. It is in thus standing with and in the Church that Plekon sees Kierkegaard truly earning the title "theologian," that is, "one who truly prays, who is in communion with God and who speaks of the God with whom he talks in the community of the Church."

But by what authority does any mere human proclaim God's will and word to the community of faith within which he or she stands? Stephen Dunning's "Who Sets the Task? Kierkegaard on Authority" takes up this question by way of an analysis of two metatheological texts, *On Authority and Revelation* and "Of the Difference between a Genius and an Apostle." These texts grew out of Kierkegaard's lengthy and intense reflection on the case of Adolph Adler, a Lutheran pastor on the Danish island of Bornholm, who claimed to be the bearer of a special revelation from God. Kierkegaard took this opportunity to make explicit the consequences already implicit in the writings under the pseudonym Johannes Climacus. Given that Christianity holds that the learner is radically alien to the truth to be learned (in contrast to the Socratic view, which holds that the truth lies within the learner, waiting for recovery by way of recollection), the learner must accept on faith a communication he or she cannot independently verify. But by denying the human capacity to verify the message or even the credentials of the messenger, doesn't Kierkegaard deprive himself (and us) of any basis on which to dismiss the ravings of the Adlers (and Jim and Tammye Bakers) of this world?

While Kierkegaard does try to provide a set of criteria for discerning the self-incrimination of false prophets, Dunning sees the fundamental significance of these texts in their rethinking of the category of authority itself. As he points out in the opening of his essay, authority is today widely perceived as inherently authoritarian. Kierkegaard's talk of the prophet as the authoritative deliverer of a paradoxical message seems initially to be a reduction to absurdity of the idea of authority; it appears to leave the recipient of such a message in the unenviable position of either making a solitary, irrational leap of faith in accepting the message or else drawing away, scandalized. Dunning argues that this reading of Kierkegaard is a caricature. The truth is that Kierkegaard portrays the authority of the message as deriving from faith, that is the presence of God in and to the recipient of the message.

> It is here, in the concept of "presence," that the key to divine authority is to be found. An apostle's message is always the same and yet always new and fresh, because the apostle is a person who lives on the basis of his relationship with God in the present. "Presence" is both temporal—meaning not merely past or future—and relational: in the present, the apostle lives in the *presence* of God.

That is, authority is not the basis of faith. Rather, that basis is faith's own reception of the ever surprising and new words God speaks to it through God's appointed messengers, the prophets. It is the immanence, the felt presence of God that validates for the believer the apostle's message. Rather than an irrational, solitary leap by an anxious individual, the recognition of authority grows directly out of just the features of Kierkegaard's theology that Plekon terms "incarnational optimism": a sense of God's presence in the good creation, in Christ, and in the Eucharistic elements. The pseudonyms who do present faith as such a solitary, irrational, anxious leap, preeminently Johannes de Silentio and Johannes Climacus, describe the life of faith from *without*. Accordingly, they could not be expected to experience the presence of God that validates as authoritative the paradoxical communications of the Christian faith. Dunning's essay clearly raises questions as to the epistemological significance of religious experience for Kierkegaard even as it clarifies for us his understanding of the nature of authority.[14]

The severest test of the revisionist portraits Plekon and Dunning paint of Kierkegaard as a nonauthoritarian affirmer of community is quite probably *Fear and Trembling*. Johannes de Silentio's paean to Abraham, after all, is persistently read as depicting the believer as a self sundered from all human communication as a result of a decision to obey blindly a divine decree contravening the most basic standards of human community.[15] Mark Lloyd Taylor's "Ordeal and Repetition in Kierkegaard's Treatment of Abraham and Job" calls just that interpretation into question. Taylor argues that the key to a correct reading of *Fear and Trembling* is the simultaneously published but largely ignored *Repetition*. Taylor finds the ties between *Repetition* and *Fear and Trembling* in the dialectic of loss and recovery, of renunciation and reacceptance, common to the stories of Job and Abraham explored in the two books. Rather than identifying faith with worldless isolation, as critics suggest, Taylor shows that Kierkegaard uses his pseudonyms to delineate a faith that leads the believer beyond the sublime solitude of the knight of infinite resignation to the full involvement with the world that characterizes the knight of faith. Taylor suggests that the teleological suspension of the ethical in which the individual stands *qua* individual outside the universal before God is an analogical figure for the human condition of sin. Where the righteous Job and Abraham are called out of the universal (the ethical) as a trial, we stand outside the ethical through the demonic suspension of the ethical that goes with sin. On this reading, faith is not a celebration of autistic solitude but the restitution beyond all reasonable expectation of communion with God and hence with other humans through a return to the universal in the form of a second ethics (that is, an ethic in which one's relations to the universal is mediated by one's direct relation to God rather than vice versa).

As diverse as their subject matter is, each of these three essays in the first section displays close attention to the dialectic of immanence and transcendence in Kierkegaard's religious thought. Kierkegaard has always been known as a philosopher of transcendence. No plausible interpretations of his thought can overlook that dimension of his thought. Kierkegaard's God is an "utterly other" God; God's authoritative revelations are paradoxical, that is, radically other than that which arises in the hearts and minds of humans; faith in this God is all-consuming, it is an absolute relation to the absolute that relativizes all relations to the world. But what these three essays show is that Kierkegaard always keeps God's transcendence in dialectical tension with God's immanence. Plekon's emphasis on "incarnational optimism," Dunning's uncovering of the basis of authority in God's presence to the believer, Taylor's interpretation of faith as a recovery of relations with God and the world, together show that transcendence is always dialectically linked for Kierkegaard to life *in* this world, *with* other people.

The three essays of the second section further develop this characteristic Kierkegaardian dialectic of transcendence and immanence, separateness and continuity, by examining some of its ethical implications. George Connell challenges Kantian readings of the letters by Judge William that make up *Either/Or II*. In the process, he calls into question the notion that Kierkegaard's ethical stage is grounded in a radically autonomous and so inescapably solitary choice of self. Taking seriously the Judge's claim to be offering only glosses on Bishop Balle's catechism, Connell sees in the letters a theonomous and therefore essentially relational ethic. On his reading of *Either/Or II*, the ethical self cuts all of its immediate ties to the world as it becomes conscious of and accepts its status as existing responsibly *coram deo* (before God), but this moment of withdrawal (despair) is immediately complemented by a return to complete involvement in and with the world (and with the others we meet there) as the given which is task (*Opgave*) because it is a gift (*Gave*) of God.

While *Fear and Trembling* clearly challenges Judge William's attempted assimilation of the ethical and the religious, Edward Mooney's "Getting Isaac Back: Ordeals and Reconciliations in *Fear and Trembling*" traces in it the same dialectic of renunciation and reacceptance Connell discerns in *Either/Or II*. Unquestionably, what is renounced and reaccepted differs markedly between *Either/Or II* and *Fear and Trembling*. In the former, the self renounces and reacquires its immediacy, its concrete particularity, in coming to exist ethically, in placing itself under the universal. In the latter, on the other hand, Johannes de Silentio describes Abraham's terrifying renunciation of the universal itself in his obedient response to God's teleological suspension of the ethical. But Mooney, like Mark Lloyd Taylor in his earlier article, laments the way the vast majority of interpreters of *Fear and Trembling* have so emphasized the aspect of renunciation and suspension that they have neglected what is said of restoration and reassertion. Where critics have heard in Kierkegaard's dialectical lyric "a rash and irrational impugnment of all ethics in the name of Absolute Obedience to Divine Command," Mooney suggests that "Ethics is not just set aside [in a teleological suspension] but revised, enlarged to include the proper spirit in which the universal is to be embraced."[16] That is, in its encounter with the Absolute, the self becomes aware that the social and cultural conventions by which it has lived are not self-validating. This encounter thereby frees the self from an assimilationist ethic to go about the task of realizing itself as an individual in the full and responsible sense of the term. But while this self wins a critical distance on those conventions, it cannot simply abandon its language, tradition, and culture without falling into impotent, mute madness. Similarly, the knight of faith may continue to act according to the ethical conventions of his or her society even after facing the fact that those conventions are not absolute or unquestionable; he or she may even be indistinguishable from a tax collector. Mooney's essay is a bold one in that he puts what he regards as Kierkegaardian claims into radically different non-Kierkegaardian language. Although it is likely to be controversial, we think his boldness is repaid by striking new insight into *Fear and Trembling*.

Louise Carroll Keeley's "Subjectivity and World in *Works of Love*" confirms Connell's closing suggestion that the dialectical juxtaposition of separation and involvement is not confined to the pseudonymous authorship but recurs in Kierkegaard's unambiguously Christian "second authorship" as well. Her article is especially important since she squarely confronts one of the most articulate and forceful indictments of Kierkegaard on the charge of asocial individualism: Louis Mackey's "The Loss of the World in Kierkegaard's Ethics."[17] Surprisingly, she spends much of her essay apparently corroborating Mackey's charge of ethical acosmism by showing that Kierkegaard consistently focuses on the subjective, interior dimensions of the works of love he considers rather than on the objective results they achieve. If Kierkegaard can be shown to be asocial and acosmic even in *Works of Love*, the book he put forward as his most complete account of the social dimension of human life, the case against him on this charge is strong indeed. But in the final pages of her essay, Keeley shows Mackey's reading to be fatally one-sided. Unquestionably, Kierkegaard stresses the subjective reality of love so as to declare love's freedom from the differences and vicissitudes of the objective order. But what Keeley stresses and Mackey overlooks is that, for Kierkegaard, "Love's subjective deepening is accompanied by—no, entails—a commensurate movement in the opposite direction." As Kierkegaard himself puts it, "What love is, it does; what love does, it is."[18]

All six of the essays so far reviewed assert the dialectical character of Kierkegaard's thought against all too common one-dimensional interpretations. But the three essays of Part II share a special attention to the dialectic of independence and involvement. When Judge William counsels *A* to despair, when Johannes de Silentio speaks of infinite resignation and the teleological suspension of the ethical, when Kierkegaard asserts in *Works of Love* that true love requires self-denial, we stand before quite similar declarations of independence from the external, the objective, the finite, the temporal. It is his pervasive attention to such a withdrawal into self that lends credibility to charges that Kierkegaard is an asocial or even acosmic individualist. Connell, Mooney, and Keeley argue, however, that the movement of retreat to the interior, the intensification of subjectivity, is only completed in Kierkegaard's view in a counter-movement of involvement in the objective order.

But is this not to attribute to Kierkegaard exactly the Hegelian dogma lampooned so lustily in *Either/Or*, that the interior is the exterior and the exterior the interior? Connell, Mooney, and Keeley answer no. Ethical selfhood, faith, and love each has its external, objective expression, but none of the three subjective states is infallibly recognizable by its external, objective expression. As Johannes de Silentio notes with amazement, the knight of faith may look and act for all the world like a philistine shopkeeper. But if, according to Kierkegaard, moral integrity, faith, and love move incognito through the world, then don't we have just the subjective, individualistic, apolitical philosophy the critics decry?

It is quite possible to defend Kierkegaard on this charge. The fact that integrity, faith, and love are not immediately and infallibly recognizable does not imply that they are utterly sundered from the objective public order. Instead, it is the natural consequence of the truism that identical behaviors may have various motivations; if acknowledging that commits a thinker to acosmism, then Kierkegaard has numerous and distinguished company.

But there is something to the charge, and this recognition led Kierkegaard himself to a significant revision of his thought in the period after 1846. That the seven articles of the third and explicitly sociopolitical part of our collection focus overwhelmingly on this latter phase of the authorship indirectly indicates that this revision engages Kierkegaard far more concretely and critically with the public order than had thitherto been the case. The articles by Westphal and Ziolkowski, with which the section opens, document this reorientation in the direction of the objective, the external, the sociopolitical. Westphal, like Plekon, Nordentoft, and Sløk, discerns a progression from an earlier understanding of Christian experience as incognito, subjective, and incommensurable with any externality, to a later view as implacably and essentially at odds with the established order. This shift is most dramatically apparent in Kierkegaard's changing view of the outward dimension of religious suffering. While in the *Postscript* Johannes Climacus denies that the scourging of the Apostles described in Acts 5 is properly religious suffering since it involves merely physical and not psychological pain, Westphal notes that, "As early as 1847 . . . Kierkegaard II begins to treat the flogging of the apostles as the archetypal expression of the suffering which is the mark or sign of true faith." This notion that the genuine

Christian, the witness to the truth, inevitably suffers persecution contains in seed the attack on the Church with which Kierkegaard's life culminates. How are we to explain this shift? What does it reveal about the relationship between the first and the second authorships?

Johannes Sløk argues in *Da Kierkegaard Tav: Fra Forfatterskabet til Kirkestorm* that two independent factors lie behind the reorientation: first, the replacement of absolute monarchy in Denmark by a constitutional monarchy in which all real power lay with an elected parliament, and, second, Kierkegaard's closer attention to the concrete life of Jesus as recorded in the Gospels. While Bruce Kirmmse's article below follows up on Sløk's suggestion of the importance of contemporary social and political developments in Denmark for Kierkegaard's thought, what we note here is Sløk's conclusion of radical discontinuity between the earlier and the later Kierkegaard. Westphal agrees that the alteration of Kierkegaard's view of Christian existence is sufficiently radical to warrant speaking of a new stage, Religiousness C, beyond Religiousness B (Transcendent Religion) as described in the *Concluding Unscientific Postscript*. But Westphal denies that the change is a simple departure from the views of the pseudonymous authorship, as Sløk suggests. Westphal writes that this change from religiousness B to C is "rather like moving from the third to the fourth movement of a carefully composed symphony." The impetus Westphal identifies behind the progressions from existence-form to existence-form is unmistakably Hegelian; the motivation is the experience of otherness that shatters illusions of self-sufficiency and ultimacy in the lower existence-form. But where Hegel sees this dialectic leading the individual beyond herself or himself into full participation in the state that is "the way of God in the world," Kierkegaard sees that the ultimate Other, the transcendent God, relativizes all human projects and institutions. Herein lies the key to the late Kierkegaard's belief that the true Christian will be persecuted—the one thing self-absolutizing human projects and institutions cannot endure is the presence of one who existentially manifests the ultimacy of God. The qualitative difference, the transcendent otherness of God is a stated theme at least as early as the "Ultimatum" of *Either/Or* and arguably as early as *The Concept of Irony*. If Kierkegaard waits until 1846 to draw the social and political implications of that transcendence, that in no way alters the coherence of the progression from his pseudonymous writings to his later works. Westphal himself argues convincingly in his *Kierkegaard's Critique of Reason and Society* that already in such apparently apolitical pseudonymous works as *Fear and Trembling, Philosophical Fragments*, and *Concluding Unscientific Postscript* Kierkegaard's fundamental agenda is to expose the self-absolutizing pretensions of his society and its elites by confronting them with the truly Absolute.[19]

Eric Ziolkowski's "Don Quixote and Kierkegaard's Understanding of the Single Individual in Society" nicely complements Westphal's essay by describing an evolution of Kierkegaard's conception of the knight of the dolorous countenance that parallels his changing conception of religious persecution. Originally, Kierkegaard takes Don Quixote's idiosyncrasy and social estrangement as comic peculiarities of the Don himself. But as Kierkegaard's view of society as self-absolutizing finitude develops, he comes increasingly to see Quixote as a tragic symbol of what one can expect to suffer when one lives for an ideal in a society intent on defending itself against ideals. Finally, Kierkegaard identifies Don Quixote with Christ and Christ's disciples. More specifically, Quixote comes to represent for Kierkegaard the comic contradiction between "whatever is essentially Christian and contemporary secularized Christendom." Ziolkowski's essay, like those of Westphal and Nicoletti, has important implications for the debate over Kierkegaard's supposed irrationalism. When rationality is equated with bourgeois calculation of personal advantage, living for an ideal generally and Christianity specifically will appear insane. When that "rationality" is the legitimating ideology of a social and political establishment, the Don Quixotes (and Christians) of that order can expect to be persecuted and derided as that establishment defends itself.

But the late Kierkegaard's contribution to our conception of social existence isn't exclusively negative. Stephen Crites underlines ironically the positive social dimension of Kierkegaard's thought by uncovering it just below the surface of a text that, in Crites' view, works explicitly to deny the validity of such a dimension of human existence, *The Sickness unto Death*.[20] Focusing on the infamous opening paragraph of the book, Crites argues that Anti-Climacus' intentions notwithstanding, the definition of spirit as self-relating self allows, nay, invites application to social phenomena—families, unions, nations—as well as to individual human beings. More to the point, he shows that one cannot discuss the individual in terms of this definition of self without taking into account the communities, institutions, and traditions in which he or she is involved; this membership, this involvement is a central aspect of the finitude, the necessity of the self-synthesis.[21] To deny it, to ignore it, is to be in despair. Crites' reading of *The Sickness unto Death* may well be termed deconstructionist in that he tries to show that the text works by subverting its own immediate meaning. However, in contrast to many self-declared works of deconstruction, Crites offers a reading of Kierkegaard that is still recognizably Kierkegaardian. His attempt to deconstruct the text works so well that it ironically calls into question whether it is indeed undermining the author's intentions or discovering them.

While Crites suggests that the pseudonymity of *The Sickness unto Death*, its authorship by the ideal, hyper-Christian, and socially unsituated Anti-Climacus accounts for the absence of these social implications from the explicit text, Bruce Kirmmse places Kierkegaard within the context of the modernization of Denmark and its attendant social and ideological changes. In the process, he shows that, ironically, Kierkegaard's championing of the individual is itself an attempt to counter the self-interested individualism of modern civil society. That is, Kierkegaard's supposed asocial individualism is in fact conceived and executed as an attempt to recall the variously competing and massing *homines oeconomici* to the possibility of being Neighbors.[22]

Michele Nicoletti's chapter, "Politics and Religion in Kierkegaard's Thought: Secularization and the Martyr," focuses, like Kirmmse's, on Kierkegaard's analysis of and response to what sociologists call modernity. After reviewing standard dismissals of Kierkegaard as an arch-conservative, he explains Kierkegaard's fervent attempt to draw a sharp distinction between the religious life of the individual, which is absolute and infinite, and the political life of the state, which deals with the finite and the relative. In previous eras, the state had a religious foundation, but the modern state has liberated itself from religion. This secularization is only apparent, however, as the political state now sacralizes itself and attributes ultimate meaning to its concerns. In such a society only the truly religious individual will be able to gain detachment from "results" so as to give society what it most needs. Paradoxically, then, the "single individual" has the absolute perspective that puts political concerns into their relative perspective. However, only the religious individual who is willing to be a martyr has such a perspective. Nicoletti's conclusion provides strong support for the thesis, increasingly clear in Westphal and Ziolkowski as well as Kirmmse, that Kierkegaard's concept of "the individual," far from an asocial individualism, was conceived in relation to and as a solution for the social crisis and as a new opportunity linked to the development of democracy and capitalism.

Wanda Warren Berry addresses an aspect of Kierkegaard's social and ideological context with which he did not deal as perceptively: patriarchy. Significantly, Berry finds in Kierkegaard himself the theoretical basis for an appropriation of his insights by those for whom Kierkegaard's view of and comments about women are highly offensive. That theoretical basis is profoundly communal. It involves, first, a forgiveness that teleologically suspends the ethical so as to sustain a relation and, second, an awareness on the part of offended women that the offending philosophical and religious traditions are nonetheless their own and so can only be cast aside on pain of their becoming fantastic, rootless, and isolated. Berry's chapter follows up nicely on the tensions that exist between the above articles by Mooney and Westphal. Mooney's stress is on the sustained participation of the developed self in its culture. Westphal accentuates the critical posture of the Christian self before the powers and principalities that rule the world. With apologies to Kierkegaard, there is no question of an either/or here. Instead, we are perpetually faced with the difficult task of balancing these two dialectically complementary truths. Berry struggles earnestly in her chapter to find the appropriate middle ground between an unrealistic stance of utter rejection of Western cultural and intellectual tradition because of its sexist taint and a conservative idolatry of the given. It is an important indication of Kierkegaard's contemporary relevance to see how germane his thought is not only to debates about gender relations but also to the ongoing disputes between the likes of Gadamer on the one hand and Habermas or, more recently, the forces of deconstruction on the other.[23]

Charles Bellinger's chapter, "Toward a Kierkegaardian Understanding of Hitler, Stalin and the Cold War" is a most striking attempt to make good on the suggestion also pressed by Crites that the categories of *The Sickness unto Death* can appropriately and fruitfully be applied to large-scale social phenomena. In fact, Bellinger goes a step further in taking the aesthetic and ethical stages as themselves applicable to nation-states. Bellinger carries on Kierkegaard's commitment to dialectical thought by refusing either to abstract individuals from their concrete social settings or to reify society by viewing it as a reality completely prior to and determinative of its constituent individual members.

The following essays do not constitute an exhaustive or systematic account of Kierkegaard's understanding of community, society, ethics, or politics. Nonetheless, individually they suggest and together they demonstrate that the long prevailing conception of Kierkegaard as the great spokesman of asocial individualism is profoundly misguided. (Cross references to chapters in this volume and some references to additional, outside materials have been added by the editors.)

George B. Connell
Concordia College
C. Stephen Evans
St. Olaf College

Notes

1. See, for example, W. T. Jones, *Kant to Wittgenstein and Sartre*, 2nd ed., rev. (New York: Harcourt, Brace, 1975), pp. 209–234; Brand Blanshard, "Kierkegaard on Faith" in *Essays on Kierkegaard*, ed. Jerry Gill (Minneapolis, MN: Burgess, 1969), pp. 113–126; and Herbert M. Garelick, *The Anti-Christianity of Kierkegaard: A Study of "Concluding Unscientific Postscript"* (The Hague: Martinus Nijhoff, 1965).

2. As one would expect, given the essential relationship between the two concepts, *rationality* is fully as elusive as *paradox* in its exact meaning. Accordingly, those who charge Kierkegaard with irrationality should be careful to state exactly how they construe that irrationality. Typically, critics have suggested that Kierkegaard calls on us to believe *p* and not *p*. Chapters in this volume by Westphal, Ziolkowski, and Nicoletti suggest instead that when Kierkegaard criticizes rationality, he usually has in mind the calculating "common sense" of bourgeois self-interest. For further discussion of this approach to Kierkegaard's supposed irrationality, see Merold Westphal, "Kierkegaard and the Logic of Insanity," in *Kierkegaard's Critique of Reason and Society* (Macon, GA: Mercer University Press, 1987); C. Stephen Evans, *Kierkegaard's "Fragments" and "Postscript": The Religious Philosophy of Johannes Climacus* (Atlantic Highlands, NJ: Humanities Press, 1983) and *Passionate Reason* (forthcoming from Indiana University Press).
3. For examples of decidedly unsympathetic critiques of Kierkegaard as an asocial individualist, see Theodore Adorno, *Kierkegaard: Construction of the Aesthetic*, trans. Robert Hullot-Kentor (Minneapolis, MN: University of Minnesota Press, 1989); and K. E. Løgstrup, *Opgør med Kierkegaard* (Copenhagen: Gyldendal, 1967).
4. Martin Buber, *Between Man and Man*, trans. Ronald Gregor Smith (New York: Macmillan, 1965), p. 50.
5. "A Philosophical Encounter with Buber," in *The Legacy and Interpretation of Kierkegaard*, vol. 8 of *Bibliotheca Kierkegaardiana* (Copenhagen: Reitzels, 1981), pp. 243–275.
6. Mark C. Taylor, *Journeys to Selfhood: Hegel and Kierkegaard* (Berkeley, CA: University of California Press, 1980), p. 179.
7. Buber, *Between Man and Man*, p. 55.
8. Hellmut Toftdahl, *Kierkegaard først—og Grundtvig så* (Copenhagen: Nyt Nordisk Forlag, 1969), p. 201.
9. For a contemporary Hegelian attempt to correct the supposed acosmism of Kierkegaard's twentieth century theological inheritors, the dialectical theologians, see Paul Lake, *The Politics of Salvation* (Albany, NY: SUNY Press, 1984).
10. See Louis Dupre, "The Sickness unto Death: Critique of the Modern Age," pp. 85–106; John Elrod, "The Social Dimension of Despair," pp. 107–120; and Sylvia Walsh, "On 'Feminine' and 'Masculine' Forms of Despair," pp. 121–134; all in *International Kierkegaard Commentary: The Sickness unto Death*, ed. Robert Perkins (Macon, GA: Mercer University Press, 1987); and all of the articles in *International Kierkegaard Commentary: Two Ages*, ed. Robert Perkins (Macon, GA: Mercer University Press, 1984). We can anticipate that the volume of essays on *The Corsair Affair* will be especially relevant to the issue of Kierkegaard's social and political thought.
11. Johannes Sløk, *Da Kierkegaard Tav: Fra Forfatterskab til Kirkestorm* (Copenhagen: Reitzel, 1980), pp. 11–12.
12. These articles fall into two groups: those dealing primarily with Kierkegaard's theology and those that focus on sociological and historical dimensions of Kierkegaard's thought. To the first category belong "The Late Kierkegaard: A Reexamination," papers of the Nineteenth Century Theology Working Group, *American Academy of Religion* 7 (1981): 13–40; "Kierkegaard, the Church and Theology of Golden Age Denmark," *Journal of Ecclesiastical History* 34(1983): 245–66; "Introducing Christianity into Christendom: Reinterpreting the Late Kierkegaard," *Anglican Theological Review* 64(1982): 327–52. To the second

group belong "Anthropological Contemplation: Kierkegaard and Modern Social Theory," *Thought* 55(September 1980): 346–69; "Kierkegaard and the Interpretation of Modernity," *Kierkegaard-Studiet* 11(1981): 3–12; "Moral Accounting: Kierkegaard's Social Theory and Criticism," *Kierkegaardiana* 12(1983): 69–82. "Kierkegaard the Theologian: The Roots of His Theology in *Works of Love*," this collection, belongs to the first group.
13. Quoted in the translator's introduction to *Works of Love*, trans. Howard V. Hong and Edna H. Hong (New York: Harper and Row, 1962), pp. 17–18.
14. It is his sense of God's presence in Scripture that explains the authoritative role the Bible plays in his thought. And in the journal entries leading up to the attack on the Church, Kierkegaard repeatedly criticizes Bishop Mynster for not speaking an authoritative word to his congregants. Dunning helps us see how Kierkegaard would take this as a manifestation of the absence of God from the institutional Church and thus goes a long way toward explaining the vehemence of the attack on the Church. For an illuminating discussion of this angle on the attack on the Church, see Sløk, *Da Kierkegaard Tav*.
15. See, for example, Blanshard, "Kierkegaard on Faith."
16. These quotations are taken from an earlier draft of Mooney's essay. We have retained them here since they still seem to us to capture the main thrust of his essay.
17. In Louis Mackey, *Points of View: Readings of Kierkegaard* (Tallahassee, FL: University Presses of Florida, Florida State University Press, 1986).
18. Kierkegaard, *Works of Love*, p. 261.
19. See also Bruce Kirmmse's "Call Me Ishmael—Call Everybody Ishmael," and Michelle Nicoletti's "Politics and Religion in Kierkegaard's Thought: Secularization and the Martyr," in this volume.
20. See also John Elrod, "The Social Dimension of Despair," in *International Kierkegaard Commentary: The Sickness unto Death*, pp. 85–106.
21. Readers will recognize the deep congruance between Crites' comments here and those of Sløk quoted above.
22. See Bruce Kirmmse, *Kierkegaard in Golden Age Denmark* (Bloomington, IN: Indiana University Press, 1990).
23. For an interesting indication of the balanced character of Kierkegaard's hermeneutical practice, note that Merold Westphal compares Kierkegaard and Habermas in his article in this volume, whereas C. Stephen Evans links Kierkegaard and Gadamer in both his *Passionate Reason* and in *Wisdom and Humanness in Psychology: Prospects for a Christian Approach* (Grand Rapids, MI: Baker Books, 1989).

PART I
The Religious Vision

1 Kierkegaard the Theologian: The Roots of His Theology in *Works of Love*

MICHAEL PLEKON

> If you are a theologian, you will pray truly.
> And if you pray truly, you are a theologian.
> Evagrios the Solitary
> *On Prayer: One Hundred and Fifty-Three Texts*, no. 62

At the heart of Kierkegaard's still-understudied yet central text, *Works of Love*, is this passage, a most compact and compelling statement of his theology:

> As Christianity's good news is contained in the doctrine about humankind's kinship with God, so its task is humankind's likeness to God. But God is love, therefore we can resemble God only in loving, just as, according to the apostle's words, we can only "be God's co-workers-in-love." (I Cor. 3:9)[1]

In the same year, 1847, he also wrote the following entry in his journal:

> You talk about wanting to find consolation in Christ. All right, but you had better watch out lest there be something egotistical here. You are supposed to be like Christ. All right then, try this—at the very moment you yourself are suffering most of all, simply think about consoling others, for this is what he did. The task is not to seek consolation—but *to be* consolation, to seek the company of the cripples, the despised, the sinners and the publicans.[2]

To hear this is to hear the essential voice of Kierkegaard, the voice of the theologian.[3] Not only was that his academic status—he was *candidatus theologicus* before he was *Magister artium* and *Doctor philosophiae*—it was also his self-understanding. His writing does not simply culminate, as he says, at the foot of the altar; it begins there, too. I agree with Johannes Sløk that all the stages Kierkegaard describes, all the perspectives on life (*Livs-anskuelser*) in the very popular pseudonymous literature, not to mention all of the explicitly religious writings (the edifying discourses, the other talks and eucharistic homilies) and the texts such as *Philosophical Fragments, Concluding Unscientific Postscript, Fear and Trembling, Sickness unto Death, Training in Christianity, Judge for Yourselves!, For Self-Examination*, and, yes, *Works of Love*—and especially the literature of the public attack on the Church—all of this, I want to claim, is theological.[4] It also happens that much more that is theological is to be found in other, perhaps unexpected places, such as Kierkegaard's journals, his literary experiments and criticism, his social and political analysis, and his intricate social-psychological descriptions.

When I say that Kierkegaard was essentially a theologian, I do not principally have in mind the ordinary modern meaning and situation of this calling. We normally think of a theologian as an academic, as a teacher and scholar in a graduate school or seminary context. However, this has not been the classic work or location of the theologian in the tradition of the Church. Whether we look to the Eastern or Western Church, the theologian's identity and task can be clearly described. In the definition given by the ascetic and Church father of the fourth century, Evagrios of Pontus, the theologian is the one who truly prays, who is in communion with God and who speaks of the God with whom he talks in the community of the Church. The theologian was first and foremost the bishop, the chief pastor of a parish, baptizing regularly, catechizing, preaching, celebrating the Eucharist, caring for a congregation. In all of these pastoral and ecclesial actions, theology was done. The theologian could also be one following the life of an ascetic or that of a teacher, a scholar, or a presbyter or deacon in the church's ministry. Obviously, we continue to have a few such theologians: Thomas Merton, Dietrich Bonhoeffer, Karl Rahner, Bernard Lonergan, Karl Barth, Alexander Schmemann, and Edward Schillebeeckx come to mind. For quite some time, however, the theologians we have read are pretty much academic professionals. There is no regular or necessary connection to the tradition, worship, and fellowship of the Church. In fact, such ties have even come to be seen as confusing and parochial, and the theologian's relationship to the Church and tradition seems more often critical and adversarial than familial and communal.

The classical pattern does not exclude criticism, the goals of reform and renewal, even the strategy of open attack. Think of John Chrysostom, Ambrose and Maximus, Dominic and Francis, Hus and Savonarola, Luther and Melanchthon, Wesley and, in our time, Bonhoeffer. A theologian is no mere spokesperson for the institutional Church, simply a reinterpreter and defender of dogma. The theologian prays, works, thinks, and finally speaks in communion with God and the rest of the baptized. The theologian proclaims and celebrates the life of God lived within the Church's Scriptures, tradition, and liturgy. The theologian is at the root ecclesial and sacramental. Alexander Schmemann has emphasized this insight that theology is best communicated in the celebration of the liturgy by the baptismal, eucharistic assembly which is the church.[5] Aidan Kavanagh has also affirmed theology's liturgical roots.[6]

My point here, and it is fundamental to any understanding of his writings and to this analysis, is that Kierkegaard was a theologian in the classical, catholic, and orthodox sense.[7] His work was not merely to describe or analyze doctrine but rather to proclaim God's relationship with us and point out the way of following Christ, of imitation as the pattern of the baptized life. Despite his criticism of the Church and highly inflammatory polemic against it at the end of his life, Kierkegaard remained a theologian of the Church even during the public attack in 1854–1855. It is true that he stopped receiving Holy Communion, so far as records indicate, in 1852 and ceased participation in public worship. Clearly, this was a significant action and not simply disgust with liturgy and preaching. Kierkegaard, as his journal shows, endured much he could not stomach in the Copenhagen churches. However, he did not cease his own life of prayer, of reading the scriptures and other spiritual literature. He is one of the few modern critics of Christianity to take a stand from within the community of faith, one that is rooted in the Scriptures.

It is important to understand Kierkegaard as fundamentally a theologian if we are to grasp his basic intention. Kierkegaard would certainly have affirmed, with Johannes Climacus, the pseudonymous author of *Concluding Unscientific Postscript*, that he wanted "to make things more difficult" in an age in which the tendency was to make life easier.[8] He also said that he had nothing new to teach, only what was handed down from the fathers, and that he wanted to reintroduce Christianity into Christendom. His writings are filled with his diagnosis of the modern Church's decay.[9] Yet the liturgical book of most American Lutherans, the *Lutheran Book of Worship* (1978), is not wrong in commemorating Kierkegaard on the day of his death, November 11, as "teacher" and "theologian."[10] For it is precisely as a teacher of the Church, as a theologian, that Kierkegaard makes his most important but regularly overlooked contribution to the life of the Church and of the individual Christian.

I see this contribution to be Kierkegaard's fundamental emphasis on the Church's and the individual Christian's communion or relationship with God and his insistence on the imitation of Christ (*Christi Efterfølgelsen*).[11] It is a striving to be and to do the works of love as Christ himself was and did these works. It is to put the "God-relationship" (*Guds-Forhold*) into practice, to make it existential, to be not only a hearer but a doer of the Word. It is no surprise that Kierkegaard called the epistle of James his favorite scriptural text.[12] There is a fascinating conversation reported by, of all people, Bishop Hans Lassen Martensen (Kierkegaard's old theology tutor, Bishop Mynster's successor, and a long-time target of Kierkegaard's invective). According to Martensen, Kierkegaard argued that he felt it more effective to use the theology of James' epistle for making inroads, in awakening (or literally, in "ploughing up") the Christian life.[13]

But this "ploughing up" was not just disruptive, it was essentially creative. Kierkegaard wanted to serve as a theological midwife, not only as a Christian Socratic gadfly. He was trying to work with the Holy Spirit and his reader for renewal and growth in the life of God. As I have argued in my writing on the last years of Kierkegaard's life,[14] alongside his stress on the imitation of Christ, suffering for the Gospel (doctrine), and the Cross is an affirmative theological vision. Of course, throughout the history of the church there has been a tradition of the *via negativa*, the apophatic tradition of the pseudo-Dionysius, Gregory of Nyssa, and others of the fathers. But Christian theology that is truly orthodox and catholic, that is, true to the tradition of the Scriptures and the Church, *always* preaches the Cross and the resurrection as inseparable. So did the theologian Kierkegaard.

I have called the other, affirmative side of Kierkegaard's theology his "incarnational optimism."[15] It is not the cure, corrective or neutralizer of Kierkegaard's demanding, ascetic, Cross-based theology. It does not obliterate or render tame Kierkegaard's insistence on the radical demands of baptismal life, the sacrificial following after the prototype or pattern, Christ. Yet, this "incarnational optimism" is essentially and authentically Kierkegaard's theology just as much as the negative, prophetic criticism we more easily read and hear in the writings of his last years. In a journal entry from 1849, we hear perhaps the most succinct and characteristic statement of this other side of the later Kierkegaard's theology:

> I must now take care, or rather, God will take care of me, so that I do not go astray by all too one-sidedly staring at Christ as the prototype. It is the dialectical element connected with Christ as the gift, as that which is given to us (to call to mind Luther's standard classification). But dialectical as my nature is, in the passion of the dialectical it always seems as if the contrasting thought were not present at all—and so the one side comes first of all and most strongly.[16]

While this "incarnational optimism" is found in many places, including Kierkegaard's journals, it is especially concentrated in *Works of Love*. From this often overlooked text, I have drawn the following elements of this dialectical, "other side" of the later Kierkegaard's theology and sketch their main lines here. These other features expand the description of Kierkegaard's theology beyond what I have called its "incarnational" character. I do this because the Incarnation of God did not occur in isolation but is entwined with his creative and sanctifying actions, with the very life of the Holy Trinity, with Christ's paschal work and with the continuance of this divine life and activity in the eucharistic community, the Church.

A CREATIONAL THEOLOGY: GODLY GOODNESS

> . . . and yet, is not God love? But does not he who created man in his image that he might be like him, might become perfect as he is perfect (Matthew 5:48) and consequently attain to the perfection which is God's own, *become like the image which is God's own*—does he not seek his own? Indeed, he seeks his own, which is love, he seeks it by giving everything, for God is good, and there is only one who is good, (Matthew 19:17), God who gives all. And was not Christ love? But he came into the world to become the prototype in order to draw all men into himself that they might *become like him*, in truth become his own.[17]

My argument here, that Kierkegaard is a genuine theologian of the Church, of the tradition, that he is both orthodox and catholic, could not have a firmer footing than this, the foundation of his theology in the creation.[18] The affirmative quality of his theological work is rooted here. Kierkegaard proclaims the goodness of God the creator and the goodness of his creation is so many places: in the *Edifying Discourses*, the sermons for Friday celebrations of the Eucharist, and especially *Works of Love*. Creation reflects the creator, creation is made to be holy. The crown of God's creation, humankind, is made in the image and likeness of God. Looking upon all of creation, God sees Himself in it. God sees that it is good. Even in the harsh, apparently world-denying writing in his later journals and in the public attack on the Church, Kierkegaard never relinquishes this conviction of the fundamental holiness and goodness of creation, of humanity.[19] Bearer of the tradition of Scripture and Church that he is, Kierkegaard also recognizes the fallen state of the human race and of the natural world. Thus standing undeniably in the classical catholic consensus, Kierkegaard constantly underscores the great gift of redemption in and through the work of Christ, and the sanctifying power of the Holy Spirit, urging each person back toward God.

Further, Kierkegaard's is not a Pollyanna theology. There will be struggle. Ultimately God wants only our good, and life in and with God is peace and joy. Yet life in the God-relationship will bring collision with oneself and with others.[20]

> . . . for Christianity, the opposition of the world stands in essential relationship to the inwardness of Christianity. In addition, the person

who chooses Christianity should in that very moment have an idea of its difficulty so he knows what it is he chooses. Nothing should be promised . . . which Christianity cannot deliver, and Christianity cannot deliver something different from what it has promised from the first: the ingratitude of the world, opposition, mockery and always to a higher degree the more earnest a Christian one becomes. This is the final difficulty in being a Christian and when one recommends Christianity there should be silence least of all about this.[21]

While much more could be said about Kierkegaard's creation theology, one last aspect must be mentioned. His is clearly *not* the "optimism" of the eighteenth century Enlightenment, based upon divine design, human reason, and their interplay. The "optimism" I have attributed to Kierkegaard is rooted in the peace of the Gospel of John and the joy in suffering of Paul. Kierkegaard's affirmative stance has its true home in the mighty acts and promises of salvation history, of creation, the Cross and resurrection, and of Pentecost. In holy baptism, one is joined to this joy and peace, one is joined to Christ.

A Trinitarian Theology: Godly Community

The fundamental goodness of God is not only expressed in the outgoing actions of creating and sustaining but also within, in the very *nature* of God. God is the Holy Trinity, a communion, a community in love. The Father, Son, and Holy Spirit are eternally united in love. The relationship of Father, Son, and Holy Spirit, their internal, mutual "economy" as the Eastern Fathers put it, is essentially love, just like the external "economy" they enact: creation, redemption and sanctification.[22] Throughout *Works of Love*, this trinitarian communion or community of love in God finds reflection in God's dealing with the world and with humankind. The trinitarian prayer at the beginning of *Works of Love* eloquently expresses Kierkegaard's vision of love as the essence of the divine life:

> How could love be rightly discussed if You were forgotten, O God of Love, source of all love in heaven and on earth, You who spared nothing but gave all in love, You who are love, so that one who loves is what he is only by being in You! How could love properly be discussed if You were forgotten, You who made manifest what love is, You, our Saviour and Redeemer, who gave Yourself to save all! How could love be rightly discussed if You were forgotten, O Spirit of Love, You who take nothing for Your own but remind us of that sacrifice of love, remind the believer to love as he is loved, and his neighbour as himself! O Eternal Love, You who are everywhere present and never without witness wherever You are called upon, be not without witness in what is said here about love or about the works of love. There are only a few acts which human language specifically and narrowly calls works of love, but heaven is such that no act can be pleasing there unless it is an act of love—sincere in

self-renunciation, impelled by love itself, and for this very reason claiming no compensation.[23]

As is his custom, Kierkegaard does not develop an extended or systematic theology of the Trinity. This is also true with respect to Christology, baptism, the Eucharist, the Scriptures, and other principal theological loci. It is not that Kierkegaard has little or nothing to say about these important elements of the Church's faith and life. On these loci, as a matter of fact, Kierkegaard's theological reflection is important. Yet, one looks in vain for a sustained treatment, say an entire volume or even a chapter, devoted to just Christology or the sacraments. Rather, Kierkegaard's method is to treat Church dogma when appropriate to the goal and style of a particular writing. Kierkegaard's eucharistic theology, for example, is not restricted to his homiletic *Discourses at the Eucharist on Fridays*, but is also put forward in journal entries, in other prayers and homilies, and even in the polemical literature of the public attack on the Church of 1854–1855.[24]

Kierkegaard's theology, I therefore want to claim, is trinitarian, *informed* by the communion of Father, Son, and Holy Spirit with each other and with us. Creation, redemption, and sanctification are inextricably linked with each other as are the three Persons and their total saving action for us.

An Iconic and Incarnational Theology: Godly Resemblance, Christlikeness

Kierkegaard's theology is trinitarian. It is also powerfully incarnational in two ways. First, there is the creation-identity of the human person with the Creator. Although Kierkegaard does not explicitly use the language of the Eastern Church, he nevertheless recognizes the human person as image (*Billede*) or icon of God. Each person bears the likeness of the Holy One.[25] The iconic relationship between God and the human person comes out even more dramatically in another passage from *Works of Love*, cited at the beginning of this essay, the one in which Kierkegaard speaks of humankind's kinship, likeness and co-working with God.[26] God has always been and continues to be incarnate in His people. Yet (secondly), God distinctively and definitively enters flesh and time, becomes part of His creation in Christ.

> Here one rightly sees the subjectivity in Christianity. Generally the poet, artist, etc. is criticized for introducing himself into his work. But this is precisely what God does; this he does in Christ, and precisely this is Christianity. Creation is really fulfilled only when God has included himself in it. Before Christ, God was included, of course, in the creation, but as an invisible mark, something like the watermark in paper. But in the Incarnation, creation is fulfilled by God's including himself in it.[27]

Kierkegaard's perspective is incarnational, not only because it is based on creation but also because it is so thoroughly Christological, a Kierkegaardian characteristic all too often ignored in studies but emphatically and undeniably present in the texts. Christ is the Redeemer and the pattern for imitation, the one who invited his followers to suffering. But He is also the risen Lord, the giver of the life and power of God. The Cross and Resurrection are always there together in Kierkegaard, in a truly catholic, orthodox way. Even though deliberately and strategically, the Cross is stressed in his proclamation; especially in the last years, the Cross is still the bearer of joy and paschal life into the world. Such a dialectical Christology, indeed, a truly paschal theology, is put forward in *Training in Christianity*, *For Self Examination, Judge for Yourselves!*, and the journals and polemical publications of Kierkegaard's last years.[28]

A PRACTICAL THEOLOGY: GODLY BEING AND DOING

For Kierkegaard, despite the fall and sin, those who bear God's image are called and helped to grow in likeness to Him by the baptismal and eucharistic indwelling of God. Kierkegaard does not explicitly use the language of the Eastern Church Fathers, that of "theosis," to describe our sanctification by God.[29] This "deification" or "divinization" of humanity is God's work of granting us participation in His life, so that we may grow in likeness to Him. Yet, while not speaking of theosis, Kierkegaard does describe the same process of the sanctification of the person in the God-relationship. We respond to God's work of sanctifying by doing God's works, the works of love. Doing the works of love is, for Kierkegaard, precisely *metanoia* or returning. It is never merit-seeking or merit-earning work but doing the Gospel, living out the life of the Kingdom given as gift.

Much of the text of *Works of Love* consists of Kierkegaard's use of scriptural descriptions of these works. Among the texts on which Kierkegaard bases his writing in *Works of Love* are Luke 6:44; Matthew 22:39; Romans 13:8, 10; I Timothy 1:5; I John 4:7, 20; I Corinthians 8:1, 13; Hebrews 13:16; Ephesians 6:13. Loving like God means believing all things while never being deceived, hoping all things without being put to shame, not seeking one's own fulfillment but that of the one loved. Furthermore, to love with God's heart is to cover even a multiplicity of sins, to be merciful even when one has nothing else to give, to always seek reconciliation, to remain faithful in one's love. Along with the late Danish scholar, Kresten Nordentoft, I take Kierkegaard's description of love, "building up," to be the summation of all the rest and perhaps that which most closely identifies the unique character of divine love.[30] The passages in which we find this description are among Kierkegaard's most beautiful:

> Love builds up. To build up is to construct something from the ground up. In the simple illustration of a house, a building, everyone knows what

is meant by ground and foundation. But spiritually understood, what are the ground and foundation of the life of the spirit which are to bear the building? In very fact it is love; love is the origin of everything, and spiritually understood love is the deepest ground of the life of the spirit. Spiritually understood, the foundation is laid in every person in whom there is love. And the edifice which, spiritually understood, is to be constructed, is again love; and it is love which edifies, . . .

Therefore, when the discourse is about the works of love in building up, it must mean either that the lover implants love in the heart of another person or that the lover presupposes that love is in the other person's heart and precisely with this presupposition builds up love in him—from the ground up, insofar as in love he presupposes it present as the ground. One of the two must exist for building up. But I wonder whether or not one person can implant love in the heart of another person. No, this is a more-than-human relationship, a relationship unthinkable between man and man; in this sense human love cannot build up. It is God, the creator, who must implant love in each person, he who himself is love.[31]

For Kierkegaard, to do the works of love, like God, is to act as God does. It is to presuppose love to be there in the omnipresent neighbor. Such loving is God-like in "enticing forth" the good in the neighbor, "presupposing that it is present at the base," that is, at the very foundation of the other's being and person, "like the germ in a kernel of grain."[32] While it cannot be elaborated here, this work of love, the Godly presupposing of love in the neighbor, is perhaps one of Kierkegaard's most insightful "finds" in the Church's and Scripture's tradition, and, as such, it is probably one of his most valuable theological gifts to us.

A COMMUNAL THEOLOGY: GODLY INTERACTION

The trinitarian, iconic, and incarnational relationship between God and humankind that Kierkegaard understands from Scripture and tradition has another consequence for his theology. Kierkegaard does not separate or dichotomize the love of God and the love of neighbor. These always intersect and interpenetrate. They are truly one, as the New Testament, especially the letters and Gospel of John, insist. What is radical about Christian or God-like loving is that God and humankind are inseparable. God is the "middle term" and "third party" in every relationship.[33]

> The God-relationship is the mark whereby love towards men is recognized as genuine love. As soon as a love-relationship does not lead me to God, and as soon as I in a love-relationship do not lead another person to God, this love, even if it were the most blissful and joyous attachment, even if it were the highest good in the lover's earthly life, nevertheless is not true love. The world can never get through its head that God in this way not only becomes the third party in every relationship of love but

essentially becomes the only loved object, so that it is not the husband who is the wife's beloved, but it is God, and it is the wife who is helped by the husband to love God, and conversely, and so on. The purely human conception of love can never go further than mutuality: that the lover is the beloved and the beloved is the lover. Christianity teaches that such a love has not yet found its proper object: God. The love-relationship is a triangular relationship of the lover, the beloved, love—but love of God. Therefore to love another person means to help him to love God and to be loved means to be helped.[34]

Just as God permeates all creation through the act of making and ultimately permeates the flesh, through Christ, just as God has penetrated humankind and each human person as the image and likeness, so too there is no human relationship that goes untouched by God. As Alexander Schmemann has put it, with God's creation, incarnation, and the Spirit, nothing is neutral any longer. So too for Kierkegaard, there is nothing that God has not taken to Himself. Contrary to so much of his caricature, Kierkegaard is not anti-human, not at all opposed to creation, to this world.[35] So much of his writing attests to precisely this, the *Edifying Discourses*, the homilies or discourses for the Friday celebrations of the Eucharist; the innumerable journal entries, many of which are prayerlike affirmations of God's love for us and the world; and of course, *Works of Love*. When Kierkegaard does bring forward the Cross, when he does speak of the need for "dying to the world," when he seemingly casts everything off and envisions Christianity as "the hatred of all that is human," it is not a rejection of what has been described here. Rather, it is consonant with a classical, catholic, and orthodox Christian stance, one solidly within tradition. In the end and at the end, Kierkegaard attacks the human resistance to God's permeability, the rejection of our trinitarian, iconic, incarnational relationship with God and with each other. To go on with the trappings of the faith, of the Church, the Scriptures, liturgy, and sacraments, having abandoned the always entering, ever-present God is what Kierkegaard really means when he speaks of "playing at" Christianity and "making a fool of God." Everything is different, everyone is touched by the relationship with Father, Son, and Holy Spirit.

A Full Theology: Paschal, Eucharistic, Ecclesial

Finally, contrary to so much of the hyperindividualism of which he is accused, Kierkegaard's theological optimism is essentially communal or social. It is not difficult to see why. If the life of the Church and of every Christian is the life of God, then it *must* be communal. The Holy Trinity is the community of love, and the image of God is formed in every person, in every neighbor. Thus the trinitarian, iconic, incarnational, Christological, and communal qualities of the life of God and of the human person demand that we "love those we see." *Works of Love* contains abundant examples of Kierkegaard's communal theology.

> How deeply the need for love is grounded in the nature of man! The first observation, if we dare call it that, made about man, an observation made by the only one who could truly make it, by God, and about the first man, expresses just this. For we read in Holy Scripture: "God said, it is not good that the man be alone." Then woman was taken from man's side and given to him for community—for love and companionship first take something from a man before they give. All through the ages everyone who has thought deeply over the nature of man has recognized in him this need for community. . . .
>
> So deeply is this need grounded in the nature of man and so essentially does it belong to being a human being that even He who was One with the Father and the Spirit, He who loved the whole race, our Lord Jesus Christ, even He felt in a human way this need to love and be loved by an individual human being. Truly he is the God-man and thus eternally different from every human being, but he nevertheless was also a true human being and tried in everything human. On the other hand, the fact that he experienced this need is the very expression of its belonging essentially to man. He was an actual human being and therefore could participate in everything human.[36]

Although I cannot elaborate upon it here, I am convinced that it is in these elements of Kierkegaard's later, affirmative theology that we can locate his authentic ecclesiology. Especially in light of his attack on the Danish Church, it is often thought that Kierkegaard rejected the ecclesial base of Christianity. Kierkegaard's ecclesiological substance, his fundamental understanding of the Church as life in and with God, is to be found here, in this "other side" of his later theological thinking.[37]

There is more to Kierkegaard than the intricacies of his early pseudonymous writings. There is more to his theology than even the brilliance of *Philosophical Fragments* and the *Concluding Unscientific Postscript*. Finally, the theology of Kierkegaard is not simply the negative, polemical, apparently suffering-obsessed version that seems to dominate his writing in the later years, especially during the public attack on the Church of Denmark. As I have argued in other studies, there is more to Kierkegaard's theology, even in these tumultous last years. In my understanding, Kierkegaard quite deliberately opted for a strategy in which "the one side comes first of all and most strongly."[38] However, what I have described here is just as much a part, and a constitutive one at that, of Kierkegaard's theology, as the better recognized later themes of martyrdom, the imitation of Christ in suffering for the Gospel, and dying from the world and being reviled and rejected. His affirmative theology was restrained, even submerged, in both published writings and unpublished journals. Yet it was never repudiated, nor was it ever completely concealed. Kierkegaard's strategy of understatement may have worked too well. We have heard only the side he put first and very strongly. But to locate and hear the rest, we need to read the thirteen homilies he wrote (and in several cases, actually preached) for the weekday celebrations of the Eucharist in Copenhagen's cathedral, Vor Frue Kirke.[39] In these, and in other writings, one can hear the other side, indeed, the fullness of Kierkegaard's theology. One will hear of God's yearning for relationship with us, the Eucharist as the heart of the Church, and the giving of God's life, blessing, forgiveness, community, and the responsibility to enact what we have received.[40]

Finally, we must read the discourses/homilies for Ascension and Pentecost and the seven expositions on John 12:32 in *Training in Christianity* to recognize that Kierkegaard's theology is truly paschal.[41] There is no opposition of the Cross and the Resurrection, as Bonhoeffer once argued.[42] Kierkegaard cannot be faulted for ignoring or downplaying the risen Lord in favor of the one that was crucified. For him, the text of the dismissal after distribution of the bread and cup in the eucharistic liturgy of the Church of Denmark expressed theological fullness. It was the crucified and risen Christ Jesus who fed the faithful with His body and blood, by which He made satisfaction for sin. Kierkegaard affirmed the paschal nature of the Eucharist, of baptism, and of the life of faith in the Church. One is baptized, going down into Christ's death to rise to new life, a sacrificial life, like His.[43] Kierkegaard's discourse for the feast of the Ascension is filled with this paschal motif: Christ is the way, the narrow way, the way of the Cross and suffering. But it is the way by which we ascend with Him into heaven.[44]

There is a telling sign that Kierkegaard clung to this full theology, that he could be affirmative while also hurling prophetic invective at the Church. Right in the middle of the publication of *The Instant* (*Øieblikket*), between numbers 7 and 8, on September 3, 1855, Kierkegaard published a homily he had preached four years earlier, on May 18, 1851, at the Eucharist in the Citadel Church in Copenhagen. It was based on the epistle appointed for that day, the fourth Sunday after Easter, what Kierkegaard called "my first, my dear text," James 1:17–21 ("Every good and perfect gift. . . .").[45] The title, taken from the epistle, is "God's Unchangingness" (*Guds Uforanderlighed*). Kierkegaard concentrates on the uniqueness of God's unchanging nature, and such absolute consistency and constancy are contrasted with all the human tendencies toward change. There is fear and trembling in the recognition that God knows and sees all and does not change. Yet the thrust of Kierkegaard's preaching runs directly counter to the expected conclusion and counter to the tenor of the polemics just previously published and already written for subsequent publication. Kierkegaard does not proclaim God's wrath and punishment and humanity's deserved condemnation.

Rather, he stresses God's unswerving pursuit of us, his relentless love for us. The sermon is a most affirmative proclamation of God's communion with His people, even though it is placed in the middle of the intense negativity of the Church attack.

CONCLUSION

All too often we freeze Kierkegaard's theology on the negative frames most visible in the writings of the last years. Likewise, his incessant praise for the "single individual," his apparent contempt for anything collective, his prescription that we become ourselves by renouncing all that is joyful, his ruthless attack on the Church and the clergy, and his boycott of the liturgy toward the end of his life—none of this seems to help when we look for what is constructive and affirmative in his theology. We therefore see him as a sort of anti-theologian, an enemy of the Church and its tradition, clergy, and liturgy. It is little wonder that some have seen in him the continuation of the radical portion of the Reformation,[46] an exclusively spiritual Christian author, a leveller of all except the individual's one-to-One relationship with God. Kierkegaard has become some kind of superprotestant, a caricature of the tortured, lonely, alienated modern soul. It is not too far to jump from this to the extreme evaluations in which Kierkegaard becomes not only post-ecclesial, post-protestant, but also post-Christian.[47] But there is more—what Kierkegaard also said, indeed, what Kierkegaard principally said, found abundantly in the numerous, less academically popular works I have mentioned, not the least of which is *Works of Love*. In these we find that for all his ingenuity and invective, Kierkegaard loved and preserved the Church's tradition and was its speaker, a theologian of the Church. Moreover, we find that his theology is truly orthodox and catholic (and therefore, allow me to say, Lutheran, for that is all that "Lutheran" really means).[48] In other words, Kierkegaard's theology is paschal, eucharistic, and ecclesial. It is rooted in the Cross and Resurrection, in the pure sacramental word and right eucharistic worship and spirituality of the Church.[49] It strives to express the fullness (*pleroma*) of the paschal mystery, conveyed in the assembly's continued life of saying the Gospel, giving thanks, and becoming the body of Christ. Even in his negations, Kierkegaard affirms the core of all this: God's communion/relationship with his community and the communion of each, of all that community with Him.

Notes

1. Throughout I cite from *Works of Love* (hereafter WL), ed. and trans. Howard V. Hong and Edna H. Hong (New York: Harper Torchbooks, 1964), p. 74.
2. VIII-1; A 4321; JP 1841. In citing journal entries, the first citation is from the

Danish edition, *Søren Kierkegaards Papirer*, ed. Niels Thulstrup, index by N. J. Cappelørn (Copenhagen: Gyldendal, 1968–1978) and the second from *Søren Kierkegaard's Journals and Papers* (hereafter JP), ed. and trans. Howard V. Hong and Edna H. Hong (Bloomington, IN: Indiana University Press, 1967–1978).
3. For released time essential to the preparation of this study, I want to thank Dean Martin Stevens of the School of Liberal Arts and Sciences, Baruch College of the City University of New York. I also want to thank the Rev. Ronald F. Marshall, pastor, and the people of the First Lutheran Church of West Seattle. As the lecturer at their eighth annual commemoration of Søren Kierkegaard, I had the opportunity to prepare five presentations of Kierkegaard's theology. This study is derived from that series. I also want to thank my own bishop, the Rev. Dr. William H. Lazareth, of the Metropolitan New York Synod of the Evangelical Lutheran Church in America, in which I serve as a pastor. Bishop Lazareth serves the Church as just the kind of theologian I describe in this essay.
4. Johannes Sløk, *Kierkegaard—humanismens tænker* (Copenhagen: Hans Reitzel, 1978); *Da Kierkegaard tav* (1980); *Kierkegaards univers: en ny guide til geniet* (Copenhagen: Hans Reitzel, 1985).
5. Alexander Schmemann, *For the Life of the World* (1973); *Of Water and the Spirit* (1974); *Introduction to Liturgical Theology* (1966); *Church, World, Mission* (1979); *Liturgy and Life* (1974); *The Eucharist* (1988) (all from Crestwood, NY: St. Vladimir's Seminary Press).
6. Aidan Kavanagh, *On Liturgical Theology* (1984); *Elements of Rite* (1982) (both from NY: Pueblo).
7. I have described and illustrated the work of Kierkegaard as such a theologian in a paper, "Kierkegaard and the Eucharist," forthcoming in *Studia Liturgica*.
8. Søren Kierkegaard, *Concluding Unscientific Postscript*, trans. Walter Lowrie and David F. Swenson (Princeton, NJ: Princeton University Press, 1968), p. 166.
9. On this see Howard A. Johnson, "Kierkegaard and the Church," in Kierkegaard's *Attack upon Christendom*, Walter Lowrie, trans. (Princeton, NJ: Princeton University Press, 1968), pp. xix–xxxiii; Berndt Gustafsson *I den Natt: Studier till Søren Kierkegaards forfallsteorier* (Stockholm: Diakonistyrelsens Bokförlag, 1962); Emanuel Skjoldager, *Den egentlige Kierkegaard: Søren Kierkegaards syn på Kirken og de kirkelige handlinger* (Copenhagen: Søren Kierkegaard Selskabet, 1982); and my articles, "Prophetic Criticism, Incarnational Optimism: On Recovering the late Kierkegaard," *Religion* 13(1983): 137–53; and "Kierkegaard, the Church and Theology of Golden Age Denmark," *Journal of Ecclesiastical History* 34, no. 2 (April 1983): 245–66.
10. See Philip H. Pfatteicher, *Festivals and Commemorations* (Minneapolis, MN: Augsburg Publishing House, 1980), pp. 421–25.
11. This emphasis on the centrality of love in Kierkegaard is echoed in several papers in this volume, particularly those by Louise Carroll Keeley and Wanda Warren Berry.
12. See *Edifying Discourses*, trans. David F. Swenson and Lillian Marvin Swenson (Minneapolis, MN: Augsburg, 1943–1946), vol. 1, pp. 35–55, vol. 2, pp. 27–66; *For Self Examination* and *Judge for Yourselves*, trans. Walter Lowrie (Princeton, NJ: Princeton University Press, 1974), pp. 35–74. See Merold Westphal's essay in this volume for further discussion of the role of imitation of Christ in Kierkegaard's religious thought.
13. H. L. Martensen, *Af mit Levnet* (Copenhagen, 1882–1883), vol. 2, pp. 137–47, vol. 3, pp. 12–23.

14. "Prophetic Criticism, Incarnational Optimism: On Recovering the Later Kierkegaard," *Religion* 13 (1983): 137–53.
15. See my article in note 10 above as well as my other studies, "Protest and Affirmation: The Late Kierkegaard on Christ, the Church and Society," *Quarterly Review* 2/3 (1982): 43–62; "Introducing Christianity into Christendom: Reinterpreting the Late Kierkegaard," *Anglican Theological Review* 64 (1983): 327–52; and "Blessing and the Cross: The Late Kierkegaard's Christological Dialectic," *Academy* 39(1983): 25–50.
16. *Søren Kierkegaards Papirer*, X-1 A 246; JP 1852.
17. WL, p. 247. Emphasis added.
18. The essays by Charles Bellinger and George Connell in this volume also emphasize the role the doctrine of creation plays in Kierkegaard's thought.
19. *Søren Kierkegaards Papirer* XI–2 A 8; JP 2450.
20. This essential collision is the major theme of the essays by Westphal and Ziolkowski in this volume.
21. WL, 187.
22. See Vladimir Lossky, *The Mystical Theology of the Eastern Church* (Crestwood, NY: St. Vladimir's Seminary Press, 1976); and *In the Image and Likeness of God*, ed. John H. Erickson and Thomas E. Bird (Crestwood, NY: St. Vladimir's Seminary Press, 1985). On the icon of the Trinity by Andrei Rublev (1425) see Egon Sendler, *The Icon: Image of the Invisible*, trans. Steven Bigham (Redondo Beach, CA: Oakwood Publications, 1988); and L. Ouspensky and V. Lossky, *The Meaning of Icons* (Crestwood, NY: St. Vladimir's Seminary Press, 1982), and Paul Evdokimov, *The Art of the Icon: A Theology of Beauty* (Redondo Beach, CA: Oakwood Publications, 1990).
23. WL, p. 20.
24. See *The Attack upon Christendom*, trans. Walter Lowrie (Princeton, Princeton University Press, 1968), pp. 205–7; 268–70.
25. See WL, p. 247, quoted earlier.
26. Ibid., p. 74.
27. *Søren Kierkegaards Papirer*, X–1 A605; JP 1391.
28. See the discussion in my articles cited in notes 9, 14, and 15 above.
29. See the works of Lossky cited in note 22 above and the following: Jaroslav Pelikan, *The Christian Tradition*, vol. 2, *The Spirit of Eastern Christendom (600–1700)* (Chicago, IL: University of Chicago Press, 1974); A. M. Allchin, *Participation in God* (Wilton, CT: Morehouse-Barlow, 1988); Georgios I. Mantzaridis, *The Deification of Man* (Crestwood, NY: St. Vladimir's Seminary Press, 1984); Lars Thunberg, *Man and the Cosmos: The Vision of St. Maximus the Confessor* (St. Vladimir's Seminary Press, 1985). For an especially helpful analysis, with East-West comparisons, see William G. Rusch, "How the Eastern Fathers Understood What the Western Church Meant by Justification," in *Justification by Faith: Lutherans and Catholics in Dialogue VII*, ed. H. George Anderson, T. Austin Murphy, and Joseph A. Burgess (Minneapolis, MN: Augsburg, 1985).
30. See Kresten Nordentoft, *Kierkegaard's Psychology*, trans. Bruce Kirmmse, (Atlantic Highlands, NJ: Humanities Press, 1978) pp. 323–386; and *Søren Kierkegaard: Bidrag til kritiken af den borgerlige selvoptagethed* (Copenhagen: Dansk Universitets Presse, 1977), pp. 168–83, 238–43.
31. WL, 204–5.

32. Ibid., 206–7. Also see Louise Carroll Keeley's discussion of this point below, on pp. 101–5.
33. See WL, pp. 112–13, 117.
34. Ibid., p. 124.
35. Admittedly, a few of the remarks at the end of the *Attack upon Christendom* are jarring and not easy to reconcile with the overall thrust of Kierkegaard's work.
36. WL, 153–54.
37. On ecclesiology, see Jaroslav Pelikan, *The Christian Tradition*, vol. 1, *The Emergence of the Catholic Tradition (100–600)* (Chicago, IL: University of Chicago Press, 1971); Alexander Schmemann, *For the Life of the World* (1973), *Church, World, Mission* (1979), *The Eucharist: Sacrament of the Kingdom* (Crestwood, NY: St. Vladimir's Seminary Press, 1988); Carl E. Braaten, *The Apostolic Imperative* (Minneapolis, MN: Augsburg, 1985); John D. Zizioulas, *Being as Communion* (Crestwood, NY: St. Vladimir's Seminary Press, 1985); Robert W. Jenson, "Sovereignty in the Church," in *The New Church Debate*, ed. Carl E. Braaten (Philadelphia, PA: Fortress, 1983).
38. *Søren Kierkegaards Papirer*, X–1 A246; JP 1852.
39. They are collected, in translation, in *Christian Discourses*, trans. Walter Lowrie (Princeton, NJ: Princeton University Press, 1974); and in *Training in Christianity*, trans. Walter Lowrie (Princeton, NJ: Princeton University Press, 1972).
40. Again, I will put forward Kierkegaard's eucharistic theology in a forthcoming essay.
41. See *For Self-Examination* and *Judge for Yourselves*, pp. 75–106; and *Training in Christianity*, pp. 151–254.
42. *Letters and Papers from Prison*, trans. and ed. Reginald Fuller et al. (New York: Macmillan, 1967), pp. 197–98.
43. *Attack upon Christendom*, pp. 205–6. See also journal entries IA 60 (JP 5089) and XI–1 A556 (JP 5047).
44. *For Self-Examination* and *Judge for Yourselves*, pp. 228–40.
45. See journal entry X–4 1323 (JP 6769). The sermon is in *For Self-Examination* and *Judge for Yourselves*, pp. 228–40.
46. Vernard Eller argues for this view in his *Kierkegaard and Radical Discipleship* (Princeton, NJ: Princeton University Press, 1968).
47. Such a claim was made as early as Georg Brandes' *Søren Kierkegaard* (Copenhagen: Gyldendals, 1877), the first book of Kierkegaard interpretation.
48. On the constitutive catholicity and orthodoxy of Lutheranism, see Eric We. Gritsch and Robert W. Jenson, *Lutheranism: The Theological Movement and its Confessional Writings* (Philadelphia, PA: Fortress, 1976); Carl E. Braaten, *Principles of Lutheran Theology* (Philadelphia, PA: Fortress, 1983); William H. Lazareth, "Evangelical Catholicity: Lutheran Identity in an Ecumenical Age," in Braaten, *The New Church Debate*, pp. 15–38; and "Evangelical Episcopate: An Argument from the Lutheran Confessions," *Lutheran Forum* 22, no. 4 (Advent/November 1988): 13–17; and *Christian Dogmatics*, 2 vols., ed. Carl E. Braaten and Robert W. Jenson (Philadelphia, PA: Fortress, 1984).
49. This is, of course, the ecclesial language of the Augsburg Confession, the Lutheran movement's statement of its own identity within the one, holy, catholic, and apostolic church. See, in particular, articles 5–15 of the Confession in *The Book of Concord*, trans. and ed. Theodore G. Tappert et al. (Philadelphia, PA: Fortress, 1959).

2 Who Sets the Task? Kierkegaard on Authority

STEPHEN N. DUNNING

INTRODUCTION: THE PROBLEM OF AUTHORITY

Perhaps no category of traditional Christian theology is more problematic—or subject to more misunderstanding—than the concept of authority. A survey of the prominent debates of our time, including everything from such gender- and sex-related issues as the ordination of women and the blessing of homosexual relationships to ethical issues involving questions of the sanctity of human and nonhuman life, quickly shows that at the heart of the disagreements is always a conflict over authority. For some, Christian faith is to be defined as life-under-authority, whether that authority be construed as Scripture, the teaching office of the Church, or some more local form of leadership. For others, authority is virtually indistinguishable from authoritarianism; hegemony belongs only to the individual conscience, and it is considered inappropriate if not dangerous whenever efforts to persuade escalate into invasive pressures to conform.

One of the more articulate critics of those who would appeal to authority in theological debates is the prominent Harvard theologian, Gordon D. Kaufman. In a contribution to the recent *Festschrift* for Basil Mitchell, Kaufman condemns the notion of believing in absurdities and paradoxes, which he associates with Tertullian and Kierkegaard, as nothing more than a "demand for an unqualified fideism."[1] In his view, the submissive trust in God of a suffering Job requires too high a price, nothing less than a "sheer acceptance of overwhelming *authority*,"[2] an authority that, according to the likes of Barth and Bultmann, offers "no experiential grounds for faith."[3] Kaufman protests that this blind faith, based upon appeals to authority and revelation, is no longer viable. His well-known alternative is that we understand faith, like all human thought, to be made up of constructs of the human mind, not of symbols or concepts that have fallen from on high.

The difficulty with Professor Kaufman's attack is his assumption that submission to authority requires an abdication of intellectual responsibility and results in blind faith. That may characterize Kaufman's view of "unqualified fideism," but I'm not sure who really qualifies as an unqualified fideist! Certainly not Barth, not Bultmann, not Tertullian, and, above all, not Kierkegaard.

If we were to inquire among Kierkegaard's readers about his view of authority, the most frequent response might well be that it is something he claims not to have. Again and again throughout both authorships—the "aesthetic" or pseudonymous works and those ethical and religious writings published under his own name—we are reminded that he speaks without authority. One obvious meaning of that disclaimer is that he was never ordained, and therefore he could not preach with ecclesiastical authority. But that, I think, is no more the real crux of authority for Kierkegaard than it is for Kaufman. A close look at what he had to say about authority in several of the texts written during the late 1840s will show how much deeper is his understanding of the relation between authority and faith. Whereas many, with Kaufman, assume that authority generally serves as a foundation and warrant for faith, Kierkegaard, I will argue, reverses that relation: it is faith that constitutes the foundation and warrant; divine authority can only occur within a context in which faith is already established.

I take my title for this essay from *Works of Love*, where Kierkegaard remarks that "authority means precisely to set the task."[4] But it is in his relatively little-known book about Magister Adler, *On Authority and Revelation*,[5] that he really spells out what he means by the concept. Out of consideration for the disgraced priest, Kierkegaard published only a short section of the book—in which Adler is not even mentioned—under the title, "Of the Difference Between a Genius and an Apostle."[6] This appeared in 1849 as the second part of *Two Minor Ethico-Religious Treatises*, attributed to the pseudonym "H. H." It is a brief essay that goes into the matter of authority in great detail. A short while later, Kierkegaard wrote in his journal: "[H]e [H. H.] rightly understood and explained perhaps the most important ethical-religious concept: authority."[7] (I will not refer to the author as H. H., since I do not believe that this pseudonym has the same standing as those in Kierkegaard's earlier works.)[8]

KIERKEGAARD: WHAT AUTHORITY IS NOT

A first approach to Kierkegaard's understanding of authority is available by a sort of *via negativa*—a characterization of authority in terms of what it is *not*. Such descriptions are admittedly formal, but they provide a helpful prolegomenon, and they also serve the very important function of dispelling prevalent misunderstandings.

1. Kierkegaard's "difference" essay distinguishes its two types in terms

of their appropriate spheres. The genius, we are told, belongs to the sphere of immanence, whereas the apostle belongs to the sphere of transcendence.[9] This is tantamount to saying that the authority of the genius remains merely human, whereas that of the apostle is divine. Kierkegaard develops this distinction in a paragraph in which every word is emphasized. He observes, first, that the original contributions of genius will eventually be assimilated by others, whereas those of an apostle retain forever their startling newness; second, that genius is what it is out of its own nature and resources, but apostles are apostles only by virtue of being appointed by divine authority; and third, that the goal of genius is fulfilled in the completion of an immanent work of genius, while an apostle carries out his work only in order to fulfill an "absolute paradoxical teleology" or purpose that transcends the work itself.[10]

By this brief preliminary synopsis, Kierkegaard has provided an outline of the structure of the remainder of his essay. He has also made clear that he is indeed approaching his subject as a "negative" theologian. All we have been told is that divine authority is not human and not immanent, whether initially or after some process of assimilation, or even when viewed in terms of motivation. What it means to say that authority can be divine or transcendent has not yet been specified.

2. Another negative characteristic has also been signaled in the use of the term *paradoxical*. Here we come to the aspect of Kierkegaard's legacy that is criticized by Gordon Kaufman. Throughout his discussion of Adler, Kierkegaard attacks modern exegesis, dogmatics, and speculative philosophy. They are accused of weakening the call to obedience through "the parenthetical,"[11] by which he seems to mean the endless qualifications placed by modern scholarship upon both scriptural and foundational formulations. Even more serious, in Kierkegaard's view, is the assumption of modern interpreters that Christian revelation is to be *understood*, fully comprehended in the manner of something immanent.[12] This is illustrated by the tendency to use Christian language, which deals with qualitative or transcendental categories, for "pretty much everything" in the world.[13] All these traits of modern religious thought represent efforts to "thrust back the sphere of paradox into the aesthetic sphere."[14] Moreover, it is not simply an aberration of modernity, for the insistence that Christianity must be made intelligible begins with orthodoxy itself, which "has the intent to make Christianity plausible. . . . But to make Christianity plausible is to misinterpret it."[15]

This is not the place to review scholarly discussions of Kierkegaard's alleged irrationalism.[16] There are, however, several points that are clearly made in the literature under consideration and that help to clarify what is meant by the rejection of thought as a criterion for divine authority.

First, it is clear that Kierkegaard disagrees totally with the modern infatuation with doubt. From Descartes to Tillich, doubt has been held to be the primary credential of a person of intelligence and reflection. Such a position is parodied by Anti-Climacus in *Training in Christianity*, where one of those who objects to the claims of Jesus does so on the grounds of their circularity: if Jesus is God, then he possesses divine authority; and if he possesses divine authority, then his claim to be God must be believed; but either way there is the *if*.[17] The problem with such doubt is forcefully stated in a journal entry of 1847: "People try to persuade us that the objections against Christianity spring from doubt. That is a complete misunderstanding. The objections against Christianity spring from insubordination, the dislike of obedience, rebellion against all authority."[18]

Second, the fact that an apostle or someone who is the exception (*extraordinarius*) submits to authority in no way means that such a person cannot also be reflective. On the contrary, the truly exceptional person will be one who "must have the presupposition of his age constantly at his service." Since the presupposition of the modern age is reflection and intelligence, "it is unthinkable that the divine governance has not itself taken note of this fact."[19] In short, apostles to this reflective age will be able to comprehend and utilize reflective reason for their divinely appointed task just as apostles to a more emotional age would equally utilize emotion to communicate their message. But they would not be bound to reflection or to emotion as their own spiritual presupposition.

Finally, and perhaps most important in answering the objections of rationalistic thinkers, divine authority in no way precludes thought, for its opposition to thought comes only after and as a result of thought. In a long passage that deserves to be quoted at length, Kierkegaard writes:

> *The paradox-religious relationship* (which, quite rightly, cannot be thought but only believed) *appears when God appoints a particular man to divine authority*, in relation, be it carefully noted, to that which God has entrusted to him. The man thus called is no longer related as man to man *qua* man; his relationship to other men is not that of a quantitative difference (such as a genius, exceptional gifts, positions &c.), he is related paradoxically by having a specific quality which no immanence can resolve in the equality of eternity; for it is essentially paradoxical and *after* thought (not before, anterior to thought), [but] contrary to thought.[20]

The result of all this is not to posit either irrationalism or fideism, in which thought is simply rejected. On the contrary, here thought is exhausted, taken to its limit. Kierkegaard endorses that which is contrary to thought only after thought. When thought comes up against a wall, then thought as such becomes irrelevant; only a leap of faith (to borrow a phrase from elsewhere in Kierkegaard's writings) can take us over that wall.[21]

3. A similar irrelevance appears with the third negative characteristic: no authority is ever based upon the profundity or cleverness or even the truth of a doctrine.[22] We cannot judge a teaching to be true and conclude therefore that the teacher must have authority. As Kierkegaard emphasizes: "*Authority is a specific quality which, coming from elsewhere, becomes qualitatively apparent when the content of the message or of the action is posited as indifferent.*"[23] This is why Adler was so misguided when he defended his alleged revelations on the basis that, under further scrutiny, they demonstrated "'meaning and connection'."[24] To Kierkegaard, this claim evades the most important issue, namely, that Adler had claimed his utterances to be revelations from God. Thus their apparent meaning and connection, like the frame of mind he was in when he received and uttered them, is ultimately irrelevant. It is the same with Christ himself. The authority of Christ's statements derives from the fact that it was Christ who made them; apart from him, as propositions in their own right, they have no divine authority at all.[25]

This allusion to the biblical record of Christ's statements raises a very important question, one that can be only briefly noted in this paper: What is the authority of Scripture for Kierkegaard? As much as Kierkegaard quotes Scripture, and as much as it obviously shapes his thinking in countless conscious and unconscious ways, it is clear that it, too, like every other message, has only a derivative authority. Even in *Works of Love*, no doubt one of Kierkegaard's most scripturally based writings, it is made clear that the special quality of Scripture resides not in *what* it teaches, but rather in *how* it teaches, in the fact that it makes a demand of its reader, for "with invisible letters behind every work in Holy Scripture a disturbing notice confronts him—for there it reads: go and do likewise."[26] Scripture offers little in the way of a doctrine of friendship to the casual or poetic enquirer. "But let a Christian search, one who wants to love his neighbor, he will certainly not search in vain; he will find each word stronger and more authoritative than the last, serving to kindle this love in him and to keep him in this love."[27] In short, the authority of Scripture is not an external, objective fact. It exists only in the relationship between the Word of Scripture and the obedient heart of the listener or reader. It is, as it were, a form of address that must always be expressed in the second person singular: "For the divine authority of the Gospel speaks not to one man about another man, not to you, the reader, about me, or to me about you—no, when the gospel speaks it speaks to the single individual."[28]

To return to the three negative characterizations of divine authority, we found that they are all qualitatively dialectical: authority is not immanent but transcendent; it is not rational but paradoxical; it is not a matter of content but of otherness or heterogeneity, of coming from elsewhere.

There are also two final characteristics that are not dialectical, for, in both cases, their negation does not carry with it a corresponding affirmation.

4. The first of these is the famous Kierkegaardian category of offense. A person familiar with his many discussions of the offense of Christianity might well assume that offense itself is a sign of divine authority. But such is not the case. The apostle certainly does give offense; but so does the genius, particularly in a society that is dominated by the mentality of the masses.[29] Moreover, no alternative to offense is affirmed. The apostle does give offense, but that does not distinguish him as one having divine authority.

5. The other nondialectical negative characteristic is even more surprising, for it would seem to contradict Kierkegaard's insistence upon the "reduplication" of our thinking in our lives as the mark of authenticity.

> If a dedicated teacher is enthusiastically conscious that he has expressed [in his life] the doctrine which he is proclaiming at the sacrifice of all else, this consciousness may give him determination, but it does not give him authority. His life as a proof of the right of the teaching is not 'the other' (τὸ ἕτερον); it is a simple reduplication.[30]

Kierkegaard goes on to contrast such a teacher with a policeman who, although ethically quite unscrupulous, has authority when he is on duty by virtue of his appointment. Likewise, in relation to Adler, he remarks that the fact that a person has become "awakened in an extraordinary way" in a "revival" in no way gives his thought the divine authority of a revelation.[31] Such spiritual renewal is a purely personal matter and entails no dialectical opposites. Both reduplication and renewal are, as it were, assumed of the apostle (unlike the policeman). But they in no way guarantee his divine authority. (They may, however, enhance his human authority. Divine authority inheres in the divine commission. But human authority does require reduplication, as in the case of the voluntarily poor person who has authority to teach about voluntary poverty, whereas a wealthy person does not.)[32]

To sum up this survey of the negative characteristics of divine authority: it is not immanent but transcendent; not rational but paradoxical; and not a matter of content but heterogeneous to its own message. In each of these pairs, the second term is presented dialectically as the contrary of the first. Kierkegaard has not told us what substantive affirmations are involved in speaking of divine authority as transcendent, paradoxical, and heterogeneous. The final two negative characteristics are offense and reduplication. Unlike the first three, dialectical contraries are not presented, for although offense and reduplication will normally accompany divine authority, they do not in themselves guarantee its presence.

Adler: A "Sign" of Contemporary Confusion

The occasion for these reflections upon authority was, of course, the hapless Magister Adler. In 1843 Adler had published a collection of his sermons in which he distinguished between those written in the customary manner and those he had written "by the direct assistance of the Spirit."[33] The following year Adler was suspended by Bishop Mynster, and in 1845, following an inquiry, he was deposed. Kierkegaard's tone in writing about Adler is a mixture of sympathy for one who has suffered a great deal and impatience with a man he considers to be utterly confused. His analysis of Adler offers him an opportunity to employ the categories he had so carefully worked out in the pseudonymous writings on the stages of aesthetic, ethical, and religious consciousness. In the process, he presents Adler as a representative or "sign" of the times, a man who embodies all the confusions about authority and revelation that typify the modern world. Adler is not to be affirmed as one of "the elect" who has, as he claimed, received a revelation, nor dismissed as "an offended man demonically shrewd." Rather, Adler is, more than any of his contemporaries, "a phenomenon . . . an anticipation of the dialectic which is fermenting in our age."[34] However, this should not be taken to mean that Adler has no significance as an individual, or that the essay is merely a political analysis of social trends. On the contrary, Kierkegaard insists that his treatise on Adler is "ethico-religious" in the sense that *the point of departure is FROM ABOVE, from God*, and *the formula is this paradox that an individual is employed.*"[35]

There are three primary dimensions of Kierkegaard's discussion of Adler, all of which involve ethical matters, and are therefore related to the question of reduplication discussed above. These are the issues of Adler's Hegelianism, the depth of his inwardness, and the confusion in his understanding of the concept of revelation. Together, they present a picture of Adler as a sign of the situation in Christendom, where "one may in a way become a Christian, and even a Christian priest, without having the least impression of Christianity in the way of . . . becoming a Christian."[36] Kierkegaard doubts that Adler really had an experience of "Christian awakening," but he is sure that "the catastrophe of his life must be able to exert some awakening effect upon everyone" in Christendom.[37]

That Magister Adler had some sort of profound religious experience, however, Kierkegaard does not doubt. He writes: "[T]here arose before him a light, and it was not by thinking it arose but by the Spirit."[38] Adler claimed that this experience included not only a light but also specific doctrinal revelations that were imparted to him directly by Jesus. In Kierkegaard's view, although it may not have been a specifically Christian awakening, it was certainly a "leap . . . into the sphere of religious inwardness" by which he became for the first time "concerned about himself."[39] This experience brought him to the "turning-point of decision, whether he will become a Christian" or not.[40]

Adler's response to this experience is one that Kierkegaard finds laden with irony: he burned all his Hegelian manuscripts! It is ironic precisely because his subsequent behavior confirmed rather than denied his earlier commitment to Hegelianism.[41] It is doubly ironic, because it was an effort to express outwardly what is purported to be an inward transformation, and the adequacy of the external to express the internal is one of Hegel's claims that Kierkegaard condemns most often.[42] This claim is symptomatic of the fundamental disease of Hegelianism, according to Kierkegaard's diagnosis, namely, that it lacks an ethical dimension and therefore encourages a fanciful and speculative leaping back and forth between the external categories of the aesthetic sphere and the expressions of inwardness that characterize the religious.[43] Corresponding to this is the confusion of objective and subjective categories. Prior to his experience, Adler had studied only Hegelian thought, and this had taught him that the separation of the objective from the subjective had been overcome. Therefore, when he had a powerful subjective experience, Kierkegaard reasons, Adler assumed that it must also have brought with it new objective content.[44] He was totally lacking in those "presuppositions" by which he would have been able to judge the Hegelian philosophy and to interpret his experience in relation to the question of revelation.[45] Therefore his interpretation of his experience became equivocal. He tried to mediate it through reason, with the result that his later accounts of it are nothing more than a "volatilization" of his earlier claim that he had received a revelation.[46]

One of the things that most fascinates Kierkegaard about Adler is the way in which his religious experience is undermined by his Hegelian education. Whereas "[m]ost men live in relation to their own self as if they were constantly out, never at home. . . . [Adler] was fetched home by a higher power."[47] If this sort of experience can be thought of as a spiritual rebirth, then Magister Adler's rebirth seems to have been aborted! As a child of Christendom, he had been "born" a Christian and "raised" as a Christian.[48] After his experience of genuine inwardness, he had to choose between living in inwardness before God or living in externality before men.[49] He chose to burn his Hegelian manuscripts and then dealt with the continuing tension in an equally external manner—by literary activity.[50] All of this simply confirms Kierkegaard in the conviction that it is impossible for anyone to arrive at self-understanding through Hegelian categories, at least not until one is dead![51]

If the external expression of Adler's tension is literary activity, its internal reality is a sort of "dizziness" that promotes fantastic speculation. Kierkegaard concludes that Adler was not really much of a thinker at all, that he had "the habit of putting himself into an exalted mood," of using emotional and monotonous repetition in order to find some inspiration.[52] This dizziness is another way of avoiding the ethical, of replacing decision with sentiment and thought with fantasy.

In the end, Adler retreated into the self-contradictory position of refusing to retract his claim to revelation but at the same time interpreting himself as a genius rather than as an apostle.[53] It is this utter confusion about the nature of revelation that is, according to Kierkegaard, at the root of the other confusions that abound in his books and all the works of Hegelianism. Anyone—pagan, Jew, or Christian—can be moved by an experience of something spiritual, something higher. Although there may be a distinctively "Christian emotion" or "Christian experience," and Magister Adler may in fact have had it, what is crucial is that the Christian has a clear grasp of Christian concepts by which to interpret the experience.[54] The fact that Adler did not have such a grasp is evident in his subsequent claim: that he had received a revelation from Jesus that instructed him to believe precisely what all Christians are to believe on the basis of faith. In other words, he was set apart by a revelation that told him to be just like everyone else! This is especially silly in relation to his ordination, for it means that Adler thought he had been especially commissioned to preach exactly what he had previously been ordained to preach.[55] All understanding of the logic of revelation and the call to be an apostle is lacking here, just as it is lacking in Hegel's philosophy of religion.

FAITH AS THE BASIS FOR DIVINE AUTHORITY

We have seen that Kierkegaard rejects Adler's claim to have received a revelation from God. That rejection is based upon the fact that Adler so equivocated about his own claim that he could not possibly be taken for a "true *extraordinarius* . . . [who] is concerned only about his instruction and his relationship to God." Whereas most people lack conviction and are concerned only for success, the apostle possesses a "heterogeneous certainty, the certainty of eternity" that frees him from interest in questions of temporal success.[56] Adler's own concessions about the strange style and need for development of his alleged revelations, and his total silence about their revealed nature in his four last books, show that he himself did not really believe them to have been revealed. Moreover, had he believed in them fully, he would no doubt have resigned his position as a priest of the Church.[57]

But what is it that Adler might have done or written had his revelation and divine authority been genuine? To answer this question, it is necessary to set the discussion of Adler's case in the context of some of Kierkegaard's other writings from the late 1840s. Adler himself came to refer to his religious experience as a "consciousness of being *rescued* in a miraculous way." Kierkegaard accepts this, and adds only that such a consciousness would always keep him humble by reminding him that he had gone so far into sin as to have needed such a miraculous rescue.[58] But Adler showed no such humility. Moreover, such an awareness of being blessed with a revelation of the eternal who entered temporal existence would certainly be remembered as a paradox that tests men; but Adler wrote about his revelation as if it were something that could be tested by human criteria.[59] So, although Adler's experience of being "shaken" by the Spirit gives him a definite advantage and accounts for everything good in his writings, the way in which he views it as merely a past event to be assimilated as fully as possible indicates that he has not really become an apostle, a spokesperson for God: "[T]here is not the fresh outpouring of an experienced religion which now at the moment . . . arises to a present life."[60]

It is here, in the concept of "presence," that the key to divine authority is to be found. An apostle's message is always the same and yet always new and fresh, because the apostle is a person who lives on the basis of his or her relationship with God in the present. "Presence" is both temporal—meaning not merely past or future—and relational: in the present, the apostle lives in the *presence* of God. Kierkegaard is not to be thought of as a mystic who advocates a disciplined striving after experiences of union with God. But he does make clear that, for him, the presence of God is not merely a scriptural or liturgical formula. It is an experienced reality, the foundation of the faith relation, and thus a prerequisite for any and all claims to divine authority.

The sense of humility mentioned above echoes a passage in *Purity of Heart*, where Kierkegaard writes of the need for a sense of shame before the "transfigured one." This encounter is profoundly subjective yet clearly not just a matter of blind faith based upon authority: "But the transfigured one exists only as transfigured, not visibly to the earthly eye, not audibly to the earthly ear, only in the sacredly still silence of shame."[61]

This idea is repeated in *Works of Love*, where we read that the only way to understand the eternal is to have "stillness around you while you wholly concentrate your attention upon inwardness."[62] A constant theme of that book is the centrality of the God-relationship, which must be the point of departure for every individual: "Because the man belongs first and foremost to God before he belongs to any other relationship, the first question put to him must be whether he has deliberated with God and his conscience."[63] The mark of divine authority is that it speaks only *within* this relationship, grasping the one addressed. Just as Scripture does not speak to us about others, so also in every communication with Christ "it is infinitely important that it is Christ who has spoken it, and when it is spoken to an individual it is precisely to *him* that it is spoken."[64]

Finally, perhaps the most famous Kierkegaardian formulation of the presence of God in the life of the believer is the one attributed to Anti-Climacus in *Sickness unto Death*: "Faith is: that the self in being itself and in willing to be itself rests transparently in God."[65] For a Christian, God is present in the very act of being or willing to be a self. That is why a believer will never defend Christianity: "To defend something is always to disparage it,"[66] precisely because the defense presupposes that the one being defended is absent and unable to defend himself. But Christian faith means to stand every moment in the presence of God. In an earlier time, writes Anti-Climacus, when Christianity "exercised dominion over men and with heretofore unknown severity brought them up with the fear and trembling of the punishment of eternity,"[67] it had not yet occurred to Christians (as it would in Christendom) that one can be a Christian without living in God's presence.

Conclusion: The Difference between an Apostle and a Religious Author

Unlike Adler, Kierkegaard never claims to have received a revelation. He does not view himself as an apostle or as in any way possessing divine authority. We have seen that this authority is characterized by him primarily in terms of what it is not, but that it also presupposes the positive presence of God. Divine authority is transcendent, paradoxical, and heterogeneous. This means that the apostle is an individual whose words seem to come from God himself, a person through whom God draws us into His presence. Only because of this is the apostle's claim to divine authority accepted by the believer. That authority is transcendent, for it is not based upon any human characteristic or immanent possession of the apostle; it is paradoxical, for it is an instance of the eternal revealing itself in a moment of time, the universal through a particular person; and it is heterogeneous, for there is no way to judge the apostle's claim simply by the content of his message. That the apostle is certain to give offense to many and that his life will certainly reduplicate his teaching cannot be viewed as warrants of divine authority, for both facts are equally true of the genius. Several warrants of a negative sort are mentioned, reminiscent of the "inverted dialectic" of suffering in *Concluding Unscientific Postscript*.[68] Thus suffering is hailed as a "proof" of apostleship;[69] the bizarre notion of commanding that which everyone already desires is said to be proof of the divine origin of the commandment to love; and the unpromising nature of the first disciples of Jesus is claimed to enhance "the impression of divine authority" granted to them.[70] But Kierkegaard does not dwell upon any of these inverted dialectics of authority. Rather, it is the presence of God that certifies the words of an apostle or of Scripture as the Word of God. That is the foundation, the faith relationship upon which all claims to divine authority must rest. Faith can never be based upon authority, for it is only by faith as a living relationship with God that divine authority ever enters into human life.

What does this imply for Kierkegaard's constant reiteration that he writes as one "without authority"? On the one hand, he was never ordained, and so he cannot claim ecclesiastical authority. On the other, however, he was trained in critical and dialectical analysis, and this gives him the authority to analyze Adler's errors. In this sense, he is like the physician who can diagnose on the basis of the authority of his knowledge even though he has not shared the experience of the sick patient.[71] But this is a merely human authority, available to anyone who will submit to the rigors of philosophical and theological training. It is often suggested that Kierkegaard's denials of authority show his respect for the existential demand that each individual has to decide for himself about his relationship with God.[72] This is true, but it must never be allowed to eclipse what is central here, namely, Kierkegaard's own self-understanding as a religious author in relationship with God. He is, as he himself writes in a famous passage in *Purity of Heart*, only a "prompter" in a theater where the listeners/readers are those who are prompted, the stage is eternity, and God is the audience.[73] Thus:

> God's presence is the decisive thing that changes all. As soon as God is present, each man in the presence of God has the task of paying attention to himself. The speaker must see that during the address he pays attention to himself, to what he says; the listener, that during the address he pays attention to himself, to how he listens, and whether during the address he, in his inner self, secretly talks with God.[74]

The genius of Kierkegaard's second authorship lies not, like that of the first, in his indirect communication and the dialectic of existence. The genius of these "direct" works is that they are addressed not only to men and women but also to God. They do not have divine authority, for divine authority occurs only when God sets the task, when God gives one person a message for others. In contrast, it is Kierkegaard who is addressing God on behalf of himself. And we, his readers, are, in a sense, listeners who are only eavesdroppers—unless we are willing to be "prompted" to become speakers ourselves.

Notes

1. Gordon D. Kaufman, "Mystery, Critical Consciousness, and Faith," in *The Rationality of Religious Belief: Essays in Honor of Basil Mitchell*, ed. William J.

Abraham and Steven W. Holtzer (Oxford: Clarendon Press, 1987), p. 57.
2. Ibid., p. 56.
3. Ibid., p. 57.
4. Søren Kierkegaard, *Works of Love: Some Christian Reflections in the Form of Discourses*, trans. Howard and Edna Hong (New York: Harper Torchbook, 1962), p. 104 (hereafter cited as WL).
5. Søren Kierkegaard, *On Authority and Revelation: The Book on Adler, or a Cycle of Ethico-Religious Essays*, trans. Walter Lowrie (Princeton, NJ: Princeton University Press, 1955) (hereafter cited as AR). This work is not dealt with in many discussions of Kierkegaard's thought. However, two very fine articles on it are available in English: Stanley Cavell, "Kierkegaard's *On Authority and Revelation*," in *Kierkegaard: A Collection of Critical Essays*, ed. Josiah Thompson (Garden City, NY: Doubleday Anchor, 1972), pp. 373–93; and Ronald Hustwit, "Adler and the Ethical: A Study of Kierkegaard's *On Authority and Revelation*," in *Religious Studies* 21 (1985): 331–48.
6. Søren Kierkegaard, "Of the Difference between a Genius and an Apostle," in *The Present Age*, trans. Alexander Dru (New York: Harper & Row, 1962), pp. 89–108 (hereafter cited as PA).
7. *The Journals of Søren Kierkegaard*, ed. and trans. Alexander Dru (London: Oxford University Press, 1938), no. 940 (hereafter cited as JSK).
8. I have discussed the problem of pseudonymity in *Kierkegaard's Dialectic of Inwardness: A Structural Analysis of the Theory of Stages* (Princeton, NJ: Princeton University Press, 1985), especially p. 3 and p. 253, note 2.
9. See Mark Lloyd Taylor's discussion of the connection between repetition and transcendence in his essay in this volume, pp. 42–43.
10. PA, pp. 90–91.
11. AR, pp. 26–27.
12. Ibid., p. 102.
13. Ibid., p. 103.
14. Ibid.
15. Ibid., p. 59.
16. On the question of Kierkegaard's irrationalism, see C. Stephen Evans, *Kierkegaard's Fragments and Postscript: The Religious Philosophy of Johannes Climacus* (Atlantic Highlands, NJ: Humanities Press, 1983), Chap. 11; and Merold Westphal, "Logic of Insanity," in *Kierkegaard's Critique of Reason and Society* (Macon, GA: Mercer University Press, 1987) pp. 85–103.
17. Søren Kierkegaard, *Training in Christianity and the Edifying Discourse which "Accompanied" It*, trans. Walter Lowrie (Princeton, NJ: Princeton University Press, 1967), p. 49 (hereafter cited as TC). This is reminiscent of the "if" in Luke 20:1–8: if John the Baptist has divine authority, then his testimony about Jesus must be believed; if Jesus has it, then John must be believed; and so on.
18. JSK, no. 630. Note that in Danish doubt (*tvivl*) is etymologically linked to despair (*fortvivl*). Kierkegaard sees this as no accident.
19. AR, pp. 46–47.
20. PA, p. 99. There is an unfortunate misprint in this edition, where "qualitative" is printed for "quantitative." See Søren Kierkegaard, *Samlede Værker*, vol. 15: *Tvende ethisk-religieuse Smaa-Afhandlinger*, ed. A. B. Drachmann (Copenhagen: Gyldendal, 1963), p. 58 (hereafter cited as SV).
21. Although Kierkegaard does say faith is a form of immediacy, to use Hegelian language, he constantly argues that it is not a "first" but a "later" or higher immediacy.

22. See Merold Westphal's chapter in this volume.
23. PA, p. 96.
24. AR, pp. 72–73.
25. PA, p. 102.
26. WL, p. 60.
27. Ibid., pp. 59–60.
28. Ibid., p. 31.
29. PA, p. 107.
30. Ibid., p. 97. The Danish for "reduplication" is often *Reduplikation*, but the word in question here is *Fordoblelse*, (literally: redoubling). SV, 15, p. 56.
31. AR, p. 24.
32. JSK, no. 993. It is this necessity of reduplication that eventually leads Kierkegaard to the conclusion that the witness to the truth, the true Christian, must collide violently with the established order. See the articles in this volume by Merold Westphal and Eric Ziolkowski.
33. AR, p. 19.
34. Ibid., p. 67. Stanley Cavell seems to confuse the issue when he remarks that "Kierkegaard is . . . no less a phenomenon than Adler." Broadly construed, that may be true. But Adler's confusion about basic religious concepts qualifies him as a type of his age, whereas Kierkegaard's estrangement from that same age makes him a "phenomenon" in a very different sense. See Cavell, "Kierkegaard's *On Authority and Revelation*," p. 392.
35. AR, pp. 192–93.
36. Ibid., p. 189.
37. Ibid., p. 179.
38. Ibid., p. 150.
39. Ibid.
40. Ibid., p. 149.
41. Ibid., pp. 87, 170.
42. Ibid., pp. 151–53. Note that Kierkegaard himself later comes to demand some external expression of the internal, although he never claims that the internal can be exhaustively so expressed or that any specific external expression is a guarantee of the corresponding inwardness. See the essays by Merold Westphal and Louise Carroll Keeley in this volume.
43. AR, pp. 133, 129.
44. Ibid., pp. 168–70.
45. Ibid., p. 145.
46. Ibid., p. 77.
47. Ibid., p. 154.
48. Ibid., pp. 181–88.
49. Ibid., p. 152.
50. Ibid., p. 173.
51. Ibid., p. 176.
52. Ibid., pp. 131, 135, 136.
53. Ibid., pp. 101–2.
54. Ibid., pp. 68, 163–64.
55. Ibid., pp. 78–79.
56. Ibid., p. 41.
57. Ibid., pp. 90, 92, 99. Kierkegaard frequently insists that he is basing his entire treatment of Adler entirely upon the latter's own concessions (p. 70 *et passim*).
58. AR, p. 82.

59. Ibid., p. 58.
60. Ibid., p. 156.
61. Søren Kierkegaard, *Purity of Heart Is to Will One Thing: Spiritual Preparation for the Office of Confession*, trans. Douglas V. Steere (New York: Harper & Row, 1956), p. 92.
62. WL, p. 304. See Louise Carroll Keeley's chapter in this volume in which she discusses whether Kierkegaard's emphasis on inwardness in *Works of Love* and elsewhere is so great and so undialectical as to constitute acosmism.
63. WL, p. 141.
64. Ibid., p. 104.
65. Søren Kierkegaard, *The Sickness unto Death: A Christian Psychological Exposition for Upbuilding and Awakening*, trans. Howard V. and Edna H. Hong (Princeton, NJ: Princeton University Press, 1980), p. 82 (hereafter cited as SD). See the discussions of this passage in the chapters in this volume by George Connell, Stephen Crites, Wanda Warren Berry, and Charles Bellinger.
66. SD, p. 87.
67. TC, p. 224.
68. Søren Kierkegaard, *Concluding Unscientific Postscript to the Philosophical Fragments*, trans. Walter Lowrie and David F. Swenson (Princeton, NJ: Princeton University Press, 1941), p. 467. On the "inverted dialectic," see Sylvia Walsh Utterback, "Kierkegaard's Inverted Dialectic," *Kierkegaardiana* 11(1980):34–54; and my *Kierkegaard's Dialectic of Inwardness*, pp. 193–95.
69. PA, p. 195.
70. WL, pp. 41, 56, 126.
71. AR, p. 11.
72. WL, p. 361, note 37.
73. Ibid., p. 180.
74. Ibid., p. 181. See the chapter by George Connell in this volume, where it is argued that God's watchful presence is a precondition of the responsible self-relation that is the essence of ethical selfhood.

3 Ordeal and Repetition in Kierkegaard's Treatment of Abraham and Job

MARK LLOYD TAYLOR

October 16, 1843, was an unusual day in the unusual career of Søren Kierkegaard. On that day he published two pseudonymous works: *Fear and Trembling* by Johannes de Silentio and *Repetition* by Constantin Constantius. Despite their simultaneous publication, the books have met very different fates in Kierkegaard scholarship. The one has lived up to Kierkegaard's prediction: "Oh, once I am dead, *Fear and Trembling* alone will be enough for an imperishable name as an author."[1] The other has lived down to his ironic remark: "*Repetition* was insignificant, without any philosophical pretension, a droll little book, dashed off as an oddity."[2] While *Fear and Trembling* has been the subject of innumerable self-contained essays by philosophers and theologians of all persuasions, interpretations of *Repetition* have been restricted largely to books on the entire pseudonymous authorship by Kierkegaard specialists.[3] In any case, the usual interpretations seem to be problematic on several counts.

What is striking about discussions of *Repetition* is the amazing elasticity with which the book is endowed by its interpreters.[4] On the one hand, it is discussed within the context of Kierkegaard's early aesthetic productions and is linked back to Volume 1 of *Either/Or* and ahead to the banquet of *Stages on Life's Way*. On the other hand, the book is seen as expressing in the concept of repetition an ultimate category within Kierkegaard's understanding of Christian existence. But how is the presence of such an ultimate category in such an early work to be accounted for? After all, *Repetition* followed *Either/Or* by a mere eight months. Isn't it curious that the rebirth of the self in Christian existence, which presupposes sin, incarnation, atonement, and faith, can be described using a concept developed in a book that, apparently, lacks all such religious categories?

Although the sheer number of competing readings of *Fear and Trembling* makes generalization dangerous, it would seem safe to say that, until recently, most discussions of the book have focused on the issues of rationality and absurdity, ethical duty and religious obedience raised by the first two problemata.[5] But isn't it curious that such a voluminous secondary literature, full of radically conflicting views as to what is being said in the text, should have developed concerning a work whose pseudonymous author's very name, Johannes de Silentio, implies silence and concealment, not speech and revelation; whose author consistently denies he has, or can even understand, the faith of Abraham; whose author chooses as an epigraph an anecdote about a messenger who conveyed an indirect message he himself did not understand?

If the usual interpretations of the two books individually are curious, then the treatment of their relationship to, and significance for the understanding of, one another is even curiouser. Their simultaneous publication is considered, almost by default, to be accidental, since it is rare that either work is treated as integral to the understanding of the other. When they are treated in relation to one another it is almost always either in discussions of the entire pseudonymous authorship or in biographical studies of Søren Kierkegaard the man. In such discussions, the order of presentation—more importantly, the logic of evaluation—is always *Repetition* first, then *Fear and Trembling*. The consensus is that the point made by *Repetition* requires completion in *Fear and Trembling*. For example, one interpreter bases his view of the relationship between the two books on what he takes to be the significance of the two biblical stories in the books:

> In one of the letters in *Repetition* the Young Man observes, "Job's significance is that the border conflicts incident to faith are fought out in him." This is a highly astute observation about Job, who is after all neither a saint nor a hero of faith. It is appropriate that he should be the Biblical focus of *Repetition*, whose concern is precisely these "border conflicts." But now in *Fear and Trembling* Kierkegaard is pressing an exploratory foot over the "boundaries of the marvelous" into the proper territory of faith itself. It is only proper that Job should recede into the background while Abraham takes his place. For Abraham is beyond the "border conflicts"; he is a faithful man; he is the very paradigm of faith—the "knight of faith." In shifting his focus from Job to Abraham, Kierkegaard moves from a consideration of the boundaries of faith to a consideration of its center.[6]

But isn't it curious that whenever the two books are discussed in relation to each other in Kierkegaard's later works, both under pseudonyms and in his own name, the order in which they are presented— more importantly, the logic by which they are evaluated— is always *Fear and Trembling* first, and then *Repetition*, never the reverse?[7] Yes, curious indeed.

The problematic state of the interpretation of the two books, coupled with their recent publication together as Volume 6 of *Kierkegaard's Writings*, suggests the fruitfulness of an alternative reading. The purpose of this essay is to lay the foundation for such a reading. My central thesis is as follows. Careful study of the striking similarities between the Abraham and Job stories in *Fear and Trembling* and *Repetition* indicates that the two books are not accidentally related but, in fact, are companion pieces that have the same goal: the introduction of the concept of repetition.

ORDEAL: THE ABRAHAM AND JOB STORIES IN *FEAR AND TREMBLING* AND *REPETITION*

A superficial reading of *Fear and Trembling* and *Repetition* might suggest more differences than similarities. The former is Johannes de Silentio's dialectical lyric on the story in Genesis 22 of God's command to Abraham to sacrifice his son Isaac. The latter is subtitled "a venture in experimenting psychology" and, initially, seems to be a grab bag of observations by Constantin Constantius on a host of unrelated subjects: repetition and recollection, love and betrothal (specifically of a young man), trips to Berlin, the theater. Within Constantin's observations are the young man's letters concerning his relationships to his beloved and to Constantin, as well as his interest in the Book of Job.

A closer reading, however, reveals considerable similarities between the two authors. Both Johannes and Constantin are characterized as silent, although this badge of silence is ironic since, after a fashion, the silent ones do speak.[8] Both hint that their statements cannot be taken simply at face value, but must be understood to communicate indirectly.[9] The two loquacious silent authors, who write misleadingly, express a similar attitude toward their readers: they don't want any; and toward their subject matter: they don't understand it.[10] Johannes and Constantin use virtually the same words to describe their inability "to make a religious movement."[11] But this inability does not keep them from admiring and praising those who can make a religious movement.[12]

Before an examination can be carried out of the Abraham and Job stories—stories which involve religious movements—two other preliminary remarks about *Repetition* need to be made. First, in this work one faces the problem of multiple pseudonymity, for although Constantin is the author of the book, it is in the young man's letters to Constantin that the story of Job is told. In this *Repetition* is more like *Either/Or*, where one author is "enclosed within the other like the boxes of a Chinese puzzle,"[13] than *Fear and Trembling* with its single pseudonymous author. Just as the editor *malgré lui* of *Either/Or*, Victor Eremita, hints that the profusion of poetic individuals in that book are all his own creation,[14] Constantin says, in a concluding letter to his "real reader," that he not only experimented with the young man, but, in fact, created him.[15] Whatever the differences between the standpoints represented by Constantin and the young man, especially with regard to Job and the meaning of repetition, it must be remembered that the young man is a poetic creation of Constantin, designed to illustrate certain existential possibilities, just as Constantin, Johannes de Silentio, and all the other pseudonymous authors are poetic creations of Kierkegaard serving a similar purpose. Second, the young man's story of Job occurs within a book that is about repetition, in obvious and not so obvious ways. Constantin may despair of realizing repetition in his own life, but he is able to analyze the concept. There are three explicit discussions of repetition in the book.[16] A brief summary of these is crucial.

At the beginning of his book, Constantin indicates that he has been "practically immobilized" by the question "whether a repetition is possible and what importance it has."[17] He says that repetition is a modern concept that will be discovered, one which will be the opposite of the concept of recollection in Greek philosophy. The Greeks taught that all knowing is a recollecting; modern philosophy will teach that all life is a repetition, although it has not yet done so, since in Leibniz alone can an intimation of the concept be found. In recollection, that which has been is repeated backwards; in repetition, it is repeated forwards. Repetition makes one happy in the "blissful security of the moment," while recollection makes one unhappy.[18] Constantin employs a series of metaphors to contrast recollection, repetition, and hope. Hope is a stiff, unworn garment of uncertain fit; recollection is an ill-fitting, worn-out garment that is discarded; repetition is a perfectly fitting garment that is indestructible. Hope is a lovely woman who slips away; recollection an old woman with whom one is never satisfied; repetition a beloved wife of whom one never grows weary. Hope cowardly chases butterflies; recollection is voluptuous, but never leaves its spinning wheel; repetition is mature, profound, courageous, and genuinely alive. Hope is a beckoning fruit, recollection petty travel money—neither of which satisfy. And repetition? To finish this comparison, Constantin uses religious language: "Repetition is the daily bread that satisfies with blessing."[19] Indeed the world would not have existed at all if God had not eschewed hope, as well as recollection, and instead willed repetition. Constantin concludes: "Repetition—that is actuality and the earnestness of existence. The person who wills repetition is mature in earnestness."[20]

The second discussion of repetition also opens with the contrast between Greek and modern philosophy.[21] But this time Constantin is critical of modern (Hegelian) philosophy, saying that repetition proper has been mistakenly called "mediation." He praises "repetition" (*Gjentagelse*) as a good Danish word, unlike the foreign import "mediation" (*Ophævelse*, from German *Aufhebung*). Mediation does not account for the motion, the transition, the change accomplished in repetition. Constantin suggests that, at this point, the Greeks have something important to offer with their category of *kinesis* (motion, change). He proceeds to describe the *kinesis* of repetition, saying that repetition involves novelty, the coming into being of the new, the re-new-al of that which has been.

> The dialectic of repetition is easy, for that which is repeated has been—otherwise it could not be repeated—but the fact that it has been makes the repetition into something new. When the Greeks said that all knowing is recollecting, they said that all existence, which is, has been; when one says that life is a repetition, one says: actuality, which has been, now comes into existence.[22]

Then comes another important concluding statement:

> Recollection is the ethnical [pagan] view of life, repetition the modern; repetition is the interest of metaphysics and also the interest upon which metaphysics comes to grief; repetition is the watchword in every ethical view; repetition is the *conditio sine qua non* for every issue of dogmatics.[23]

Once again, a connection between repetition and religious categories is suggested. The statement concerning "interest" reveals Constantin's view that repetition is not a natural, mechanical process, but is grounded in human freedom. He also hints that there is something about repetition that is inaccessible to the theoretical exercise of human reason.

Constantin returns a final time to the concept of repetition in the second part of his book, appropriately titled, "Repetition." He writes that he was surprised suddenly to begin receiving letters from the young man, who had, sometime earlier, abruptly left his beloved and vanished. In the letters, the young man speaks of his desire to reestablish the relationship, even though he knows it to be humanly impossible, given his shame over the way he broke up with the girl. The issue that brings the young man to a halt is none other than repetition. Once again a contrast is drawn between Greek and modern philosophy. But here the *novum* that comes into being in repetition is explicitly connected with a religious figure, Job. Constantin says that the young man is right not to seek a clarification of repetition in either Greek or modern philosophy. The Greeks made the opposite movement of recollection, while modern philosophy makes no motion at all, only a commotion. And, in any case, the immanent categories of philosophy are useless, since "repetition is and remains a transcendence."[24] Constantin confesses his inability to clarify the concept further, praises the fact that the young man has turned to Job, and reports the young man's belief that he has found repetition in Job's story. With this, the two biblical stories can now be considered.

Johannes de Silentio and the young man are captivated, even obsessed, by the Old Testament stories of Abraham and Job, respectively. Johannes says, of himself presumably, that there was once a child who heard the story of God's test of Abraham.

> The older he became, the more often his thoughts turned to that story; his enthusiasm for it became greater and greater. . . . Finally he forgot everything else because of it; his soul had but one wish, to see Abraham, but one longing, to have witnessed that event.[25]

But for all this consuming interest, the man was unable to understand Abraham. "Every time he returned from a pilgrimage to Mount Moriah, he sank down wearily, folded his hands, and said, 'No one was as great as Abraham. Who is able to understand him?'"[26] *Fear and Trembling* represents Johannes' amazed praise of Abraham.

The young man finds the story of Job to be a unique comfort in the pain of breaking off the relationship with his beloved.[27] He calls Job his "unforgettable benefactor" and says, "I do not read him as one reads another book, with the eyes, but I lay the book, as it were, on my heart and read it with the eyes of my heart, in a clairvoyance interpreting the specific points in the most diverse ways."[28] Like a school child, he takes Job to bed with him, so that he can learn while he sleeps. Every word from Job is food and clothing. He transcribes phrases from Job and lays them on his "sick heart as a God's hand-plaster."[29] In his eight letters to Constantin, the young man reveals his understanding of Job and narrates his own situation in light of Job's story.

The stories of Abraham and Job told by Johannes and the young man are remarkably similar. Johannes' summary of Genesis 22, "that beautiful story of how God tempted Abraham and of how Abraham withstood the temptation, kept the faith, and, contrary to expectation, got a son a second time,"[30] introduces the three central concepts used by both storytellers to illuminate their Old Testament heroes: ordeal, faith, and repetition.

The key to the situation of Abraham is that he undergoes an ordeal, one imposed by God, whereby God tests or tempts him. Johannes makes this point in each section of his dialectical lyric.[31] An ordeal is a paradoxical category, one that goes beyond the ordinary categories of reason. Johannes is fond of saying that Abraham is a prodigious paradox. Abraham can be admired, and he can certainly arouse passion, but he cannot be understood, or, rather, he can be understood only as one understands a paradox. The three problemata display the paradoxical nature of Abraham's ordeal.

In Problema I, Johannes shows that an ordeal involves a collision of a person with the demands of ethics in which the ethical is suspended by something higher. But since the ethical is the universal, is binding on all individuals without exception and, thus, has no *telos* beyond itself, but is itself the *telos* of all individual acts, such an ordeal is paradoxical indeed. It places the individual beyond the universal through a teleological suspension of the ethical. This is Abraham's situation. God's command to sacrifice Isaac collides with Abraham's ethical duty not to harm his son. God's command "suspends" the ethical demand. It is clear that Johannes does not understand this teleological suspension of the ethical to mean that Abraham was given license, and an easy conscience, to murder his son. He is not so much freed to violate his ethical duty as prohibited from obeying it by the voice of God. All the while, Abraham recognizes and, with the most intense pathos, feels the binding character of ethical duty. Indeed, the clarity and validity of the ethical demand tempts Abraham to disobey God. This is why the situation is an ordeal. Johannes concludes: "Either Abraham was a murderer every minute or we stand before a paradox that is higher than all mediations."[32]

Johannes goes on to say in Problema II that an ordeal, a teleological suspension of the ethical, places the individual in an absolute relation to the absolute, to God, that is higher than the individual's relation to the ethical. In an ordeal, "the single individual . . . determines his relationship to the universal [the ethical] by his relation to the absolute [God], not his relation to the absolute by his relation to the universal."[33] Unlike a tragic hero, Abraham would not accomplish a higher ethical purpose by his "sacrifice." Johannes concludes: "either there is an absolute duty to God, and if there is such a thing, it is the paradox just described . . . or else faith has never existed because it has always existed, or else Abraham is lost."[34]

At the climactic point of each of the first two problemata, where Abraham stands under a teleological suspension of the ethical in a purely individual but absolute relationship to God, the only defense available is to say that his situation is an ordeal, by which he is being tested. Johannes indicates, however, that such a defense is not effective at all, because Abraham cannot prove it is only an ordeal that forces him to sacrifice Isaac and not his own murderous intent. This reveals a final characteristic of an ordeal for Johannes: as a paradoxical category, an ordeal cannot be mediated by thought so as to make the one undergoing an ordeal understandable to others. To say, "It is an ordeal," explains nothing, for the very nature of an ordeal places a person beyond the universal, communicable, understandable categories of ethical rationality. Problema III explores the "pledge of silence"[35] extracted from Abraham by his ordeal.

The question raised by this final problema is: "Was it ethically defensible for Abraham to conceal his undertaking from Sarah, Isaac, and Eliezer?"[36] Either there is a silence that brings us face to face with the paradox of an individual who stands higher than the universal, or Abraham is lost. Johannes demonstrates that Abraham's silence has nothing to do with aesthetic secrecy and can only be condemned by ethics, which demands self-revelation at any cost. "Abraham cannot speak, because he cannot say that which would explain everything (that is, so that it is understandable): That it is an ordeal such that, please note, the ethical is the temptation."[37] Even when Abraham does speak he is not understood. In response to Isaac's question, "Where is the lamb for sacrifice?" Abraham's answer, "God himself will provide the lamb for the burnt offering," simply restates, and does not do away with, the paradox.[38] Why? Because Abraham's response to Isaac is ironic or, more precisely, an instance of the "speaking in tongues" that is the proper language of an ordeal.[39] And so Johannes ends where he began, marveling at the paradox of Abraham.

The young man's story of Job is not nearly as detailed, as dialectically relentless, or as passionately charged as Johannes' tale of Abraham. Nevertheless, he understands Job's situation to be an ordeal and describes an ordeal very much as Johannes does. In the letter of December 14 he says: "How then is Job's position to be explained? The explanation is this: the whole thing is an ordeal."[40] An ordeal is an "altogether transcendent" category and cannot be illuminated aesthetically, ethically, or dogmatically.[41] The young man describes the genesis of an ordeal in terms familiar from *Fear and Trembling*, saying that an ordeal occurs through a collision with ethics caused by some higher religious telos:

> How does the individual discover that it is an ordeal? . . . First of all, the event must be cleared of its cosmic associations and get a religious baptism and a religious name, then one must appear before ethics for examination, and then comes the expression: an ordeal.[42]

In Job's case, the ethical is represented by his "comforters," who try to convince him that his misery and misfortune are the punishment for some sin, of which Job must repent. Job steadfastly maintains this is not the case and thus "avoids all cunning ethical evasions and wily devices,"[43] a phrase reminiscent of Johannes' statement that for Abraham the ethical constituted a temptation. Job is an exception. The view that he has violated the ethical and needs to repent cannot help him, for, like Abraham, the ethical has been suspended by a higher power, God.

An ordeal, the young man continues, "places a person in a purely personal relationship of opposition to God, in a relationship such that he cannot allow himself to be satisfied with any explanation at second hand."[44] Job, like Abraham, stands in an absolute relationship to God that is beyond the universal demands of ethics.[45] Likewise, try as he might, Job cannot communicate to his comforters that his situation is an ordeal. The explanation causes more difficulties than it solves. An ordeal cannot be caught within the rational categories of any science, for an ordeal applies to the exception, not the rule. Even dogmatics does not explain an ordeal, but simply begins with the assumption that such and such an event is an ordeal.

And once one knows that an event is an ordeal, "the resilience of the ordeal is impaired, and the category is actually another category."[46]

To say that their situations are ordeals implies, contrary to all appearances, that Abraham and Job are innocent of any wrongdoing. Johannes reminds the reader that "Abraham was God's chosen one, and it was the Lord who imposed the ordeal."[47] Later, he says: "[O]nly a person of that kind is put to such a test."[48] The young man's evaluation of Job is similar:

> [T]he secret in Job, the vital force, the nerve, the idea, is that Job, despite everything, is in the right. . . . He affirms that he is on good terms with God; he knows he is innocent and pure in the very core of his being, where he also knows it before the Lord.[49]

The second similarity between Johannes' Abraham and the young man's Job, then, is that both Old Testament figures withstand their ordeals and thus can be held up as illustrative of faith.

The ordeals of Abraham and Job involve sacrifice and loss. Johannes and the young man marvel at the composure of their heroes in the midst of such loss and speak of the comfort their example gives to all others who suffer loss. But both storytellers make it clear that what ultimately interests and amazes them is not the resilience of their heroes in loss, but the way in which they regain what has been lost, their restorations. This is the third similarity between their stories.

Johannes explores the marvel of the restoration of Isaac to Abraham in the "preliminary expectoration" that precedes the three problemata. Abraham, Johannes says, "through a double movement . . . attained his first condition, and therefore . . . received Isaac more joyfully than the first time."[50] This double movement occurs "by virtue of the absurd, for all human calculation ceased long ago."[51] Isaac is bound and lying on the altar. Abraham has the knife in hand and is prepared to sacrifice his son. It is only the voice of God that stays his hand; it is only after God speaks that Abraham sees the ram caught in the thicket. And yet the paradoxical faith of Abraham is that even with knife in hand, against all reason and evidence, he believed God would not require Isaac. "By faith Abraham did not renounce Isaac, but by faith Abraham received Isaac."[52]

Johannes illuminates the double movement by virtue of the absurd that constitutes faith through his well-known contrast between the knight of infinite resignation and the knight of faith. The initial movement is a negative one, whereby actuality is given up or renounced or resigned. The knight of infinite resignation has renounced all of actuality and, therefore, exists within finitude as a stranger. The knight of faith also makes the movement of resignation, but goes on and makes a second movement, a movement in which the actuality previously negated or renounced is restored. The knight of faith "after having made the movements of infinity, makes the movements of finitude" or, more exactly, continuously receives the finite as a result.[53]

How does this happen? How does the knight of faith receive back again the finite which has been resigned? This is the paradox, the marvel of faith. According to Johannes, "it takes purely human courage to renounce the whole temporal realm," while it takes "a paradoxical and humble courage to grasp the whole temporal realm by virtue of the absurd, and this is the courage of faith."[54] The phrase, "by virtue of the absurd," indicates that the second moment of the double movement, the moment that is faith proper, unlike the Stoic self-starvation of the knight of infinite resignation, is not an immanent human possibility at all. It occurs only "by virtue of the fact that for God all things are possible."[55] This paradoxical second movement transcends the categories of human reason.

> The absurd does not belong to the differences that lie within the proper domain of the understanding. . . . The moment the knight executed the act of resignation, he was convinced of the impossibility, humanly speaking; that was the conclusion of the understanding . . . [F]or the understanding continues to be right in maintaining that in the finite world where it dominates this having was and continues to be an impossibility. The knight of faith . . . can be saved only by the absurd, and this he grasps in faith.[56]

While Johannes can describe the way others, prototypically Abraham, make this movement, he says he is incapable of making it himself.

For Johannes, therefore, faith is characterized not by giving something up, but by receiving something. The knight of faith is so far from being a stranger in the finite world that the knight can be mistaken for a tax collector, fully immersed in finitude, with no external sign of heterogeneity.[57] The difference, and it is an absolute difference, is that the knight of faith does not live in the finite immediately, but in the second immediacy of the double movement of faith whereby the finite is received from the hand of God. Abraham received Isaac back, but in a wholly new way. It is the same Isaac, the same finite world, and yet not the same, for now Isaac, the finite, is received from the hand of God by virtue of the absurd, when impossible in human terms. The double movement of faith is nothing less than "a new creation by virtue of the absurd."[58]

The young man's view of Job's restoration is found in his letter of January 13. He writes:

> The storms have spent their fury—the thunderstorm is over—Job has been censured before the face of humankind—the Lord and Job have come to an understanding, they are reconciled, "the confidence of the Lord dwells again in the tents of Job as in former days"—men have come to understand Job. *Now* they come to him and eat bread with him and are

sorry for him; his brothers and sisters, each one of them, give him a farthing and a gold ring—Job is blessed and has received everything *double*.—This is called a *repetition*."[59]

It is significant that the young man uses the concept of repetition to describe the restoration that Job experiences. Recall Constantin's claim that repetition is the *kinesis* in which actuality that has been is re-newed or re-born, not immanently, but transcendently. Job receives back again all that he had lost, not through his own effort, but by God's act. Job's repetition occurs only when it is impossible, beyond all human calculation.

> Who could have imagined this ending? Yet no other end is thinkable, and not this one, either. When everything has stalled, when thought is immobilized, when language is silent, when explanation returns home in despair—then there has to be a thunderstorm. Who can understand this? . . . So there is a repetition, after all. When does it occur? Well, that is hard to say in any human language. When did it occur for Job? When every thinkable human certainty and probability were impossible. Bit by bit he loses everything, and hope thereby gradually vanishes . . . [T]he knot and the entanglement are tightened and can be untied only by a thunderstorm.[60]

The paradox of Job is that he was found to be in the right only through God's rebuke in the thunderstorm: "How blessed to be rebuked by God! . . . Was Job proved to be in the wrong? Yes, eternally, for there is no higher court than the one that judged him. Was Job proved to be in the right? Yes, eternally, by being proved to be in the wrong before God."[61]

The preceding analysis suggests that Constantin's category of repetition applies not only to the young man's story of Job, but also to Johannes' tale of the restoration of Isaac to Abraham. "Repetition" names and describes formally the double movement of faith lyricized by Johannes. Both Abraham and Job reveal the same double movement: loss, negation of actuality, followed by negation of that negation, which entails a new creation, a rebirth, a repetition of actuality. This double movement occurs only by virtue of the absurd beyond all immanent possibility. It is just this transcendent possibility, inexplicable in terms of either Greek or modern philosophy, to which Constantin's concept of repetition refers. It can be concluded, therefore, that the stories of Abraham and Job told by Johannes and the young man are, in fact, two versions of the same story: the story of an ordeal that ends with a repetition by virtue of the absurd, which, in some fashion, illustrates religious faith.[62]

REPETITION: *FEAR AND TREMBLING* AND *REPETITION* IN KIERKEGAARD'S AUTHORSHIP

Thus far, the similarities between the stories of Abraham and Job in *Fear and Trembling* and *Repetition* have been examined. A further similarity between the two books can now be asserted, namely, that Johannes and Constantin employ the two biblical stories to introduce the concept of repetition in the same indirect fashion. While both authors indicate, formally, the meaning of repetition, neither depicts the material content of the repetitions of Abraham and Job directly. Materially, directly, they only show what repetition is not by presenting analogues to Abraham and Job that the reader must finally transcend as inadequate if the point of the biblical stories is to be grasped.

Johannes' book is full of such analogues, although by far the most sustained set is to be found in Problema III. There a whole host of characters from folk, classical, and religious literature are brought forward: married couples from Aristotle's *Poetics* and *Politics*, Agamemnon and Iphigenia, Axel and Valborg, Agnes and the merman, Sarah and Tobit, Richard III, and Faust, among others. Like Abraham, these characters face issues of secrecy and revelation, but their secrecy or silence can be explained in the immanent terms of aesthetics and ethics, which do not apply to Abraham's paradoxical silence. What is striking is the comical way their stories interrupt the discussion of Abraham. Johannes says of all his aesthetic and ethical analogues to Abraham: "I got involved in the previous discussion to make that subject [i.e., Abraham's silence] an obstacle, not as if Abraham could thereby become more comprehensible, but in order that the incomprehensibility could become more salient."[63] What Johannes has done is to bring the reader to a boundary through his story of Abraham. He has given a name to the unknown territory, "faith," and has indicated something of the ordeal, the pathos associated with the passage into the new territory. Johannes has not described materially the territory of faith, the new birth or repetition of the self. The detailed examination of aesthetic secrecy, of the tragic hero's ethical self-revelation, and of the demonic silence of the merman has removed all possible aesthetic or ethical (that is to say, all immanent) explanations of Abraham's ordeal. By showing the inadequacy of all immanent categories for understanding Abraham, Johannes has indirectly prepared the reader to discover the transcendent character of faith and the repetition it involves. The reader does not come to understand Abraham, faith, and repetition from Johannes' book, but she or he has been shown very clearly what Abraham, faith, and repetition are not.

A similar form of comical indirection is to be found in *Repetition*. There the analogue to Johannes' misleading analogues is Constantin's technique of revealing repetition as a transcendent concept having to do with the final wholeness of human existence, only to hide it, simultaneously, under mundane examples. Constantin's initial discussion of repetition involves the contrast between repetition and recollection, but what follows is a portrayal, not of repetition, but of recollection and recollection's love in the person of the young man. This leads to Constantin's "investigative journey" aimed at testing "the possibility and meaning of repetition."[64] Curiously, he tests the possibility and meaning of his transcendent category within the sphere of immanence by trying (and failing) to repeat a trip to Berlin. In the second part of *Repetition*, the device used, at one and the same time, to reveal and conceal the meaning of repetition is no longer Constantin's failure, but the young man's apparent success, in achieving repetition. The young man likens his broken relationship with his beloved to Job's ordeal and believes he too has experienced a thunderstorm (reading in a newspaper that the girl has married someone else). But the young man's thunderstorm makes him a poet. His "repetition" is really a poetic recollection of himself.[65] Constantin sums this up when he says of the young man:

> In the earlier letters, especially in some of them, the movement was much closer to a genuinely religious resolution, but the moment the temporary suspension is terminated, he gains himself again, but as a poet, and the religious founders, that is, becomes a kind of inexpressible substratum. If he had had a deeper religious background, he would not have become a poet. Then everything would have gained religious meaning. The situation in which he was trapped would then have gained meaning for him, but the collision would have come from higher levels, and he would also have had a quite different authority, even though it would have been purchased with still more painful suffering.[66]

The young man is not Job. His experience, like Constantin's investigative journey and even the name "Constantin Constantius," is a parody of the concept of repetition, one which points beyond itself to the story of Job.

There are hints in both books that just as the previously mentioned aesthetic and ethical analogues point toward the ordeals of Abraham and Job, so the two biblical stories point beyond themselves to an as yet unknown standpoint. In the middle of his digressive third problema, Johannes refers cryptically to sin.

> Now here I would like to make a comment that says more than has been said at any point previously. Sin is not the first immediacy; sin is a later immediacy. In sin, the single individual is already higher (in the direction of the demonic paradox) than the universal, because it is a contradiction on the part of the universal to want to demand itself from a person who lacks the *conditio sine qua non*.[67]

This remark is amplified in a footnote:

> Up until now I have assiduously avoided any reference to the question of sin and its reality. The whole work is centered on Abraham, and I can still encompass him in immediate categories—that is, insofar as I can understand him. As soon as sin emerges, ethics founders precisely on

repentance; for repentance is the highest ethical expression, but precisely as such it is the deepest ethical self-contradiction.[68]

Sin represents a higher analogue to Abraham, an even more paradoxical ordeal in which a person becomes an exception and experiences a teleological suspension of the ethical, not by means of God's testing, but through her or his own inability to fulfill the universally binding ethical demand. Because sin indicates "another sphere and cannot explain Abraham," it is not pursued further by Johannes.[69]

The young man also leaves a tantalizing comment in his discussion of Job. Job can only be understood in terms of the paradoxical, transcendent category "ordeal." And yet this very category is relativized, for the young man suggests that an ordeal is temporary:

> That this category could tend to cancel out and suspend all actuality by defining it as an ordeal in relation to eternity, I readily perceive. But this doubt has not gained the upper hand over me, because, inasmuch as ordeal is a *temporary* category, it eo ipso is defined in relation to time and therefore must be annulled in time.[70]

One is left wondering if there might be an analogous category to an ordeal, one defined in relation to eternity. The nature of such a permanent ordeal remains an unexplored possibility beyond the scope of *Repetition*, just as the nature of sin transcends Johannes' discussion in *Fear and Trembling*. But these hints suggest that the standpoints represented by Abraham and Job themselves must be transcended if the ultimate significance of the two books is to be understood.

These oblique hints left hanging in *Fear and Trembling* and *Repetition* are filled out in the two crucial discussions of the books in Kierkegaard's later pseudonymous works: the long footnote in the introductory chapter of Vigilius Haufniensis' *The Concept of Anxiety*[71] and the review of the entire pseudonymous authorship to date (1846) by Johannes Climacus in *Concluding Unscientific Postscript* ("A Glance at a Contemporary Effort in Danish Literature").[72] These two texts both clarify the relationship between Johannes de Silentio's and Constantin Constantius' books and indicate how they function within the pseudonymous authorship. Vigilius Haufniensis begins with Johannes de Silentio's remarks about sin, asserts that the story of Abraham shows that "either all of existence comes to an end in the demand of ethics, or the condition is provided and the whole of life begins anew . . . through a transcendence," and argues that it is precisely Constantin's concept of repetition that elucidates this new birth of the self.[73] Johannes Climacus also adopts a similar reading. He suggests that *Repetition* serves as a "repetition" of *Fear and Trembling*, ensuring that Johannes de Silentio's indirect message about Abraham is not misconstrued in aesthetic or ethical terms, and claims that because "an ordeal is a transitional phase" Abraham and Job return "to an existence in the ethical," while the sinner remains in a state of permanent heterogeneity with the ethical, related to it not "as possibility to actuality, but as impossibility."[74]

The concept of sin is crucial for Climacus. Sin is "the decisive expression for the religious mode of existence; it is not a moment within something else, within another order of things, but is itself the beginning of the religious order of things."[75] Neither *Fear and Trembling* nor *Repetition* takes sin directly into account. Johannes de Silentio perceives that sin is a possibility beyond Abraham; Constantin and the young man explore the temporary ordeal of Job and merely hint that there might be a permanent ordeal defined in relation to eternity. It follows, therefore, that neither book and neither biblical story penetrates into the religious mode of existence as defined by Climacus, since the necessary point of entrance, sin, is lacking.

What, then, is the purpose of the two books and their biblical stories if it is not to describe religious faith? Climacus has an answer:

> Just as *Either-Or* had made sure that the teleological suspension of the ethical should not be mistaken for aesthetic secrecy, so the three pseudonymous books [*Either/Or, Fear and Trembling*, and *Repetition*] had together made sure that sin, when it came to be brought forward [in *The Concept of Anxiety*] should not be mistaken for this or that weakness and imperfection; sorrow over it should not be confounded with sighs and tears and blubbering over ourselves and this vale of tears; the suffering involved in it not confounded with a *quodlibet*.[76]

In an age that has mixed together Christian religious categories and the immanent categories of aesthetic and ethical existence in "a confusion of tongues,"[77] the first step in an effective communication of religious truth must be to forestall such confusion. Using aesthetic and ethical categories alone, Climacus says, an author must demonstrate that sin, the entryway into religious existence, is a paradoxical state of being that cannot be encompassed in aesthetic or ethical terms. This suggests that *Fear and Trembling* and *Repetition* function within Kierkegaard's authorship in exactly the same way that Johannes' analogues to Abraham and Constantin's analogues to repetition function within the two books. Just as those lower analogues announce Abraham and Job as religious exceptions by showing what Abraham and Job are not—tragic heroes or poets—so the books announce the desperate heterogeneity of sin by showing what sin is not—an ordeal, a temporary suspension of the ethical, such as that experienced by Abraham and Job.

Here is conclusive evidence that the usual interpretations of the two books are mistaken. It just will not do to say that the Job of *Repetition* represents the boundary of faith, while Johannes' Abraham represents its center. Nor does it make sense to view *Fear and Trembling* as the resolution of issues raised in *Repetition*. In fact, Abraham and Job represent exactly the same category or possibility: the ordeal. There is no qualitative difference between them. The suspension of the ethical they experienced did not involve their own sinfulness, but God's testing. Their temporary ordeals are lower analogues, which announce indirectly the permanent suspension of the ethical that is sin. One could view *Fear and Trembling*, with its story of Abraham, as completing *Repetition*, with its story of Job, only by mistaking the indirect method of communication employed by Johannes and Constantin.

If it is true that the two books prepare for an understanding of the crucial category of sin through the stories of the ordeals of Abraham and Job, without portraying sin materially, then it is equally true that the restorations of Abraham and Job are but lower analogues to the rebirth of the self in faith that is true repetition. Sin is a more radical suspension of the ethical than an ordeal. If a repetition is to be possible for the sinner, if she or he is to regain herself or himself in *statum pristinum*, it can only be by virtue of an absurd even more radical than God's suspension of the ethical demand in an ordeal. The repetition of the sinful self is the forgiveness of sin, received and lived out in faith. The absurd, by virtue of which this takes place, is the absolute paradox of God made flesh in Jesus Christ. Kierkegaard's understanding of repetition in this eminent sense is expressed perfectly by the Johannine *gennethenai anothen* (born anew/born from above; see John 3:3). The double meaning of this phrase captures both the radical newness of the life of faith as well as the fact that it comes to a person as a gift from God.

Two consequences follow from this. First, the interminable debate as to whether or not Kierkegaard is right that religious faith is antithetical to rationality, allegedly the point of Johannes' story of Abraham, is completely beside the point. The purpose of the story of Abraham in *Fear and Trembling*, as well as the story of Job in *Repetition*, is not at all to offer a portrayal of the content of religious faith but, rather, is to take away from the reader the possibility of any application of aesthetic or ethical categories to religious existence. While Abraham and Job are exceptions and cannot be comprehended using aesthetic or ethical categories either, they do not represent the exception that is the person of faith, for faith can only exist on the other side of sin, a category that applies neither to Abraham nor to Job.

Second, repetition is indeed an ultimate category, one that is central to Kierkegaard's understanding of Christian existence. However, this ultimate category is present in *Fear and Trembling* and *Repetition* only indirectly. Johannes and Constantin speak of repetition as the new birth from above in an unknown tongue. Not only do they speak about Abraham and Job in tongues, but even the point made indirectly about Abraham and Job in their books is an instance of speaking in tongues, one that points beyond itself. An interpretation of Johannes' and Constantin's glossolalia concerning repetition must wait for Kierkegaard's later works. Repetition as the new birth from above is hinted at in Vigilius' *Concept of Anxiety* and described "from below" in the Climacus works *Philosophical Fragments* and *Postscript*. An adequate portrayal is available only from the ideal Christian standpoint of the Anti-Climacus works *Sickness Unto Death* and *Training in Christianity*. And, even there, it is made clear that any description of the new birth from above remains an indirect communication, for such a description serves only to invite the reader to appropriate repetition herself or himself.

ORDEAL, REPETITION, AND SCRIPTURE

My purpose in this essay has been to provide the foundation for a more adequate reading of *Fear and Trembling* and *Repetition*. Given the nature of Kierkegaard's authorship, however, it would not seem out of place to suggest, even if briefly and incompletely, one area in which these books might contribute to contemporary theology.

At the beginning of his book, Johannes de Silentio comments that if he had been an exegetical scholar and had known Hebrew, "he perhaps would easily have understood the story of Abraham."[78] This remark ought to be taken as one more example of Kierkegaard's penchant for irony. In fact, the treatment of the Abraham and Job stories in *Fear and Trembling* and *Repetition* would seem to be quite appropriate. The stories are horrible, frightening ones, stories which, if read directly, can be very destructive. Kierkegaard does not read them this way, but seems, rather, to understand them to communicate indirectly. One application that might be derived from *Fear and Trembling* and *Repetition* is that the stories of the ordeals of Abraham and Job are ordeals for the reader or hearer of the stories. Their purpose is to test us and take from us traditional, but inadequate views. The story of Abraham's ordeal negates any attempt on our part to domesticate or own the promise of God's grace. Job's ordeal negates any view of God as the coercive yet manipulable ruler of a universe in which the good always prosper. By taking away such inadequate views, the stories open up space for a new discovery of God, or, a discovery of a new God.[79] This God is not to be found in the stories directly, but only beyond the traditional options made impossible by the stories. To use Kierkegaard's concepts, one could say that the stories of Abraham and Job provide the absurd by virtue of which a repetition, a new birth, of our view of God can be accomplished.[80]

The concept of repetition, employed in a noneminent sense to be sure, is applicable more generally to an understanding of the way in which scripture functions within the community of faith. All scripture, not just the stories of Abraham and Job, must undergo something analogous to a repetition if it is to speak truly. Scripture can be neither recollected, nor passed by; it must be born anew by virtue of the absurd.[81] The absurd by virtue of which scripture undergoes such a repetition is nothing less than the reality of God. As Kierkegaard suggests under the pseudonyms Johannes de Silentio and Constantin Constantius, the finite can be appropriated as the finite only when it is received absurdly from the hand of God. If the finite is not repeated, born anew from above, it will either be grasped in an idolatrous stranglehold or evacuated of all significance through infinite resignation. Likewise, only as scripture is negated as God, by God, can it be repeated, reborn, as the gift and the demand of God's word to us, in, under, and through the human words of the text. The call for a recognition of this is one small part of the life work of Søren Kierkegaard.

Notes

1. *Søren Kierkegaard's Journals and Papers*, 7 vols., ed. and trans. Howard V. and Edna H. Hong (Bloomington, IN: Indiana University Press, 1967–1968), entry 6491 (hereafter cited as JP plus citation number).
2. *Søren Kierkegaards Papirer*, 20 vols., ed. P. A. Heiberg, V. Kuhr, and E. Torsting (Copenhagen: Gyldendal, 1909–1948), IV B 20 (hereafter cited as *Papirer* plus volume and citation number).
3. Although Louis Mackey is certainly a "specialist," his "Once More with Feeling: Kierkegaard's *Repetition*," in *Kierkegaard and Literature: Irony, Repetition, and Criticism*, ed. Ronald Schliefer and Robert Markey (Norman, OK: University of Oklahoma Press, 1984), pp. 80–115, is one of the few "free-standing" studies of *Repetition* available. The *International Kierkegaard Commentary* series volume on *Repetition*, which should appear soon, will help fill the gap.
4. See, for example, Mark C. Taylor, *Kierkegaard's Pseudonymous Authorship: A Study of Time and the Self* (Princeton, NJ: Princeton University Press, 1975), pp. 172, 181, 329–30; John W. Elrod, *Being and Existence in Kierkegaard's Pseudonymous Works* (Princeton, NJ: Princeton University Press, 1975), pp. 229–32; and Louis Mackey, *Kierkegaard: A Kind of Poet* (Philadelphia, PA: University of Pennsylvania Press, 1971), pp. 262–63.
5. Jerry H. Gill has offered a helpful characterization of this literature in his essay, "Faith Is as Faith Does," in *Kierkegaard's Fear and Trembling: Critical Appraisals*, ed. Robert L. Perkins (University, AL: University of Alabama Press, 1981), pp. 204–9. There are two other excellent contributions in this collection: Robert L. Perkins, "For Sanity's Sake: Kant, Kierkegaard, and Father Abraham," pp. 43–61, and Mark C. Taylor, "Sounds of Silence," pp. 165–88. Along with Gill's essay, the efforts of Perkins and Taylor help overcome some of the traditional misunderstandings of the book.
6. Josiah Thompson, *The Lonely Labyrinth: Kierkegaard's Pseudonymous Works* (Carbondale, IL: Southern Illinois University Press, 1967), pp. 126–27. See Gregor Malantshuk, *Kierkegaard's Thought*, ed. and trans. Howard V. Hong and Edna H. Hong (Princeton, NJ: Princeton University Press, 1971), p. 234.

7. *The Concept of Anxiety*, trans. Reidar Thomte in collaboration with Albert Anderson (Princeton, NJ: Princeton University Press, 1980), pp. 17–19n (hereafter cited as CA); *Concluding Unscientific Postscript*, trans. David F. Swenson and Walter Lowrie (Princeton, NJ: Princeton University Press, 1941), pp. 234–40 (hereafter cited as CUP); *The Point of View for My Work as an Author*, trans. Walter Lowrie (New York: Oxford University Press, 1939), p. 21 (hereafter cited as PV); JP, 6:6357.
8. *Fear and Trembling* and *Repetition*, trans. Howard V. and Edna H. Hong (Princeton, NJ: Princeton University Press, 1983) (hereafter cited as FT, R). Here the references are to FT, pp. 1, 8; and R, pp. 134–35, 188.
9. FT, p. 3; R, pp. 19, 225.
10. FT, p. 7; R, p. 226.
11. FT, p. 37; R, p. 187.
12. FT, p. 15; R, p. 187.
13. *Either/Or*, trans. Howard V. and Edna H. Hong (Princeton, NJ: Princeton University Press, 1983), vol. 1, p. 9 (hereafter cited as EO plus volume and page number).
14. EO, vol. 1, pp. 8–10.
15. R, p. 228.
16. Ibid., pp. 131–33, 148–49, 184–87. For a helpful study of "repetition" in relation to the Hegelian notion of "mediation" see André Clair, "Médiation et Répétition: La Lieu de la Dialectique Kierkegaardienne," *Revue des Sciences Philosophiques et Théologiques* 59(1975): 38–78.
17. R, p. 131. It is worth noting that *Gjentagelse* ("repetition") literally means to "re-take" or "to take again." Unfortunately, this sense of activity is not immediately conveyed in the English word.
18. R, p. 132.
19. Ibid.
20. Ibid., p. 133.
21. Ibid., p. 148.
22. Ibid., p. 149.
23. Ibid.
24. Ibid., p. 186. See Stephen Dunning's discussion in this volume on the connection between transcendence and authority, pp. 20–21.
25. FT, p. 9.
26. Ibid., p. 14.
27. R, p. 213.
28. Ibid., pp. 198, 204.
29. Ibid., p. 204.
30. FT, p. 9.
31. Ibid., pp. 9, 19–22, 31–32, 58–60, 74, 76–77, 115.
32. Ibid., p. 66.
33. Ibid., p. 70.
34. Ibid., p. 81.
35. Ibid., p. 21.
36. Ibid., p. 82.
37. Ibid., p. 115.
38. Ibid., p. 116.
39. Ibid., pp. 118–20.
40. R, p. 209.
41. Ibid., p. 210.

42. Ibid., p. 209.
43. Ibid., p. 210.
44. Ibid.
45. Compare Edward Mooney's account of this relation in his essay in this volume.
46. R, p. 210.
47. FT, p. 19.
48. Ibid., p. 31.
49. R, p. 207.
50. FT, p. 36.
51. Ibid.
52. Ibid., p. 49.
53. Ibid., pp. 38, 40–41. See Edward Mooney's chapter in this volume for further discussion of this dialectic as it is played out in *Fear and Trembling*. Also, George Connell's essay discusses a similar dialectic of loss and recovery in *Either/Or*.
54. FT, p. 49.
55. Ibid., p. 46.
56. Ibid., pp. 46–47.
57. On the incognito character of faith in *Fear and Trembling* and in Kierkegaard's later writings, see the chapters in this volume by Edward Mooney, Merold Westphal, and Eric Ziolkowski.
58. FT, p. 40.
59. R, p. 212.
60. Ibid., pp. 212–13.
61. Ibid., p. 212. See also the "Ultimatum" at the conclusion of EO, vol. 2.
62. Kierkegaard is not alone in linking the stories of the ordeals of Abraham and Job. There are several interesting rabbinic parallels. According to a Talmudic text, *Sanhedrin* 89b, the testing of Abraham narrated in Genesis 22, like that of Job, was instigated by Satan. After observing Abraham's failure to offer sacrifice at a banquet celebrating the weaning of Isaac, Satan comments that the father of faith's joy over the gift of the child has caused him to forget God the giver. God responds that Abraham would be willing to sacrifice the child of promise, if asked to do so. The ordeal recounted in Genesis 22 follows immediately and vindicates both Abraham and God (see *The Babylonian Talmud*, 6 parts, ed. and trans. Isidore Epstein [London: Soncino Press, 1935] part 3, vol. 4, p. 595). Commenting on Genesis 57:4, one rabbi says that Job was a contemporary of Abraham. Others teach that Satan originally planned to test and denounce all of Israel and had to be persuaded by God to impose the ordeal only on Job. Job is likened to a goat thrown to an attacking wolf in order to save the flock (see *The Midrash*, 8 vols., ed. and trans. H. Freedman and Maurice Simon (London: Soncino Press, 1951), vol. 1, pp. 505–7.
63. FT, p. 112.
64. R, p. 150.
65. Ibid., pp. 221–22.
66. Ibid., p. 229.
67. FT, p. 98.
68. Ibid., p. 98n.
69. FT, p. 112. See Ronald M. Green, "Deciphering *Fear and Trembling's* Secret Message," *Religious Studies* 22(1986): 95–111, for a discussion of the hidden role sin plays in the book. Also see Edward Mooney's discussion of hidden inwardness in his essay below, pp. 86–89.

70. R, p. 210.
71. CA, pp. 17–19n.
72. CUP, pp. 225–66.
73. CA, pp. 17–18n.
74. CUP, pp. 234–36, 238–39.
75. Ibid., p. 239.
76. Ibid., p. 240.
77. CUP, p. 240.
78. FT, p. 9.
79. See Merold Westphal's chapter in this volume for more on Kierkegaardian strategies to discredit notions of God developed to our specifications.
80. Nelly Viallaneix's "Kierkegaard, l'Ancien Testament et Israel," *Etudes Théologigues et Religieuses* 54(1979): 547–77, demonstrates the constitutive role of Old Testament themes in Kierkegaard's thought and offers resources for an evaluation of his relation to the Jewish tradition. See Walter Strolz, "Die Hiob-Interpretation bei Kant, Kierkegaard und Bloch," *Kairos* 23(1981): 75–87, for a view of Job similar to the one I have sketched here.
81. An elaboration of this idea is suggested in Jaroslav Pelikan's discussion of tradition as idol, as token, and as icon in *The Vindication of Tradition* (New Haven, CT: Yale University Press, 1984), pp. 54–56. According to Pelikan, tradition becomes an idol when it directs us to itself, demands the preservation of the past as an end in itself, and claims to have transcendent reality captive in that past. Tradition as a token is a purely arbitrary, accidental representation that does not embody transcendent reality at all. Tradition functions as an icon "when it does not present itself as coextensive with the truth it teaches, but does present itself as the way we who are its heirs must follow if we are to go beyond it—through it, but beyond it—to a universal truth that is available only in a particular embodiment, as life itself is available to each of us only in a particular set of parents" (p. 56). Kierkegaard's concept of repetition would seem to offer a description of the dialectical process by which tradition, specifically the normative tradition we call Scripture, becomes an icon, rather than an idol or a token. Compare this line of thought to that developed in this volume by Stephen Dunning in his discussion of the way authority presupposes an encounter with the presence of God in living faith.

PART II
Ethics

4 Judge William's Theonomous Ethics

GEORGE B. CONNELL

While Kierkegaard understood his stages of existence to represent the essentially invariant structures of human existence,[1] he often endowed his literary realizations of those possibilities with the specific characteristics of their most representative contemporary examples. Thus, the aesthete of *Either/Or I* is modeled after the romantic ironists, especially Friedrich Schlegel. The aesthete's ethical counterpart, Judge William, is in turn widely believed to be inspired, at least broadly, by the thought and person of Immanuel Kant.[2]

It is easy to understand the popularity of this view. At the personal level, the same (somewhat oppressive) atmosphere of Hanseatic rectitude clings to the two. In terms of ethical theory, the points of coincidence are striking: both identify the ethical with the universal, insist that ethical volition is autonomous, value ethical personality as first and foremost an end in itself, locate moral worth in volition rather than result, and sharply dichotomize an internal (or noumenal) realm of freedom from an external (or phenomenal) realm of necessity.[3]

As plausible as the association of Judge William with Kant may seem, we should be wary. None of the points of coincidence listed above speaks directly to the central issue of how each ethicist accounts for the existence and authority of moral obligation. Accordingly, the agreement between the two may be superficial, covering fundamental disagreement. I will argue that this is in fact the case and that a too hasty association of Judge William with Kant has prejudiced readings of the former's writing. In particular, many assume that because Judge William characterizes ethical volition as free and as guided by an internal teleology, he follows Kant in denying that God's authority grounds moral obligation. This, in turn, has fostered a dismissive attitude, if not outright neglect, in reference to the invocations of God, examples from the life of the Church, appeals to theological principles, and quotations from the Bible that are rife in Judge William's letters. At most, interpreters have taken these passages as indicating an ancillary role for God in human ethical life and a corresponding status for religious beliefs as "practical postulates."[4]

I will argue that these largely neglected passages instead betoken a theonomous ethic, that is, an ethic that, while grounding obligation in the agent's relation to God, is not heteronomous.[5] Unfortunately, these specifically religious passages are too fragmentary and anecdotal to build a case for such a position directly upon them. Instead, in the paradoxical spirit of Kierkegaard, I propose to demonstrate the fundamental disagreement between Kant and Judge William by exploring a point at which the two are in startling agreement: their shared belief that one becomes an ethical person by choosing to do so. Not only will the parallelism of their views on this point help the fundamental differences stand out more clearly, but by concentrating on this most fundamental of all ethical choices we will be taken to the heart of both ethicists' theories of obligation.

At first glance, the suggestion that moral character originates in choice may seem unremarkable. Philosophers have long insisted that virtue or vice is imputable to an agent only insofar as those states of character result from freely undertaken actions. The causal relation between choice and character is usually supposed to be indirect. One directly makes particular ethical or unethical decisions and gradually becomes the sort of person for whom such actions are characteristic. One need not have any project of becoming a certain sort of person, but if one does, it is generally not supposed to have a corresponding basic action. Instead, acquiring a certain character is regarded as a second-order action that exhausts itself completely in first-order actions such as behaving in characteristic ways, associating with certain sorts of people, reading appropriate books, and meditating on particular thoughts.

Kant and Judge William turn this accepted, broadly Aristotelian view on its head. One does not become virtuous by and through particular virtuous actions; rather, one chooses to be ethical and only then is one able to carry out particular ethical actions. Judge William does not, à la Pascal, ask A to go through the motions of ethical life (to marry, get a job, etc.) on the supposition that by and by a transformation of character will follow. Instead, he exhorts A to despair, choose himself, and embrace ethical existence.[6] So discrete an action is this choice that Judge William tells A to cast the letter aside and resolve without delay should he feel the moment of decision ripe. So fundamental to ethical existence is this choice that first with its execution can we truly characterize the self in ethical terms. As Judge William puts it, the original choice is not of good *or* evil but of good *and* evil as the categories in terms of which one understands oneself.[7] Thus, the original choice is the choice to exist in a moral universe. All individual moral actions are in essence reaffirmations and applications of that fundamental choice.

Kant similarly asserts that particular virtuous actions are phenomenal manifestations of a single noumenal decision to make respect for the law the agent's motive. This decision is an "intelligible act" of the faculty of free choice (*Willkür*) ranking the two incentives of human action, inclination and respect, in the supreme maxim (*Oberste Maxim*) by means of which lower-level maxims fitted to more determinate situations are formulated.[8] As one's supreme maxim is, so is one's disposition (*Gesinnung*). It is in this disposition that true virtue or vice, purity or impurity of heart, lies—phenomenal virtue being at best true virtue's inadequate expression in an alien medium, at worst whitewash on a tomb filled with corruption. Kant acknowledges that at the phenomenal level, practice can make perfect, but even in *The Doctrine of Virtue*, where he stresses our duty to develop character traits conducive to the moral life, he repeatedly rejects the association of virtue with habit and asserts that "the resolution to practice virtue must be made all at once and in its entirety."[9]

Given the distance from both common sense and the tradition of moral philosophy of Kant's and Judge William's notions of character formation as a basic action, and given their susceptibility to infinite regression (If in order to choose ethically in a given situation I must have chosen to make such choice my policy, why is it not necessary to choose to choose to choose ethically?), we must at least briefly say why the two subscribe to this view. Judge William's notion of choosing to exist ethically is not surprising since the essential role of the will in passing from one existence-form to another is a standard Kierkegaardian theme. In contrast to Hegel's descriptions of necessary, immanent transitions in the life of spirit, Kierkegaard and his pseudonyms stress the discontinuities between existence-forms and argue that passionate, total resolutions of will are the only means of passing from one to the other. Aesthetic existence, even in the form of a prudential, eudaemonistic "ethic," is qualitatively distinct from true ethical existence. Only a revolution effected by the will in the self's structures of thought, feeling, and volition can achieve the transformation.[10]

While Kant's notion of a single noumenal act giving rise to either a pure or impure maxim fits naturally with his rigorism (the rejection of "anything morally intermediate whether in actions [*adiophora*] or in human characters"),[11] his two-tiered structure of volition develops fully only in his late works, notably *Religion within the Limits of Reason Alone*, to deal with major difficulties in the volitional psychology of the earlier ethical works. In the *Groundwork*, Kant defined the will as practical reason and correspondingly identified freedom with the agent's obedience to the law. But if inclination-motivated action is completely unfree and strictly necessitated by the laws of nature, then it makes no sense to impute guilt to the heteronomous self. To avoid this Platonic conundrum, Kant broadened his conception of the will to reflect more fully that it "stands, as it were, at the crossroads half-way between its a priori principle which is formal and its a posteriori incentive which is material."[12] That is, as an integral part of a finite rational creature, the faculty of choice (*Willkür*) feels the pull of both reason and inclination.

But how is it possible to combine in one faculty absolute spontaneity and susceptibility to influence by inclination? Are Kant's alternative definitions of *Willkür* as transcendental freedom and as the faculty of desire consistent? Kant avoids contradiction here only by postulating two roles for *Willkür*: first as a *liberum arbitrium* spontaneously ranking the two incentives (since neither can be wholly absent in any human action, there is no question of excluding either), and second as the faculty of desire acting on the prompting of its strongest impulse (as determined by itself in its former capacity). "The freedom of the will [*Willkür*] is of a wholly unique nature in that an incentive can determine will [*Willkür*] to an action *only so far as the individual has incorporated it into his maxim.*"[13] The first aspect of *Willkür* corresponds to the noumenal choice of a pure or impure supreme maxim while the second corresponds to the phenomenal manifestations of the disposition so chosen. Thus, Kant posits this two-tiered structure of volition to explain how a finite rational being can be both free and subject to temptation.[14]

Having looked at the structures and motivations of these theories of volition, we must ask how Kant and Judge William account for the obligatory character of the original choice of ethical existence. Kant explains the "objective necessity" of ranking respect for the law above inclination in one's supreme maxim in exactly the same way he explains the objective necessity of the actions that follow from it: in terms of the legislative form of the maxim involved. Theorem III of the second critique reads, "If a rational being can think of its maxims as practical universal laws, he can do so only by considering them as principles which contain the determining ground of the will because of their form and not because of their matter."[15] That is, only when an action has a universalizable maxim and is chosen by the agent for this reason is it morally good. When only one action is open to the agent that meets the former criterion, that action is obligatory. All of these conditions hold in reference to the formulation of a moral supreme maxim. Making respect for the law one's motive is clearly universalizable since its universal adoption is what is envisioned in the idea of the kingdom of ends. Since no sensuous incentive could motivate a choice relating exclusively to form, this noumenal act is the faculty of choice (*Willkür*) responding to the demands of pure rational will (*Wille*). Finally, its only alternative, the promotion of inclination to a position of dominance, is not universalizable because it is self-contradictory, involving as it does the use of freedom to surrender the self to natural necessitation.

In identifying the ethical with the universal, Judge William shows that he too recognizes a formal requirement of consistency as integral to his ethics.

Upbraiding A for living according to principles different from those he would recommend to a similarly situated youth, he writes, "What an enormous contradiction! Your whole being contradicts itself."[16] However, in an ironic reversal of Kant's notion that people make exceptions of themselves out of excessive self-love, Judge William finds A guilty of treating himself worse than he, as an essentially good-hearted person, could bear to treat others!

There is, however, no indication that Judge William regards this formal requirement of consistency as more than a minimal, necessary condition of ethical action. Instead, he traces specific duties back to the self's choice of itself (which is simply another expression for its choice of ethical existence). In thus accounting for the self's duties in terms of its responsible relationship to itself in all its particularity, Judge William seems to promulgate a far richer, more concrete theory of obligation than does Kant.[17]

We should be wary of uncritically embracing this conclusion, however. First, Kant is not the formalist he is often caricatured as being. Although it is the form of a maxim that accounts for its moral status, its material content (the end toward which it aims) cannot but reflect the particular situation of the agent. Second, Judge William's ethic is in the first analysis fully as formal as Kant's. It is only after this first moment is grasped that we can properly appreciate its concreteness. Judge William nicely captures this dialectical character of his ethic: "But what, then, is this self of mind [which I choose]? . . . It is the most abstract of all, and yet in itself it is also the most concrete."[18]

To shine light on this darkly paradoxical expression, I turn to Judge William's first admonition to A: despair. This advice at first seems strange given that Judge William diagnoses aesthetic existence as despair. He is, however, using the term in two very different senses in the two cases. The former is a suffered condition, the latter a voluntary action. In fact, despair in the second sense is simply the negative expression for choosing oneself: "When I choose absolutely, I choose despair."[19] Judge William does not here advocate standardization. Instead, the despairing self retains all its individuating characteristics but "he who has them is as one who does not have them."[20] What he has in mind here is that in choosing oneself, it is not the particular characteristics that one has that motivate the choice, it is the simple fact that one has them. It is not the "content" of the choice—that one is rich or poor, clever or slow—that matters in the first instance, it is that those features stand in a certain formal relation to the self: that the self can say of them, "mine." To choose oneself is to take up a stance of responsible attention toward oneself as one finds oneself. As Kierkegaard frequently puts it, the given (*Gave*)—a purely formal designation—is the task (*Opgave*). It is out of this formal relationship of the self to itself that particular duties arise. Although all ethical selves are formally identical (they relate in the same way to their given characteristics and situations), they are materially diverse (their given characteristics and situations vary). In taking responsibility for its given aspects, each self finds itself faced with a unique set of duties. This positive moment in the process Judge William colorfully describes as the self clothing itself in itself. Only by appreciating both the negative-formal and the positive-concrete moments of the choice of self can we understand Judge William's statement that the self attains the universal by becoming the particular self that it is.[21]

The question we must now ask is whether and why the self is obligated to take up such a stance toward itself. Judge William clearly thinks the self is so obligated. He describes "the path of duty" as one that selves "are not only permitted to take . . . but are commanded to take."[22] But, unlike Kant, Judge William is not able to explain this objective necessity in terms of a formal consideration such as consistency. Such radically different stances toward one's given circumstances as Stoic apathy, Sartrean nausea, or Camus' metaphysical rebellion are perfectly consistent. To help us determine why Judge William believes this particular stance toward oneself to be obligatory, I turn again to the question of how determinate duties arise out of it.

As noted above, the self that chooses itself adopts a stance of responsible attention to itself. This form of reflection not only discovers the self as it is, it reveals the self as it might become. The ability to conceive of possible but nonactual states of affairs is a function of the faculty of imagination. In the specific context of the ethical self's reflection on itself, imagination does not project possibilities indiscriminately but presents visions of future states the self may achieve through its own agency. But even after eliminating those possibilities that are logically, physically, emotionally, and morally impossible, the self is still presented with numerous possible futures. How is it that any of the corresponding possible projects becomes obligatory and not simply permissible?[23]

Judge William's answer is choice (*Valg*) and resolution (*Forsæt, Beslutning*). The self contracts determinate obligations by choosing to undertake specific projects. In undertaking such commitments the self closes for itself a variety of equally permissible possibilities. A's failure is not so much that he, like Johannes the Seducer, undertakes immoral projects, as that he experiments; that is, he only playfully and tentatively undertakes projects, thereby keeping his options open. According to Judge William, this has its price. The self is volatilized and made fantastic in its attempt to be everything and nothing. In order to become a self, as it is morally obligated to do, the self must commit itself, close many possibilities by actualizing a few. The decision so to resolve is none other than the choice of ethical existence we have been discussing. Thus, to choose oneself is to resolve to resolve or, as Judge William would put it, to choose to choose.[24]

But what is it that makes any particular resolution or, for that matter, the resolution to undertake resolutions binding on the self that makes it? What is it that keeps an ethical self's projects from being just as experimental as the aesthete's? Can a self by virtue of its willpower alone reach into its future to close otherwise permissible options and make obligatory actions not otherwise required? Can the self, as Kant's quotation of Juvenal suggests, "let [its] will be voucher for the deed"?[25] Kierkegaard clearly did not think so and focused his critique of Kant's notion of autonomy on exactly this issue. In a journal entry from 1850, he writes:

> Kant was of the opinion that man is his own law (autonomy)—that is, he binds himself under the law which he himself gives himself. Actually, in a profounder sense, this is how lawlessness or experimentation is established. This is not being rigorously earnest any more than Sancho Panza's self-administered blows to his own bottom were vigorous. It is impossible for me to be really any more rigorous in A than I am or wish to be in B. Constraint there must be if it is going to be in earnest. If I am bound by nothing higher than myself and I am to bind myself, where would I get the rigorousness as A, the binder, which I do not have as B, who is supposed to be bound, when A and B are the same self.[26]

Every indication is that Judge William is in complete agreement with his creator on this point. The specific project he singles out as archetypal for ethical existence is, of course, marriage. Given the ecclesiastical setting of wedding vows, this would be a very poor choice indeed if he were trying to illustrate an ethics grounded in strict autonomy. In fact, he explicitly insists that only because the wedding vows are spoken before a priest in his capacity as a minister of God are they serious and binding.

> After all, the wedding ceremony is not something the lovers themselves thought up in an opulent moment, something they could abandon if they thought of something else along the way. Hence, it is a power that we encounter.[27]

It is in this very consideration that Judge William locates much of A's aversion to marriage. After conjuring up an aesthetically inspiring vision of A meeting his betrothed on their wedding day, he describes A as seized with dread at the thought of going before God's altar to take his vows. He imagines A angrily demanding, "What kind of authority is it that dares to thrust itself between me and my bride, the bride I myself have chosen and who has chosen me?"[28] How striking that A stands here with Kant against Judge William in pressing the demands of untrammeled autonomy. This is precisely the secret alliance Kierkegaard suggests in the previously cited journal entry.

While these passages indicate that the watchful presence of a higher authority—as Judge William puts it, "eyes that see in secret"—is a necessary condition of binding, nonexperimental choice, it remains to be explained why the resolution to make such choice one's policy (i.e., the adoption of the specifically ethical stance toward one's given circumstances) is obligatory.[29] Since God is invoked as the authority who holds the self to vows undertaken before God, one might reasonably expect that in explaining the obligatory character of the choice of ethical existence Judge William will similarly refer to divine authority. This I will argue is the case. What Judge William does not do is promulgate a crude and undialectical divine command theory of obligation. Rather, he joins Kant in condemning such a theory as heteronomous.[30] But how can Judge William both invoke divine authority in explaining obligation and describe himself as the champion of freedom?[31] He can only escape the charge of self-contradiction here by showing that grounding obligation in God need not nullify human freedom but rightly understood serves as its precondition and support. His discussion in "The Aesthetic Validity of Marriage" of the self's duty to love supports just such a theonomous view of ethics.

First, by taking its vow to love before a power that will hold it to its resolution, the self is freed from itself. The unbound self, the self that knows no higher authority than itself, is subject to its own whims and moods.[32] In contrast, the self bound by duty looks to duty (and thus to the divine source of that duty) as security against itself in its moments of temptation. Since Judge William defines freedom as being "raised above the moment,"[33] the God-relationship is freeing, not confining.

Second, by referring their love to God, the lovers are freed from each other. Without such a transforming reference to God, love can degrade into an excessive closeness in which the stronger smothers the weaker, thereby robbing the latter of his or her status as individual. Whereas Kant proposes respect for the other as a moral agent as the way to counteract love's tendency toward excessive familiarity,[34] Judge William invokes God's presence as the mediating third in the relationship who simultaneously holds the two together (by making love a duty) and holds them apart (by either humbling or encouraging). In his stereotyped vision of the sexes, it is the man who threatens to dominate and the woman who stands in danger of being absorbed. Accordingly,

> When . . . he thanks God [for the couple's love, the man] humbles himself under his love . . . [while] when she thanks God for the beloved [the woman] places enough distance between herself and her beloved so that she can, so to speak, breathe.[35]

Judge William here anticipates *Works of Love* in so describing the liberating power of the God-relationship.[36]

But even if in relating to God one is freed from a deleterious vulnerability to oneself and to other humans, is not a relationship of obedience to a transcendent Other, no matter how benevolent, fundamentally unfree? Put specifically in terms of the love-relationship, how can reference to God not subvert the "internal teleology" of first love? William recognizes and responds to this challenge: "[I]f [duty] has not already existed in embryo in first love, then its appearance is naturally very disturbing."[37] But under what circumstances could duty so subsist as germ? How can it be that in resolving before God to undertake a task (*Opgave*) one is somehow making explicit and developing the innermost potential of the given (*Gave*) as it relates to the self?

The answer lies in taking the word "given" literally. For Judge William, the given denotes one element of a two-place relationship whose complement is the giver. That is, the given does not designate the brute contingency of the self's thrownness but rather the circumstances of the self's existence as provided by Providence itself.[38] In taking responsibility for oneself, in choosing oneself, one is simultaneously entering into a relation to the Giver of those circumstances. (As Anti-Climacus puts it, when a derived relation relates itself to itself it also relates itself to the power that established it.)[39] In attempting to do justice to both dimensions of the choice of self, Judge William is driven into the contortions of thoroughly dialectical language.

> The choice here makes two dialectical movements simultaneously—that which is chosen does not exist and comes into existence through the choice—and that which is chosen exists; otherwise it was not a choice. In other words, if what I chose did not exist but came into existence absolutely through the choice, then I did not choose—then I created. But I do not create myself, I choose myself. Therefore, whereas nature is created from nothing, whereas I myself as immediate personality am created from nothing, I as free spirit am born of the principle of contradiction or am born through my choosing myself.[40]

That is, one's choice of oneself is simultaneously creative and receptive. This juxtaposition of the active and the passive is implicit in the *Gave/Opgave* (gift/task) association noted above. Judge William repeatedly underlines just this duality in his descriptions of the choice of self as "receiving oneself out of the hand of God."

> When around one everything has become silent, solemn as a clear, starlit night, when the soul comes to be alone in the whole world, then before one there appears . . . the eternal power itself, then the heavens open and the I chooses itself or, more correctly, receives itself.[41]

It is an earnest and significant moment when a person links himself to an eternal power for an eternity, when he accepts himself as the one whose remembrance time will never erase, when in an eternal and unerring sense he becomes conscious of himself as the person he is.[42]

But since he has not created himself but has chosen himself, duty is the expression of his absolute dependence and his absolute freedom in their identity with each other . . . [H]e will be an autodidact just as he is a theodidact.[43]

Judge William's characterizations of wedding vows as simultaneously resolution and thanksgiving repeats this fundamental theme. In fact, he uses identical language to express the choice of one's spouse as he used to express the choice of oneself: "to take the beloved as a gift from God's hand."[44] According to Judge William, it is only because the self regards this love as given by God that it can appropriately ask God to vouch for that love by holding the lovers to their vows. He specifically condemns any self that makes an "attempt to deceive God, to sneak into something for which it thinks it does not need his help, and by having recourse to him only when it feels that things are not going well otherwise."[45] That is, only under its aspect as a *gift* of God can first love be chosen before God as *task* by the lovers. Thus, the pairing of thanksgiving and resolution is essential to Judge William's understanding of marriage and by extension all other ethical projects. (Using a very different metaphor to make the same point, Judge William writes that as with government bonds, all true resolutions, including marriage, are "signed in heaven and then . . . countersigned in time.")[46]

We are now in a position to see how Judge William grounds obligation in the God-relationship without compromising the self's freedom. In creating free agents, God not only gives an existence characterized by concrete circumstances, he assigns that existence as task. This divine mandate is not an arbitrary exertion of superior power; it is the natural relation between a finite free agent and its creator. Because freedom for Judge William is not indifference but responsibility, the self created to be free can only become itself by taking responsibility for itself as it finds itself. God figures in two distinct ways as the *conditio sine qua non* of this acceptance of self. First, as we said above, the self can only take responsibility for itself in an earnest, nonexperimental manner if this choice is taken before a higher authority able to hold the self to its choice. Since this recognition of God's authority is a precondition of the self's freedom, such an appeal denotes not a heteronomous but a theonomous ethic. Second, the specific character of the act of accepting oneself in all one's particularity as described by Judge William is only possible and appropriate when that particularity appears in the light of belief in a Creator-God. As we saw above, enlisting God as guarantor of a vow is only appropriate when the given from which the task arises is seen as God's gift and the undertaking of the task as the obedient response to that gift. This background determines the fundamental tone of the choice. Although Judge William's choice of self has marked affinities with Heidegger's resoluteness, the terms in which the two describe acceptance of one's situation are worlds apart. Instead of facing an irremediably tragic and brutely contingent situation with grim determination, Judge William's choice is simultaneously an act of thanksgiving. While it is under their aspect as gifts of God that particular circumstances naturally give rise to projects and tasks, their status as the self's *own* circumstances ensures that moral obligation springs from the very being of the self and does not represent an externally imposed set of rules.

In confirmation of this interpretation of his ethic, I call attention to a story from Judge William's boyhood that captures vividly his theological vision. In describing one of his formative impressions of obligation, Judge William tells of being enrolled in Latin school by his father. The father, having purchased his son's schoolbooks, places them in the young man's hands and says, quite simply, "William, by the end of the month, you are to be third in your class."[47] The task established and the means for its completion supplied, William is left to himself. He is allowed to play or work as he wishes. He is neither encouraged nor threatened. The fact that his father nonetheless keeps an eye on things so impresses the child with a sense of duty that he never loses it.

This little autobiographical sketch is a perfect allegory of Judge William's theological vision. In both, a patriarchal authority figure gives William his existence, situates him in a demanding milieu, supplies him with the requisite means, commands him to undertake on his own initiative to do what is required, and remains as an "eye that seeth in secret" to lend seriousness to his exertions. All the rest is up to William.

It is in this exaggerated emphasis upon human ability to fulfill the demands of ethics and not in an exclusion of God from a foundational role in ethics that Kierkegaard locates the theological inadequacy of Judge William's views. Specifically, William's ethical self-confidence runs aground on the twin reefs of human sin and divine omnipotence. Kierkegaard begins to adumbrate the former shipwreck in *Repetition*, in which the young man wants nothing more than to follow the course prescribed by Judge William to A. The youth finds, however, that he no longer is possessed of an unsullied immediacy that William speaks of lifting up into a "higher concentricity." In *Fear and Trembling's* analysis of the merman's similar plight, this predicament is more specifically identified as sin. As Johannes de Silentio points out, sin carries with it a "suspension of the ethical" in that it involves the radical inability of the self to meet the demands of the law.[48] It is interesting to note that Judge William shows a dim sense of this inability in endorsing the "Ultimatum" he appends to his letters to A. As a representative of immanent religiousness, the Jutland pastor locates this inability only in the qualitative difference between God and humans and not in a self-initiated fallenness.

In overestimating human ability, Judge William further implicates himself in a sin of lese majesty against God. Humans are able to fulfill on their own the demands of morality only if those laws are fixed. Thus, Judge William's self-confidence depends upon the assumption that God cannot change the ground rules of His relation to humans. This is just the condition Johannes de Silentio describes in *Fear and Trembling*:

> The whole existence of the human race rounds itself off as a perfect self-contained sphere, and then the ethical is that which limits and fills at one and the same time. God comes to be an invisible vanishing point, an impotent thought; his power is only in the ethical which fills all of existence.[49]

The problem here is not that the authority figure fails to play a role in grounding obligation, it is that the obligation that figure grounds so mediates the relationship to the subject self that the authority figure effectively disappears into the mediating element. Quoting Johannes de Silentio again, "The duty becomes duty by being traced back to God, but in duty itself I do not enter into relation to God."[50] In reporting on his relationship to his father, Judge William describes exactly such a loss of ability to distinguish between an authority figure and his commands, "Under this influence, when I reflected on my father, he seemed to me the incarnation of the rule."[51]

Thus despite their very different theories of obligation, Judge William and Kant are in important agreement: duty to God is reducible to ethical duties and humans are possessed of the ability to fulfill these duties. Nonetheless, in evaluating Judge William's writings, we should not forget that there is an element of truth in his statement that his letters are but glosses on Bishop Balle's *Lærebog i den Evangeliske-christelige Religion*.[52] Despite all its theological shortcomings, Judge William's thought is built squarely on the doctrine of creation.[53] This is why his ethic is so much better able to include the full concretion of human life than is Kant's. This is also why Kierkegaard saw fit to place in William's mouth so many of the views developed more fully in the unambiguously Christian phase of his authorship.[54]

Notes

1. The qualifier "essentially" is added in recognition of the fact that one existence-possibility, the Christian, first opened at a determinate point in history: the Incarnation. But as Johannes Climacus argues, the subsequent passage of time has in no way qualitatively altered the character of even this most historically adventitious of existence-forms.
2. See, for example, George Schrader, "Kant and Kierkegaard on Duty and Inclination," in *Kierkegaard: A Collection of Critical Essays*, ed. Josiah Thompson (Garden City, NY: Doubleday, 1972); James Collins, *The Mind of Kierkegaard* (Chicago, IL: H. Regnery, 1953); Alasdair MacIntyre, *After Virtue* (South Bend, IN: University of Notre Dame Press, 1981), p. 42. See also in the volume, Edward Mooney, "Getting Isaac Back: Ordeals and Reconciliations in *Fear and Trembling*.
3. It is this sharp dichotomization, together with Judge William's explicit polemic against Hegel, that leaves me unconvinced by interpretations of *Either/Or* II as representative of the bourgeois *Sittlichkeit* of Hegel's *Philosophy of Right*. Perhaps the popularity of such interpretations stems from the undoubtedly correct notion that the ethical as described by Johannes de Silentio in *Fear and Trembling* is at least broadly Hegelian. While I hope in a future essay to respond directly to Hegelian readings of *Either/Or* II, the conclusions I reach in this essay will make clear the gist of my disagreement.
4. See John Elrod, *Being and Existence in Kierkegaard's Pseudonymous Works* (Princeton, NJ: Princeton University Press, 1975), p. 117; and Mark Taylor, *Kierkegaard's Pseudonymous Authorship* (Princeton, NJ: Princeton University Press, 1975), pp. 242, 279–80.
5. While the term "theonomy" was popularized by Tillich, Kierkegaard was well aware of the concept. See his notes from Martensen's lectures on speculative theology, *Søren Kierkegaards Papirer,* 22 vols., ed. P. A. Heiberg, V. Kuhr, and E. Torsting, rev. Niels Thulstrup (Copenhagen: Gyldendal, 1968–1970), II C 28. Stephen Dunning's chapter in this volume develops the compatibility of human freedom and divine authority in the context of another Kierkegaardian text, *On Authority and Revelation*.
6. Søren Kierkegaard, *Either/Or*, 2 vols., trans. Howard V. Hong and Edna H. Hong (Princeton, NJ: Princeton University Press, 1987), II, p. 208.
7. Ibid., p. 224.
8. Immanuel Kant, *Religion Within the Limits of Reason Alone*, trans. Theodore M. Greene and Hoyt H. Hudson (New York: Harper and Row, 1960), p. 26.
9. Immanuel Kant, *The Doctrine of Virtue*, trans. Mary J. Gregor (Philadelphia, PA: University of Pennsylvania Press, 1964), p. 149.
10. It is the very totality of this choice that nullifies the threat of infinite regression. The self, though free and responsible, is not at its own disposal in the simplistic sense that it can without difficulty convert the wish to be ethical into effective willing. It is not in a prior act of the self but rather in a spontaneous gathering together of all the aspects of the self in taking responsibility for itself that ethical selfhood originates. Thus while the self chooses to choose, it does not choose to do so.
11. Kant, *Religion*, p. 18.
12. Kant, *Foundations of the Metaphysic of Morals*, trans. Lewis White Beck (Indianapolis, IN: Bobbs-Merrill, 1959), p. 16. It is interesting to note that Judge

William also uses the crossroads metaphor in describing ethical existence. See *Either/Or* II, p. 172.
13. Kant, *Religion*, p. 19.
14. For a further comment on the development of Kant's notion of freedom, see John Silber, "The Ethical Significance of Kant's Religion," in *Religion Within the Limits of Reason Alone*; and Robert Paul Wolff, *The Autonomy of Reason* (New York: Harper and Row, 1973), p. 122.
15. Immanuel Kant, *Critique of Practical Reason*, trans. Lewis White Beck (Indianapolis, IN: Bobbs-Merrill, 1956), p. 27.
16. Kierkegaard, *Either/Or* II, p. 162.
17. Such a claim is made by George Schrader in "Kant and Kierkegaard on Duty and Inclination."
18. Kierkegaard, *Either/Or* II, p. 214.
19. Ibid., p. 213.
20. Ibid., p. 210.
21. See the chapters in this volume by Mark L. Taylor and Edward Mooney for discussions of a similar dialectic of loss and recovery in other Kierkegaardian texts.
22. Kierkegaard, *Either/Or* II, p. 149. This shows that Alasdair MacIntyre is on the wrong track in criticizing Kierkegaard for suggesting that the authority of the ethical resides wholly in the arbitrary decision of the self. Judge William is asserting, like Kant, that the objectively necessary laws of human action become subjectively necessary only through the choice of the agent. See *After Virtue* (South Bend, IN: University of Notre Dame Press, 1981), pp. 38–42.
23. Compare this with Mooney's discussion of the issue on p. 83.
24. Kierkegaard, *Either/Or* II, p. 178.
25. Kant, *Critique of Practical Reason*, p. 3.
26. Kierkegaard, *Journals and Papers*, 7 vols., trans. Edna H. Hong and Howard V. Hong (Bloomington, IN: Indiana University Press, 1967–1978), entry 188 (I, p. 76).
27. Kierkegaard, *Either/Or* II, p. 89.
28. Ibid., II, p. 52.
29. Ibid., II, p. 287. See Stephen Dunning's chapter in this volume, pp. 22, 29. For a recent cinematic treatment of the relationship between moral obligation and a watchful God, see Woody Allen's *Crimes and Misdemeanors*.
30. Kierkegaard, *Either/Or* II, p. 214.
31. Ibid., II, p. 176.
32. Ibid., II, pp. 67n, 68.
33. Ibid., II, p. 179.
34. Kant, *The Doctrine of Virtue*, p. 141.
35. Kierkegaard, *Either/Or* II, pp. 57–58.
36. For more on Kierkegaard's treatment of gender questions see Wanda Warren Berry, "Finally Forgiveness," in this volume, and Sylvia Walsh, "On 'Feminine' and 'Masculine' Forms of Despair," in *The International Kierkegaard Commentary on The Sickness unto Death*, ed. Robert Perkins (Macon, GA: Mercer University Press, 1987).
37. Kierkegaard, *Either/Or* II, p. 146.
38. Edward Mooney devotes much attention to the grateful acceptance of the given in Chapter 5. He specifically considers the coherence of a gratefulness that is *not* directed toward any giver. See p. 76. See also Louise Carroll Keeley, Chapter 6.

39. See *The Sickness unto Death*, trans. Howard V. Hong and Edna H. Hong (Princeton, NJ: Princeton University Press, 1980), p. 13.
40. Ibid., II, pp. 215–16.
41. Ibid., p. 177.
42. Ibid., p. 206.
43. Ibid., p. 270.
44. Ibid., p. 57.
45. Ibid., p. 36.
46. Kierkegaard, *Stages on Life's Way*, trans. Edna H. Hong and Howard V. Hong (Princeton, NJ: Princeton University Press, 1983), p. 68. For more on the significance of thanksgiving in Kierkegaard's thought, see Paul Minear, "Thanksgiving as Synthesis of the Eternal and the Temporal," in *A Kierkegaard Critique*, ed. Howard A. Johnson and Niels Thulstrup (New York: Harper and Row, 1962), pp. 297–308.
47. Kierkegaard, *Either/Or* II, p. 269.
48. See Mark Lloyd Taylor, Chapter 3, this volume, for a more detailed analysis of the crucial role sin plays in undermining the ethical life.
49. Kierkegaard, *Fear and Trembling*, trans. Edna H. Hong and Howard V. Hong (Princeton, NJ: Princeton University Press, 1983), p. 68.
50. Ibid.
51. Kierkegaard, *Either/Or*, p. 269. See the chapters in this volume by Westphal, Taylor, and Mooney for more discussion of the inadequacy of this conflation of the ethical and the divine.
52. *Either/Or* II, p. 323.
53. For a discussion of the centrality of the doctrine of creation to Kierkegaard's thought, see Michael Plekon's "Kierkegaard the Theologian: The Roots of His Theology in *Works of Love*", Chapter 1, this volume, and Charles Bellinger, Chapter 13, "Kierkegaard on Hitler, Stalin, and the Cold War."
54. I wish to thank the National Endowment for the Humanities for sponsoring the 1985 Summer Seminar on Kierkegaard during which research for this essay was begun. I also wish to express thanks to participants in the seminar and especially the seminar director, Sylvia Walsh Perkins, for much helpful discussion.

5 Getting Isaac Back: Ordeals and Reconciliations in *Fear and Trembling*

EDWARD MOONEY

> [The knight of faith] knows it is beautiful to be born as the particular with the universal as his home, his friendly abode, which receives him straightaway with open arms when he wishes to stay there.
> Johannes de Silentio
Fear and Trembling

> This possessing [of a self] is not—it is the reverse of—possessive; . . . it is the exercise not of power but of reception. Then the question is: On what terms is the self received?
> Stanley Cavell
The Senses of Walden

> In faith, I receive everything.
> Johannes de Silentio
Fear and Trembling

Abraham's crisis—the demand from God that he sacrifice his son Isaac—is hypnotic. Johannes de Silentio, the pseudonymous author of *Fear and Trembling*, spares none of his considerable talent depicting, dialectically and lyrically, the wonder and horror of Abraham's lonely journey to the mountain. He can barely contain his restless, ambivalent fascination. But this focus on a single terrifying moment of truth can blot out a wider vision.[1] Is faith *primarily*, or *only*, the heroic weathering of ordeals? Mesmerized by the terror, we may forget that faith is not relinquishing Isaac, or not *only* that. Unlike the knight of resignation, the faithful knight embraces the hopeful trusting expectation that *Isaac will be restored*. He anticipates and is granted the return of simple worldly life.[2]

The resigned knight gives up the worldly. This recalls an otherworldly "yearning for the beyond," the alienation Hegel called "unhappy consciousness."[3] But from Johannes' standpoint, a monastic or stoic estrangement from the world is in fact *unfaithful*: "[the knight of faith] is *happy*, only he is *heir apparent to the finite*, whereas the knight of resignation is a stranger, a foreigner."[4] If the image of Abraham raising his knife is paralyzing, there are less terrifying pictures to contemplate. Quite ordinary people—tax collectors, poor serving maids, even professors of philosophy—can be knights of faith.[5] The shopkeeping knight is at home in the world, apparently beyond dilemma, crisis, or any spectacular suspensions of ethics. But how can a pedestrian shopkeeper also be an immortal hero? Is his ordeal a distant memory? Does he become, shall we say, a *retired warrior*?

Kierkegaard fears the complacency that can arise if our attention drifts from terror and suffering to the comforting daily.[6] But he is clear that the return of Isaac is also the return of the mundane social matrix within which particular ordinary lives can flourish. There is an ethics deeper and fuller than the one shattered in the midst of Abraham's ordeal. To lose the reconciliatory, worldly dimension of faith is to lose half the truth.

RESIGNATION, HUMILITY, AND VALUE

However difficult it may be to perform an act of resignation, it is at least intelligible. Johannes understands a "movement of infinity," a transfer of devotion from worldly objects to something beyond. A knight of resignation's "estrangement," in its way, is admirable. There is honor in relinquishing a world that identifies faith with a child-like absence of doubt, difficulty, or sacrifice; that encourages the conflation of God's will and Reason; that lets ethics collapse into social convention. But admiring Abraham's faith is not so simple. Faith transfers devotion *away* from the world, but simultaneously contains hospitality *toward* it. "On the strength of the absurd" Abraham can do "the impossible." He gives Isaac up and gets him back.

This "absurdity" can be sketched as an ordeal of love that tests conflicting measures of care.[7] Alastair Hannay provides an alternative formulation. The Abraham story symbolizes the "formal features" of the "compound attitude" of faith. The belief that Isaac must be resigned suggests that "nothing in the world has value simply because one values it." The opposed belief, that Isaac will be returned, suggests that "things have their value nonetheless, but . . . on their own account and from God." In faith, we are ready to accept things of value back "on a new basis," their "status clarified."[8]

The first element in this "compound attitude" of faith corresponds to resignation, glossed by Hannay as the view that *"nothing in the world has value simply because one values it"* (my emphasis). I take this to mean that however important to us our cares may be, anything that possesses real value will possess it independently of our attitude toward it. Johannes presupposes an objectivity of moral value.[9] He never doubts that fathers should love their sons or that Abraham should love his God. Without this moral objectivity we could not account for the possibility of error in evaluative judgment. We can misplace our cares, mistake our values. Second, this objectivity accounts for the fact that we cannot dictate or determine at will the meaning of evaluative concepts whose supportive web provides sense for our lives, individually and collectively. Third, it reflects the sense that meaning *dawns*, comes to us unbidden, in wonder, insight, or surprise. At moments it seems to arise from a source deeper and other than ourselves. This truth remains even when such bestowal appears so apt to our particular subjective needs and aspirations that it seems virtually to have been chosen. The valuable is not just what we happen at the moment to value. This insight is linked to the first movement of faith, resignation. But how?

Abraham, being only human, is liable to become trapped in his own desires, his own care for Isaac. However intense and sincere his attachment, Abraham must acknowledge Isaac's independent worth, his value apart from a father's heartfelt care. Love can mask a self-preoccupation, a distorting proprietary claim. In this light, what we lose is objectivity, appreciation of the real separateness of the other. The truly valuable is a radiant center of energy and worth independent of our immediate subjective response. Resignation silences such self-preoccupation, or the thought that value issues from our command or is a possession over which we have a proprietary claim. In our receptive love for others and for the ordinary, we shift to a welcoming, selfless concern.

This move toward a reflective, moral objectivity is linked to humility.[10] While acknowledging risk, uncertainty, and the possibility of error, I also acknowledge a standard, an absolute, by which I can measure growth toward a more fitting perception of persons and the world. This standard, rather than my subjectivity, appears as the center of things. What I admire, cherish, or respect I do not scheme to possess, manipulate, or control.

The humbling of the will through resignation is a kind of Socratic wisdom of ignorance. We know not whence value dawns. But we acknowledge an objective source that transcends our powers to possess or fully comprehend. But as Johannes has it, faith is more than this acknowledging of ignorance, this resigning of presumption. As much as one relinquishes a worldly control of mundane value, one affirms its value nonetheless. With this second, receptive movement of faith, Johannes believes that worldly things have value not on *his* account but, in Hannay's phrase, "on their *own* account and from God." The "second element" in the "compound attitude" of faith readies us to accept things back, "on a new basis," their "status clarified."

Resignation is a preparatory move, not a final resting place. We are readied not for despair or estrangement from the finite, through and through. That would be to *remain* a knight of resignation, or worse. We are readied to exercise a virtue Cavell calls *reception*.[11] The readiness is all.[12] The faithful knight opens toward bestowed meaning, is prepared for whatever may be given. He sees that things are of inexplicable, abundant value, present to be received and cherished in their own right.

SUSPENDING THE UNIVERSAL: INDIVIDUAL WORTH

If value is in some sense independent, there to be welcomed or acknowledged, it is also independent of "the universal"—those norms that are, in Hegel's view, implicitly rational, and are embedded in social convention and practice.[13] Since these norms reflect only an aggregate of individual values, they are no more solid than a string of any individual's relatively capricious choices. A ground of value must lie deeper.

Within a Hegelian or conventionalist context, the universal is the locus of act-governing public rules. It names evolving social conventions and the rational structures that underlie them. But it is also the purported home or final resting place of the self in its journey toward meaning or fulfillment. But if, as in the Hegelian scheme, assimilation to the universal becomes "the absolute," the object of our aspiration and worship, then the individual must become insignificant, a vanishing point. A conventionalist-rationalist goal, at least as Kierkegaard sees it, eliminates anything like separate, individual persons, each of priceless worth. Personal realization becomes a travesty, for how can it be distinguished from being lost in the crowd?

"Giving up the universal" is giving up an assimilationist goal of human development. In faith, the importance of individual identity or character, the importance of subjectivity, outranks conventional practice. Individuals are more than abstract vanishing points whose significance hinges on absorption into a social matrix. Persons in their solitary integrity become a primary focus. But a focus on particular persons in their uniqueness will appear unethical to one who adopts the standpoint of the rationalist system. Moving beyond the assimilationist goal will appear possible only "on the strength of the absurd."

"Becoming subjective" is in part renouncing the universal for the particular. The structure of one's particularity, one's priceless worth, can be spelled out as a complex of virtues that provide standards for self-evaluation. To abjure the universal as the dominant seat of value is to see that individuals generally and, more especially, the particular individual you or I happen to be, become "justified." We acquire some ultimate, inalienable standing in the broadest scheme of things. This standing or worth is constituted by a triad of personal virtues: freedom, integrity, and trusting receptivity or faith. To move beyond the universal is to approach the stage of faith.

We discover, as Johannes has it, that "the individual is *higher* than the universal" and "*justified* over against it"; the particular person is "not subordinate but *superior*" to the universal.[14] Faith is "higher" than social, civic, or rational morality, but not because it provides grounds for overriding ethics or because it marks out a specific way of life that can easily be distinguished from a more conventional life. Faith is "higher" because for someone having weathered its ordeals, it can be felt, retrospectively, to have transformed and completed an all-too-familiar yet finally provisional moral outlook.[15] Faith provides the setting for a new ethics, established on a new basis. Conventional practices are complemented by a self-structure of inward virtues.

Throughout the period of writing *Fear and Trembling*, Kierkegaard worried if there could be legitimate exceptions to morality. Could one, say, break a marriage engagement without moral fault? Dilemmas provide one model of a person's inability to fulfill moral demands and so of "exceptions." But we can now sketch a different model of an "exception" to moral requirement. On this reading, the teleological suspension of ethics describes a phase in individual development, where the crucial issue is becoming an individual distinguishable from, and possessed of worth " higher" than, the universal.[16] One lives "outside" convention to the extent that one finds one's worth and identity to be irreducible to convention. This is quite compatible with living happily (and perhaps invisibly) within convention.

The universal is a necessary but not sufficient source of personhood. If freedom from the universal can be achieved by will alone, to establish or get back a self requires more. One cannot just "bootstrap" oneself into a new identity by an "existential choice." A rich and abundant self draws on powers bestowed. Neither chosen nor possessed, it is received. And the power that bestows significance to the individual also returns the universal, making possible a religious life amid worldly goods. John D. Glenn Jr. puts it this way:

> . . . recognizing the contingency and relativity of every finite good [the knight of faith] neither takes it as secure and absolute nor expends all his energy in spiritually distancing himself from it; but he accepts all that he possesses as a gift from the hand of God, to be enjoyed and loved as such, yet to be released, if need be.[17]

And he adds: "faith both relativizes and restores the self's ethical self-relation."[18] One becomes an individual by relating to an absolute Good. The receptive self then becomes curator of the values of the everyday, values whose easy acceptance marks the faith and joy of the simple shopman.

Later we will complete this picture of suspending and then getting back the universal in the ongoing development of particular selves. But here let me comment on the religious idea of bestowal of value.

Gift and Giver

To attack assimilation as a proper absolute for orienting life is commendable enough. Equally, one might join Johannes in protesting the idea that persons are entirely self-creating.[19] Apart from biological and sociological realities, at crucial moments in self-development we often seem to draw on powers larger than ourselves. And perhaps things do have value in their own right, intrinsic value that can be pictured as flowing from some deeper source. To recognize a kind of Platonic or Christian absolute Good can seem an appropriate acknowledgment of the experience of inspiration or empowerment. And it can seem an appropriate brake on our familiar and excessive self-preoccupations. There is surely a place in the panoply of human virtue for a receptive humility, whether cognitive, moral, or spiritual. But whatever the value of humility or receptivity to bestowed goods, one might think it both risky and unnecessary to articulate these virtues in the specific terms suggested, to presuppose a Beneficent Other.[20]

That there is an absolute or God so placed as to return Isaac, or to provide a ground of value or to underwrite individuality is for Kierkegaard an assurance of faith.[21] A bare objective belief in the existence of such a God or absolute holds little moral or religious interest for him. The question is *how* such an absolute becomes acknowledged or refused, becomes or fails to become the orienting frame for a self under way and at risk. The conceptual and narrative resources of biblical theism provide a natural context for elaborating a number of personal virtues, among them the virtue of trusting receptivity, a welcoming openness to value bestowed. But gratitude for the gift of a new life, a new Isaac, a new universal, cannot underwrite or prove the presence of a Giver.[22] One might embody a rich gratitude for life, take it thankfully as a gift bestowed, and yet be quite agnostic about the proper target of one's thanks. Perhaps, as Cavell suggests, Thoreau, Emerson, or Heidegger exercises a virtue of reception: "[T]he question is: On what *terms* is the self received?"[23] Clearly, they need not be theistic.

For most humans, at least those we admire, the sense of an absolute or set of absolutes that confer meaning and set direction is an inescapable feature of their lives. A Good that provides orientation, or in Cavell's phrase, sets "the terms on which the self is received," seems essential. So Charles Taylor argues convincingly in *Sources of the Self*:

> We come here to one of the most basic aspirations of human beings, the need to be connected to, or in contact with, what they see as good, of crucial importance, of fundamental value. And how could it be otherwise, once we see that this orientation in relation to the good is essential to being a functional human agent?[24]

God or Reason, fame or history, artistic expression or family life are goods that make possible the identification and elaboration of daily pleasures, honors, and failures. They set standards against which relative honors, pleasures, or fulfillments of common life are measured. These "absolutes," goods of intrinsic and preeminent worth, can be displayed in narrative visions of a complex and fulfilling life. They will typically be several, in degrees of disharmony. The task of selfhood is their discovery, articulation, and coordination. Their discords and harmonies sketch the drama and repose of the everyday, as well as the sufferings and conciliations of life's larger tragedies and tales of faith. They chart the distant, often elusive, and largely unattainable stars of aspiration and regard.

Such ideals or goods are absolute in the sense that there is no greater good, no higher standard, no more encompassing frame in terms of which our lives make sense, or gain importance and direction. Again, as Taylor has it:

> The issue for us has to be not only where we are, but where we are going. And although the first may be a matter of more or less, the latter is a question of towards or away from, an issue of yes or no. So an absolute question always frames our relative ones.[25]

To respond to our absolute question, Where are we going? we articulate or attempt to articulate the loose array of absolutes that frame a way of life, that infuse *my* life, with meaning.

How we conceive of such absolutes, how we articulate their moral or aesthetic or religious detail, and how we frame or resolve the conflicts between them, will vary from person to person and remain contestable. But the requirement that there be such absolutes, such fundamental frames or standards, seems inescapable. This is my sense of Johannes Climacus's *Postscript* remark: "The postulate [of God] is so far from being arbitrary that it is precisely a life-necessity. It is then not so much that God is a postulate as that the existing individual's postulation of God is a necessity."[26] Climacus speaks of dialectic as the "ministering power" that *"discovers and helps find where the absolute object of worship is."*[27] Dialectic, lyric or otherwise, reflective and self-interpreting, discovers our gods, our cares. We are readied for reception of self. Although it may not compel others—in fact, it may provoke scorn—a biblical God is the absolute for Kierkegaard or Johannes.[28] Their sense of this absolute is embedded in their readings, selective, critical, and affirming, of numerous narratives, creeds, and traditions. These readings, in turn, shape the presence and absence of meaning in the currents and still spots of their lives.

The idea of a self bestowed may be given weight by stories of God; and stories of God may give weight to the virtue of alert, trusting receptivity. There is a natural, if not necessary, connection between the ideas of gift and giver, of reception and bestowal, of gratitude and acknowledgment of God.[29] These pairs are not arbitrarily coupled but joined in reciprocally reinforcing perspectives, each projecting some ground, some legitimation or intelligibility on the other. The interpretative circle is auspicious. Lyrical dialectic brings out the connections or clears the view for trusting their perception.

Absent the possibility of proofs or the legitimacy of brute indoctrination, two questions stay open: Can *this* absolute provide us, one by one, with orienting conviction? If it cannot, or not immediately, what more in the way of philosophical or lyrical explication could lead us to embrace a specifically theistic or Christian faith? Acknowledging uncertainty about the conferred grounds of our identity, our lives, is a central theme of Kierkegaardian faith. Its trusting assent is given amid ultimate risk. To forego closure on this issue is itself dialectically apt. Philosophy cannot force acknowledgment or deliver the object of its concern or veneration; it can only minister or assist.

Let me turn now to speculate on the structure of our bestowed individuality as a cluster of virtues and its compatibility with a social matrix or the universal.

Essential Humanity: The Universal Returned

If conventional value must be "suspended," why not reject it, or adopt an utterly new table of value? For Abraham, wanting Isaac back is clear enough. But why generalize? Is there a broader point in welcoming back the universal, more or less *in toto*? And if it is welcomed back, how, specifically, can a knight whose essence is at least partially separate from the world nevertheless be happily immersed in it?

There is a sense in which Kierkegaard's critique does not undermine but bypasses attack on the bulk of commonplace social, rational, or civic morality. One should keep one's promises, care for one's kin, and neither lie, steal, nor kill. The mistake is to absolutize these tenets or think they form an ordered whole whose unity is transparent to reason. This bulk of civic morality provides threshold requirements of decency and in that sense is more or less indispensable. But these requirements are not supreme or complete ideals in terms of which a human life can be defined. Having been initiated into some degree of moral sociability, we embark on the larger project of becoming subjective, becoming selves. At that point, these minimal requirements will seem dethroned but not destroyed. A child will learn not to lie or punch or play with fire before the exceptions fit in. In any case, social morality alone is often insufficient for moral action or understanding. It is not simple or univocal but ambiguous and complex. We find that obligations can conflict and that our self-assessments and readings of our setting can be agonizingly uncertain.

A faithful knight might appear ordinary because she accepted the bulk of commonplace social virtue and by good luck avoided any spectacular, publicly notorious dilemma or crisis. But we could still ask how such a life is possible. Apart from outward marks, what will distinguish this knight from the thousands who have never made even the first step toward faith? What will distinguish her from a backsliding conventionalist?[30]

Whether a person's bearing is dramatic or unassuming, heroic or quite ordinary, the absolute gives to the individual the varied and complex resources of the universal, resources through which she or he will express an identity. Johannes de Silentio puts this idea dauntingly as follows: "the single individual who, having been subordinate to the universal as the particular, now by means of the universal becomes that individual who as the particular stands in an absolute relationship to the absolute."[31] Being first subordinate to the universal (while the goal was assimilation), the individual now exploits the universal and is beholden only to the absolute, which underwrites his individuality. Hannay expands on this passage:

> Abraham acts as though someone could be properly human prior to the expression of his or her humanity in the universal, so that the universal becomes an expression in turn of a humanity pre-established, as it were, at the level of the particular and no longer the category in which humanity is established.[32]

The universal does not establish our "particular humanity" but is a vehicle for its expression. What gets expressed "predates," at least logically, the occasions of its expression.

This is a formulation of faith that Johannes de Silentio cannot fully grasp. Abraham remains largely an enigma to him. But *Fear and Trembling* reflects forward to the *Postscript* and *Sickness unto Death*. Taking a field of vision wider than Johannes himself can enjoy, we can sketch the process whereby one's essential humanity is expressed.

Any characterization of the essentially human must give due recognition to language, biology, tradition, training, and culture. A raw, minimally fashioned outcome of these acculturating processes we could call a "proto-self," or as Kierkegaard might call it, an "immediate self."[33] One's essential humanity can then be taken as a dual capacity that one exercises in relationship to this initial, proto-self. First, one can step back and reflect on what is bequeathed by biology, training, or convention. One can then take the proto-self one finds oneself more or less saddled with in a particular way. Inwardly in reflective judgment and outwardly in action, we alter, endorse, or deny portions of the immediate self. This is a uniquely human capacity, the essence of personhood. As Harry Frankfurt puts it in a classic series of papers, it is the capacity for "second-order" care or desire, the capacity to care about our (more or less given) cares, and to have that second-order care alter or articulate a self.[34]

Here is how Judge William puts the matter in *Either/Or*:

> [The person] has himself, then, as an individual who has these talents, these passions, these inclinations, these habits, who is under these influences, who in this direction is affected thus, and in another thus. Here then, he has himself as a task, in such a sort that his task is principally to order, cultivate, temper, enkindle, repress, in short, to bring about a proportionality in the soul, a harmony, which is the fruit of the personal virtues.[35]

Being able to occupy such a position over against the given proto-self (the self with these habits, these passions, and so forth) is a moral virtue, a uniquely human excellence. And the exercise of this virtue brings forth a harmony, a proportionality in the soul. To inhabit a position permitting the exercise of such virtue is both to possess (at least part of) one's essential humanity and to be in a condition of expressing that humanity through the universal.

Judge William calls this an exercise of the personal virtues. They in fact form a family of virtues, each having a familiar name:

Freedom. One acknowledges and exercises one's capacity to endorse or reject (aspects of) the proto-self and its projects conditioned by the universal.

Responsible Individuality or Integrity. One renounces the assimilationist ideal and endorses responsible individual development ("becoming subjective") as the properly human goal.

Trusting Receptivity or Faith. One exercises not power but reception. Through a newly acquired humility, one finds oneself vulnerable both to the intrinsic value of persons or things and to an ultimate source of their value and life-bestowing power; one establishes (or finds oneself established in) "an absolute relationship to the absolute."

This trio of freedom, integrity, and faith constitutes our essential humanity. The progressive acquisition, articulation, and strengthening of these virtues mark the movements from proto-self to full selfhood, from a premoral or "aesthetic" through an ethical stage, and then on to a faithful position in the world. Although there may be an inward heroism in growth toward fuller selfhood, a free, faithful, and responsible person need not appear extraordinary or heroic, like the wonder and terror that is Abraham.

The idea of our humanity as a cluster of moral and religious virtues is not something upon which Johannes de Silentio has a firm grasp. After all, he is baffled by the knight of faith. Nevertheless, this reading of our "essential humanity" has considerable textual support, complements Johannes' aims in *Fear and Trembling*, and strengthens our overall grasp of this dialectical text. In addition, it fits well with later Kierkegaardian themes found in the *Postscript* and in *Sickness unto Death*. But this reading also presents a relatively static picture of human essence. How does this square with the familiar Kierkegaardian theme of movement, of development by stages and conflict between perspectives? Can it be squared with the central idea of a teleological suspension of ethics? Finally, if the crowning virtue is receptivity, how does this square with the idea that virtues are excellences we strive to attain?

FAITH AND MORAL VIRTUE: CLARIFICATIONS

The tasks of selfhood—realizing our humanity, suspending the ethical, getting Isaac and the universal back—are processes of character or identity formation, more or less grounded in and constituted by the personal virtues of faith, freedom, and integrity. Such excellences of self are ideals and always achieved as a matter of degree, in one respect or another. There is no once and for all in getting faith, transcending conventionality, or achieving one's essential humanity. And we should expect some uncertainty in determining whether minimal levels of achievement have been attained in the exercise of each of these person-shaping virtues. For each has its cheap if sometimes barely distinguishable counterfeit.

Furthermore, we have been speaking throughout of movements or steps toward selfhood, of temporal sequences. One is immersed in aesthetic life before the ethical emerges. One suspends the ethical, then gets it back. Resignation precedes receptivity. The paradigms of faith are ordered: Socrates, Abraham, Christ. But this reliance on sequence is partly a heuristic narrative device. Change in self may be more or less instantaneous and may or may not involve discrete steps in an antecedently determined order of development. What is crucial is a logical or structural rather than a temporal priority.

If this is so, then the individual may express the aesthetic life view in some parts of her life, failing thereby to possess or exercise the full virtues of her humanity. Yet in another part of her life she may fully express an ethical or religious virtue. Kierkegaard depicts characters more or less representative of a life view. But our actual lives typically lack such tidy narrative unity and completeness. We are admirable or ethical in this respect, shameful or aesthetic in that. The familiar Kierkegaardian "stages," "spheres," or "life views" may be taken as the elaboration of one or another voice in this trio of personal virtues. But although each virtue may be conceptually distinct and "all or nothing," it is unrealistic to suppose that it becomes embedded in an individual, concrete life either instantaneously or through and through. We work to increase the areas of our strengths or excellences and to diminish the domains of weakness or vice, to develop the color, power, and flexibility of each voice, and to be attuned to, if we cannot always control, their rhythmic and tonal ensemble, whether fortuitous or intended, classically poised or racked in unsettling disharmony.

The apparently intractable conflict between ethics and faith, captured in the "teleological suspension of ethics" does not describe a permanent, destructive rupture in the self. Instead, it marks the ever-present possibility of conflict among virtues and principles, especially in moments of change and crisis. From a position sufficiently distanced from the tensions of an ordeal, a disharmony between ethics and faith marks only a passing phase in individual development.[36]

Evidence for a rough harmony among the religious and moral virtues lies in the images of "domestic" knights of faith—the shopman, the serving maid, the professor. As we have seen, Glenn speaks of relativizing finite goods and the restoration of the self's "ethical self-relation." Apparently the virtues of affiliation and civic virtue can be harmonized with faith. It is put this way by Hannay:

> by adopting a *telos* outside the ethical [the knight of faith] is not putting himself above morality so much as extending morality's universe; and although he places himself outside the self-sufficient universalist ethics [and hence inside an ethics of inward virtue], he still feels the contrary feel of that [universalist] ethics.[37]

The faithful knight is not proposing that "the value ordinarily attributed to conventional moral practice may be revoked at any time by non-moral divine imperative . . . [but that] there can be *morally* motivated exceptions to the rule that ethical norms apply universally."[38] The moral (and, in part, religious) virtues of faith, responsibility, and freedom may provide a subjective basis for questioning the dominance of an objective universal ethical rule. But that is not to posit an overall, inescapable rupture between ethics and faith. The return of the (now dethroned) universal coincides with the embrace of an enhanced ethical position—one that has space for the personal virtues.

Leaving a rupture between ethics and faith would cripple Johannes' account of both. The universal, as Johannes occasionally acknowledges, is essential for the formation and maintenance of what we have called a proto-self and for the subsequent expression of our essential humanity. It provides roles and rules that define the broad array of possibilities for relationship, for conduct, and for varying life strategies through which, for better or worse, one can hope to project a worthy humanity. True, the individual for Kierkegaard is of preeminent worth. Nevertheless, the social matrix is the inescapable field of one's endeavor, the arena wherein that worth, however problematically, can find its expression.

Expressing oneself through the universal does not mean that all of its possibilities are endorsed or exploited. For one who has "suspended the ethical," convention or tradition is a highly variegated and complex set of options, materials, or opportunities that one may use to greater or lesser effect in the pursuit and expression of a particular life. Being ready to express myself through the universal does not yet tell me (what could?) which portions, and in what measure, are to become my vehicles for expression. The career I pursue, the way I reveal my filial concern, the form my civic participation assumes, the friends that I seek—each will become part of my identity made intelligible by social norms and possibilities. But there is room within that social matrix for an unimaginably large number of possible lives, only one of which will be mine. From the standpoint of faith, to accept the universal is not to accept a rigid life plan that imprisons the self in deadening uniformity. It leaves ample elbow room for particularity of expression.[39]

Let me consider another set of questions. Is Kierkegaardian faith merely trusting receptivity? And if virtue is by and large a matter of disciplined accomplishment, how can faith qualify as a virtue? After all, we are repeatedly reminded that faith is attained not on the knight's strength, but on "the strength of the absurd."

To interpret faith only as a trusting receptivity is to simplify its complexity for Kierkegaard. The virtue of receptivity is a minimal requirement for a kind of elementary faith. Such openness toward bestowed goods can be given a secular or nonbiblical articulation. And for someone becoming a Christian, faith will involve the "offense" of the "absolute paradox," the Incarnation, and the intractable obstacle of sin. These complexities in the specification of Christian faith might prompt us to divorce Christian faith from the broader virtue of trusting receptivity. On the other hand, we could take these complexities as an invitation to deepen our grasp of at least one prominent and familiar articulation of elementary trust. On this view, the virtue of trusting receptivity lays the groundwork for more detailed articulations, among them, specifically Christian expressions. These might contain complex creedal affirmations that entwine the images of Incarnation or sin. In that case, a narrative continuum might link elementary, secular, or moral faith with Christian trust or faith.[40]

Linking faith and virtue can be challenged from other directions. Is faith really an achievement?[41] One objection to taking it as an attainment is that faith provides what the will alone cannot, for example, forgiveness. Some defects of action or character or circumstance just cannot be overcome by effort. Yet with increased moral consciousness we can develop a painful sense of responsibility for ineradicable fault, for something the striving self cannot overcome on its own. Such moral stain can be somewhat cleansed by personal efforts of restitution or repentance. But often it can only be forgiven, not worked off.[42] And there are related reasons for separating faith from achievement, and thus, perhaps, from virtue.

If there is a "double movement" of faith, the second movement seems to be initiated by another, or at least not by the unaided self, which is primarily receptive. It is not executed on the basis of our strength, but on the strength of the absurd. But the common view is that moral virtue involves a kind of active striving and commitment. The aesthete, to escape his corruption, must pursue virtue. Resignation and faith require weathering ordeals; strength and effort are required. But striving for faith might seem to be self-defeating, like trying to be effortless. How can humility, spontaneous thankfulness, or receptivity be *pursued*? Can we *exercise* receptivity? If the self is mainly the active pursuit of ideals, virtues, or absolutes, then becoming a self will be a task that is self-initiated and sustained. Yet the enablement that gets us through dilemmas frequently appears as a gift, as power bequeathed. It seems to dawn unaided. Perhaps faith is like the action of keeping still, cousin to a stunned and quiet submission, an alert but yielding immobility.

Our ability to master the world or ourselves is limited. Secular and religious faiths can concede this. Perhaps not all virtue is a matter of striving, mastery, or possession. To possess a virtue like good-heartedness or humility need not mean that we can bring about at will the specific excellence the virtue names or the particular good it provides. Jon Elster makes this point epigrammatically: "There is hubris in the view that one can be master of one's soul—just as there is an intellectual fallacy in the view that everything that comes about by action can also be brought about by action."[43] Happiness or love or understanding may come about through our varied actions. But we may lack an effective recipe, a procedure to bring them about. There may be rough guidelines for the achievement of some end or the cultivation of some trait of character. To the initiate these may appear as platitudes; to others, deep obscurities or paradoxes ("Just be natural!"). Whatever the steps recommended, it does not follow that they can be implemented at will by the self to whom they are addressed.[44]

As any lover or musician, parent or teacher knows, our excellences are not entirely at our command. Nor do we always understand their source. We can wonder at the genesis of our artful phrase, our social touch, our way with tools. Kierkegaard conceives the self as an uneasy tension between autonomy and dependence, self-initiative and other-dependent discovery. Self and surrounding world are at last as much gift as heroic achievement. Isaac is returned, not wrested back by force or rhetoric.

Another source of hubris is a misplaced stress on critical self-consciousness. What appears as ethical commitment can in fact be aesthetic self-regard: Am I looking well? David Wisdo describes this danger in an insightful essay on Simone Weil. And his description also suggests a rationale for the invention of quite ordinary, unheroic faithful "knights." Perhaps the knight could be a simple peasant:

> . . . the sophisticated moral agent, who possesses a rich and highly nuanced vocabulary to describe his actions and give shape to his moral life, runs the risk of making this kind of activity an end in itself. The temptation is to aspire to a kind of moral virtuosity by attending to the many ways his actions might enhance the richness and depth of his moral repertoire. Although the moral vocabulary of the ignorant peasant might be much more limited and impoverished than that possessed by the Aristotelian person of virtue, the peasant is much less likely to succumb to the temptation of viewing his actions as a means to render his life a moral work of art.[45]

There is a real risk in characterizing Johannes' hero *as* a hero, a knight of faith joining the battle for moral and religious virtue. If faith is a quest, Johannes also correctly depicts it as "absurd," quixotic.[46] But it is far from inevitable that the pursuit of virtue degenerate into narcissistic self-regard or that it involve an inflated presumption of self-sufficiency. To recognize the limits of one's virtue is a virtue. One must know, as Johannes reminds us, "what one can and cannot do."[47]

The knight of faith is not a proud, resourceful champion, jousting for his princess before an assembled crowd of spectators. With his invention of the shopman, Johannes nearly makes this point explicit. Were Johannes closer to faith, not merely an admiring outsider, he might have seen outright that faithfulness is distinct from the colorful world of warriors. Yet as unhappy romantics, poets in search of celebrity, adventure, and the spectacular, this is the world toward which we and Johannes so easily gravitate. These heroes of faith and resignation can seem to promote an absurd will to power, an overweening will to master mortality and time. Yet faith is cultivating the opposite: a trusting receptivity, an openness toward whatever may be given. It is the simplicity, humility, and playfulness of the shopman: no hero, but a "poet of the ordinary," who gives his loving regard toward the least of finite objects.[48] The shopkeeper or serving maid embody virtue without needing a grandstand or raising a banner to accomplishment. Attaining self is not a task to master solo. Whatever the knight's ordeal, work, or suffering, at last he receives himself, welcomes himself thankfully as a gift.

KANT, KIERKEGAARD, AND HIDDEN INWARDNESS

Various mainstream philosophers appear in discussions of Kierkegaard: Hegel, Socrates, and Kant lie powerfully in the background. Although I have tried to minimize historical comparisons, it will help to consider a parallel between Kant and Kierkegaard. One might assume that these two moralists—one a champion of Reason, the other a celebrated "irrationalist"—could only meet as adversaries. This is far from true. On a number of issues their perspectives converge.[49]

To be trained to keep promises and refrain from cheating is a central part of conventional morality. We are acculturated into taking a number of practices as self-evident, binding duties. But Kant proposes that one could be perfectly trained in this respect and yet express nothing of moral worth. For Kant, one's essential humanity involves acting from a particular stance, from a particular motive. The state of my subjectivity, the purity of my will, is the crucial factor. However praiseworthy my conduct may be from a conventional point of view, without proper motivation it will fail to have moral worth. An aspiring moral agent must learn to supplement conventionally approved behavior with inward moral virtue, with purity of will.

How to alter or clarify a mixed or muddled will is not something Kant spells out. He avoids a developmental approach; he is not a stage theorist. Nevertheless one might imagine a critical moment in becoming a Kantian when conventional, appropriate, and "dutiful" conduct becomes "teleologically suspended." One could imagine a moment of crisis when one sets aside the presumption that conventional acts of promise-keeping, say, or truth-telling represent moral achievements. The pretence of the universal, that keeping one's word in accord with duty has moral worth, would be suspended in the light of a higher good—purity of individual will. One would grasp, then, that allegiance to conventional morality *per se* is misplaced. One would grasp, or be grasped by, a "higher good," a quite superior *telos* that then defines our humanity. Relating absolutely to this absolute, each person is bequeathed a priceless worth, a ground for self-respect, and a basis for respect for others. For Kant, this absolute is purity of will or Reason.

Acknowledging or having faith in this "higher good" is suspending one's tendency to absolutize conventional moral conduct, but it is also a readiness to accept "duty" back on a new basis. After the teleological suspension, I keep my promise not just in accord with, but from duty. For both Kierkegaard and Kant the moral and spiritual center is how I, as a particular, express myself through convention. For both, "the universal becomes an expression . . . of a humanity pre-established, as it were, at the level of the particular."[50] And the structure of that "pre-established" humanity is strikingly similar: freedom, integrity, and trust in (or respect for) an absolute are virtues that define a fully human self, at home in a conventional matrix.

To become truly moral, Kant requires that our motives reflect Reason's categorical imperatives. Kierkegaard finds the transcendental locus of unconditional obedience elsewhere, giving the absolute another name. For his part, Kant makes an explicit critique of Abraham, one that challenges Johannes' account. Reason, Kant writes, ought to have halted Isaac's sacrifice. In the *Groundwork* he suggests that confronted with a choice between Reason and Christ, our allegiance should be to Reason.[51] Nevertheless, the structural parallel remains. If Reason is the absolute for Kant, then it is an absolute relationship to *this* absolute, and a recognition of one's dependence on it, that underwrites one's full humanity.[52]

Finally, both Kant and Kierkegaard depict an unsettling tension between normative urgency and epistemic uncertainty. Our salvation hinges on purity of motive construed as a correct relationship to God or Reason. Yet the marks of having attained this inward purity remain tantalizingly obscure. Objective uncertainty will accompany our passionate commitment to the new *telos* governing our lives. Although our aim is purity of motive, there can be no proof that our motives are pure. Here is the Kantian parallel to Johannes' problem of detecting the simple knight of faith. There are conceptual—and to the trained or sensitive observer, perceptual—differences between pure and mixed motive, between Philistine and knight of faith. But in neither case is a sure-fire criterion for identification spelled out.

Moral contrasts can rest on perceptual cues that defy translation into explicit differentiating criteria. We can hear unmistakable irony in a voice or know a scream is false, like a child's mimic of a cry of terror. We can see a lie written on a person's face, feel the hatred in a "playful" tease. If perceptual cues are not salient, if they fail to strike a chord, it may be difficult, if not impossible, to spell them out. So with the essential moral cues at hand. How do we *know* that what we intend in good will or good faith has not been subtly infected by self-interest? There is risk, uncertainty, and moral anxiety at the heart of these accounts.[53] Yet despite the dark, we strive for a purity, God, or good we can never know we have attained or are even reliably approaching.

Self-assessment is primary for both the faithful knight and for Kant's moral agent. The beam in one's own eye should loom larger than the mote in one's neighbor's. Nevertheless, this uncertainty applies equally to our assessments of others. And this suggests, once more, due caution in assessing the tale of Abraham. Rather than providing a model for outward behavior, the startling horror of an upraised knife is intended symbolically to highlight an otherwise elusive aspect of virtue. It can mark the moment when will is purified.

> The story of Abraham and Isaac need not be taken . . . as a literal description of what a person must be prepared to do if he is to be said to have faith. It can be read as an allegory in which Abraham's actions symbolize some general features of a religious consciousness rather than illustrate the sort of deeds expected of someone who has that consciousness.[54]

Are there marks to tell us when an allegorical or symbolic interpretation is appropriate? Johannes warns against readings that provide "tasteful explanations," readings that water down words "to be taken in as terrifying a sense as possible." Such misplaced effort "ends up in drivel rather than terror."[55] But who dares say which inward transformations do not raise nightmares, which shifts in moral perception are unterrifying?

Upraised knives are unmistakable objective evidence. A more inward teleological suspension is harder to spot. Abraham is kin to the shopman; he cannot be that terrifyingly out of line. The upraised blade threatens a severing of allegiances; and its remaining only upraised reminds us that the severing, however crucial, is only a prelude to welcoming reconciliation.

THE INVISIBLE KNIGHT

Johannes de Silentio has promised to focus on the lonely journey to the mountain. That itself shifts our gaze from the moment of sacrifice. And the shopkeeping knight reminds us that there is not just a journey to the mountain, but also a return, a return of and to a simple life in the embrace of the universal. This ordinary fellow is gracefully reconciled with the world and conventional ethics. Here is the portrait, beautifully drawn:

> "Good God, is this the person, is it really him? He looks just like a tax-gatherer." . . . He is solid through and through. His stance? Vigorous, it belongs altogether to finitude, no smartly turned-out townsman taking a stroll out to Fresberg on a Sunday afternoon treads the ground with surer foot; he belongs altogether to the world, no *petit bourgeois* belongs to it more. One detects nothing of the strangeness and superiority that mark the knight of the infinite. This man takes pleasure, takes part in everything, and whenever one catches him occupied with some-

thing his engagement has the persistence of the worldly person whose soul is wrapped up in such things.[56]

What chilling test has this burgher undergone? What qualifies him as a knight of faith?

> He drains in infinite resignation the deep sorrow of existence, he knows the bliss of infinity, he has felt the pain of renouncing everything, whatever is most precious in the world, and yet to him finitude tastes just as good as to one who has never known anything higher, . . . he has this sense of being secure to take pleasure in it, as though it were the most certain thing of all.[57]

The shopman is not *in extremis* or subject to agonizing ordeals. He has received the universal back, and leads an outwardly unexceptional life. But he is faithful and therefore exceptional. His acting in accord with convention has in no way tricked him into a false unqualified or absolute respect for convention. His loyalty lies elsewhere, not with the assimilationist ideal. In some inner gesture, hidden from our view, the shopman resigns the universal, undergoes its "teleological suspension," and then joyfully welcomes it back as a vehicle for the expression of his humanity:

> Faith's knight . . . knows that it is glorious to belong to the universal. He knows it is beautiful and benign to be the particular who translates himself into the universal, the one who so to speak makes a clear and elegant edition of himself. . . . He knows it is beautiful to be born as the particular with the universal as his home, his friendly abode, which receives him straightaway with open arms when he wishes to stay there.[58]

Yet the possibilities of suffering, isolation, or dilemma are ever present, occasioned by the stringent demands of freedom, integrity, and receptivity. Johannes adds a sobering caution: "But [the faithful knight] also knows that higher up there winds a lonely path, narrow and steep; he knows it is terrible to be born in solitude outside the universal, to walk without meeting a single traveller."[59] Together, solitary crisis and answering reconciliation animate Johannes' lyrical, dialectical effort. And the last word is worldly affiliation: "It must be wonderful to get the princess, and yet it is only the knight of faith who is happy, only he is heir apparent to the finite."[60]

THE TALE RETOLD

Isaac comes from his father's loins. Abraham has his rightful claims. Then in a shattering event, the son is lost, only to be returned, no longer now his father's possession. He rests in Abraham's keeping, on loan, as it were, from God. Here is a test of reason and care, a humbling of possessive will, an ordeal to confirm his essential humanity. The story challenges a number of Hegelian assumptions: for example, that morality is adherence to social norms, that duty to God is essentially social duty, and that moral action must be "transparent," must wear its justification and intelligibility on its sleeve. But the tale also models a process of self-formation.

As a distillate of biology, tradition, and convention, a proto-self appears, only to suffer the trials of self-articulation, the ordeals of resignation and faith. Woven from countless social practices, our projects, essential segments of our identity, are repeatedly put at risk. They encounter resistance from circumstance and competing ideals. Inevitably they become subject to critical reflection. Then, to varying degrees, they are reaffirmed or welcomed back, transformed. With luck, effort, and aid, we tend an increasingly moral self, nourished by a relationship to a barely articulable but powerfully present absolute good. The trials of faith are linked to this process of socialization and identity formation, for as Kierkegaard writes in *Training in Christianity*: "[T]here is *no established order* which can do without fear and trembling. Fear and trembling signifies that one is in the *process of becoming*."[61] The ongoing movements of giving up and getting back are given their essential social context.

The tale sharply mocks complacency. We grandly assume ownership or mastery or certainty of saving power, say, through membership in the crowd or through pursuits of pleasure or learning or status. There can be complacency about the objects I pursue. Chasing status, I neglect the tasks of selfhood. Or there can be complacency in presumption. I attempt to will or attain success of the relevant sort on my own. To achieve virtuous self-sufficiency, one envisions the triumph and glory of knighthood. Blind to the limits of one's competence, to the pervasive possibility of dilemmas and defeating circumstance, one expects to erase evil through goodwill and strength alone. But this is vain. For Johannes or Kierkegaard, the world is morally and spiritually unmasterable. The recognition of limits may trigger a crisis of morale. Why continue the battle? But it may also open and empty the self. Enablements that seem to flow from an absolute may dawn, enter to enlighten, and restore.[62] Values are conferred upon me as the particular individual I am, appropriate to my needs midway in the unfolding of my humanity.

As if to forestall a confusion between convention and the true basis of our humanity, Kierkegaard avails himself of a biblical story of similar intent. We confront the primordial human frighteningly stripped of the comforts of the ordinary. It is an essence both terribly fragile and terribly strong. Like the moment of vision delivered from the whirlwind at the end of Job,[63] the person is silenced, now a vessel of trusting receptivity, strong in integrity, fragile in buffeting circumstance. Through the medium of a dream, a song, a tale in the night, we see allegiance, virtue, stripped bare. But a story meant to make unmistakable this contrast between our humanity and the context of its expression is not a proposal to reject common decency.

Startling revelations help us see. They are not prescriptions to teach us what to do.⁶⁴ The exposure of fragile virtue is not a command to cast off all that clothes our humanity, protects our vulnerability: "[The individual] does not . . . divest himself of the manifold composite garment of the finite in order to clothe himself in the abstract attire of the cloister."⁶⁵ We suffer skepticism, withdrawal, and retreat—the loss of the finite and our Isaacs. But the garments of the everyday—decencies, good food, friends, and play—are not abjured. Abraham and shopmen are inside and outside of a single fabric. As Kierkegaard confesses, "If I had had faith, I would have married Regina."⁶⁶ In faith, the sustaining values of the everyday are offered for our care. As Johannes has it, we taste "the sublime in the pedestrian."⁶⁷ Nothing less than disaster may awaken us to our humanity; but nothing less than reconciliation lets it be realized.⁶⁸

Notes

1. Compare Rousseau: "Sensation-mongering philosophers have a great fondness for deeds that make noise." Jean-Jacques Rousseau, *The Government of Poland*, trans. Willmoore Kendall (Indianapolis, IN: Hackett Publishers, 1972), p. 96.
2. Of course, to speak of the expectation that Isaac will be returned as being "consoling" cannot mean that Abraham can have forgotten the pain of the trial, or that God is justified in setting the ordeal, or that Abraham is justified in his response; nor can referring to the expectation as "hopeful" mean that Abraham is exempt from anguish. See "Abraham and Dilemma: The Teleological Suspension of the Ethical Revisited," *International Journal for the Philosophy of Religion* (October 1987), appearing revised in my *Knights of Faith and Resignation: Reading Kierkegaard's Fear and Trembling* (Albany, NY: State University of New York Press, 1991), Chapters 4 and 5. See also Mark Lloyd Taylor's chapter in this volume.
3. "Hegel explains that in [faith] . . . 'What is present is only this going out on my part, this aiming to reach what is remote; I remain on this side with a yearning after the beyond.' For Kierkegaard, this 'longing is the umbilical cord to the higher life'; for Hegel, it is 'the ceaseless sigh of the self-estranged spirit.'" Mark C. Taylor, *Journeys to Selfhood* (Berkeley, CA: University of California Press), p. 269.
4. p. 79 [50]; emphases added. The first page citation is to *Fear and Trembling*, Introduction and trans. Alastair Hannay (Harmondsworth, U.K.: Penguin Books, 1985); the second, in brackets, is to *Fear and Trembling* and *Repetition*, ed. and trans. Howard V. Hong and Edna H. Hong (Princeton, NJ: Princeton University Press, 1983). Johannes Climacus discusses monastic otherworldliness as a failure of faith in *Concluding Unscientific Postscript*, trans. David F. Swenson (Princeton, NJ: Princeton University Press, 1941), for example, p. 359. Johannes de Silentio makes a similar point, *Fear and Trembling*, p. 126 [100].

5. *Fear and Trembling*, p. 67 [38].
6. He warns repeatedly against a "consequentialist" focus on "the outcome," as if Isaac's return could justify faith. Justification, in that sense, is out of the question. See my *Knights of Faith and Resignation*.
7. See my "Understanding Abraham: Care, Faith, and the Absurd," in *Kierkegaard's Fear and Trembling: Critical Appraisals*, ed. Robert L. Perkins (Birmingham, AL: University of Alabama Press, 1981).
8. Hannay, Introduction, *Fear and Trembling*, p. 24.
9. The frequent picture of Kierkegaard as a subjectivist about values is not grounded in the actual text. For an extended Wittgensteinian defense of realism or objectivity in ethics, see Sabina Lovibond, *Realism and Imagination in Ethics* (Minneapolis, MN: University of Minnesota Press, 1983). See also Charles Taylor, *Sources of the Self: The Making of Modern Identity* (Cambridge, MA: Harvard University Press, 1989).
10. See Iris Murdoch, *The Sovereignty of Good* (New York: Schocken Books, 1972); Lovibond, *Realism and Ethics*; Thomas Nagel *The View from Nowhere* (Oxford: Oxford University Press, 1976), Chapter 11; and my review of Nagel, "Living with Double Vision: Objectivity and Subjectivity in Human Understanding," *Inquiry* 31 (1987).
11. Stanley Cavell, "Thinking of Emerson," in *The Senses of Walden* (San Francisco, CA: North Point Press, 1981), p. 135.
12. Shakespeare, *King Lear*.
13. Compare with Merold Westphal, this volume, p. 113.
14. *Fear and Trembling*, p. 84 [55ff.]. Emphasis added.
15. Compare with Westphal's claim (this volume, p. 111) that in Kierkegaard's writings there is an implicit dialectical progression, in which the aspirations of earlier stages are finally fulfilled in a life of faith.
16. Merold Westphal suggests that "teleological suspensions" occur at each Kierkegaardian stage shift. These transformations both cancel and preserve the form and content of a lower stage as one rises dialectically in a kind of repeated Hegelian *aufhebung*. So, for example, the passage into the ethical can be seen as a "teleological suspension" of the aesthetic. See Westphal, this volume, p. 112.
17. John D. Glenn, Jr., "The Definition of the Self and the Structure of Kierkegaard's Work," in *International Kierkegaard Commentary. Sickness unto Death* (Macon, GA: Mercer University Press, 1987), p. 20.
18. Ibid., p. 21.
19. On the limits and powers of bootstrapping, see Ronald de Sousa, *The Rationality of the Emotions* (Cambridge, MA: MIT Press, 1986). His account of the possibility of simultaneously feeling contrary emotions is also helpful. In *Sickness unto Death*, trans. Howard V. Hong and Edna H. Hong (Princeton, NJ: Princeton University Press, 1980), pp. 13–14, Kierkegaard speaks of the Power or Other that constitutes the self.
20. For a good discussion of some of these issues as they arise in *Either/Or*, see George Connell, "Judge William's Theonomous Ethics," in this volume, and Louise Carroll Keeley's "Subjectivity and World in *Works of Love*, also in this volume. Also see Alastair Hannay, "Refuge and Religion," in *Faith, Knowledge, and Action: Essays to Niels Thulstup*, ed. George L. Stengren (Copenhagen: Reitzels Forlag, 1984).
21. An alternative to taking Kierkegaard to have dogmatically or uncritically presupposed Christian belief is to take him as proposing Christianity as a

solution to a universal spiritual problem that precedes this specific solution. See Hannay, "Refuge and Religion." This saves Kierkegaard from the charge of having been curiously uncritical about adopting the Christian standpoint. Having diagnosed the hypocrisy and thoughtlessness of his time, why not just chuck the religious framework and its daunting tasks altogether? Kierkegaard believes that there is a deep fissure in our existence, an emptiness that familiar answers to "the problem of existence" merely gloss over or deny. Only recourse to the extranatural resources of Christianity, in his view, can heal this breach.

22. Confucius, Thoreau, and Heidegger endorse the virtue of a receptivity without specifying in detail the features of a correlative Giver. For an interesting discussion, focused on rehabilitating the idea of gratitude for the beneficence of nature, without positing an agent to whom one addresses the gratitude, see Lloyd Reinhard, "Gratitude and Blasphemy: Some Gaps in Moral Space," in *Environmental Philosophy*, ed. Don Mannison et al. (Canberra: Australian National University, 1980).
23. Cavell, "Thinking of Emerson," p. 135.
24. Taylor, *Sources of the Self*, p. 42.
25. Ibid., p. 47. Compare Kierkegaard's *Concluding Unscientific Postscript* claim that the task in life is to relate absolutely to absolute ends, and relatively to relative ones (p. 371); and the discussion by C. Stephen Evans in *Kierkegaard's Fragments and Postscript: The Religious Philosophy of Johannes Climacus* (Atlantic Highlands, NJ: Humanities Press, 1983), pp. 163*ff*.
26. *Concluding Unscientific Postscript*, p. 179 n.
27. Ibid., p. 438. My emphasis.
28. See Michael Plekon, this volume, who affirms that Kierkegaard stands squarely within the tradition of orthodox Christianity.
29. See George Connell, this volume, on this same theme, pp. 64–65.
30. See Merold Westphal, this volume, for an account of the way this exact concern guided the development of Kierkegaard's thought in the years after 1846.
31. *Fear and Trembling*, p. 84*f* [56].
32. Hannay, Introduction, *Fear and Trembling*, p. 30.
33. C. Stephen Evans, in *Søren Kierkegaard's Christian Psychology* (Grand Rapids, MI: Zondervan, 1990), discusses this developing self and calls this proto-self the "pre-self."
34. See Harry Frankfurt, "Freedom of the Will and the Concept of a Person," *Journal of Philosophy* (January 1971), collected with other related papers in *The Importance of What We Care About* (Cambridge: Cambridge University Press, 1988); Charles Taylor, "Responsibility for Self," retitled, "What Is Human Agency?" in *Human Agency and Language* (Cambridge: Cambridge University Press, 1985). I discuss these in "Kierkegaard Our Contemporary: Reason, Subjectivity and the Self," *Southern Journal of Philosophy* (Fall 1989). Cf. also R. Z. Friedman, "Morality and the Morally Informed Life," *Midwest Studies in Philosophy* 13 (1988).
35. *Either/Or*, II, pp. 266–267, trans. Walter Lowrie and David F. Swenson (Princeton, NJ: Princeton University Press, 1971). George Connell, this volume, discusses such second-order choice in Judge William and Kant.
36. McKinnon argues that the pseudonymous works generally present "contradictions" or disharmonies only for pre-Christian life views, conflicts that are resolved in the final move into Christianity. That is, a Christian would find no

destructive opposition between ethics and faith. He also argues that Kierkegaard's remark regarding his love for Regine, that "If only I had had faith, I would have married," shows Kierkegaard's belief in the compatibility of conventional or civil virtue and faith. Alastair McKinnon, "Kierkegaard," *19th Century Religious Thought in the West*, vol. 1, ed. Ninian Smart et al. (Cambridge: Cambridge University Press, 1985).
37. Hannay, *Kierkegaard*, p. 78.
38. *Ibid.*, p. 79.
39. See George Connell, this volume, p. 66.
40. K. E. Løgstrup develops just such a Christian ethic in *The Ethical Demand* (Philadelphia, PA: Fortress, 1971). Løgstrup, however, reading Kierkegaard in a way that contrasts dramatically with the essays in this volume, criticizes his fellow Dane for excluding the virtue of trusting receptivity from his thought.
41. For an excellent discussion of this issue, see Robert M. Adams, *The Virtue of Faith* (Oxford: Oxford University Press, 1987), especially Chapter 1.
42. I follow up Johannes' hints on this matter of sin in *Knights of Faith and Resignation*, Chapter 8. See also Evans, *Kierkegaard's Fragments and Postscript*, Chapter 12.
43. Jon Elster, *Sour Grapes: Studies in the Subversion of Rationality* (Cambridge: Cambridge University Press, 1985), p. vii. I thank David Wisdo for calling this to my attention.
44. In his article in this volume, George Connell argues that both Kant and Judge William speak in terms of just such a direct choosing to be virtuous. For more on virtue and the "athletic virtues" subject to the will, see Robert C. Roberts, "What Is a Virtue," *Philosophical Review* 93 (April 1984).
45. David Wisdo, "Simone Weil on the Limits of Virtue," *Religion and Intellectual Life* (July 13, 1989).
46. The aptness of this adjective in reference to Kierkegaard's knight of faith is documented in Eric Ziolkowski's essay, this volume.
47. *Fear and Trembling*, p. 127 [101].
48. I thank James C. Edwards for the ideas in the last three sentences, conveyed to me in private correspondence.
49. For an attempt at rapprochement between Kant and the sort of "virtue ethics" I describe here as Kierkegaardian, see Robert B. Louden, "Can We Be Too Moral?" *Ethics* (January 1988). Direct and extended comparisons with Kant are found in Peter J. Mehl, "Kierkegaard and the Relativist Challenge to Practical Philosophy," *Journal of Religious Ethics* 14 (1987); R. Z. Friedman, "Kierkegaard: Last Kantian or First Existentialist," *International Journal for Philosophy of Religion* (1982) and "Morality and the Morally Informed Life," *Midwest Studies in Philosophy* 13 (1988); Robert L. Perkins (ed.), "For Sanity's Sake: Kant, Kierkegaard, and Father Abraham," in *Kierkegaard's Fear and Trembling: Critical Appraisals* (Birmingham, AL: University of Alabama Press, 1981); Evans, *Kierkegaard's Fragments and Postscript* and *Subjectivity and Religious Belief* (Grand Rapids, MI: Eerdmans, 1978; reprinted by University Press of America, 1982); and George Schrader, "Kant and Kierkegaard on Duty and Inclination," in *Kierkegaard: A Collection of Critical Essays*, ed. Josiah Thompson (Garden City, NY: Doubleday, 1972), pp. 324–41.
50. Hannay, Introduction, *Fear and Trembling* (Harmondsworth, UK: Penguin Books, 1985), p. 30.
51. Kant, *Strife of the Faculties*, Prussische Akademie Ausgabe, 7:43, quoted in Perkins,

"For Sanity's Sake," p. 59; and *Groundwork*, Sect. II, many editions.
52. Kierkegaard might well wonder whose this "Reason" really is, echoing Alasdair MacIntyre's *Whose Rationality, Which Justice?* (South Bend, IN: University of Notre Dame Press, 1989).
53. See *Concluding Unscientific Postscript*, p. 150.
54. Hannay, Introduction, *Fear and Trembling*, p. 23.
55. *Fear and Trembling*, p. 100 [72].
56. Ibid., p. 68 [39].
57. Ibid., p. 69f. [40].
58. Ibid., p. 103 [76].
59. Ibid.
60. Ibid., p. 79 [50].
61. Søren Kierkegaard, *Training in Christianity*, trans. Walter Lowrie (Oxford: Oxford University Press, 1941), p. 89. My emphasis.
62. Compare here the thoughts of Stephen Crites and Charles Bellinger in their essays in this volume on the role of God as the source of possibility.
63. Notice the way Mark Lloyd Taylor in his essay in this volume ties the Abraham story to Job's story as recounted in *Repetition*.
64. Charles Taylor (*Sources of the Self*) joins Iris Murdoch (*The Sovereignty of Good*) in lamenting the obsession in moral philosophy with rights, acts, and obligation to the exclusion of visions of animating goods. See also Evans' contrast between a "soul making" and a "society transforming" ethic in *Kierkegaard's Fragments and Postscript*, Chapter 5.
65. *Concluding Unscientific Postscript*, p. 367. Johannes de Silentio contrasts monastic resignation and faith, p. 126 [100].
66. Quoted in McKinnon, "Kierkegaard."
67. *Fear and Trembling*, p. 70 [41].
68. I'd like to thank David Wisdo for suggesting the resonance with Thoreau and the way of putting things in these last two sentences. A Thoreauvian pattern of skepticism, withdrawal, and reconciliation through writing is discerned by Stanley Cavell in *The Senses of Walden*. See also Cavell, "The Uncanniness of the Ordinary," *The Tanner Lecture on Human Values* (Salt Lake City, UT: University of Utah Press, 1988), reprinted in *In Quest of the Ordinary* (Chicago, IL: University of Chicago Press, 1989). Kierkegaard explores this pattern of being stripped of the world as a necessary preparation for acknowledging a deeper ground of the self in *Sickness unto Death*.

6 Subjectivity and World in *Works of Love*

LOUISE CARROLL KEELEY

Kierkegaard's authorship is alleged by many to be acosmic. Ordinarily, this charge of worldlessness is a consequence of a prior and more fundamental objection. At bottom, what is at issue is Kierkegaard's particularly strident form of ethical individualism. For Kierkegaard, the ethical is the event of self-development; for its study, one's assignment is to oneself. To assume that the ethical is more accessible in the big numbers provided in the panorama of world history is a delusion that the self invents to evade the ethical challenge. In Kierkegaard's view, that which is world-historical deceives rather than merely distracts. Moreover, one's relationship to the ethical reality of another is the same as one's relationship to something that one proposes to do but has not yet done—that is, both are conceived realities or mere possibilities. To put the matter simply, ethical partnership is prohibited: "[T]here is no immediate relationship, ethically, between subject and subject."[1]

With his customary prescience, Kierkegaard anticipated the chief objection made against him: "[T]o make the ethical reality of the subject the only reality might seem to be acosmism."[2] But this remark, with the tantalizing word "seem," is inconclusive. No less a critic than Louis Mackey reflects upon the difficulties in his study, "The Loss of the World in Kierkegaard's Ethics." Rejecting the charge of metaphysical acosmism, he attributes, nonetheless, a kind of ethical acosmism to Kierkegaard.

Typically, acosmism refers to the metaphysical theory that advocates the nothingness of the world. Mackey argues that, for Kierkegaard, the charge is both irrelevant and improper. Because it abstracts from the central ethical concerns of the individual, it is irrelevant; whether the world is real or not is not ethically pertinent. Mackey hastens to note that Kierkegaard is not denying the world's reality, either; in fact, he proceeds with the assumptions of Greek realism and assumes what the commonsense classicist would assume.[3] But preoccupation with such metaphysical matters, Kierkegaard cautioned, distracts one from the real ethical task. Hence the charge is dismissed as improper as well as irrelevant.

Mackey contends that Kierkegaard's concern to uphold freedom necessitates his position, and hence the governing motive is ethical rather than metaphysical. But Mackey goes further. He argues that the freedom Kierkegaard advocates is essentially "separative" such that his position, not excluding the religious dimension of his ethics, is acosmic in this new sense:

> [Kierkegaard] means to say that the individual is really isolated from other beings, receiving from them neither support, insistence, opposition, nor allurement. The world is only a cluster of possibilities for him, and as such does not offer him matter, content, locus, opportunity, or exigence for action—these he must generate out of his own freedom . . . his will to preserve freedom untrammeled led him to sweep away all order, participation, and community. His insistence that the question of the reality of the world is ethically irrelevant, and that only an indirect possibility-relation holds between the ethical subject and other realities, implies a sort of freedom that is separative only and is not supported by the cosmos.[4]

Mackey concludes: "The effect of Kierkegaard's position is *to infinitize the freedom of the individual and thereby to absolutize human subjectivity.*"[5]

Thus far Kierkegaard's acosmism has been tied to his ethical authorship. With regard to his religious writings a different suspicion seems in order: surely holiness need not entail the kind of separative worldlessness that Mackey charges. *Works of Love*, it might seem, would provide a ready antidote to the acosmic emphases of his ethical literature. Surely love as work must be worldly, that is, it must involve a relationship to another and presuppose a shared context. And Kierkegaard's observations concerning method seemed to support this competing thesis: "[W]hen I have first presented one aspect sharply, then I affirm the other even more strongly. Now I have my theme of the next book. It will be called: 'Works of Love'."[6]

What follows is a detailed investigation of certain of these works of love. It entails a surprising discovery: Kierkegaard consistently "subjectivizes" these movements of love. Mackey is close to being correct. More exactly, the works of love are found to be themselves subjective. The performance of the action as a literal enactment in the world that effects certain consequences is not given much emphasis. Instead, it is, at least in part, the inwardness of the lover that makes of the work a work *of love*. On Mackey's interpretation, *Works of Love*, too, is acosmic. But acosmism, thus understood, need not be the final word. The final section of the paper will suggest one way of seeing the worldly significance of the works of love. Thus I argue, in the end, that Kierkegaard's thought is not acosmic but relevant to real actions in a real world.

Kierkegaard's indirection is nowhere better apparent than in this cursory journal entry: "[I]n no case is cosmism Christianity," he observed.[7] (Whether or not Christianity is acosmic he does not venture to decide.) At any rate, a Christian ethics that did accent the individual's situation in the world might begin by treating of the corporal works of mercy, such as feeding the hungry, visiting the imprisoned, or caring for the sick. Kierkegaard nowhere discusses such matters. Instead, he praises works which, although familiar in a nominal way to everyone, have this substantive difference: they are stripped of most objective determinants and recast as subjective. What follows is a documentation of the subjectivity of these works.

Works of Love begins in a way that appears to highlight objective results; the fruits of love are featured. But even Kierkegaard's claim that love is recognizable by its fruits attests to love's hidden life: "There is a place in the human being's most inward depths; from this place proceeds the life of love."[8] *Works of Love* continues with a summons to love one's neighbor, an imperative that should surprise no one in Christian reflections of this sort. But it is neither accidental nor irrelevant that neighbor-love should figure so prominently at the outset. Love of the neighbor is the paradigmatic form of Christian love.[9] It is so because it maintains a complete impartiality toward its object and is constituted instead as self-renunciation. Neighbor-love is the kind of love in which the object is not determinative; instead it is shaped by its form, which is subjectivity. Kierkegaard sketches the following contrast: unlike erotic love or friendship, which are entirely inclinational, neighbor-love tolerates neither preference nor aversion. Because one's neighbor is precisely every other, all categorical distinctions are irrelevant. Neighbor-love presupposes equality, the mark of the eternal. Hence its object is not determinative of it at all. Put differently, it confers an equivalence upon every object, thereby privileging none. Preferential love, on the contrary, elects one object as worth attaining. In Kierkegaard's view, this establishes it as self-love and amounts to a kind of duplicity:

> All other love, therefore, is imperfect in that there are two questions and thereby a certain duplicity: there is first a question about the object and then about the love, or there is a question about both the object and the love. But concerning love to one's neighbor there is only one question, that about love. . . . Erotic love is determined by the object; friendship is determined by the object; only love to one's neighbor is determined by love. Since one's neighbor is every man, unconditionally every man, all distinctions are indeed removed from the object. Therefore genuine love is recognizable by this, that its object is without any of the more definite qualifications of difference, which means that this love is recognizable only by love.[10]

Both Kierkegaard's discussion of neighbor-love, which helps frame the opening of the text, and his analysis of the work of love in praising love, which closes it, affirm the subjective character of love's works. Given the fact that *Works of Love* is itself a work of love in praising love, it seems appropriate that Kierkegaard ends the text by analyzing the very process that produced it. This work presupposes not poetic talent but inward self-renunciation:

> If praising love is to be done effectively, one must persevere for a long time in thinking one thought, in maintaining it, spiritually understood . . . with the most punctilious and dutiful renunciation of every other thought. But this is very strenuous.[11]

The work of love in praising love entails thinking only one thought; the thought is of love and hence God. To think only of God in the inwardness of one's own situation is to renounce oneself so as to allow the thought of God to penetrate one's consciousness. For Kierkegaard, the transparency that real thinking yields is, in this case, a becoming conscious of one's own condition as nothing before God. Self-renunciation is the consequence for subjectivity of thinking only one thought. Similarly, sacrificial disinterestedness is Kierkegaard's expression for the same kind of selflessness exercised in the direction of the neighbor. One is disinterested in oneself to the extent that one is interested in another. Because the other is never finally exhausted, self-disinterestedness, carried to its logical extreme, is sacrificial.[12] Both self-renunciation and sacrificial disinterestedness represent a profound deepening of subjectivity rather than a forfeiture of it.

Even when the announced topics might encourage us to suspect otherwise, the same subjective emphasis recurs in the passages anchored by the two works of love just discussed. If law is understood in its customary way as a series of prohibitions, then love as the fulfillment of the law would seem to have an objective grounding. Similarly, on the assumption that conscience has an objective basis, one would expect an account of love's relationship to conscience to include an objective treatment. But Kierkegaard's emphasis, in both cases, is thoroughly subjective.

In Kierkegaard's discussion of love as the fulfillment of the law, the law *per se* is given a rather cursory treatment. When he does speak about the law as a body of provisions, he calls it indeterminate—like a shadow in comparison with an actual object, or a sketch matched against a completed drawing. In Kierkegaard's view,

> The law starves out . . . one never gets his fill by its help, for its character is precisely to take away, to demand, to exact to the uttermost, and the continuous regression of indefiniteness in the multiplicity of all its provisions constitutes an inexorable collection-statement of demands. With every provision the law demands something, and yet there is no limit to the provisions.[13]

These provisions exact requirements that can never be satisfied short of love. Hence Kierkegaard foregoes any further discussion of them and turns instead to love's completion of the law. Inwardness and perseverance are the subjective postures he examines. Kierkegaard's conception of love divinely understood is formulated with geometric rigor: to love oneself is to love God; to love another is to assist that other in loving God; to be loved by another is to be helped by that other to love God.[14] This triangulated love presupposes a self-renouncing inwardness. The perseverance of love is the summons to maintain this same sacrificial inwardness through time—to uphold in breadth of time what one does in depth of inwardness.[15] It compounds the strenuousness of inwardness and hence intensifies the lover's self-renunciation. Once again, Kierkegaard has centered his attention on the subjective dimension of love as the fulfillment of the law rather than the law's objective enactments.[16]

This subjective emphasis reappears in Kierkegaard's discussion of conscience. In Kierkegaard's view, conscience is the individual's relationship to God. To say that love is a matter for conscience means that one's love relationships must be transformed in accordance with one's God-relationship.[17] This transformation effects a new inward orientation; love's scrutiny by conscience does not seek to make external changes. In brief, by subjecting erotic love and friendship to the unflinching gaze of conscience, Christianity achieves an interior transformation rather than an exterior revision.[18] Once again, Kierkegaard's analysis has taken a decidedly subjective turn.

This subjective focus might seem to be compromised in Kierkegaard's discussion of "Our Duty to Love Those We See"; after all, the one seen—who presumably has some objective status—determines our duty to love. But Kierkegaard's position is more subtle. It is a mistake to focus on the lovableness of the object, he cautions; instead, it is love's development that must be tended. When properly developed, love finds the already given or chosen object lovable. This work of love, then, does not begin with the lovableness of the object—quite the opposite. Whoever "brings love with him when he seeks an object . . . will easily . . . find it to be such that it is lovable."[19] The challenge is not merely to love another in spite of that other's imperfections; no, the task is to find the other—together with his or her imperfections—lovable. Continually discovering the lovableness of the one seen is this work's concrete task. Once again, it is a task that only the subjective-minded lover can fulfill.

Kierkegaard's analysis of "Our Duty to Be in the Debt of Love" turns upon a similar subjective emphasis. Being indebted ordinarily implies another to whom one owes some repayment.[20] Debt, thus understood, has an objective component. Kierkegaard reverses the debtor-creditor relationship. He argues that it is not by being loved but by loving that one acquires an infinite debt. Thus debt, which it is one's duty to be in, is effectively tied to one's subjective decision to love. Infinite loving yields infinite debt. For Kierkegaard, indebtedness and giving are commensurate rather than inverse, for the criterion is the infinite rather than the finite, the subjective rather than the objective.

Love's duty to remain in infinite debt has its temptation in the comparative. To compare love with another's love or one's own prior expression of it, for example, is to reduce love to an object. Comparison finitizes what is essentially infinite; it makes objective what ought to be subjective. Further, whoever is caught in the calculative mindset of the comparative cannot act.[21] But Christian love, in Kierkegaard's view, *must* act.[22] But even action finds its terminus "in the depths of inwardness where love is related to God."[23]

In Part II, Kierkegaard's text is organized around his praise of love that builds up, believes, hopes, seeks not, hides, and abides. Although Kierkegaard might seem to be praising what love does, his focus is not on what love does objectively but on what love is subjectively. Put simply: its work is to love. Brief examples will suffice.

Love Builds Up. But "love which builds up has nothing to point to, for its very work consists only in presupposing."[24] The true lover makes no claim to implant love in the other. His project is more humble: he trusts in love's prior presence as a ground that can in turn be built up. Kierkegaard's formulation is apt: love loves forth love. That is, it does not put love where there was none but rather entices love forth in a new, subjective expression.[25]

Love Believes All Things. Although opposites, both love and mistrust begin in knowledge. Thereafter, both convert this knowledge into belief, mistrust electing to believe nothing at all and love choosing to believe all things:

> Love is the very opposite of mistrust, and yet it is initiated in the same knowledge. In knowledge the two are, so to speak, not distinguished from each other . . . only in conclusion and decision *in faith* (to believe all things, to believe nothing), are they directly opposite to one another.[26]

Neither result can be attributed to the understanding; to believe all or to believe nothing is a choice that reveals the subjectivity of the one who makes it. Once again, it is not the result that determines the work as a work of love but the subjectivity that precedes and forms it.

Love Hopes. Compared to actuality, the future is always a duality; that is, its possibilities include both good and evil. Expectation, in Kierkegaard's view, is a relationship to pure possibility that preserves this essential duality. But the equanimity of pure expectation can be altered by a choice: "[T]o relate oneself expectantly to the possibility of the good is to *hope* . . . to relate oneself expectantly to the possibility of evil is to *fear*."[27] Once again, Kierkegaard does not look to the result to vindicate hope, but rather understands hope to originate in the subject's decision for the eternal.[28]

Love Seeks Not Its Own. Kierkegaard claims that love revolutionizes the relationship to "one's own" by recognizing no distinction between mine and yours. Because this revolution takes place in inwardness, the subjective is again his focal point. In love, justice's demand for equal shares is overcome in the direction of self-sacrifice. Hence "the deeper the revolution is, the more justice shudders."[29] That justice should shudder is appropriate. Justice promises an objectively calculated fairness. Even the image of justice (blinded and with balanced scales) promotes this view. The love that seeks not its own, on the other hand, employs no such objective tallies; mine and yours are identified in subjectivity as the same.

Love Hides the Multiplicity of Sins. "Forgiveness takes away that which nevertheless is."[30] That is, the sin that is seen is made unseen by being forgiven in love. Forgiveness, for Kierkegaard, has no institutionalized format; it takes place in the inward recesses of the heart.[31]

Love Abides. Because the true lover, who is in compact with the eternal, can never cease loving, love, by its very nature, abides.

Once Kierkegaard has discussed the being of love as its work (that is, its building up, believing all things, etc.) he returns to a more explicit consideration of additional works of love. He praises "mermaimfulness, a work of love, even if it can give nothing and is capable of doing nothing."[32] Mercifulness is Kierkegaard's alternative to a very pedestrian form of charity that amounts to nothing more than a literal donation of one's temporal goods. Or, more positively, mercifulness is the subjective ground from which real charitable donations proceed. Being merciful need not entail the alleviation of another's suffering or the satisfaction of a single need. It may effect some worldly assistance to another, but these consequences are not constitutive of it. Instead, Kierkegaard shifts the focus away from any consequences to the subjectivity of mercifulness itself. Being able to be merciful is distinct from and more loving than being able to do something. In the language of Kierkegaard's *Concluding Unscientific Postscript*, mercifulness is a "how" of being rather than a "what" of doing. No one is excluded from its practice for want of goods; any exclusion is a self-exclusion accomplished in inwardness.

In his account of "The Victory of Reconciliation in Love Which Wins the Vanquished," Kierkegaard distinguishes between two different but related struggles, the first a combat between good and evil, the second a struggle for the reconciliation of the one vanquished. He posits, in the first instance, a victory for the good: the battle against the enemy has been won and the unloving one is in defeat. It is now that the second struggle must be waged, the battle for the enemy. The lover's objective is to evoke in the vanquished a recognition of his need for forgiveness, a willingness to be reconciled, and an acceptance of the forgiveness offered, but to evoke these sentiments in such a way that this experience is an experience of love. Better still, in the second struggle, the lover's task is to get the other to accept the forgiveness that he needs, to permit himself to be reconciled. But human emotions like resentment conspire against him; after all, the vanquished may see in the lover only the victor who has defeated him. Hence this second struggle, "the most inward"[33] one, requires a new strategy. The lover, although present, must conceal himself before the vanquished. In his place he puts forward the good, confident that the good will conquer.

Kierkegaard's account of "The Work of Love in Remembering One Dead" is taken up toward the end of *Works of Love*. Its position is a fitting one on two counts. First, it intimates a continuum between life and death such that love's work knows no bounds: in love, the eternal rather than the temporal is the measure. Second, the work of love in remembering one dead is a task that only subjectivity can undertake. Objectively, there is nothing to be gained. Unlike many of the preceding works whose subjectivity is not readily apparent, this work's subjective requirement is obvious. It provides, therefore, a retroactive endorsement of our subjective emphasis throughout the text.

Kierkegaard's position is striking but simple: if one would test the Christian character of one's love, the work of love in remembering one dead provides three thoroughly reliable criteria. First, because all possibilities for repayment are curtailed, this work of remembrance is the most unselfish love; it yields no objective gain, nor would the lover expect it to.[34] Second, loving remembrance of one dead is an instance of the most free love. The lover can never be constrained to love; the beloved, being dead, cannot exert the slightest influence to compel the prospective lover. To remember one dead is to love on one's own initiative. Third, this work of love exhibits faithfulness. If the relationship is altered, the lover cannot protest that it is the other who has provoked the change. To be dead is to remain unchanged. If fidelity is compromised the former lover is alone accountable:

> The work of love in remembering one who is dead is thus a work of the most disinterested, the freest, the most faithful love. Therefore go out and practise it; remember one dead and learn in just this way to love the living disinterestedly, freely, faithfully.[35]

It is significant that Kierkegaard counsels a return to the living and exhorts us to a certain practice. If *Works of Love* is thoroughly acosmic, as Mackey argued, then such a summons could seem, at best, half-hearted. But Kierkegaard's tone is enthusiastic and urgent. Although Mackey had argued that Kierkegaard's acosmism had led to the sabotage of community, Kierkegaard attends to the community of the living—and even to the community of the dead![36] We are left with this difficult question: are Kierkegaard's works of love acosmic or not?

Thus far the argument in every case suggests the work of love is essentially subjective; that is, to love is a feature of inwardness. Correlatively, these works of love are not given objective determinants in the sense of results or consequences. If mercifulness, for example, effects no improvement in someone's worldly circumstances, it is not thereby disqualified as mercifulness. But Kierkegaard speaks, too, of the outgoing movement of love and claims that *Works of Love* takes special note of this.[37] In what way can these two movements be reconciled?

The key to the riddle may lie in the distinction between the temporal and the eternal that runs as a subtext throughout *Works of Love*. In Kierkegaard's view, the works of love are not merely temporal occurrences. It is in this sense that he is not overly interested in the worldly consequences of loving works. Temporal, worldly, and human obstacles can conspire to jeopardize the lover's work. Time might intervene in one's intention to aid one's neighbor before assistance can be rendered. Institutional obstacles not of one's making might sabotage one's project for reconciliation. And human will, inspired by malice, can engineer ill results elsewhere. Of course, in another sense, Kierkegaard *is* interested—it does matter whether one's neighbor's affliction is alleviated or not. But he is opposed to any kind of consequentialism that sees in the outcome a vindication of the work that produced it.[38] The work of love is not merely what it achieves in the world or in time; its characteristic mark is the eternal.

It is perhaps another instance of Kierkegaardian indirection that the relevant citation occurs in his discussion of how "love hides":

> If . . . the eternal is in a man, the eternal reduplicates itself in him in such a way that every moment it is in him it is in him in a double mode: in an outward direction and in an inward direction back into itself, but in such a way that it is one and the same, for otherwise it is not reduplication. . . . *So it is with love.*[39]

Kierkegaard's meaning is not easy to understand. Because language by its very nature is temporal, it must use temporal devices to give expression to the eternal. Hence the difficulty is intrinsic to the project undertaken—to articulate what eternity means. Whenever the eternal is present in a person, its outward direction and its inward direction, though seemingly plural, are in fact one and the same. The self attentive to the eternal in itself is simultaneously attentive to the eternal being who sustains it. And "so it is with love," Kierkegaard observes. Love, too, manifests the reduplication of the eternal such that its outward direction and its inward direction are identical:

> What love does, it is; what it is, it does—at one and the same moment; simultaneously as it goes beyond itself (in an outward direction) it is in itself (in an inward direction), and simultaneously as it is in itself, it thereby goes beyond itself in such a way that this going beyond and this inward turning, this inward turning and this going beyond, are simultaneously one and the same.[40]

The argument thus far maintains that Kierkegaard does not mean that the objective performance of an action, that is, its literal enactment in the world, is love's measure, or that love is what is successfully enacted in the world. But this position must be qualified in an important way. The decisive phrase, upon which the qualification turns, is "in the world." Throughout Kierkegaard's authorship, time and world figure prominently as being capable of both deceit and sabotage. What looks like neighbor-love, for example, might be calculated to ensure one's own gain; love's striving might be undercut by worldly obstacles before it can be realized in time. Common sense, then, urges us to dispute the unlikely pairing of love's doing and love's being in the world.[41]

But Kierkegaard's context is different; love's proper referent, he notes repeatedly, is the eternal. It is in this sense that "what love does, it is; what it is, it does."[42] The work of love, as distinct from love itself, is love's outward direction made manifest in the world. Kierkegaard's point is that love strains in the direction of a doing, that its nature is to go beyond itself. What love does when it has undergone the reduplication of the eternal is a work of love; what this work of love does in the world of temporal experience is a second and quite different question. It may or may not achieve its end. In either case its temporal success or failure is not the same as love's doing eternally understood.

Love's going beyond is simultaneously an inward turning. It is this inward turning of love that has been documented thus far. Love's subjective deepening is accompanied by—no, entails—a commensurate movement in the opposite or outward direction. Love opens out to works of love. In this respect, *Works of Love* is not acosmic. Paradoxically, it is love's designation as eternal that implies a relationship to the world. The impress of the eternal, characteristic of true love, makes love's being and its doing one. The love that goes beyond itself gains inward strength; likewise, when love's inward direction is strengthened, its outward direction is strengthened too.

Hence world and community are not lost in *Works of Love* but rather subject to renewal through that love.

Notes

1. Søren Kierkegaard, *Concluding Unscientific Postscript*, trans. David F. Swenson and Walter Lowrie (Princeton, NJ: Princeton University Press, 1974), p. 285.
2. Ibid., p. 305.
3. See John Wild, "Søren Kierkegaard and Classical Philosophy," *The Philosophical Review* 49 (1940): 537–51.
4. Louis Mackey, "The Loss of the World in Kierkegaard's Ethics," in *Kierkegaard: A Collection of Critical Essays*, ed. Josiah Thompson (Garden City, NY: Anchor Books, 1972), p. 279.
5. Ibid., p. 282.
6. Søren Kierkegaard, *Søren Kierkegaard's Journals and Papers*, vol. 5, no. 5972, ed. Howard and Edna Hong (Bloomington, IN: Indiana University Press, 1978), p. 364. Prominent examples of twentieth century reflections on the theme of love include Anders Nygren, *Agape and Eros*, trans. Philip S. Watson (New York: Harper and Row, 1969); and Gene Outka, *Agape: An Ethical Analysis* (New Haven, CT: Yale University Press, 1972). See also Karl Barth, *Church Dogmatics*, vol. 4, "The Doctrine of Reconciliation," Part II (Edinburgh: T. and T. Clark), pp. 782–83. Barth objects to the "inquisitorial and terribly judicial character" of Kierkegaard's conception of love in *Works of Love*. A more recent and sympathetic treatment of the theme of love in Kierkegaard's thought is offered by Sylvia Walsh, "Forming the Heart: The Role of Love in Kierkegaard's Thought," in *The Grammar of the Heart*, ed. Richard H. Bell (San Francisco, CA: Harper and Row, 1988).
7. Kierkegaard, *Journals*, vol. 3, no. 2712, p. 195.
8. Søren Kierkegaard, *Works of Love*, trans. Howard and Edna Hong (New York: Harper and Row, 1962), p. 26 (hereafter cited as WL).
9. Outka contends that Kierkegaard "sets out with exceptional clarity and force a content found repeatedly elsewhere." *Agape*, p. 16. But Kierkegaard's contributions to the discussion of agape are not reducible to a recapitulation of central themes in the Christian tradition. "His further moves are increasingly subject to controversy," Outka maintains (pp. 16–17), including agape's assessment of an inherent flaw in natural love, the reduction of preferential love to self-love, the incompatibility of neighbor-love with friendship, and so on.
10. WL, p. 77.
11. Ibid., p. 331.
12. Outka maintains that interest in and attention to another's needs and the consequent self-disinterestedness are not the same as submission to the exploitation of another. Kierkegaard does not advocate "indiscriminant self-abnegation" (p. 21), in part because it would not be beneficial for the neighbor if his aggressive tendencies were encouraged and in part because it compromises the development of true self-love. Walsh ("Forming the Heart," p. 248) points out that Kierkegaard's emphasis on the self-sacrificial character of Christian love leads him to neglect another feature of love, namely, "our need to *be* loved as well as to love."
13. WL, pp. 111–12.

14. Cf. WL, p. 113. See Walsh, "Forming the Heart," pp. 236–37:

    What the presence of a God-relationship within human love relations means is that God—or love, since for Kierkegaard love is God and God is love—becomes the object of love; that is, love itself, rather than either lover in the relation, becomes the focus of the relation. . . . love forms the proper object of love relations precisely by putting the focus of those relations on helping one another learn *to love rather than seek to be loved* in and through the relation. In other words, the ultimate goal of a love relation should be to assist both parties in learning to love themselves, each other, and other persons in a proper manner. That is what it means to love God.

    John W. Elrod also discusses the relationship between self-love, love of neighbor, and love of God in *Kierkegaard and Christendom* (Princeton, NJ: Princeton University Press, 1981).
15. As Outka puts it, "self-renunciation or self-sacrifice is the only fully appropriate 'temporal' embodiment or the inevitable 'historical' manifestation of agape" (*Agape*, p. 19).
16. Cf. Jeremy Walker, *Kierkegaard: The Descent Into God* (Montreal: McGill-Queen's University Press, 1985), p. 44. Walker underscores Kierkegaard's contention that the Dominical injunction to love one's neighbor as oneself "cannot be understood simply as an injunction to perform certain acts or certain kinds of acts. The injunction is to be understood as enjoining a certain *spirit* in one's actions, a certain spirit which will inform and direct one's actions."
17. Compare with Stephen Dunning's chapter in this volume, and George Connell's chapter in this volume.
18. That Kierkegaard himself comes to question this neat juxtaposition is the thesis of Merold Westphal's chapter in this volume.
19. WL, p. 156.
20. See George Connell, in this volume, pp. 64–66, and Edward Mooney, pp. 76–78, who discuss this question specifically in terms of the debt of gratitude.
21. See Bruce Kirmmse, this volume, pp. 168–70, for a discussion of Kierkegaard's view that the modern age is afflicted with a pathological spirit of comparison. This takes the form of envy, leveling, and conformism.
22. Outka points out that Kierkegaard's position allows for a distinction between agape as indiscriminate acceptance of each person as neighbor and discriminant expression, attention, and responses to those neighbors in accordance with their respective needs:

    Agape prohibits discriminatory judgments where these determine whether the other is to be cared about at all, but it allows and perhaps requires that he be cared about appropriately. In the latter case diverse assessments and actions may be in order. . . . In short, equal consideration is not the same as identical treatment.
    Agape, pp. 19–20.
23. WL, p. 183.
24. Ibid., p. 206.
25. See Michael Plekon, this volume, pp. 9–10.
26. WL, p. 216. On love as a possible and right basis for belief, see Walker, *Kierkegaard*, pp. 76ff.
27. WL, p. 234.

28. See Stephen Crites, this volume, pp. 153–55, and Charles Bellinger, p. 219.
29. WL, p. 249.
30. Ibid., p. 274.
31. Compare with Wanda Warren Berry's essay in this volume.
32. WL, p. 292.
33. Ibid., p. 308.
34. Thinkers who defend the mutuality of agapeistic love find Kierkegaard's "complete indifference to any kind of response" problematic. See Outka, *Agape*, pp. 279–85. Walsh reminds us that it is Kierkegaard's position that the mutuality and reciprocity essential to preferential love make these forms of love selfish. She claims that Kierkegaard has an ambivalence toward reciprocity in love, although he presupposes it in others and seeks to elicit it ("Forming the Heart," p. 248). "Yet surely reciprocity would be the ideal in Christian love, even if it cannot be demanded."
35. WL, p. 328.
36. Cf. Johann Baptist Metz, *Faith in History and Society: Toward a Practical Fundamental Theology*, trans. David Smith (New York: Seabury Press, 1980), pp. 37–38.
37. WL, p. 263.
38. Outka notes that Kierkegaard has been criticized for being overly preoccupied with the "thanklessness" that attends neighbor-love; worldly consequences do not matter. He points out, however, that "within eschatological limits the concept of 'reduplication' or 'like-for-like' rigorously applies" (*Agape*, p. 67). As Kierkegaard puts it: "But the lover, who forgets himself, is remembered by love. There is One who thinks of him, and in this way it comes about that the lover gets what he gives" (WL, p. 262).
39. WL, p. 261. Emphasis added.
40. Ibid., p. 261. Emphasis added.
41. Kierkegaard's example is initially problematic. "When we say, 'Love makes for confidence,' we thereby say that the lover by his own makes others confident . . . we also say something else: that the lover has confidence" (WL, p. 262). I do not think that Kierkegaard is suggesting that the lover as a matter of fact always inspires confidence or that the cunning person always evokes anxiety. Sometimes the lover is shunned and the cunning one is approached. (Christ is an example of the former.) But when the lover as lover loves—and this necessitates the presence of the eternal—every action is matched by a subjective deepening and every subjective deepening is matched by an action. Kierkegaard is pointing to the constitutional peculiarity of love: what it does, it is; what it gives, it acquires.
42. WL, p. 261.

PART III
Social and Political Thought

7 Kierkegaard's Teleological Suspension of Religiousness B

MEROLD WESTPHAL

In Acts 5 we read that the apostles were arrested and forbidden to teach in "that name" and about "that man." Upon their release they returned to the temple and resumed their teaching. In reply to the angry consternation of the authorities, Peter simply replied, "We must obey God rather than men." The keepers of the Established Order, the bishops and professors of the time, wanted to put them to death; but upon the advice of a certain Gamaliel they released them after flogging them and repeating the injunction "to give up speaking in the name of Jesus." As for the injunction, the apostles "went steadily on with their teaching in the temple." And as for the flogging, "they went out from the Council rejoicing that they had been found worthy to suffer indignity for the sake of the Name."

Kierkegaard gives us two quite different comments about this flogging. In *Concluding Unscientific Postscript*, where suffering emerges as an essential category of religious experience, Kierkegaard I has Johannes Climacus tell us that the flogging "is not a case of religious suffering" but merely an instance of misfortune, since "the individual is secure in his God-relationship and suffers only outwardly." Because misfortune is an aesthetic category, the courage of the apostles is not essentially different from that of Mucius Scaevola, the Gordon Liddy of pagan antiquity.[1]

As early as 1847, however, Kierkegaard II begins to treat the flogging of the apostles as an archetypal expression of the suffering that is the mark or sign of true faith.[2] I want to suggest that the contradiction here is a dialectical one and that it provides us with the hermeneutical key to understanding the unity and continuity of Kierkegaard as a religious author. By Kierkegaard's religious authorship I do not mean that subset of his writings in which he speaks in his own name and in the mode of direct address about various religious matters. I mean his authorship as a whole, for I think he was right in *The Point of View* in insisting that the pseudonymous authorship be understood as informed by a religious teleology.[3]

So my suggestion is not that the theory of the stages is the key to the pseudonymous authorship (Kierkegaard I), while the dialectical contradiction about apostolic suffering is the key to the religious authorship (Kierkegaard II). It is rather that the dialectical contradiction about apostolic suffering points to the completion of the theory of the stages, which, in its complete form, reveals to us the unity and continuity of Kierkegaard's entire authorship. There is a real break between Kierkegaard I and Kierkegaard II. But whether one dates Kierkegaard's *Kehre* in 1846 with the completion of the pseudonymous authorship proper or in 1848 with his Easter week experience of forgiveness, the suggestion I want to make is that it is not like abandoning work on an opera to begin on a symphony. It is rather like moving from the third to the fourth movement of a carefully composed symphony.

The symphony I have in mind is dialectical, and its movements are the stages on life's way. The dialectical progression is Hegelian in several senses:[4]

1. Like the dialectic of the *Phenomenology* and *Philosophy of Right* (and possibly that of the *Logic* as well), it is an experiential dialectic. Concepts are considered only as forms of possible experience and conceptual schemes as forms of life. The necessity of the rise and fall of various language games as forms of life is no merely conceptual, logical necessity, but an experiential necessity that is in itself quite unnecessary. That is simply to say that one may not experience the necessity at all. For example, if dullness of sensibility anesthetizes us to the aesthetic atrocities that surround us, we will feel neither the inadequacy of the squalor or kitsch in which we live nor the necessity of passing beyond it. Such a dialectic presents us less with logical necessities than with experiential possibilities that may be experienced as practical necessities.

2. The "refutation" of any moment in a dialectical progression consists in overcoming its immediacy. A mode of experience or form of life is immediate just to the degree that it takes itself to be self-sufficient, complete, absolute. The necessity of passing beyond it is the experience of its other as such, as the other that reveals its insufficiency, incompleteness, and relativity. As each of the three previous sentences implies, in an experiential dialectic mediation is not something a subject does to an object, internalizing its other and thereby overcoming its otherness. It is rather something that happens to or within the subject as it is overcome by its other. If any internalizing takes place, it is the other that does it. Such is the relationship, for example, between consciousness and its other, self-consciousness, in the *Phenomenology*; between *Moralität* and its other, *Sittlichkeit*, in the *Philosophy*

of Right; and between the esthetic and its other, the ethical, in *Either/Or*.

This is why Hegel describes the dialectical process in language reminiscent of Jesus' notion of finding one's life by losing it (Matthew 16:21–28; cf. John 12:22–26) and Augustine's idea that God's exalted Word "raises up to Itself those who are subdued" through the work of Jesus in His humility, whose work it was to "detach from themselves those who were to be subdued and bring them over to Himself, healing the swelling of their pride."[5] In Hegel's account, dialectical progress toward the goal of wholeness is

> unhalting, and short of it no satisfaction is to be found at any of the stations on the way. Whatever is confined within the limits of a natural life cannot by its own efforts go beyond its immediate existence; but it is driven beyond it by something else, and this uprooting entails its death. Consciousness . . . is something that goes beyond itself. . . . When consciousness feels this violence, its anxiety may well make it retreat from the truth, and strive to hold on to what it is in danger of losing. But it can find no peace.[6]

3. The falsehood of the "refuted" moment is not the simple falseness of a binary logic but the relational falseness of the part that takes itself for the whole. Hence the "refuted" moment is not fixed, divorced, or executed, but reassigned, given a new, subordinate role to play. Hegel calls such refutation *Aufhebung*, in which the false moment is transcended and restored to its (limited) truth by being both negated (as putative whole, as absolute) and preserved (as designated part, as relative). Kierkegaard's name for this is teleological suspension. For example, the teleological suspension of the ethical does not mean that it is "relinquished" but "preserved in the higher, which is its *telos*."[7] If there is such a thing as an absolute duty to God, "then the ethical is reduced to the relative. From this it does not follow that the ethical should be invalidated [abolished; Lowrie]; rather, the ethical receives a completely different expression."[8]

To speak of the teleological suspension of the ethical as an "example" is to recognize that each transition in Kierkegaard's dialectic has this shape. To take another example, one can just as fruitfully speak of the teleological suspension of the aesthetic in relation to the ethical. From the ethical point of view "it by no means follows that the esthetic is excluded . . . it is excluded as the absolute, but relatively it is continually present."[9] The esthetic is not abolished but "dethroned,"[10] "for the art of mastering desire is not so much in exterminating it or utterly renouncing it as in determining the moment."[11] Similarly, with respect to sorrow, the task is "not to wipe out the aesthetic in sorrow but to control it ethically."[12] In short, the ethical "does not want to destroy the esthetic but to transfigure it" so that, with reference to the matter at hand, love may "transfigure itself in a higher sphere."[13] Romantic love does not overcome its other here. It is overcome by it as it is dethroned and controlled and thereby transfigured.

The theory of the stages of existence presented in Kierkegaard's pseudonymous authorship is a series of teleological suspensions in which a form of life that takes itself to be self-sufficient and thereby absolute is overcome and transfigured in this manner by the other that shows it to be incomplete and thus only relative. For the esthetic that other is the claim of moral categories upon my life. The voice of conscience, if it gets through to me, reveals the futility of the desire to preside over my own happiness.

At the ethical stage it is as the desire to preside over my own goodness that I try and fail to be self-sufficient. My aspirations to moral autonomy take two closely related forms. First, I interpret the moral life in a triumphalist manner as a series of tasks I can (at least in principle) accomplish. The thrill of victory prevails over the agony of defeat. Second, in order to render this plausible, I interpret the universality of the moral claims on particularities of my life in a Hegelian-bourgeois manner, restricting those claims to the expectations in terms of which my society defines middle-class decency. The ethics of my station and its duties requires that I incorporate the social "We" into the personal "I." I accept the voice of the people as my voice because it is, after all, "our" voice. Moreover, by identifying with the social self of the ethical rather than with the exclusively particular self of the esthetic, I gain the advantage of moral status without having to listen to any voice but my own. As Rousseau, Kant, and Hegel have taught us, freedom is obedience to a law we prescribe to ourselves. By making the voice of the people the voice of God, I seek, as part of "us," to retain my moral autonomy.[14]

The other by whom this attempt is overcome is, of course, the God who is not the echo of our own social mores, the God who called upon Abraham to offer up Isaac. The teleological suspension of the ethical is the relativizing of social morality before the absolute claims of God. In this *Aufhebung* the self loses its moral life and identity, dying away from the immediacy of the ethical, and is regenerated or resurrected to the new life and identity of the religious.

We know that in the writings of Johannes Climacus Kierkegaard poses the question of what it means to become a Christian and in doing so subdivides the religious stage into Religiousness A and specifically Christian Religiousness B. This distinction in the *Postscript* continues his reflection in the *Fragments* on the difference between the Socratic assumption that the truth is within us (immanence) and the Christian assumption that only one who is both Teacher and Savior can give us access to the truth, which lies beyond our powers of recollection and recognition (transcendence).[15] We misunderstand this complication of the theory of the stages both if we find sectarian motivations at its root and if we think that this distinction brings the theory of the stages to completion.

What lies at its root is Kierkegaard's perception of how extraordinarily difficult the teleological suspension of the ethical really is. In order to thematize that difficulty adequately, Kierkegaard finds it necessary to subdivide the religious stage into three, not merely two distinct moments. It is only with the teleological suspension of Religiousness B in what I shall call Religiousness C that we get the answer to the question of what it means to become a Christian and with that answer the completion and unification of Kierkegaard's work as a religious author.[16] This is because it is only with Religiousness C that the teleological suspension of the ethical is accomplished or, to speak more guardedly, that we really understand how difficult it would be to accomplish such a task. For there is nothing about the gods of Religiousness A and B to keep them from being the echo of our social mores, the legitimizing servant of the Established Order, while the God of Religiousness C is essentially a danger to every Established Order.[17]

By contrast with both Religiousness A and B, Religiousness C shows (1) why Johannes de Silentio was so careful to identify himself as an admirer but not a follower of Abraham, (2) why he thought it so absurd, if Abraham be given as the paradigm of faith, to aspire to go beyond him, and (3) why he found it the ultimate absurdity to think that this could be accomplished in an act of intellectual comprehension, however profound.

To show how Religiousness C is the teleological suspension of Religiousness B and thereby the completion of the teleological suspension of the ethical, it is necessary to show two things: first, how these two religious stages differ from each other, and second, how B is "preserved in the higher, which is its *telos*,"[18] that is, how B is incomplete (in the Hegelian sense, abstract and false) until it is incorporated into C as part of a more inclusive whole.[19]

To spell out the differences between Religiousness B and Religiousness C, I turn to the three major texts of which Walter Lowrie was most fond, *Training in Christianity, For Self-Examination,* and *Judge for Yourself!*, all written after the Easter week experience of 1848 and in the mode of direct discourse, in spite of the pseudo-pseudonym of the first. I agree with Lowrie that these "last and most trenchant of his *religious* writings" not only "belong intimately together" but are "the books which most clearly reveal him."[20] Nor can I quarrel with his suggestion that they are "so clear and definite in their aim that they may serve to define the tendency and purpose of the earlier, the strictly pseudonymous works."[21] I would only add that if they have this importance in the authorship as a whole, it is precisely because by defining Religiousness C they spell out for us the meaning of the teleological suspension of Religiousness B.

We know from Johannes Climacus that for Religiousness B Christ is the Paradox.[22] From the works just mentioned we learn that for Religiousness C Christ is the Pattern[23] or the Paradigm.[24] As Paradox Christ is to be believed; as Pattern or Paradigm he is to be imitated. This basic difference expresses itself in radically disparate meanings for such basic Kierkegaardian categories as *offense, objectivity,* and *outwardness.*

The concept of *offense* in Kierkegaard has its roots in his Augustinian understanding of sin as pride. We are the selves who wish to preside over our lives. Our attempt as esthetic selves not to notice the claims of the right and the good expresses our offense at these claims. We wish to preside over our happiness without interference from anyone who would be an authority over us. We compete willingly with those who wish the same wealth, honor, or pleasure we seek. But we are offended at anyone who tells us what we unconditionally ought or ought not to do.

The internal failure of this project or the external pressure of socialization leads (some of) us (some of the time) to the ethical as a negotiated compromise. I will accept the claims of the right and the good if they can be restricted to what we as a social order find necessary for public order and middle-class decency. In this way I can still preside, more or less, over my own goodness. I've had to pay a price, but I have retained a significant measure of autonomy. This is a price I am willing to pay. Through this collective bargaining process the ethical has become a real bargain.

If society is the other to the esthetic project of absolutizing the individual, God is the other to the ethical project of absolutizing the social order. But which God?—only the God whose voice is not the voice of the people disguised by some acoustic illusion to seem like a divine voice. (Images from the end of *The Wizard of Oz* seem appropriate here.) But such a God is offensive to human pride, and it is now in the interest of the social order, not just the individual, to negotiate a compromise. The goal of the negotiation is to permit lots of God talk while leaving us free collectively to preside over our own goodness without any real interference. We need a theological ideology and a God who will rationalize or legitimize our customary modes of behavior.

Religiousness A is the first such negotiated ideology. Human cleverness realizes that the Platonic notion of recollection could be quite useful. If we could preside over our truth by acknowledging as true only the truth we find within ourselves, we could continue to preside over our goodness without seeming to do so. For, to use a concrete example, Abraham will never find within himself a divine voice calling for the sacrifice of Isaac. Such a voice is the antithesis of knowledge as recollection and vice versa. With help from Plato, Religiousness A can filter out all those putative divine voices that do not echo the voice of the people. As the *Postscript's* account of resignation, suffering, and guilt shows us, Religiousness A is capable of intense subjectivity. But the epistemological immanence in which it operates blurs the distinction between a genius and an apostle[25] as well as the difference between the voice of the people and the voice of God (Reason).[26]

Religiousness B is the repudiation of this religious ideology. In the attempt to be honest about the nature of biblical faith, it acknowledges that it belongs to the object of faith to be the object of offense and that all attempts to make Christianity reasonable by removing the offense do so by abandoning the heart of the Christian faith. That heart, the other before which Religiousness A is *aufgehoben*, is God in the flesh. The Incarnation in its historical particularity is beyond recollection. In Religiousness B we cannot preside over our truth but in humility must accept as a gift the truth we cannot discover or even recognize apart from God's grace. Christianity is doubly supernatural. The Incarnation is itself a miracle, and the faith by which I acknowledge it is also a miracle.[27]

This is the point where Kierkegaard explicitly links the concepts of contemporaneity and offense, which belong essentially together.[28] Contemporaneity with Christ means that we must decide whether this individual is God or not under circumstances where certainty is impossible. For the first generation presence is not proof; for all the rest of us proofs are not presence. The gap between evidence and certainty, signifier and signified, requires a leap that is offensive to our desire to preside over our truth. Faith is not the athletic ability of a great leaper; it is the humble willingness to give up epistemic autonomy.[29] As far as the pseudonymous authorship can take us, this is what it means to be a Christian.

By invalidating the negotiated compromise that is Religiousness A, this humble faith *might* open the way for completing the teleological suspension of the ethical. But it could play quite a different role. What if Religiousness B is only a second negotiated compromise to render the teleological suspension of the ethical more apparent than real? What if it is the bargain in which we agree to give up the claim to epistemic autonomy, not in order that our ethical autonomy may be overcome by God as the truly absolute Right and Good, but precisely as the price we are willing to pay to be able to hold on to our ethical autonomy? If we could restrict the divine voice, which is not the echo of our human voice (transcendence), to the area of metaphysics (and the liturgical celebration of that metaphysics once a week or so), the God of bargains might be good enough to leave the social order to be run by us the rest of the time (immanence). This is precisely the project that Religiousness C shows Religiousness B to be, at least in Christendom.

For Religiousness C Christ is not merely the Paradox to be believed but the Pattern to be imitated. This is because for Religiousness C truth is not merely beyond recollection and a gift of divine grace; since the world wishes to be the source of its own truth, God's truth must always suffer in the world.³⁰ Truth is a way and a life, and since the disciple is not above the master,³¹ if that way and that life are the suffering first of misunderstanding and then of persecution, the disciple (as in Acts 5) can only find truth (and joy) in sharing these sufferings of the master.

For Religiousness C it is not the bare facticity of the life of Jesus that are most important.³² Rather, the specific content of that life as a threat to the established order is what matters.³³ By challenging the hierarchical structure of that order Jesus guarantees the opposition of the powers that be. He is not just an individual who claims to be God. That is problematic enough. What is worse, he claims to be the Expected One without recognizing the Established Order as an authority or the People as God.³⁴ The best and the brightest are offended. But the worst is yet to come. Beyond placing himself above the Established Order, he lives a divine compassion that in lowliness, humiliation, poverty, and impotence lives with and cares for the little people of the world and does so without the "cruel pleasure" of blaming the victim.³⁵ This is the way that leads to the Cross, and he invites us to follow him on that path. That is what it now means to be contemporary with Christ, and that is the invitation which offends.³⁶

The other before whom the immediacy of Religiousness B is exposed is a triune other. It is Jesus as the way of the Cross, the neighbor as the lowly one in need, and the world as the union of power, privilege, prestige, and persecution of the truth. It is in this trinity that we encounter the God of Abraham, who is not the (disguised) voice of the people. This is the God without whom the ethical is not teleologically suspended.

Religiousness B knows the offense of loftiness, that an individual human being should claim to be God.³⁷ But only Religiousness C knows the offense of lowliness, "that the one who gives Himself out to be God shows Himself to be the poor and suffering and at last the impotent man" and, as the one who suffers, gives himself as the Paradigm for our lives.³⁸ The sign of the first offense is miracle.³⁹ Religiousness B has no problems with the supernatural. The sign of the second offense is danger.⁴⁰ Religiousness B knows nothing of this. Only Religiousness C knows how to rejoice in those avoidable sufferings that come from imitating Christ. The first Christ, a Paradox to be sure, belongs to a church triumphant and is worshipped by his admirers. The second Christ, a Pattern and a Paradigm, belongs to a church militant and is imitated by his followers.⁴¹ The bourgeois complacency of the admiring church triumphant goes just as well with Religiousness B as with Religiousness A. Conservative orthodoxy, even fundamentalism, is less different from liberal, enlightened Christianity than it supposes.

Just as Religiousness C entails a sharply different meaning for the category of *offense* (and its inseparable partner, *contemporaneity*), so it requires that *objectivity* be understood anew. In the first instance, objectivity is what distinguishes the aesthetic and speculative forms of life from the subjectivity, that is to say the distinctive unity of seriousness, strenuousness, and inwardness, of the ethical and religious forms of life. Objectivity is the aloofness of those who, in order to preside over their lives and to be fully in charge of every situation, find it useful always to remain above the fray. For aesthetic objectivity life is always play and never work. For speculative objectivity the subject is knower while all others are known. Nor does this knowledge occur in the midst of the others, as if the subject were one of them. It occurs from outside the world, *sub specie aeternitatis*, commanding the view from nowhere in particular and everywhere in general.

Just as the religious is in constant danger of lapsing back into the esthetic, so the speculative is a perpetual temptation for the believing soul. In spite of the subjectivity of which it is capable, as already noted, Religiousness A is highly vulnerable to this temptation. By assuming that knowledge is recollection, that the truth is within us in the sense that we have within us the condition for recognizing it, Religiousness A is the ongoing project, if not of reducing faith to knowledge, at least of grounding faith in knowledge and containing it within the bounds of recollection. It seeks the security of absolute certainty and is skittish about the risk involved in venturing far enough out from shore to swim suspended over 70,000 fathoms of epistemic risk. It suffers such a fear of flying that it will never leap over Lessing's "ugly, broad ditch,"[42] requiring instead that the Paradox be dissolved in the syllogism and that the ditch be bridged by proofs of various sorts and their "incontrovertible ergo."[43]

In contrast to this relapse of the religious into objectivity and in light of its own understanding of contemporaneity and offense, Religiousness B understands that Christ can only be believed, never known.[44] It does not merely permit *doxa*, which cannot show itself to be *episteme*; it defines the truth of faith as the passionate, inward appropriation of "objective uncertainty."[45] It insists that faith is a risky venture, logically speaking. Again the question arises, is this openness to cognitive risk in the service of openness to the behavioral risk involved in a genuine teleological suspension of the ethical? Or is it rather just the opposite? Perhaps it is a new proposal for collective bargaining that says to God, in effect, "We're willing to accept this element of epistemic risk (especially now that Christian doctrine is part of the all but official ideology of our society) if in turn you will drop the suggestion that we accept the ethical risk involved in actually carrying out the teleological suspension of the ethical. You can have metaphysics and all the supernaturalism you feel your dignity requires, if you'll leave ethics to us, with all the autonomy we feel our dignity requires."

Of course it is not part of the definition of Religiousness B that it play this role. But then, nothing that does belong to its definition, as given by Johannes Climacus, provides any defense against its being co-opted by Christendom to function in this way.

Once again Religiousness C is the claim that the God of bargains is an idol and the theology that emerges from such collective bargaining is but an ideology of the privileged who wish to remain complacent, no matter how orthodox its metaphysics. Religiousness C does not deny that the epistemic dimension of faith can never be reduced to knowledge in the objectivist sense.[46] It unequivocally sides with Religiousness B against Religiousness A on this point. But it goes on to protest the objectivity that occurs, not on the Platonic spectrum that runs from knowledge to opinion, but on the biblical spectrum that runs from knowledge to action, where action is understood as the imitation of Christ in his suffering.

The knowledge that Religiousness B is tempted to substitute for genuine, biblical faith cannot be proofs. That was the strategy of Religiousness A, which it has repudiated. Its objectivity consists in replacing faith with doctrine. Its church growth strategists know that if faith means imitation there will be few Christians, while if faith means assent to doctrine, even doctrine about the Paradox, there will be many Christians. Whereas Luther understood faith as imitation, Lutheranism has reduced Christianity to a doctrine, leaving the impression that Christ came into the world as a professor.[47] Since the scribes and Pharisees who were Jesus' bitterest enemies inhabited a life world where only a professor could be Messiah, it looks as if Christendom, as Dostoyevsky also recognized, identifies more easily with the crucifiers than with the Crucified.[48]

From the standpoint of Religiousness C, the attempt by Religiousness B to make Christianity into a doctrine, restricting the offense of faith to epistemic matters, is a special sort of "misunderstanding," more specifically, "a device to mitigate the shock of offense at the scandal," namely, the real scandal that "Christ's life here upon earth is the paradigm; it is in likeness to it that I along with every Christian must strive to construct my life."[49] Christianity as doctrine is Christendom's defense against Christ as Pattern, a way of reducing the price at which Christian consolation can be bought.[50]

Kierkegaard wishes neither to deny such doctrines as incarnation and atonement nor to make them unimportant. He wishes only to see truth as doctrine teleologically suspended in the way and the life it is meant to inform.[51] Doctrine should define discipleship rather than defend against it. Religiousness C seeks to expose two specific strategies of Religiousness B that work against this. One is the importance it places on the doctrine of grace.

> There is always with us a worldliness which would have the name of being Christian, but would have it at a price as cheap as possible. This worldliness became observant of Luther. It listened, and . . . it said, "Capital! That suits us exactly." Luther says, "It is faith alone that matters." . . . Let us take then his word, his doctrine—and we are liberated from all works. Long live Luther![52]

Luther, of course, knew that faith is deeply perturbing, that it entails sacrifice and persecution, that it calls the believing soul to be a witness that will be most unwelcome in Christendom. The craftiness of Religiousness B is to make Luther a hero, while managing not to hear the perturbing parts of his message.[53] Far from having a monopoly on this craftiness, Lutherans are not even its inventors. That honor goes to Peter, James, and John, for whom the coming of the Messiah meant power and glory but not danger and death (Mark 8:27–38, 9:30–41, 10:32–45).

A second strategy employed by Religiousness B for keeping doctrine and discipleship apart is the importance it places on biblical scholarship. Once again, Kierkegaard seeks not to disparage erudition *per se* but only the "pitiable misuse" to which it is put.[54] The Word of God is to be a mirror in which we see ourselves. But when we would rather not see what the mirror shows, we look at the mirror instead of looking at ourselves in the mirror. Scripture becomes the object of our knowledge rather than the means of our self-knowledge and transformation.

Kierkegaard invites us to imagine a king who publishes a command that generates neither acts of obedience nor acts of rebellion but a huge body of interpretative literature and whole schools of competing interpretation.

> All this interpretation and interpretation and science and newer science which is introduced with the solemn and serious claim that this is the way rightly to understand God's Word—look more closely and thou wilt perceive that this is with the intent of defending oneself against God's Word.

Switching metaphors in midstream, Kierkegaard tells us that it is human to beg God for patience and compassion vis-à-vis our slow and incomplete obedience.

> It is not human, however, to give the matter an entirely different turn—that I insert layer upon layer, interpretation and science and more science (pretty much as a boy inserts a napkin, or several of them, under his pants when he is about to get a thrashing), that I insert all this between the Word and myself, and then bestow upon this commentating and scientific method the name of seriousness and zeal for the truth . . . the truth is that precisely thus, in the slyest way, I remove God's word to the farthest possible distance from me, infinitely farther than it is from him who never saw God's Word, infinitely farther than from him who was so

much in dread and fear of God's Word that he cast it as far away from him as possible.[55]

Against both of these strategies, Religiousness C is the reminder that Christians are called to be "doers of the Word, and not hearers only."[56] It reminds us that "there is nothing more deceitful than the human heart, and never perhaps does it display itself more clearly than by this disproportion between our understanding and our action." Then it calls us to the sobriety for which "knowing is acting" and to the severity in which these insights are not applied to everyone except ourselves.[57]

This is not the end, however, of the critique of objectivity in Religiousness B. As we have seen, its mode of objectivity is the separation of words from deeds, and this is not restricted to the university, where professors of theology devote themselves to biblical and theological scholarship with special attention to the doctrine of grace and special inattention to the imitation of Christ on the way of the Cross. This separation also occurs in the church, Christendom's church triumphant, where the worshippers of Christ are admirers rather than followers.[58] Because it is content to be admiration, such worship is itself the means by which the worshippers keep themselves "personally aloof" from all claims that they should strive to resemble or imitate the one whom they admire.[59] The words of such worship are, of course, themselves deeds by which the worshippers defend themselves from the deeds to which they are called. At least that is how it looks from the perspective of Religiousness C.

The words that mediate between the scholarship of the university and the worship of the church are the oratory of the clergy. Evoking the Socrates of the *Gorgias* and the *Apology*, Kierkegaard notes that oratorical expertise and the service of the Deity are not necessarily the same thing. Preaching that moves us to tears but not to action is the preaching by which "we who call ourselves Christians" are "coddled." Such Christians, and Kierkegaard includes himself among them, as do I, "cannot endure the true impression of reality." And such preaching forgets that "the sermon ought not to establish an invidious distinction between the [oratorically] talented and untalented, it ought rather . . . to fix attention exclusively upon the requirement that actions must correspond with words."[60] The preacher shares with the professor the task of insulating Christendom from "the true impression of reality" that Christianity brings. This is why Bishop Mynster was able to say of *Training in Christianity* that "one half of the book is an attack upon [Professor] Martensen, and the other half on me."[61] For all the difference between the professor's Hegelianism (akin to Religiousness A) and the bishop's orthodoxy (akin to Religiousness B), Kierkegaard sees them as co-conspirators (with each other and with the people they lead) in objectivity as a defense strategy.

This conspiracy can succeed only if it solves one final problem. Unlike Religiousness A, Religiousness B has a high view of Scripture, for it places biblical revelation, not human reason, at the center of its faith. So it cannot simply ignore the biblical texts that give rise to Religiousness C. What has it to do with them? Given its skills of scholarship and oratory, it should not be difficult to give them a safe interpretation that calls for only that contemporaneity that is in keeping with its understanding of the offense and for only that subjectivity that is compatible with its practice of objectivity.

In general,

> the requirement must be changed to correspond with what we have shown we can do by the fact that we have actually done it—more cannot be required. And therefore we require a Christianity which can be brought into harmony with all the rest of our existence.[62]

This lowering of ideal standards until they correspond to what we already are, this lowering of the price so as to make Christianity a bargain, this spiritual apathy is for Kierkegaard the definition of bourgeois. The moral heroism of bourgeois Christianity is as follows: "a thoroughly worldly life, avoiding great crimes rather for prudence than for conscience' sake, artfully seeking life's pleasures—and then once in a while a so-called pious mood." From the standpoint of Religiousness C this is Christianity "in the same sense that a bit of nausea and a slight belly-ache is [sic] cholera."[63]

Apparently Kierkegaard was well acquainted with the Wall Street broker who, in the midst of the recent scandals there, was asked how his Christian faith made a difference in his business life. "I don't allow any cussing in this office," he said.

Religiousness B has a theory of suffering to match its theory of action.

> Inasmuch as in the sermon one cannot very well entirely avoid saying something about the following of Christ . . . one does it by suppressing the really decisive thing and substituting for it something different; that one ought to endure the adversities of life with patience, &c.[64]

The preacher preaches about the necessity of suffering "because of the word" or "for righteousness' sake" and about the possibility of being offended thereby.

> But listening more closely, one discovers with surprise that these many tribulations are nothing else but illness, financial difficulties, anxiety for the year to come, what one has to eat, or anxiety about "what one ate last year—and has not paid for," or the fact that one has not become what one desired to be in the world, or other such fatalities. About these things one preaches Christianly, one weeps humanly, and one crazily connects them with Gethsemane.[65]

Hearing such sermons, "one might seriously believe that in paganism men must have lived entirely without earthly sufferings and adversities," since these are given out as "specifically Christian suffering" by the preacher.

A man's wife dies. So the parson preaches about Abraham who offered up Isaac, and the widower is portrayed by the reverend orator as a sort of Abraham, a pendant to Abraham. Naturally, there is not a trace of sense in the discourse . . . but the man is pleased by it and cheerfully gives ten dollars; and the congregation has no objection, for each one expects his turn to come. Might not one cheerfully give ten dollars for the honour of resembling Abraham in such an easy way?[66]

In these interpretations of biblical action and suffering, the "endless yawning difference between God and man," upon which Religiousness B seemed to stand in its combat with Religiousness A, is teleologically suspended in the religion of a "nice . . . human God."[67]

Finally, we see the difference between Religiousness B and C with reference to the category of *outwardness*. The word grates on our ears, for even the beginner knows that inwardness is Kierkegaard's category. But the religious subjectivity he opposes to objectivity has the form of inwardness only for Religiousness A and B. When we come to C inwardness is teleologically suspended in outwardness, which becomes the encompassing category.

This brings us back to our point of departure, the flogging of the apostles in Acts 5. We do well to note the chronology of Kierkegaard's contradictory comments on this episode. The denial that the apostles' flogging is a matter of religious suffering comes from the *Postscript* (1846), at the very conclusion of the pseudonymous authorship proper, while the claim that it is quintessential religious suffering comes almost immediately thereafter, in *Edifying Discourses in Varying Spirits* (1847). (*The Gospel of Suffering* is Part III of this work. The related passage from the journals is from 1848.) This change marks the emergence of Religiousness C.

What is at issue, clearly, is the relation of inwardness to outwardness with reference to religious suffering. By virtue of what we might call a phenomenological definition, dying away from immediacy is the suffering that belongs to ethico-religious inwardness.[68] Although this definition occurs in the account of Religiousness A and although its immediate reference is to the transition from the objectivity of the aesthetic and speculative forms of life to the generic subjectivity of the ethico-religious forms, it applies to each dialectical death described by the theory of the stages. Moreover, it adequately accounts for the suffering involved in transitions that take us both to Religiousness A and then on to Religiousness B.

It is inadequate only for the final transition to Religiousness C. For while each transition is itself, as a dying away from some immediacy, an inward suffering, only the final transition is a dying away from all immediacies in which outward suffering is involuntary and accidental to a new life in which outward suffering is both voluntary and essential.[69] For either Religiousness A or Religiousness B the flogging of the apostles is merely misfortune, for religious suffering remains purely inward. But in terms of Religiousness C it is an instance of the voluntary, outward suffering that is the essential mark or sign of the faith for which the offense that needs to be overcome in contemporaneity is ethical, not merely epistemic, and for which objectivity is overcome not only in the movement from knowledge to belief, but more basically in the movement from word to deed. That the apostles greet their flogging with joy indicates both that they have this faith and that they understand it well enough to have no desire to go beyond it. At this point the task is not to go beyond the stage one has reached, but simply to remain there. And this is the task of a lifetime.

Ironically, Christendom as the church triumphant is the triumph of the spirit of the scribes and the Pharisees over this apostolic spirit. In the deified established order to which Christ could come only as a Professor, the notion that "piety and godly fear must suffer in the world" has become "something quite antiquated." In the world of the scribes and Pharisees, as in the world of the professors and bishops who have replaced them,

> People were suspicious of everything that wanted to keep hidden in inwardness—and in this perhaps they were not far wrong. But they had also done away entirely with the conception that the mark of true piety, when it is not kept hidden, is precisely the fact that it goes ill with it in the world.[70]

We are not surprised when the powers that be do not want to hear how the truth suffers at their hands. But why are they suspicious of inwardness? After all, it can be a useful tool in the three-way conspiracy between the professors, the clergy, and the people to do away with the dangers of being a follower and not merely an admirer of Christ. These dangers

> they have also wanted to do away with by endeavouring falsely to transform the Christian life into hidden inwardness, kept so carefully hidden that it does not become noticeable in one's life. One should be willing to deny oneself in hidden inwardness . . . but (for God's sake! shall I say?) one must not let it be observed. In this way, established Christendom becomes a collection of what one might call honorary Christians, in the same sense as one speaks of honorary doctors who get their degree without having to take an examination.[71]

Although Religiousness B is unashamed to employ inwardness in this manner, it remains wary, and Kierkegaard thinks it may have good cause to be. Both suspect that inwardness has utopian as well as ideological possibilities, that it may lead to undeifying the established order. Kierkegaard distinguishes two ways in which faith is perturbing. There is the "disquietude in the heroes of the faith and the witnesses for the truth who aim to reform the established order." It belongs to a life of sacrifice and suffering. Then there is "disquietude in the direction of inward change." Kierkegaard acknowledges both that his work has been for the latter and that it is quite compatible with a very comfortable life, externally speaking. But he also suggests that this "mildest, the lowest form of godliness" properly belongs to a higher, more strenuous disquietude. Far from inwardness being an immediacy that insulates faith from the imitation of Christ in his humiliation, its proper function is to point beyond itself to that task.[72]

"The very first condition for becoming a Christian is to be absolutely introverted," to be turned inward. The falseness of this claim on the lips of Religiousness B lies in its incompleteness.[73] On the lips of Religiousness C its truth is salvaged, as inwardness becomes the servant of a certain kind of outwardness. The true claim includes what the first version neglects to mention. For Religiousness C,

> the very beginning of the test of becoming and being a Christian [is] for one to be so introverted that it is as if all the others do not exist for one, so introverted that one is quite literally alone in the whole world, alone before God, alone with the Holy Scripture as guide, alone with the Pattern before one's eyes.

It is only when the last phrase is not omitted that "endless introversion teaches a man to understand to the utmost what the task is . . . that to be a Christian is to believe in Christ and to suffer for the sake of this faith."[74]

More could be said, but scarcely needs to be, about the difference between Religiousness B and C. As already noted, however, B can be said to be teleologically suspended in C only if it can be shown not only that the two are different but also that B is preserved in C as "the higher, which is its *telos.*"[75]

There can be no question about the preservation of B. It permeates the shorter discourses published with the three longer works we have been considering. But it is just as present in the longer works themselves. *Training in Christianity* begins with a reaffirmation of Johannes Climacus' interpretation of Christ as Paradox and therefore as an object of both offense and faith. And this trio of books ends with the following sentence:

> No, the Pattern must be brought to the fore, for the sake at least of creating some respect for Christianity, to get it made a little bit evident what it is to be a Christian, to get Christianity transferred from learned discussion and doubt and twaddle (the objective) into the subjective

sphere, where it belongs, as surely as the Saviour of the world, our Lord Jesus Christ, brought no doctrine into the world and never lectured but as the "Pattern" required imitation—casting out, however, if possible, by his atonement all anxious dread from men's souls.[76]

The consolation of the atonement has not been "relinquished"; but in this setting it has been given "a completely different expression."[77] Different from what? Different from anything one would hear from either Professor Martensen or Bishop Mynster.

The only question concerns how C can be said to be higher than B in the sense of being the latter's *telos*. It is possible to be very brief on this point, for the answer has been given already. C is the telos of B because (1) both B and C are modes of the religious; (2) the religious is distinctive by being the teleological suspension of the ethical; (3) like Religiousness A, Religiousness B is defenseless against becoming a "religious" way of being irreligious, that is, of resisting the teleological suspension of the ethical by working out a negotiated compromise to save as much ethical autonomy as possible; and (4) only in Religiousness C is "religious" resistance overcome and only there does the teleological suspension of the ethical actually occur. No doubt this means that Religiousness C never actually occurs. It is rather the task of a lifetime, an appropriation that is always an approximation and never an accomplishment. But Kierkegaard makes it as clear as he can that this task is the teleological suspension of the ethical as the teleological suspension of Religiousness B.

Notes

1. *Concluding Unscientific Postscript* (cited hereafter CUP), trans. David F. Swenson and Walter Lowrie (Princeton, NJ: Princeton University Press, 1941), p. 405.
2. *Søren Kierkegaard's Journals and Papers*, 7 vols, trans. Howard V. Hong and Edna H. Hong, with Gregor Malantschuk (Bloomington, IN: Indiana University Press, 1967–1978) IV 4617 (cited hereafter as JP, by Hong's volume number followed by entry number (not page number). See also *The Gospel of Suffering* (cited hereafter as GS), trans. David F. Swenson and Lillian Marian Swenson (Minneapolis, MN: Augsburg Publishing House, 1948), pp. 146–147.
3. Here I take issue with authors such as Louis Mackey, who affirms in "Points of View for His Work as an Author" that Kierkegaard's reading of his authorship in *The Point of View* is fundamentally mistaken. See *Points of View* (Tallahassee, FL: Florida State University Press, 1986).
4. Several authors have discussed the Hegelian character of the progression in the stages in Kierkegaard, among them Stephen Dunning, in *Kierkegaard's Dialectic of Inwardness* (Princeton, NJ: Princeton University Press, 1983); and George Connell, *To Be One Thing* (Mercer, GA: Mercer University Press, 1985).
5. *Confessions*, VII, 18. Cf. Thomas Merton: "We do not detach ourselves from things in order to attach ourselves to God, but rather we become detached *from*

ourselves in order to see and use all things in and for God." *New Seeds of Contemplation* (New York: New Directions, 1972), p. 21. Edward Mooney, in this volume, discusses Abraham's loss and recovery of Isaac as analyzed in *Fear and Trembling* as a seeing beyond one's own set of self-serving valuations.
6. *Hegel's Phenomenology of Spirit* (cited hereafter as PS), trans. A. V. Miller (Oxford: Clarendon Press, 1977), p. 51.
7. *Fear and Trembling* (cited hereafter as FT), trans. Howard F. Hong and Edna H. Hong (Princeton, NJ: Princeton University Press, 1983), p. 54.
8. FT, p. 70.
9. *Either/Or* (cited hereafter as EO), 2 vols., trans. Howard V. Hong and Edna H. Hong (Princeton, NJ: Princeton University Press, 1987), vol. II, p. 177.
10. EO II, p. 226.
11. Ibid., p. 250.
12. Ibid., p. 238.
13. Ibid., pp. 253, 256.
14. See Edward Mooney's essay, this volume, for further discussion of Kierkegaard's critique of a Hegelian assimilationalist ethic. While George Connell agrees that Kierkegaard's ethical stage is unrealistically self-confident, he questions the aptness of its identification with the ethics of Kant and Hegel.
15. See Stephen Dunning's comments on transcendence in relation to authority in his chapter in this volume.
16. I first used the term "Religiousness C" in a paper titled "Kierkegaard's Phenomenology of Faith as Suffering," which was presented to the Society for Phenomenology and Existential Philosophy in Toronto in the fall of 1986. It will be published by SUNY Press with the proceedings of that meeting in a volume edited by Donn Welton and Hugh Silverman. A friend tells me he has seen or heard the term elsewhere in relation to Kierkegaard, but neither he nor I know where.
17. Compare Bruce Kirmmse, this volume pp. 171–72. In *A Political Dogmatic* (Philadelphia, PA Fortress Press, 1985), Jens Glebe-Møller argues that Christianity can become politically relevant only by ridding itself of all talk of a transcendent God. Kierkegaard, in contrast, shows that a truly transcendent God is of enormous political significance in that such a God relativizes all human institutions and projects and stands in judgment over all human efforts at self-deification. For further development of this idea see Merold Westphal, *Kierkegaard's Critique of Reason and Society* (Macon, GA: Mercer University Press, 1987); Jacques Ellul, *Politics of God and Politics of Man*, trans. and ed. Geoffrey Bromiley (Grand Rapids, MI: Eerdmans, 1972); Søren Krarup, *Demokratisme* (Copenhagen: Gyldendal, 1968), and *Loven* (Copenhagen: Lindhardt og Ringhof, 1980); Alain Besançon, *The Rise of the Gulag*, trans. Sarah Mathews (New York: Continuum, 1981); and Alexander Solzhenitsyn, *The Gulag Archipelago* (New York: Harper & Row, 1974–1976).
18. FT, p. 54.
19. See Eric Ziolkowski's chapter, this volume, for a description of a parallel development in Kierkegaard's view of Don Quixote.
20. *Christian Discourses*, trans. Walter Lowrie (Princeton, NJ: Princeton University Press, 1971), p. v (cited hereafter as CD). *For Self-Examination* and *Judge for Yourself*, trans. Walter Lowrie (Princeton, NJ: Princeton University Press, 1944), pp. v, vii (cited hereafter as FSE/JFY).
21. *Training in Christianity*, trans. Walter Lowrie (Princeton, NJ: Princeton Univer-

sity Press, 1944), p. vii (cited hereafter as TC).
22. TC, pp. 28–29, 33, 67, 85, 123.
23. Ibid., pp. 195, 198, 219, 232, 238; JFY, pp. 161–217.
24. TC, pp. 109–11.
25. *On Authority and Revelation*, trans. Walter Lowrie (Princeton, NJ: Princeton University Press, 1955), pp. 103–20 (cited hereafter as OAR).
26. Compare with Ziolkowski, this volume pp. 137–40.
27. *Philosophical Fragments*, trans. David Swenson, rev. Howard V. Hong (Princeton, NJ: Princeton University Press, 1962), pp. 65, 81 (cited hereafter as PF).
28. See Per Lønning, *Samtidighedens Situation* (Oslo: Landog Kirke, 1954).
29. See Stephen Dunning, this volume, for a discussion of the connection between contemporaneity with Christ and acceptance of revelations as authoritative.
30. TC, pp. 37, 153–54, 194–95; JFY, pp. 132, 144, 179–80.
31. Ibid., p. 108.
32. PF, p. 130.
33. See Johannes Sløk, *Da Kierkegaard Tav: Fra forfatterskab til Kirkestorm* (Copenhagen: Reitzel, 1980), Chap. 4.
34. TC, pp. 50–52.
35. Ibid., pp. 19–20.
36. Ibid., pp. 9–72.
37. Ibid., pp. 96*ff*.
38. Ibid., pp. 105*ff*.
39. Ibid., pp. 97, 125, 135; cf. PF, pp. 65, 81.
40. TC, p. 243.
41. Ibid., Part III, Sections V and VI.
42. CUP, p. 90.
43. TC, pp. 33, 98.
44. Ibid., pp. 36–38.
45. CUP, p. 182.
46. TC, pp. 26–39, 96–100.
47. JFY, pp. 197–204.
48. TC, pp. 89–90.
49. Ibid., pp. 108–9.
50. JFY, pp. 215–17.
51. TC, pp. 200–205.
52. FSE, p. 41. For a twentieth century development of these ideas see Dietrich Bonhoeffer, *The Cost of Discipleship* (New York: Macmillan, 1963).
53. FSE, pp. 42–50.
54. Ibid., pp. 53, 57.
55. FSE, pp. 59–60; cf. CUP, 179–80.
56. James 1:22; FSE, p. 39.
57. JFY, pp. 134–35.
58. TC, pp. 231–50.
59. Ibid., pp. 234–35, 237, 245.
60. FSE, pp. 35–37. Also see Stephen Dunning, this volume, p. 22.
61. TC, p. xxv.
62. JFY, p. 166.
63. Ibid., pp. 207–11; cf. p. 198.
64. Ibid., p. 198.
65. TC, p. 115.

66. Ibid., p. 110.
67. Ibid., pp. 66–67 (Kierkegaard's ellipsis).
68. CUP, p. 386ff.
69. TC, pp. 111, 173; FSE, p. 87; JFY, p. 209.
70. Ibid., pp. 90–91.
71. Ibid., pp. 245–46.
72. FSE, pp. 45–49.
73. See the conclusion of Louise Carroll Keeley's chapter in this volume, in which she claims that love, although subjective, is of a nature to go beyond itself in objective acts.
74. TC, pp. 219–20.
75. FT, p. 54.
76. JFY, pp. 216–17.
77. FT, pp. 54, 70.

8 Don Quixote and Kierkegaard's Understanding of the Single Individual in Society

ERIC J. ZIOLKOWSKI

> I am fighting almost like a Don Quixote—it never occurs to them that it is Christianity.
>
> Søren Kierkegaard

Although I assume among my readers at least a passing acquaintance with the character, theme, and plot of Miguel de Cervantes' *Don Quijote de la Mancha* (in English *Don Quixote*), some prefatory remarks are in order about this Spanish classic, whose bearing upon Kierkegaard's thought and struggle as a Christian individual against society I will consider.

Don Quixote, written in two parts which appeared respectively in 1605 and 1615, is generally regarded as the first modern novel and has surely been the most widely read and most studied representative of that genre. Having assumed one of the highest ranks among Western classics, it has gone through some 2,300 editions in at least 68 dialects and languages, becoming after the Bible the world's most translated book.[1]

No work of fiction has elicited more numerous and varied responses over the centuries than the *Quixote*, and no literary hero has been viewed in such widely contrasting ways as the knight of La Mancha, who has been interpreted variously as a comic, tragic, and tragicomic figure. It is impor-

---

This essay is dedicated to Langdon Gilkey.

tant for us to note that by the beginning of Kierkegaard's century, the *Quixote* was so widely known throughout Europe that its German translator Ludwig Tieck could claim that it was *"von ganz reputirlichen Leuten gelesen."*[2] Most significant is the way the novel and its hero were read by Tieck and his fellow Romantics in Germany, most notably the Schlegels, Schelling, and Jean Paul Richter. Whereas Cervantes' seventeenth century readers had seen his masterpiece as a funny burlesque of the outmoded books of chivalry, the Romantics considered it in serious terms as an "ironic romance" (Tieck), a "romantic epic" (Jean Paul), or a powerful "myth" (Schelling). While the Romantics did not deny that some aspects of the *Quixote* were amusing, they had much loftier concepts of humor and irony than their predecessors and regarded Cervantes as the quintessential humorist and ironist. Moreover, while the author's contemporaries had viewed his hero as simply a ridiculous, mad buffoon, the Romantics converted him into a noble or even tragic emblem of the idealist individual struggling in an unworthy society,[3] a transformation that led eventually to the comparison of Don Quixote to Christ.[4]

These points should be kept in mind because the German Romantics held such great sway over Kierkegaard, whose own interest in the *Quixote* will now be examined.

In our century, Don Quixote has often been called a "knight of faith," an epithet drawn from Kierkegaard's *Fear and Trembling* (1843). Miguel de Unamuno and W. H. Auden were two of the best-known authors to characterize the Manchegan knight by this term.[5] And when Franz Kafka composed his parable "Abraham," in which the first Hebrew patriarch is transformed into a comical Don Quixote, Kafka had already read *Fear and Trembling*, whose presentation of Abraham as the paradigmatic knight of faith had led him to construe Cervantes' hero as an embodiment of the same religious type.[6]

As theologically provocative as such a view of Don Quixote might be, any application of the term "knight of faith" to him should be qualified insofar as it might seem to identify Kierkegaard's understanding of that term with Don Quixote. To be sure, certain points in Johannes de Silentio's description of the knight of faith are reminiscent of Don Quixote. When Silentio claims that "The knight of faith is assigned solely to himself; he feels the pain of being unable to make himself understandable to others,"[7] we are reminded of numerous scenes in the *Quixote* where the mad knight, solemnly discoursing upon some lofty subject in his archaic "high" dialect, baffles his listeners—for example, his nostalgic lecture on the Golden Age to a group of illiterate shepherds in Part I, Chapter 11. However, it should not be forgotten or overlooked, as it sometimes seems to be, that nowhere in

Fear and Trembling is Don Quixote mentioned by name and that nowhere in Kierkegaard's other writings—including, as far as I am aware, all his published works, private journals, and papers—is Don Quixote called a "knight of faith" or vice versa.

This certainly does not mean that Kierkegaard never speaks of Don Quixote in his works or that his understanding of the mad knight does not come to bear importantly upon his theological thinking. On the contrary, rare but suggestive allusions to Don Quixote are found in several of Kierkegaard's so-called aesthetic writings. More crucially, his journals from the period 1835–1854 contain well over a score of entries in which Cervantes' novel is alluded to or discussed.[8] Although there is no evidence by which to determine when Kierkegaard first read the *Quixote*, of which he kept both a Danish and a German translation in his library,[9] these journal entries reveal that from no later than Kierkegaard's twenty-second year through the penultimate year of his life, Don Quixote remained an important object of his contemplation.

As we will see, Kierkegaard not only viewed Don Quixote as a symbol of the "comic" principle that is present in every stage of existence, but, toward the end of his life, he also came to regard him as an analogue to Christ, Christ's disciples, and the true Christian individual struggling within modern secular society.

Before discussing Kierkegaard's conception of Cervantes' knight, we should address a question that naturally arises: Why should Kierkegaard have been attracted to *Don Quixote* in the first place? I can think of at least three reasons for that attraction.

First, there was a spiritual affinity between Kierkegaard and Don Quixote, of which the former himself was aware. Like the chaste Manchegan knight, the quite possibly virginal Kierkegaard had his own Dulcinea, that is, a young woman whom he transformed into an ideal: Regine Olsen. It is perhaps no mere coincidence that in a journal entry of 1838, the year after he met her, he identifies himself with Cervantes' love-sick knight. Recording an encounter he had one morning with a pair of girls who were dancing to the flute music of two boys, he writes: "I almost began to dance with them—so there is still such poetry in the world.—If I encounter more such phenomena, I will certainly become a Don Quixote who sees such things in everything."[10] Of course, to imagine himself as a Don Quixote was not exceptional for a young man as poetically inclined and as thoroughly steeped in the German Romantics as was Kierkegaard; after all, the Romantics had made it fashionable for poets to identify with Cervantes' knight, who symbolized for them the conflict of poetry with prose and the ideal with the real.

A second factor that must have enhanced Kierkegaard's appreciation of the *Quixote* is suggested by his tendency to publish under pseudonyms. Besides serving a serious function in his maieutic technique of indirect communication, this tendency is intimately related to his love of humor and irony. He undoubtedly took delight in Cervantes' humorous and ironical use of the fictitious Arab author, the Moorish translator, and the Castilian editor who are first mentioned in Part I, Chapter 9 of the novel. As an ironist and humorist, Kierkegaard was deeply akin to the German Romantics. Given his early immersion in their writings and their profound formative influence on his thinking (although he soon transcended Romanticism),[11] it is easy to explain how he absorbed their reverence for Cervantes. Kierkegaard's research for his two-part dissertation, *The Concept of Irony* (1841), whose second part examines the Romantic irony of F. Schlegel, Tieck, and K. W. F. Solger, would have been enough to bring him into early contact—and sympathy—with the typical Romantic perception of Cervantes as a sublime humorist and ironist.[12]

This brings us to the third and most crucial reason for Kierkegaard's attraction to the *Quixote*: its hero's status as a classic comic figure. Kierkegaard conceived of irony and humor as existential phases situated between the three stages of existence, with irony as the border between the aesthetic and the ethical and humor as the border between the ethical and the religious. Active in all stages of existence, according to Kierkegaard, is the principle of contradiction and the comic.[13] In Johannes Climacus' words, "The comical is present in every stage of life . . ., for wherever there is life, there is contradiction, and wherever there is contradiction, the comical is present,"[14] for, as Kierkegaard puts it elsewhere, "the comic is essentially contradiction" and "is always based upon contradiction."[15] This makes Kierkegaard's special interest in Don Quixote all the more understandable, since the latter's persona revolves around the comical contradiction of his trying to be a knight-errant in an age when chivalry is dead. Conceived therefore as a comic type, the Manchegan knight differs qualitatively from the various historical, legendary, and literary figures who symbolize particular stages of existence—for example, Don Juan, the aesthete; Judge William, the ethicist; and Abraham, the religious man of faith. Unlike each of them, Don Quixote cannot be consigned to any one specific existential stage because he embodies a principle that is present in every stage.

Let us turn now to consider Kierkegaard's conception of Don Quixote, a conception through whose development the knight can be seen to shift gradually from the aesthetic stage to the religious.

Kierkegaard's earliest mention of Don Quixote occurs in a journal entry of October 1835. The entry begins by discussing "the Christian" as "a person with a particular fixed idea," meaning "primarily those Christians who have not so much sought to bring Christianity into the world as to take themselves out of the world in order to live in Christ." The problem Kierkegaard then takes up has to do with the Christian's tendency, once he "achieves conviction," to avoid any further "spiritual trial [*Anfægtelse*]" by passing off as the work of "the devil" any "doubt" that he himself might experience from the confrontation of his "faith" with the assertions of "reason." To mistake the challenge of reason for the devil's work is in Kierkegaard's view "a great Christian evasion" and suggests a person who has become "spiritually deaf in one ear." Like "a person with defective vision," such a Christian "has occupied his whole life with living into a particular idea."[16] His spiritual condition "takes on the appearance of happy madness," and so he becomes comparable to Don Quixote, who with "ease . . . discovered that it must have been the evil demons who always followed on his heels, [as] when, for example, he mistakenly took windmills for giants."[17]

In this entry Don Quixote is likened to the sort of Christian whom Kierkegaard opposes. Each of these figures, Don Quixote and the Christian, is consumed by a "fixed idea,"[18] and each of them, through "happy madness," simply evades whatever might challenge his faith in that idea: the Christian, upon finding his religious faith challenged by rationalistic doubt, evades that doubt by associating it with the devil, just as Don Quixote, upon finding his chivalric illusions subverted by reality, dismisses reality as the work of wicked enchanters. Nine years later, in an 1844 entry, Kierkegaard draws a similar analogy: "For a long time now rigid letter-of-the-law orthodoxy has reverted to being a counterpart to Don Quixote, whose ridiculous hair-splitting sophistries will provide excellent analogies."[19] This sophistic Don Quixote is a far cry from a knight of faith; several years pass before we find evidence of anything resembling that conception of him in the journals.

During the years between those two entries of 1835 and 1844, Kierkegaard's allusions to the *Quixote* in his journal indicate that he is impressed by its comic and ironic qualities and utterly fascinated by its theme, on which he even contemplates composing a narrative variation. In an entry of March 1836, he imagines writing "a comic *novel*, 'A Literary *Don Quixote*,'" and considers the "irony" and "whole raft of comic ideas [that] . . . could evolve from this."[20] A second variation on Cervantes' theme is suggested seven years later by "A" in a footnote to *Either/Or* (1843). Evidently having never heard of Charlotte Lennox's highly popular English novel, *The Female Quixote* (1752), "A" calls for "a female counterpart to Don Quixote in European literature."[21]

Aside from the sheer comicality of the knight's mad antics,[22] one aspect of the *Quixote* that particularly interests the young Kierkegaard is the relationship between the knight and his squire. Two journal entries—dated February and March 1836—compare the master-fool juxtapositions of Don Quixote and Sancho Panza, Don Juan and Leporello, and Faust and Wagner.[23] Given these comparisons and the fact that Don Juan and Faust become two of the most prominent symbols of aesthetic existence in *Either/Or*, it is curious that this extensive book mentions Don Quixote in only one place[24] other than the aforementioned footnote.

In this connection it is significant that *Either/Or* was first published the same year as *Fear and Trembling*, the former in February 1843, the latter in October. If Don Quixote is mentioned neither as an aesthete nor as an ethicist in *Either/Or*, he goes entirely unmentioned in *Fear and Trembling*, which analyzes the religious stage as it is symbolized by Abraham and the knight of faith. Nor is any mention made of Cervantes' knight in Kierkegaard's journals between 1838 and 1844. These omissions, despite the commonplace equation of Don Quixote and the knight of faith by later authors, support our earlier assumption that Kierkegaard did not conceive of Cervantes' knight as occupying any one particular stage of existence.

Indeed, the complexity of Don Quixote's character can be seen to encompass all three existential stages. Insofar as he is preoccupied with the thought of and is in quest of worldly fame and glory, which suggests attachment to the finite, he exists in the aesthetic stage. Insofar as he commits himself wholeheartedly to the chivalric code, which constitutes his ethical absolute, he exists in the ethical stage. Insofar as he maintains, against the arguments of reason and to the extent of becoming ridiculous, his faith in Dulcinea and in his illusion that he has been sent by God to restore the Golden Age, he exists in a mode analogous to Kierkegaard's religious stage.

Our suspicion that Kierkegaard found Don Quixote to be pertinent to more than one stage of existence is borne out by his references to him from 1845 on. In *Stages on Life's Way*, which was published that year, Frater Taciturnus compares the suffering lover's state of mind in "'Guilty?'/'Not Guilty?'" (or "Quidam's Diary") with the "raging madness" (*delirium furibundum*) displayed by Don Quixote in the opening chapter of the *Quixote*'s second part, when the knight tells the priest the advice he would give the king on how to protect Christian Europe from an "impending" onslaught by the Turks. Whereas Don Quixote would populate all Spain with protective knights-errant in an age when knight-errancy is obsolete, Taciturnus' hero "has more sense, for he has understood the age in such a way that he himself becomes the only knight of unhappy love."[25] In this instance it is unclear whether Don Quixote is supposed to represent the aesthetic or the religious, since Quidam seems such a complex blending of the two; outwardly Quidam's conduct bears a striking resemblance to that of *Either/Or*'s aesthetic Seducer, while inwardly he appears to be in the midst of a religious crisis that is foreign to anything experienced by Johannes.[26]

The case is different in *Concluding Unscientific Postscript* (1846), which makes three allusions to Don Quixote.[27] Considered together, these allusions present the following conception of the knight. He is, to begin with, associated with both the "comic" (in allusions 1 and 3) and the "tragic" (in allusion 3), or "tragic–comic romanticism" (as allusion 1 combines the terms). This double association can be explained by Kierkegaard's conception of both the comic and the tragic as grounded in the principle of contradiction. While a comic, tragic, or tragicomic figure might exist in any stage, the three passages provide sufficient information to suggest that Climacus would locate Don Quixote in the aesthetic stage. According to the second allusion, Don Quixote's quest for fame ("world-historic significance") and his notion that he has been victimized by enchantment ("a jinx") would be viewed "mockingly" from the ethical perspective. As the archetype of those "stupid" individuals who, in Climacus' words, "forget themselves over their great importance in history," Don Quixote should presumably be viewed as an aesthete, since forgetting oneself is a primary symptom of aesthetic existence. Furthermore, while the first passage associates him with the bygone age of "letter-fanaticism" or "letter-theology," which seems to imply a leaning toward an ethical absolute, the same passage also associates the knight's "passion" with "romance," "poetry," and "beautiful *Schwärmerei*," which are all qualities one would expect to find in an aesthete, along with the "subjective madness" or "aberrant inwardness" that the third passage links to him.

As invoked in *Postscript*, Don Quixote, like Don Juan, Faust, and the Romantics, seems to fit more or less in the aesthetic stage, and not, like the knight of faith with whom he is so often identified by Kierkegaard's admirers, in the religious. However, a striking shift occurs after *Postscript*;[28] the allusions to Don Quixote in subsequent journal entries present him clearly as a figure of the religious stage, comparing him with Christ, Christ's disciples, and any aspiring Christian in the modern secular age.[29]

In early March of 1846, less than two weeks after *Postscript* appeared, Kierkegaard published *Two Ages: A Literary Review*, in which the section entitled "The Present Age" opens with the complaint: "The present age is essentially a *sensible, reflecting age, devoid of passion, flaring up in superficial, short-lived enthusiasm and prudentially relaxing in indolence.*"[30] The same section goes on to protest against what Kierkegaard calls the "leveling" of the individual in contemporary society, and the fact that "the age of heroes is past."[31] Together with his advocacy of enthusiasm, passion, and faith as antidotes to excessive reason and intellect, Kierkegaard's increasingly public role as a Christian individual struggling against official Christendom helps explain why he eventually compared the true Christian to Don Quixote, who epitomizes the passionate enthusiast and individual combating the unheroic society and age in which he lives. Thus, anticipating the comparisons made by numerous later authors (e.g., Dostoevsky, Unamuno, Ortega y Gasset, and Auden), Kierkegaard entered in his journal of 1848 what I believe to be the first analogy ever drawn between Don Quixote and Christ:

> When secular sensibleness has permeated the whole world as it has now begun to do, then the only remaining conception of what it is to be Christian will be the portrayal of Christ, the disciples, and others as comic figures. They will be counterparts of Don Quixote, a man who had a firm notion that the world is evil, that what the world honors is mediocrity or even worse.[32]

Here, rather than stress pejoratively Don Quixote's "subjective madness," as does the third allusion to him in *Postscript*, Kierkegaard conceives of him as a virtual sage who understands the world's "evil" and propensity toward "mediocrity." Nevertheless, Don Quixote remains "comic." What would make Christ and his disciples appear as "comic figures" and "counterparts to Don Quixote" is the contradiction between their mode of existence and ours: just as Don Quixote's chivalric existence contradicts the unchivalric world in which he lives, so the true Christian existence of Christ and his disciples would contradict the modern secular world (as, indeed, it contradicted their own world!).

Two entries in Kierkegaard's journal of the next year, 1849, follow up on this analogy. In one, which clearly anticipates his attack of 1854–1855 upon Christendom, he describes himself as "fighting almost like a Don Quixote," and adds: "Christendom as it is now makes Christ into a complete phantom as far as existence is concerned." This implies that the Christian "ideal" has become "something quixotic and visionary."[33] The other entry elaborates:

> Christianity does not really exist. Christendom is waiting for a comic poet à la Cervantes, who will create a counterpart to Don Quixote out of the essentially Christian.
> The only difference will be that no poetic exaggerations will be required at all, as in Don Quixote—no, all he needs to do is to take any essentially true Christian life, not to mention simply taking Christ or an apostle. The comic element arises because the age has changed so enormously that it regards this as comic.[34]

This new conception of Don Quixote reverses the view expressed fourteen years before in the 1835 entry quoted earlier. There, we recall, he is the figure to whom are disparagingly compared those Christians who evade spiritual trials by dismissing their doubts as the work of the devil. In the 1849 entry, however, Kierkegaard sees Don Quixote no longer as an evader of spiritual trials but, conversely, as an embodiment of them, and therefore as a symbol of the "essentially Christian." Don Quixote now epitomizes religious existence because he bases his chivalric life style on austerities, such as his constant battles and his penance in the Sierra Morena, which seem comic within his contemporary surroundings. Farther on in the second entry of 1849, Kierkegaard enumerates the qualities of the true Christian that would make him or her seem quixotic:

> That a person actually is earnest about renouncing this life, literally, that he *voluntarily* gives up the happiness of erotic love offered to him, that he endures all kinds of earthly privation, . . . that he thus exposes himself to all the anguish of spiritual trial [*Anfaegtelse*], . . . and then that he, suffering all this, submits to being mistreated for it, hated, persecuted, scorned (the unavoidable consequence of essential Christianity in this world)—to our entire age such a life will appear to be comic. It is a Don Quixote life.[35]

The views expressed in these entries of 1848 and 1849 mark a crucial shift in Kierkegaard's attitude toward Don Quixote. Whatever might account for the change, which could have resulted from his having recently reread and rethought the *Quixote*,[36] the few allusions he made to it during his remaining years reveal that Sancho Panza replaced Don Quixote as the object of Kierkegaard's disparagement,[37] while the latter retained his new concept of the mad knight as a comical analogue to the primitive, ascetic, true Christian in the secular world. Kierkegaard continues to develop this analogy in an 1851 entry, this time placing emphasis on the quality of asceticism that was highly esteemed by Christians in earlier ages but that has come to seem quixotic in modernity:

> What our age would really be most inclined to regard as a counterpart of Don Quixote would be an ascetic in the old sense, an ascetic who fasts and prays and accuses himself of even the slightest sinful thought and imposes punishment on himself for it—and then we are all Christians![38]

Kierkegaard's sarcastic addendum, "we are all Christians!", rehearses a notion that is later expressed repeatedly, and with undiminished sarcasm, in his public diatribes of the last two years of his life against the Danish Church and Christendom. An essential thesis of those writings, the earlier series of which were published in the political journal *The Fatherland*, and the later ones as pamphlets, is stated in the title of a piece that appeared in April 1855, seven months before his death: "In 'Christendom' all are Christians; when all are Christians, the New Testament *eo ipso* does not exist, yea, it is impossible."³⁹ This polemic crystallizes countless ideas and observations recorded over many years in his journals, including his conception of himself as someone "fighting like a Don Quixote."

To understand that self-image, which implies an individual struggling to uphold some venerable, idealistic cause (Don Quixote's chivalry or Kierkegaard's true Christianity) that can no longer be said to "exist" in that individual's society, we should take into account that Kierkegaard elsewhere refers to his service to Christianity as an "intellectual enthusiasm" and asserts that it necessitates his "enduring everything for the idea."⁴⁰ Like the German Romantics and their followers, for whom Don Quixote's enthusiasm (*Enthusiasmus, Begeisterung*) is one of his most appealing traits,⁴¹ Kierkegaard laments the eclipsing of enthusiasm by intellect and reason in present society. A journal entry of 1852 reads:

> On the other side of "intellect" lies enthusiasm: that is what should be fought for.
> But, alas, there is no intimation of any context in the contemporary age for the person who is going to stir up enthusiasm. Everywhere [there are] only these half-ripe and very blasé individuals who when they were very young may have had a flush of enthusiasm but soon thereafter became "reasonable."⁴²

In conjunction with his own enthusiastic struggle against society, one of Kierkegaard's last recorded allusions to Don Quixote occurs in an 1852 entry wherein he formulates his key distinction between New Testament Christianity and contemporary Christendom. The entry begins by asking: "How are we human beings and the human race now related to the whole concept of life contained in the N.T.?" He answers this question by observing that there has "been a complete qualitative change in the race and in what it means to be a man." "What is this change?" he further asks.⁴³

> It is that being-in-and-for-itself, the unconditional, has completely gone out of life, and "reason" has been substituted, so that being-in-and-for-itself . . . has become ludicrous to men, a comic extravaganza such as Don Quixote, which we would laugh at if we ever got to see it, but we never get to see it.⁴⁴

Kierkegaard's view of Don Quixote as a symbol of comical contradiction, and hence as a figure whom Christ and whatever is essentially Christian would resemble within the context of contemporary secular Christendom, helps account for his objection to the fact that Cervantes' novel ends with the knight regaining his sanity and reason, renouncing chivalry, and then dying. In an entry of 1854, which contains his last recorded remarks on the *Quixote*, Kierkegaard reiterates an opinion he had expressed seven years earlier,⁴⁵ stating:

It is a mistake that Don Quixote ends by dying and dies a rational man. Don Quixote ought to have no ending. On the contrary, Don Quixote ought to end with the momentum of a new fixed idea. . . . Don Quixote is an endless fantasy. Therefore it is prosaic to let the story end with his dying after he has become sensible.[46]

What troubles Kierkegaard most is not that Don Quixote dies, but that he "dies a rational man." The theologian's disturbance at this outcome is easy to understand. Once Don Quixote regains his reason, he ceases to exist as a contradiction to his world; on the contrary, he changes his name to Alonso Quixano, reconciles himself with the Church (the institutional emblem of Christendom) by confessing, dictates his will, and thereby reestablishes his identity with normative society. When Don Quixote no longer exists as a contradiction to his world, his situation ceases to be analogous to that which Christ and his disciples would find themselves in were they to exist in modernity. Indeed, a Don Quixote who exists in identity with his world is no longer a Don Quixote, just as, for Kierkegaard, a Christian who exists in conformity to modern Christendom is not a Christian.

Notes

1. William Byron, *Cervantes: A Biography* (Garden City, NY: Doubleday, 1978), p. 422.
2. Quoted by Aubrey F. G. Bell, "The Wisdom of Don Quixote," *Books Abroad* 21(1947): 261. Emphasis added.
3. See J.-J. A. Bertrand, *Cervantes et le romantisme allemand* (Paris: Alcan, 1914); Friedrich Schürr, "Cervantes y el romanticismo," *Anales Cervantinos* 1(1951): 41–70; Werner Brüggemann, *Cervantes und die Figur des Don Quijote in Kuntsanschauung und Dichtung der deutschen Romantik* (Münster: Aschendorff, 1958); Lienhard Bergel, "Cervantes in Germany," in *Cervantes Across the Centuries: A Quadricentennial Volume*, eds. Angel Flores and M. J. Benardete (New York: Gordian, 1969), pp. 315–52; Anthony J. Close, *The Romantic Approach to "Don Quixote": A Critical History of the Romantic Tradition in "Quixote" Criticism* (Cambridge: Cambridge University Press, 1978), especially chap. 2. See also Alfred E. Lussky, "Cervantes and Tieck's Idealism," *Publications of the MLA* 43(1928): 1082–97; Francisco Romero, "Don Quijote y Fichte," *Realidad. Revista de Ideas* 2, no. 5 (September/October 1947): 220–23.
4. See Eric J. Ziolkowski, *The Sanctification of Don Quixote: From Hidalgo to Priest* (University Park, PA: Penn State University Press, 1991), especially pp. 170–214.
5. See Miguel de Unamuno, *Our Lord Don Quixote: The Life of Don Quixote and Sancho with Related Essays*, trans. Anthony Kerrigan (Princeton, NJ: Princeton University Press, 1972), pp. 23, 45, 257, 277; W. H. Auden, "The Ironic Hero: Some Reflections on Don Quixote," *Horizon* 20 (August 1949): pp. 86–94; especially p. 93. Cf. Alexander Welsh, *Reflections on the Hero as Don Quixote* (Princeton, NJ: Princeton University Press, 1981), pp. 121–23, 289–90;

Anthony J. Cascardi, *The Bounds of Reason: Cervantes, Dostoevsky, Flaubert* (New York: Columbia University Press, 1986), p. 95.
6. Franz Kafka, *Parables and Paradoxes in German and English*, trans. Clement Greenberger (New York: Schocken, 1961), pp. 40–45; quoted by Welsh in *Reflections*, pp. 191–92. As noted by Welsh in *Reflections*, p. 239, n. 8, the source of all but the first two paragraphs of the parable is a letter of June 1921 to Robert Klopstock, in Franz Kafka, *Briefe 1902–1924*, ed. Max Brod (New York: Schocken, 1958), pp. 332–34.
7. Søren Kierkegaard, *Fear and Trembling; Repetition*, ed. and trans. Howard V. Hong and Edna H. Hong (Princeton, NJ: Princeton University Press, 1983), p. 80.
8. *Søren Kierkegaard's Journals and Papers*, 7 vols., trans. and ed. Howard V. Hong and Edna H. Hong (Bloomington, IN: Indiana University Press, 1967–1978), general index, vol. 7, "Cervantes" and Don Quixote." (Entries from the *Journals and Papers* will be cited by volume and entry number.)
9. Ibid., 2: 589, n. 451.
10. Ibid., 5: 119.
11. E.g., Søren Kierkegaard, *The Concept of Irony, with Continual Reference to Socrates*, ed. and trans. Howard V. Hong and Edna H. Hong (Princeton, NJ: Princeton University Press, 1989), p. 304: "The tragedy of romanticism is that what it seizes upon is not actuality. Poetry awakens; . . .—the romanticist falls asleep." See also Gerhard Niedermeyer, *Sören Kierkegaard und die Romantik* (Leipzig: Quelle & Meyer, 1909), chap. 4: "Kierkegaard als Überwinder der Romantik."
12. For example, from Kierkegaard's *Concept of Irony*, pp. 304, 549, n. 149, we know that he read Heinrich Heine's *Die romantische Schule* (1836), in which Cervantes' irony is praised. Also, in Heine's introduction to the German translation of the *Quixote* in Kierkegaard's library, the former speaks of "the irony, which God bestowed upon the world when he created it, and which the great poet [Cervantes] imitated in his little book-world [*gedrukten Kleinwelt*]" ("Einleitung zum 'Don Quixote,'" *Heinrich Heines Sämtliche Werke*, 10 vols., ed. Oskar Walzel (Leipzig: Insel, 1911–1915), 8: 129, trans. mine). For Kierkegaard's own concept of "divine irony," see the *Journals*, 2: 265.
13. See C. Stephen Evans, "Kierkegaard's View of Humor," *Faith and Philosophy* 4, no. 2 (April 1987) for more on humor and contradiction.
14. Søren Kierkegaard, *Concluding Unscientific Postscript to the Philosophical Fragments*, trans. David F. Swenson and Walter Lowrie (Princeton, NJ: Princeton University Press, 1941; 3rd paperback ed., 1974), p. 459.
15. Entries of 1842 and 1844, *Journals*, 2: 266.
16. Ibid., 1: 169.
17. Ibid., 1: 169–70.
18. Ibid., 1: 170.
19. Ibid., 3: 379.
20. Ibid., 1: 357. This novel's theme, he explains, would revolve around the fallacy of placing "primary stress . . . on reading as many [books] as possible." Of the hero, he says: "Every time he would say something which *he thought* was something new but eventually turned out to be something old he had read . . ., someone else would already have said it" (ibid.).
21. Søren Kierkegaard, *Either/Or*, 2 vols., ed. and trans. Howard V. Hong and

Edna H. Hong (Princeton, NJ: Princeton University Press, 1987). 1: 256n.
22. One of Don Quixote's misadventures is specifically alluded to in Søren Kierkegaard, *Early Polemical Writings*, ed. and trans. Julia Watkin (Princeton, NJ: Princeton University Press, 1990). In a paper Kierkegaard gave in his university's Student Association on November 28, 1835 (p. 48), he compares his age's "striving" satirically to that displayed in Don Quixote's charge against the windmills (*Quixote*, Part I, Chap. 8), while in a newspaper article dated February 16, 1836 (*Early Polemical Writings*, p. 8), he compares "the swagger-booted, high-tragic posture of [the newspaper] *Kjøbenhavnsposten*" to Don Quixote's somnambular sword-attack against the wineskins (*Quixote*, part I, Chap. 35).
23. *Journals*, 2: 248–49; 4: 273.
24. In "The Esthetic Validity of Marriage," B tells A: "I certainly dare not expect much from you, because you are continually fighting, . . . just like that Spanish knight, for a bygone time. Since you are in fact fighting for the moment against time, you actually are always fighting for what has disappeared." *Either/Or*, II: 141.
25. Søren Kierkegaard, *Stages on Life's Way: Studies by Various Persons*, ed. and trans. Howard V. Hong and Edna H. Hong (Princeton, NJ: Princeton University Press, 1988), p. 402.
26. This distinction is drawn by Mark C. Taylor, *Kierkegaard's Pseudonymous Authorship: A Study of Time and the Self* (Princeton, NJ: Princeton University Press, 1975), pp. 338–39.
27. *Postscript*, pp. 35, 125, 175.
28. Note that this shift in Kierkegaard's understanding of Don Quixote parallels and is contemporaneous with the shift from Religiousness B to C that Merold Westphal describes in this volume.
29. This development in Kierkegaard's view of Don Quixote is presaged in the first and third allusions to him in *Postscript* (discussed above), where attention is called to the knight's "passion." Climacus later asserts: "It is impossible to exist without passion" (p. 276). While there are, of course, various aesthetic forms of passion (e.g., Don Juan or Faust), passion can also be ethical or religious. As a descendant, albeit a rebellious one, of the German Romantics, Kierkegaard exalts passion and enthusiasm as religious qualities in many of his writings. Like Schleiermacher, who identifies religion with feeling (*Gefühl*), Johannes de Silentio asserts that: "that which unites all human life is passion, and faith is passion" (*Fear and Trembling*, p. 67; cf. pp. 51, 121–22). As an embodiment of passion, Don Quixote undoubtedly struck Kierkegaard also as an embodiment of faith.
30. *Two Ages: The Age of Revolution and the Present Age. A Literary Review*, ed. and trans. Howard V. Hong and Edna H. Hong (Princeton, NJ: Princeton University Press, 1978), p. 68.
31. Ibid., p. 87.
32. *Journals*, 1: 132–33. Here the term "Christian" means something very different from what it does in the previously cited entry of 1835, where Kierkegaard compares "Christians" to Don Quixote. In the 1835 entry the term connotes pejoratively those so-called Christians who remove themselves from "the world" and evade spiritual trials by passing off as the work of the "devil" any doubt that they might experience in the confrontation of their faith with reason. In the 1849 entry the term may be read as "*true* Christian." The irony of this

passage stems from its hypothesis that Christ and his disciples, who are *the* true Christians, would appear "comic" in the secular world.
33. *Journals*, 2: 283.
34. Ibid., 2: 274.
35. Ibid. In emphasizing the renunciatory aspect of Don Quixote's life, Kierkegaard either ignores or forgets Climacus' emphasis on the knight's obsession with "world-historical significance." See our earlier discussion of *Postscript*'s second allusion to Don Quixote.
36. This seems indicated by an entry of 1847 (*Journals*, 1: 357), in which Kierkegaard raises objections to the way the *Quixote* ends.
37. In two entries of 1850 and 1951 (*Journals*, 1: 76 and 4: 40), Kierkegaard alludes to the half-hearted whacks that the squire, at his master's request, administers to his own posterior to achieve the "disenchantment" of Dulcinea.
38. *Journals*, 1: 68–69.
39. *Attack upon "Christendom" 1854–55*, trans. Walter Lowrie (Princeton, NJ: Princeton University Press, 1968), p. 149.
40. Quoted in the note on "Enthusiasm," ibid., 1: 528.
41. E.g., Friedrich Bouterwek, summing up the Romantic view, characterizes Don Quixote as "the immortal representative of all men of exalted imagination, who carry the noblest enthusiasm [*dem herrlichensten Enthusiasmus*] to a pitch of folly." *History of Spanish and Portuguese Literature*, 2 vols., trans. Tomasina Ross (London: Boosey & Sons, 1823), 1: 333, from Bouterwek's *Geschichte der Poesie und Beredsamkeit*, 8 vols. (Göttingen: Röwer, 1801–1809), 3: 335.
42. *Journals*, 1: 366.
43. Ibid., 1: 217.
44. Ibid., 1: 217–18. This passage is significant to the debate over Kierkegaard's supposed irrationalism. Clearly, Kierkegaard has in mind by "reason" here what others would term "worldly common sense." See Merold Westphal's essay in this volume.
45. In an entry of 1847 (*Journals*, 1: 357).
46. Ibid., 2: 206.

9 The Sickness unto Death: A Social Interpretation

STEPHEN CRITES

Of all the empty academic exercises, the most futile are perhaps the attempts to interpret a text against the grain of its own premises: The Philosophy of Schopenhauer: An Optimistic Interpretation; *Das Kapital*: A Free-Market Interpretation; St. Thomas as Process Philosopher. That sort of thing is nowadays often called Deconstruction. A text can fruitfully be criticized from an utterly alien point of view, but to *interpret* it in such a topsy-turvy way is either naive or perverse.

Now *The Sickness unto Death* is not merely individualistic in its view of the human self. It is, in many of its most passionate passages, downright antisocial. But it is also a dialectical text, ironical to the core. The meaning of such a text, which an interpretation must attempt to unearth, is not necessarily disclosed in its most passionate passages. *The Sickness unto Death* is not all of a piece. It proceeds on many levels, of which the deepest is its dialectical structure and the most shallow is the counterpoint of trivial and often crochety opinions expressed by its pseudonymous author. An example of the latter is the long footnote that seems to exempt women from having independent selves in the sense expounded by the text.[1] It is as if our public radio announcer, in an antic moment, had superimposed a few strains of "Waltzing Matilda" over a recording of the Mozart *Requiem*.

What follows is an interpretation of the text that flies in the face of many such opinions expressed in it. For it is only necessary to adhere strictly to the text's dialectical exposition of selfhood to recognize how wrongheaded many of these opinions are. If our interpretation is critical, the critique is immanent in the text itself. We need only bring out the self-criticizing resources of the text, which provides the basis for an interpretation of its meaning unrestricted by the biases of its author. But we had better begin by dealing with him.

ANTI-CLIMACUS

According to the title page a certain Anti-Climacus is the author of *The Sickness unto Death*. An exceedingly naive reader given to archival research might be perplexed that no such name turns up on the city rolls of

Copenhagen in 1849, the year of its publication. But our archivalist might be heartened to discover that the rolls do register one S. Kierkegaard, listed on the title page as editor of the work. Here at least is a piece of cheese an archivalist can get his teeth into.

In fact Kierkegaard scholars know what that mousy archivalist might only be led cautiously to suspect, that our text was really written by Søren Kierkegaard. We have even been spared the tedium of archival research by the translators of the latest English edition of the work, who have generously appended to our text evidence retrieved from Kierkegaard's own wastebasket. In this appendix we find an early draft of the title page, with S. Kierkegaard clearly designated as author.[2] Even in the final draft of the manuscript, the text was originally said to be "by S. Kierkegaard," but his name was crossed out and "Anticlimacus," and then "Anti-Climacus," was inscribed in its place, with the additional notation, "edited by S. Kierkegaard."

What could have led Kierkegaard to disclaim authorship of our text? Here again we receive useful intelligence, not only from the appendix, but also from the "Historical Introduction" of the recent English edition. From the evidence that the editors, Howard and Edna Hong, bring forward we can conclude that Kierkegaard decided at the last minute to remove his name as author of *The Sickness unto Death* because he did not find in his own life the strict Christian solution to the sickness of despair that was prescribed by the text. Lacking faith, he considered himself to be one of the despairing sufferers of the sickness unto death. He needed to be addressed by the discourse, rather than being a man who might presume to speak its words in his own voice. Kierkegaard's typically literary solution to this problem was to attribute the discourse to a new pseudonym.

The device of pseudonymity was of course an old one for Kierkegaard. But this new pseudonym was to be different from the earlier pseudonyms, both in its character and in its relation to Kierkegaard himself. The seven works that comprise the earlier pseudonymous authorship, at least as he regarded them in retrospect, are all aesthetic and ironic: aesthetic in that they are all discarnate objects with fantastical authors, distorting mirrors in which the reader may contemplate his or her own life and its apparent possibilities; ironic in that no actual author directly speaks his own convictions in them. None of them is avowed by Søren Kierkegaard, not even the Johannes Climacus literature, which clarifies the Christian categories but makes no claim for their truth; in fact Climacus tells the reader plainly that his own attitude to Christianity is none of the reader's business. After bringing this pseudonymous authorship to a close with Climacus' *Concluding Unscientific Postscript*, Kierkegaard devoted himself exclusively to his "upbuilding" literature, written in his own name, directly and, he thought, without irony. The earlier pseudonyms, that is, were literary fictions, like the fictive narrator of a novel, really one of its characters, who tells the story from his point of view. The pseudonymous voice bore no direct relation to the point of view or the situation in life of the actual writer. But in the upbuilding literature the authorial voice and the actual writer were supposedly identical. With *The Sickness unto Death*, however, Kierkegaard had a work on his hands written "for upbuilding and awakening" in an authorial voice that he was unable to claim as his own. He was convinced that it spoke the Christian truth, directly, unironically, but it was a truth that he himself did not existentially embody. Many of the things it said had already been thematized noncommitally by Climacus in describing Christianity in a purely hypothetical mode, as a "thought experiment." But in the new text (and later in *Practice in Christianity*,[3] also ascribed to Anti-Climacus) these claims were no longer hypothetical; they were axioms from which the discourse proceeded. Hence the new pseudonym:

> Johannes Climacus and Anti-Climacus have several things in common; but the difference is that whereas Johannes Climacus places himself so low that he even says himself that he is not a Christian, one seems to be able to detect in Anti-Climacus that he regards himself to be a Christian on an extraordinarily high level. . . . I would place myself higher than Johannes Climacus, lower than Anti-Climacus.[4]

In this journal entry Kierkegaard places himself in a curious hierarchical scale, between the sub-Christian Climacus and the hyper-Christian Anti-Climacus, flesh and blood between two fictions. If only the hyper-Christian can avow the faith that in our text is the sole antidote to despair, the question arises as to whether there are any nonfictive examples of such a faith. At any rate, Kierkegaard is clear that he himself is not an example of it and, therefore, cannot publish this hyper-Christian text under his own name.

So he resolves his scruples about publishing it in characteristic fashion, by resorting again to a pseudonym. All his most enduring works were published, in the end, under pseudonyms, for reasons not necessarily related to the various justifications he offers for them. I venture to suggest that his imagination was liberated from the burdens of self-seriousness only when he could adopt a fictive voice. Only retrospectively, in the case of *The Sickness unto Death*, did Kierkegaard recognize that this dialectical exposition of the Christian axiom had also been the work of an imaginative alter ego, imaginary like the others but more insistent and independent in his claims on the work, less a mere literary artifice. The earlier pseudonyms were deliberately adopted. The hyper-Christian Anti-Climacus appears after the fact to demand recognition that he, and not Kierkegaard, is the real author of *The Sickness unto Death*.

With an indecision also typical of him in such matters, Kierkegaard first appended and then deleted an "Editor's Note," in which he hinted at this strange authorial situation. On the one hand it seems presumptuous "for someone to venture to interpret the demands of ideality with respect to being a Christian, someone who in any case . . . is imperfect."[5] We may note in passing that it is odd to speak of the strictest claims of Christianity as its "demands of ideality." The gospel speaks of incarnation, not of discarnate idealities. Søren Kierkegaard, of course, needs no catechizing from us poor worldlings on this point. But he appears in this note to suggest that the incarnate God confronts the hearer of the gospel as the demand of an ideality that materializes only insofar as hearer and speaker embody it in their own lives. This Kierkegaard could not claim for himself. Yet, on the other hand, it would be equally presumptuous to let these demands of ideality go unspoken; it would be "a cunning insurrection against God, who by no means wants ideality's demands to be suppressed." The solution to this dilemma is Anti-Climacus, the fictive voice of Christian ideality: "Thus someone has ventured it, someone who is no one; I have only ventured what for me is already very audacious—to publish this presentation."[6] Only "someone who is no one" is qualified to speak "the demands of ideality with respect to being a Christian." Only a discarnate "no one" can be the author of *The Sickness unto Death*, for only such a fictive individual can represent faith in the hyper-Christian sense. Kierkegaard, our editor, acknowledges this rather odd state of affairs respecting his author, at least obliquely. He says that the author is a kind of physician. But just as "Someone who is no one cannot possibly offend anyone, cannot possibly judge anyone," so this physician is in no position to tell anyone that he or she is sick, as a physician might who lived in human society. Dr. Nobody "merely describes the sickness while he at the same time continually defines what 'faith' is, which he seems to think he himself possesses to an extraordinary degree, and this presumably accounts for his name: Anti-Climacus."[7] The precise point of this cryptic reference to the name is obscure, but it is clear enough that it is meant to imply a kind of eminence in that pursuit in which Climacus is scarcely a beginner, and probably a rebuke to Climacus' ironical and equivocal treatment of faith.[8] Still, Anti-Climacus is after all only a fictive example of the faith he describes, and such a discarnate example can hardly be said to embody it.

The Editor's Note does raise some awkward questions about the status of this hyper-Christian author and, indeed, about the faith he is supposed to exemplify to such an extraordinary degree. This awkwardness is of course implicit in the very attribution of the text to this strange pseudonym, but the Editor's Note makes it explicit. That is why we have called attention to the note here, and the unresolved problems the note raises may have had something to do with Kierkegaard's decision to suppress it, although he does not say so. In a marginal comment on his decision to suppress it, he suggests that it is superfluous, for "it is plain to see that I personally am a part of the book—for example, the part about the religious poet."[9] Kierkegaard is referring to the moving delineation of "a poet-existence verging on the religious" that opens Part Two: "Despair Is Sin." The passage is appropriately placed, since it describes "the most dialectical frontier between despair and sin."[10] Kierkegaard's own autograph is indeed obvious at this point, for it is a self-presentation that has many parallels in his journals. The passage does make it quite clear, to us if not to his contemporaries, that our editor regards himself as the incarnation not of faith but of a particularly excruciating form of despairing sin.[11] "Such a poet-existence . . . Christianly understood . . . is sin, the sin of poetizing instead of being, of relating to the good and true through the imagination instead of being that—that is, existentially striving to be that."[12] The poet has a longing for God, but he can only express it imaginatively, because he cannot give up his despair. Like an unhappy lover, he can project the life of faith poetically, imaginatively, but cannot overcome an inner obstacle to sharing it. "Nor is what he says untrue, by no means; his presentation is simply his happier, his better I."[13] Who is, in fact, the despairing poet's happier alter ego, who lives only in his discourse? Why, again, it is Anti-Climacus. So we seem to have a strange sort of symbiosis, strange because one party to the symbiosis is a fiction. But the poet-existence described is in fact just as unfleshly. For we encounter it simply in the pages of the book Nobody has written. Even if it is reminiscent of the self-presentation in Kierkegaard's journals, that, too, is a literary production that lays many snares for a reader unwary enough to suppose that he is here encountering the real Kierkegaard. So the symbiosis is perhaps not so strange, if we can regard it as literary through and through: Anti-Climacus, our Dr. Nobody, describes the poet, who in turn has created Anti-Climacus. The poet lives in the pages of a book as a kind of diagnosis by a physician who is the poet's own better self.

Why, this symbiosis sounds almost like a pure relation that relates itself to its own self.

Aside from his part in this literary relationship, "Søren Kierkegaard" will not interest us in what follows. We know too much about the private meditations and self-deceptions of this deeply flawed genius, who probably ought to have burned his journals. We even know too much about his cunning efforts to thwart people who think they know so much about him. So let us forget about him and his journals, and concern ourselves with a text that makes sense only if we read it quite differently from the way he has tried to make us read it. He has given us Anti-Climacus as the discarnate author of the text. So let us concern ourselves with the work of Anti-

Climacus, without ever mistaking him for a flawed, actual human being.

Relational Self

It is probably the densest and most crabbed passage in the entire Kierkegaardian corpus. All Kierkegaardians know the passage to which I refer, the infamous passage from the beginning of *Sickness unto Death*. It begins, "Human being is spirit."[14] So far so good, but we pause for a quibble, so as to put off the anxious moment when we must consider what we know comes next. Howard and Edna Hong translate this sentence, "A human being is spirit." That makes the subject of the sentence unambiguously singular, an individual human being, which the Danish word, *Mennesket*, does not imply. It has the definite article, literally, "The human being," but the Danish definite article gives the term a rather more indeterminate sense, comprehending the human in all its configurations; the difference between the definite and indefinite article is the same as that in German, that is, between *Der Mensch*, which can mean simply "human being," and *Ein Mensch*, which means one single human being (although not necessarily someone in particular). Howard and Edna Hong doubtless took the liberty of translating the term with the indefinite article because they were so sure that Anti-Climacus had the single person in mind, and in that assumption they were likely correct if we can suppose that a literary fiction has something in mind. In any case, "A human being" would preclude the reading we wish to suggest for the text generally, and I respectfully submit that it is a mistranslation. The indeterminacy of "human being" is correctly maintained with the word "spirit" (*Aand*, no article), which of course designates what bloweth where it listeth, pentecostal. Not even the most enthusiastic individualist would be tempted to reify spirit, which can materialize in the ecstasies of congregation or community as well as in the utterances of a prophet.

Spirit, in turn, "is the self," again not unambiguously, "a self," as if the spiritual self corresponds to an isolated body-thing. The genius of the passage, in fact, is that its language is open to unconventional connotations, refusing to define the self as a particular psycho-physical organism. Neither can we speak of "selfhood," as if the self were generic. The self is a relating activity, a pneumatic energy that asserts itself in time. "The self is a relation that relates itself to itself, or it is that in the relation such that it relates itself to itself."[15] The self is not merely a soul, an immaterial thing related to a body-thing (for that would make the relation, we learn in the next paragraph, a mere negative unity, like two elements in solution). The relating activity is a "positive third" that constitutes whatever is related by it. It constantly materializes, is in that sense physical through and through, although it is never a fixed, self-identical, material thing.

Strictly as described, in fact, the self-relating self can be what in less strict terms we call an individual human being, but it can also be a pair of lovers, or a family, or a sisterhood, or a string quartet, or a labor union. For spirit is the self-relating self wherever the relation materializes, always localized, but not necessarily localized only in this one bag of bones and water here. For sheer relation is the self. Strictly as defined, the self is intersubjective, social, and an individual human being can be a self-relation only because he or she can also be related to others.[16]

Now Anti-Climacus does not explicitly say that, even if his language admits of its possibility. There is no doubt that he would deny this intersubjective and social locus of the self-relating self. For the most part he treats the self as if it were exclusively localized in a self-isolated individual organism. When he does deign to notice that human beings sometimes get together he deplores this tendency. "What wretchedness," he says, that so many "are lumped together and deceived instead of being split apart so that each individual may gain the highest, the only thing worth living for and enough to live in for an eternity."[17] For Anti-Climacus it is axiomatic that "the highest" can only be "gained" one by one, "split apart" in isolation. Again, in the section entitled "Finitude's Despair Is to Lack Infinitude," Anti-Climacus introduces the notion of the mass man, defined by anonymous "others."

> Surrounded by hordes of men, absorbed in all sorts of secular matters, more and more shrewd about the ways of the world, such a person forgets himself, forgets his name, divinely understood, does not dare to believe in himself, finds it too hazardous to be himself and far easier and safer to be like the others, to become a copy, a number, a mass man.[18]

The introduction of the slogan "mass man" in the English text is another liberty taken by our translators (the Danish reads merely *med i Mængden*— "together in the mass"), but this is pardonable since this concept is certainly an instance of the loss of imagination and spiritual identity that Anti-Climacus considers the despair of finitude.

But the mass man is a social pathology not inherent in sociality as such. Anti-Climacus is right in considering it a form of despair, but it is precisely a collective despair. It is not merely an individual despair induced by the sociality of human life. The dialectical heart of this text is the insight that despair is a pathology of self in its freedom, a misrelation of the relational self. "The self is freedom"[19] and that is why it can despair. A stone or a lump cannot despair, and just as despair in the individual is dialectical testimony to the spiritual freedom of the individual, so the horrific social pathologies of modern times, the collective despair that is epidemic in modern experience, is dialectical testimony to the spiritual freedom inherent in the social nature of human beings. This implication of our text appears inescapable: if the social space among human beings were not a locus of freedom's possibility, the social pathology summarized in the slogan "mass man" would not be a form of despair. It would just be an objective social phenomenon, a condition under which some human beings happen to live, and not a form of collective alienation. A heap of stones does not despair.

Despair presupposes freedom; from this dialectical heart of our text it follows that its entire dialectical structure is as applicable to the intersubjective and social life of human beings as it is to the individual life finally inseparable from it. Many of the examples of despair treated in the text are in fact social pathologies, although not acknowledged as such by our author. Anti-Climacus' constant privileging of the individual, even in despair, as if there were no collective despair, follows neither from the dialectical structure of the text nor from the troubled social experience of modern life. It is a prejudice rooted in Anti-Climacus' own equivocal position as someone who is no one, for only such a fiction can represent the asocial self. It is not only that Anti-Climacus denounces every social tendency of human beings, as if the impulse to sociality were inherently despairing and inimical to faith—to which the mildest objection is that this prejudice is unscriptural! Much more commonly he simply ignores the spiritual dynamic of social life. Many of his examples cry out for social interpretation, but their exposition in the text proceeds in a social vacuum, airless and silent, as if individuals had to do with nothing but themselves. The social is treated as a temptation that tests individuals' imperviousness.

In a marginal comment on the text, Søren Kierkegaard says he thought of adding to the preface a claim on Anti-Climacus' behalf that the form of this explication is "rooted in my being who I am." But that would have been a false note to strike on behalf of this pseudonym. For "this would be going too far in transforming a fictitious character into actuality." It surely would have been odd to have someone who is no one appealing to his own personal identity. Kierkegaard goes on to suggest that there is, after all, something two-dimensional about his pseudonym: "a fictitious character has no other possibility than the one he has; he cannot declare that he could also speak in another way and yet be the same; he has no identity that encompasses many possibilities."[20] Kierkegaard appears to think that this lack of "many possibilities" contributes to the uncompromising single-mindedness of this narrative voice. No doubt it does, since only such a fictitious character can be quite this enclosed in a single angle of vision. But that is as much as to say that Anti-Climacus cannot, after all, be a relational self. He is all of a piece. Nor is it surprising that, from such an enclosure in singleness, spirit itself should appear to be exclusively narrowed to the compass of a single individual. This individualistic paradigm of saving faith is the correlative of the fictive individual who insists on it. Perhaps no actual individual would be capable of the requisite narrowness—certainly not Søren Kierkegaard, whose very use of multiple pseudonyms evidences an "identity that encompasses many possibilities."

A consequence of entrusting such a rich work as *The Sickness unto Death* to a pseudonym that makes a virtue of narrowness is that its potential value for a spiritually directed social criticism is left unrealized. Take the notion of spiritlessness which, following the lead of Vigilius Haufniensis (*The Concept of Anxiety*), Anti-Climacus treats as a pathology peculiar to modern Christendom. Spiritlessness is not merely lack of spirit—not at all; only an ethos qualified by spirit of the highest order can pervert the gifts of the spirit to the stifling complacencies of what he calls "the philistine-bourgeois mentality."[21] Spirit's very freedom energizes its own perversion, a "misrelation" of the relational self. So spiritlessness grown aggressive enforces a religiously sanctioned social class hegemony within Christendom and an exploitative cultural imperialism in the rest of the world. Yet in Anti-Climacus' exposition the recognition of the profound social pathology of spiritlessness descends into mere fulminations against the crowd. He even enlists "God in Christ" to authorize these fulminations, in a manner typical of Christendom's own exploitation of the language of faith, a blasphemy only available to people with a rich spiritual heritage; before God, "the people, the crowd, the public, etc." are "abstractions" that "simply do not exist for God; for God there live only single individuals (sinners)."[22] Even sin is the exclusive preserve of single individuals. There can be no collective sins of a people or a class, a claim that would have been news to any of the Hebrew prophets. It is also a trivialization of the other great insight of *The Sickness unto Death*: just as despair is rooted in freedom, so sin is despair before God, from which it follows that the baleful social consequences of sin are rooted in collective despair.

As for faith, the antidote for despair: Anti-Climacus' conclusion that only true Christian individuals, like himself, are recipients of redemptive grace is one of those very complacencies of spiritlessness that he deplores. But if we attend to the dialectical construction of our text, we are constrained to say that faith takes as many forms as the free motions of the spirit that inspire it. Faith can exist among nurses and patients on a ward, or in a family struggling to make ends meet, or in a community ravaged by war.

For although our text proceeds from traditional Christian axioms, each is construed in a remarkably fresh and liberating way. Self is free. That is a traditional axiom. But self is free because it exists in a dynamic network of relations. Despair is the sickness that threatens every locus of spirit, because it is the misrelation of relational self. Sin is despair before God—the most traditional of Christian axioms.

The Power That Establishes

We return to that densest of passages. We have discovered relational self, but relational self may either be self-created or "established by another." Christian teaching assumes that it has been established by another: by God.

> If the relation that relates itself to itself has been established by another, then the relation is indeed the third [i.e., the positive third, which is self], but this relation, the third, is again a relation and relates itself to that which established the entire relation.[23]

Self, spirit, collective or individual, is purely an act of relating, which in turn relates itself to what is later called "the power" that establishes and sustains the entire network of relating. For God, too, is spirit, and in this sense the traditional Christian dogma that human being is the image of God is given fresh articulation. It is not, in scholastic fashion, that self is *caused* by God and resembles its first cause. The life of spirit is a constellation of motions and a commingling, like the fiery wheels within wheels of Ezekiel's vision. Self is a relating activity that exists in freedom as part of that relational constellation founded in the pure relating activity of divine spirit.

We will return to this dense passage yet again, to draw out its implications for selves and for the morphology of despair constructed by our text. For despair will now be the misrelation of self to the divine spirit that establishes it in freedom. Despair will be the use of freedom to refuse its spiritual freedom.

But first let us get a little clearer about this relating activity that funds the entire network of relating. What does this quasi-metaphysical definition of God mean? It repudiates the scholastic definition of God as cause, with self as mere effect. What does it put in place of God as cause? To answer this question we must bring out the major theological innovation of our text, a transparently spiritual understanding of God imaged in the faith that overcomes despair.

"What is decisive is that with God everything is possible."[24] This statement is made in the section titled "Necessity's Despair Is to Lack Possibility," which will largely occupy us in what remains. For the lack of possibility is the fundamental form of despair, but with God everything is possible. This identification of God with possibility articulates the sense in which God establishes all self-relationality. When we think of how things are connected in the world, we generally and lazily think of a vast network of causality; even a St. Thomas can suppose that spiritual beings, too, are causally related and causally grounded in God. Things are connected, as it were, backward, through causal antecedents. But here Anti-Climacus is suggesting quite the opposite, at least where spiritual self is concerned. There is indeed a network of relation, the great fabric of life, but it, in turn, is related to God as to a boundless horizon of possibility. This network of mobile relating is not a backward connection of things out of their antecedents, as in the causal paradigm, but is forward-moving, drawn into the future by the lure of possibility. For God is the primal ground, not of causality, not even of being, but of that possibility that is the ever-renewed birthplace of free spiritual relation. Freedom is the condition of every spiritual configuration actively related to the God for whom everything is possible. Freedom has possibility as its ultimate ground.

This bold identification of God with possibility is not metaphysical but existential. God is freedom's possibility. Every spiritual being knows it is free insofar as in its relating activity, within itself and with others, it relates itself to the God for whom everything is possible. If our text does not presume to speak of the divine as it is in itself, apart from all relation, it is because faith cannot conceive of God apart from all relation, since faith is just the confidence in boundless possibility. Anti-Climacus culminates a little polemic against fatalism by speaking of prayer, particularly prayer *in extremis*, when all seems lost, or prayer *de profundis*, out of the depths of desperation, and just here he comes the closest to identifying God outright with possibility. For that is what God means to those at the end of their tether, where prayer begins to be serious.

> To pray there must be a God, a self—and possibility, or a self and possibility in the pregnant sense, for God is this, that everything is possible, or that everything is possible is God, and only he whose being has been so shaken that he has become spirit by understanding that everything is possible, only he has anything to do with God.[25]

Such a prayer can arise among friends painfully estranged from one another, or at a deathbed, or in a proud nation in mortal peril, when the pride that relies on its own resources has come up short. In such straits it is no longer a matter of trying out this or that. The only alternative to desperation is the lyricism of a hopeful faith that with God everything is possible. Yet such hopefulness is not merely idle wishing. Faith is action, without visible means of support, founded on possibility. Suffering and death are the crucifixion of every mortal project, but resurrection is emblematic of God's possibility for every mortal project. The power that establishes the entire fabric of spiritual relation is divine in just this sense, that it resurrects the crucified.

Such a faith is certainly open to individuals, but it is a faith that restores them to solidarity with a community. It brings them into a hopeful association with the human enterprise, indeed with the constellation of relations grounded in divine possibility. That, for instance, seems to have been the result of the resurrection faith in the early Church—it reunited the scattered and despairing followers of Jesus and empowered them again. There is indeed a reaction to the failure of common hopes, the rending of the fabric of life, that consists in the withdrawal of individuals into self-isolation. But that is not faith. That is a form of despair, all the more transparent when this despair of self-isolation expresses itself in the language of other-worldly withdrawal.

Self Given and Self Potentiated

Part I of *The Sickness unto Death* is a morphology of despair, always considered as taking two forms that reappear in a series of doubled categories: finitude/infinitude, necessity/possibility, weakness/defiance. For on the one hand the spiritual self can despairingly will not to be itself (despair of finitude, of necessity, of weakness). If relational self were not related, in turn, to a divine horizon of possibility that funds the entire relation, then, according to the dense passage to which we must turn again, this refusal of self would be the only form of despair. But since the Christian axiom of our text assumes that relational self *is* related to a divine horizon of possibility, another form of despair appears: spiritual self can will despairingly just to be itself, cut off from God's possibility. This latter form of despair insists on its own finitude (despairing of infinitude) and its own necessity (despairing of possibility) and culminates in a despairing defiance and conscious refusal of its ground of hope. So there are these two reappearing forms of despair: not to will to be oneself, and to will to be oneself in the sense of Popeye the Sailor: I yam what I yam and that's all that I yam.

These two forms of despair are so systematically developed in our text that they may appear to be quite symmetrical, of equal weight. But given the Christian axiom the second form of despair is fundamental, while the first form is a despairing illusion that prevents the recognition of the second form. The second form, willing to be only the self one is, Anti-Climacus tells us, "is so far from designating merely a distinctive kind of despair that, on the contrary, all despair ultimately can be traced back to and be resolved in it."[26] For despair is above all the "no exit" situation, the refusal of possibility and therefore the denial of God. That is why the two types traced in Part I collapse fundamentally into the second type in Part II of the text, into despair before God. Yet even there the despair before God can take the form of willing not to be the spiritual self at all.

One might wonder why the first type of despair still has any place in the analysis, if self-relation is intrinsically a relation to God. The general answer is that spirit, even in the misrelation of despair, is always incarnate in actual self, collective or individual. Especially before God, self is in despair that denies itself as it is, that refuses to avow itself or takes flight from itself in imagination. Now imagination, or the ability to entertain unrealized possibilities, is at least a psychological precondition of faith. Yet insofar as imagination is employed to deny or obscure the recognition of self as it is, it becomes an obstacle to faith.

I judge that to be a crucial dialectical point in our text. In order to bring it out more clearly, without getting lost in the somewhat confusing inversion of terms presented in the text, it will be convenient to introduce two terms not found in the text: the given self and the potentiated self. The given self is what we have called the self as it is, the result of its individual and collective past. The potentiated self is a given self that has faith in the divine horizon of possibility. The potentiated self, the potentiated community, is ready to change, but it cannot change without avowing and taking responsibility for its given self. Without that avowal it simply becomes lost in illusions, without confronting the straits it may be in, and genuine prayer will be impossible. For the potentiated self to materialize in faith, the given self must be acknowledged. Alcoholics Anonymous understands this dialectic very well. To be helped I must recognize my given self for what it is, an alcoholic utterly unable to cope with my alcoholism. If I can do that I may be ready for the God for whom everything is possible, and the potentiated self may spread its wings. If I cannot do that I am cut adrift in self-deceiving fantasies; possibility harbors my disease instead of curing it.

We return to the pair of sections of our text on possibility and necessity: "Possibility's Despair Is to Lack Necessity" and "Necessity's Despair Is to Lack Possibility." That sounds symmetrical enough, but there is an asymmetry owing to the position of the given self in the two equations. For the fundamental asymmetry of the two fundamental forms of despair registers here in one of its prime instances. The despair of not willing to be the given self is expressed here as lack of necessity. The despair of willing only to be the given self is expressed as lack of possibility. The lack of possibility is the essential form of despair, for possibility is finally the only antidote to despair.

> When someone faints, we call for water, eau de Cologne, smelling salts; but when someone wants to despair, then the word is: Get possibility, get possibility, possibility is the only salvation. . . . At times the ingeniousness of the human imagination can extend to the point of creating possibility, but at last—that is, when it depends upon *faith*—then only this helps: that for God everything is possible.[27]

In this case to stick fast with the given self and refuse possibility is to choose despair. But that is as far as possible from saying that one should refuse to avow the given self. Such a refusal is the first and, so to say, preliminary form of despair. A pair of lovers, say, or even an institution, may so lose itself in heady possibility as to become fantastical, self-abandoned. In such a case the antidote is necessity, which in our text means the given self with all its antecedent conditions, avowed in sober self-recognition. Some of the necessary conditions to which those drunk on possibility must submit are biological, environmental, and climatic; some are more cultural and social, the legacy of a common past. Communities have taken form speaking a certain language, with a certain religious heritage, a shared ethos, and historically formed institutions that are both treasures and limiting conditions.

Ingredient in the social history of the given self, furthermore, are habits and prejudices, deeply ingrained, that we may deplore but can disavow only at risk of fantastically losing track of ourselves. Just suppose in a purely hypothetical way that I myself and my family, my church, and the university in which I work exist in a society with a long history of deformities such as racism and sexism, social class oppression, and a national ethos of greed and violence. Since I and my church and so on are also ideologically liberal, we may be tempted to suppose that by deploring and disavowing these deformities we have purged them from our collective and individual souls. According to *The Sickness unto Death* the very opposite is the case. We have simply deceived ourselves about pathologies lodged in the given self we share. The result is a despairing loss of self, for our individual and collective necessity includes the social pathologies we both suffer and inflict. Even the vegetarian young are protected in the luxury of tender sensibilities by the ring of steel and death-dealing weapons against which they protest. The disavowal of such necessities, the flight into agreeable possibilities, the attempt to deal lightly and sentimentally with our pathologies, is simply a despairing failure to accept as our own the given selves that we are. What is not avowed cannot be seriously repented. The self that is only "abstract possibility," Anti-Climacus says (who should know!), "neither moves from the place where it is nor arrives anywhere, for necessity is literally the place where it is. To become is a movement away from that place, but to become oneself is a movement in that place."²⁸ A family whose relation to itself is one of mutual self-destruction cannot break out of that cycle merely by cosmetic pretences and enforced civility. It must consciously become the given self it is or despairingly deceive itself.

It is evident from these examples, however, that the necessity to which collective and therefore individual self must submit is not yet the antidote to despair. Given self avowed is not yet the potentiated self. If the submission to given self is fatalistic, in fact, as if there were no hope for it to move from "the place where it is," it will simply have proceeded to the deeper despair of necessity, or of defiance: the desperate willing of its own given self, without possibility. It is easy to say that the antidote is to turn to God. But Anti-Climacus suggests that such a turning is not serious "until a person is brought to his extremity, when, humanly speaking, there is no possibility.

Then the question is whether he will believe that for God everything is possible, that is, whether he will *believe.*"²⁹

A racist society is dangerous to itself and to others, because it is in despair. If it consciously avows its racism, it may move "away from that place" with many painful renunciations, or it may simply move "in that place," becoming aggressive and defiant in its racism. In the latter case it sinks deeper in despair and becomes still more dangerous, for it sees no way out. "At this point, then, salvation is, humanly speaking, utterly impossible; but for God everything is possible! This is the battle of *faith,* battling, madly, if you will, for possibility, because possibility is the only salvation."³⁰ Something fundamental must happen to the self-relation of such a society, related to a boundless horizon of possibility. The "battle of faith" is the movement "from that place" of potentiated self. Potentiated self is active, not because it believes it has succeeded in purging its pathologies, but because it believes in miracles. For in the end only miraculous possibility is the solution to the sickness of despair. On that point let us give Anti-Climacus the last word: "Whether a person is helped by a miracle depends essentially upon the passion of the understanding whereby he has understood that help was impossible and depends next on how honest he was toward the power that nevertheless did help him."³¹

Notes

1. Søren Kierkegaard, *The Sickness unto Death: A Christian Psychological Exposition for Upbuilding and Awakening*, ed. and trans. with introduction and notes by Howard V. Hong and Edna H. Hong (Princeton, NJ: Princeton University Press, 1980), pp. 49n–50n. All future quotations from *Sickness unto Death* (cited hereafter as SUD) refer to this edition, but I have occasionally altered the Hong translation of quoted passages, using the Danish text of *Sygdommen til Døden* in *Søren Kierkegaard's Samlede Værker*, vol. 15, ed. A. B. Drachmann, J. L. Heiberg, and H. O. Lange (Copenhagen: Gyldendal, 1963).

    The footnote in question is primarily concerned with distinguishing between the masculine and the feminine as ideal types, without suggesting that all women are "feminine" in the sense defined. But the author cannot seem to resist throwing in some observations about women derived from his social experience. For example, "However much more tender and sensitive woman may be than man, she has neither the egotistical concept of the self nor, in a decisive sense, intellectuality. But the feminine nature is devotedness, givingness, and it is unfeminine if it is not that" (pp. 49n–50n). Again: "In devotion she loses herself, and only then is she happy, only then is she herself; a woman who is happy without devotion, that is, without giving herself, no matter to what she gives it, is altogether unfeminine" (p. 50n). The footnote concludes, to be sure, with the suggestion that any such distinction between men and women is transcended in their relation to God. In this relationship, "where the distinction of man-woman vanishes, it holds for men as well as for women that devotion is the self and that in giving of oneself the self is gained. This holds equally for man and woman"—but then the author spoils the point—"although it is probably true that in most cases the woman actually relates to God only through the man" (p. 50n). So men and women are equally selves before God, though not in the case of most women! It is not surprising that in teaching this text I have had a very hard time convincing some of my ablest women students that they should not close the book at this point. I do try to convince them, not always successfully, that they should read on, because I am myself convinced that the meaning of the text transcends the apparent condescending sexism of the author and his superficial individualism and pietism as well.

For a clear treatment of this issue that deals with this footnote as well as other charges of sexism in Kierkegaard, see Sylvia Walsh, "On 'Masculine' and 'Feminine' Forms of Despair," in the *International Kierkegaard Commentary* on *The Sickness unto Death*, ed. Robert Perkins (Macon, GA: Mercer University Press, 1987). Wanda Warren Berry addresses the issue of sexism in Kierkegaard in her chapter in this volume. She analyzes Kierkegaard both from the perspective of the shortcomings revealed by contemporary feminism and as a thinker who has a positive contribution to make to feminism.

2. SUD, p. 139.
3. *Practice in Christianity* will be the new, more accurate English title of the *Kierkegaard's Writings* edition of the Lowrie *Training in Christianity*.
4. *Søren Kierkegaard's Journals and Papers*, 7 vols., ed. and trans. Howard V. Hong and Edna H. Hong, with Gregor Malantschuk (Bloomington, IN: Indiana University Press, 1967–1978), vol. 7, entry 6433.
5. SUD, p. 160.
6. Ibid.
7. Ibid., pp. 160–161.
8. Howard and Edna Hong insist that the prefix "Anti" does not in this case mean *against*, but is an archaic form of *ante*, *before*, in the sense of a superior rank (SUD, p. xxii). It is certainly plausible that the name should suggest this superiority to Climacus, but it is not clear why it might not also imply opposition to Climacus, whose noncommital presentation of Christianity would appear frivolous from Anti-Climacus' point of view. Climacus merely presents the reader with a clear choice: Socrates or Christ—either/or! For Anti-Climacus the condition of the reader is far more grave: the reader is not merely pondering a choice between honorable alternatives. He or she is in despair, sick unto death, and Dr. Anti-Climacus is prescribing faith as the only cure. That implies a radically different relation between author and reader. The physician does not invite the patient to ponder the choice between life and death, as a philosopher might on a cool afternoon. The physician's diagnosis creates quite a different tension. If there is still an implied choice, it is between these two literatures: Climacus or Anti-Climacus—either/or.

It is worth noting that Kierkegaard's name appears on both of these literatures, as editor or the one responsible for publication.
9. SUD, pp. 161–62.
10. Ibid., p. 77.
11. Although Kierkegaard deleted the editor's note referred to, he did later regret not having added a more cryptic editorial postscript: "This book seems to be written by a physician; I, the editor, am not the physician, I am one of the sick" (SUD, p. 162).

12. SUD, p. 77.
13. Ibid., p. 78.
14. Ibid., p. 13.
15. Ibid.
16. See Charles Bellinger's chapter in this volume for an interesting attempt to apply the categories of "spirit" to twentieth century nation-states, as exemplifying various forms of social pathology.
17. SUD, p. 27.
18. Ibid., pp. 33–34.
19. Ibid., p. 27.
20. Ibid., p. 140.
21. Ibid., pp. 41–42, 46–47.
22. Ibid., p. 121.
23. Ibid., p. 13.
24. Ibid., p. 38.
25. Ibid., p. 40.
26. Ibid., p. 14.
27. Ibid., pp. 38–39.
28. Ibid., p. 36.
29. Ibid., p. 38.
30. Ibid.
31. Ibid., p. 39.

10 Call Me Ishmael—Call Everybody Ishmael: Kierkegaard on the Coming-of-Age Crisis of Modern Times

BRUCE KIRMMSE

> [With the arrival of the leveling tendency of modern society,] a demon which no individual can control is conjured up.
> Kierkegaard
> *A Literary Review*
> (1846)

> Modern bourgeois society . . ., a society that has conjured up such gigantic means of production and exchange, is like the sorcerer who is no longer able to control the powers of the nether world whom he has called up by his spells.
> Marx
> *The Communist Manifesto* (1848)

"Call me Ishmael" is of course the first line of the greatest of American novels, *Moby Dick*, but it also serves as a heading under which to understand the person in modern mass society. We will return to the full meaning of Ishmael later in the present essay.

ADAM SMITH, JOHN LOCKE, AND ISHMAEL

Ever since the Enlightenment, we have been aware that society—the relations between people—is radically different from what it had been in past ages. Among those who have given the clearest and most systematic accounts of this "modernity" have been Adam Smith and John Locke. Both

Smith and Locke make it clear that we must begin with the naked, self-interested individual, abstracted from all social relations. We build upon the rational self-interest of individuals, making no moral assumptions:

> [M]an has almost constant occasion for the help of his brethren, and it is in vain for him to expect it from their benevolence only. He will be more likely to prevail if he can interest their self-love in his favor, and show them that it is for their own advantage to do for him what he requires of them. Whoever offers to another a bargain of any kind proposes to do this. Give me that which I want, and you shall have this which you want, is the meaning of every such offer; and it is in this manner that we obtain from one another the far greater part of those good offices which we stand in need of. It is not from the benevolence of the butcher, the brewer, and the baker that we expect our dinner, but from their regard to their own interest. We address ourselves not to their humanity, but to their self-love.[1]

According to Adam Smith the idea of a "just price" is a chimera of outmoded, medieval, corporatist society. Smith is an "agnostic" on the question of prices and on economic outcomes generally. What is needed is the unfettered operation of the vast multitude of rationally selfish individual inputs, of self-interested individual decisions to be a supplier or to make a demand. All this individual selfishness moves the "invisible hand," the silent, anonymous, collective fabrication that sets the price, and it is always by definition a just price. The *market* is the key concept underlying the Smithian interpretation of economic society. The market is a corporate fiction that continually synthesizes the myriad of individual acts into a single outcome, the price. Given Smith's assumptions about human beings, the market is always right, and the price is always just.

In the sphere of political power and the making of public policy, John Locke holds a position analogous to that of Adam Smith. The starting unit is the modern individual, not the corporate unit of earlier centuries. And the individual is moved by rational self-interest with the goal of protecting and extending his/her "property": "[G]overnment has no other end but the preservation of property."[2] Provided that the rights of individuals are respected, no political outcome or policy is right or wrong in itself. Like Smith, Locke is an "agnostic" about outcomes. What is needed is the unimpeded operation of the mechanism of popular sovereignty, by which myriads of individuals consult their interests and produce a policy outcome that maximizes the total of individual satisfactions. The *electoral process* is the anonymous collective fabrication of a single outcome from vast numbers of individual inputs; it is the precise political analogue of the market.

It is important to remember that no economic result or political policy is right or wrong of itself. The anonymous market forces always produce the "right" outcome. This is the core of the modern mass society described by Smith and Locke. They are both *descriptive* and *prescriptive*. The world, they say, works this way whether we like it or not, and they only want to make the existing reality fairer and more efficient by pointing out the abuses—for Smith, monopoly, and for Locke, tyranny—that impede the optimal functioning of the market mechanism. Since this is the way things are, we had best see to it that they work smoothly.

In short, this is the world of classical-liberal, bourgeois individualism. Every individual has self-interest and makes no moral assumptions about his/her neighbor, but on the contrary assumes that the neighbor is also moved by rational self-interest. The only ultimate reality is the selfish individual. Every association is a combination or group founded to promote the sum of the self-interests of its individual members or to oppose or counterbalance other such combinations. Given his assumptions, Smith rightly opposed all combinations and groups as conspiracies in restraint of trade.

The society described by Smith and Locke is built upon the continuing, relentless pursuit of self-interest. The market will encompass the globe and will engulf everyone. With the coming of popular sovereignty, everyone is a part of politics; everyone is a part of "public opinion." We cannot hide from these anonymous forces of "progress." Those who reject or ignore these forces will find themselves a part of the process anyway, as victims of an unequal partnership, and will be compelled to play the game, acting in their self-interest merely to survive.

This modern, mass-based, individualistic market society is also the world of *Ishmael*. It will be remembered (from Genesis 16) that Ishmael was the son of Abraham by his wife's maid Hagar, who, while still pregnant, was driven away into the desert by the irate and jealous Sarah. The Bible tells us (Genesis 16:12) that it will be the sad fate of this Ishmael to be "a wild man": "His hand will be against every man, and every man's hand against him." Ishmael is the prototype of the modern self-interested individual, alone and cut off from all others, who expects only selfishness from his fellows and who acts in accordance with those expectations. This is why Melville chose him as the central character of his great nineteenth century novel about a mad quest, an insatiable hunger, and the lonely individual who narrates the tale. This is also why Kierkegaard's opponent, Meir Aaron Goldschmidt, a Jew (and author of *En Jøde*), a loner, and the freebooter editor of Copenhagen's *Corsair*, nailed Ishmael's slogan on the masthead of his journal: "His hand will be against every man, and every man's hand against his." (As we will see, Kierkegaard himself also uses this description of Ishmael to characterize modern society.) This, then, is the world of modern, bourgeois-individualist market society—one against all, all against one.

FERDINAND TÖNNIES: GEMEINSCHAFT AND GESELLSCHAFT

The world of Ishmael is the world described by Smith and Locke in the eighteenth century and by the sociologist Ferdinand Tönnies (1855–1936) in the nineteenth and twentieth centuries. Tönnies, one of the founders of modern sociology, wrote his most influential work, *Gemeinschaft und Gesellschaft*, in 1887. In his work Tönnies contrasts the older, corporate-based, traditional "community" (*Gemeinschaft*), which built upon affective ties and our "natural will" (*Wesenwille*), with the modern, individualistic "society" (*Gesellschaft*), which builds upon our "rational will" or our rational self-interest.

> The theory of the *Gesellschaft* deals with the artificial construction of an aggregate of human beings which superficially resembles the *Gemeinschaft* in so far as the individuals live and dwell together peacefully. However, in the Gemeinschaft they remain essentially united in spite of all separating factors, whereas in the *Gesellschaft* they are essentially separated in spite of all uniting factors. . . . [H]ere everybody is by himself and isolated, and there exists a state of tension against all others. . . . Such a negative attitude toward one another becomes the normal and always underlying relation of these power-endowed individuals, and it characterizes the *Gesellschaft*. . . . [N]obody wants to grant or produce anything for another individual, nor will he be inclined to give ungrudgingly to another individual, if it be not in exchange for a gift or labor equivalent that he considers at least equal to what he has given.[3]

Tönnies' description of modern, market-based, individualistic society sounds as though it were compounded of equal portions of the Ishmael story and Adam Smith! Yet, despite his discernible nostalgia for *Gemeinschaft*, Tönnies sees that the modern *Gesellschaft* has an inner dynamic of its own that will lead to its eventual and universal triumph in every sphere of human life:

> [I]nherent in the concept of the *Gesellschaft* . . . [is a] tendency [which] necessarily implies a dissolution of all those ties which bind the individual through his natural will and are apart from his rational will. For these ties restrict his personal freedom of movement, the saleableness of his property, the change of his attitudes, and their adaptation to the findings of science. They are restrictions on the self-determined rational will and on the *Gesellschaft* in so far as trade and commerce tend to make property or property rights as mobile and divisible as possible and require *unscrupulous, irreligious, easygoing people*. The state, too, feels the restrictive influence of these ties, and hastens the tendency toward their dissolution, and considers *enlightened, greedy, and practical people* as its most useful subjects.[4]

Tönnies' outlook is rather bleak, to be sure, but it builds squarely on the modern individualism of his Enlightenment predecessors.

KARL MARX

Like Tönnies and the classical Enlightenment thinkers, Karl Marx also saw the progress of the individualistic market society as relentless and its triumph as inevitable:

> *the division of labour* [which was at the core of Smith's theory] *is necessarily followed by greater division of labour, the application of machinery by a still greater application of machinery, work on a large scale by work on a still larger scale.*
>
> That is the law which again and again throws bourgeois production out of its old course and which compels capital to intensify the productive forces of labor, *because* it has intensified them, . . . the law which gives capital no rest and continually whispers in its ear, "Go on! Go on!" [5]

Yet, even though Marx plainly finds this inevitable process deplorable, he also looks upon the modern bourgeois-capitalist transformation of the world with an amazement that borders on admiration or respect:

> The bourgeoisie has through its exploitation of the world-market given a cosmopolitan character to production and consumption in every country.[6]

> National differences and antagonisms between peoples are daily more and more vanishing, owing to the development of the bourgeoisie, to freedom of commerce, to the world-market, to uniformity in the mode of production and in the conditions of life corresponding thereto.[7]

> [The bourgeoisie] compels all, on pain of extinction, to adopt the bourgeois mode of production; it compels them to introduce what it calls civilisation into their midst, i.e., to become bourgeois themselves. In one word, it creates a world after its own image.[8]

> All fixed, fast-frozen relations, with their train of ancient and venerable prejudices and opinions, are swept away, all new-formed ones become antiquated before they can ossify. All that is solid melts into air, all that is holy is profaned.[9]

Yet Marx's nostalgia for the *Gemeinschaft* of earlier ages, for affective social relations *is* very marked. The bourgeois market society has utterly deracinated and denuded the worker; it

> has stripped him of every trace of national character. Law, morality, religion are to him so many bourgeois prejudices.[10]

> The bourgeoisie, wherever it has got the upper hand, has put an end to all feudal, patriarchal, idyllic relations. It has pitilessly torn asunder the motley feudal ties that bound man to his "natural superiors," and has left remaining no other nexus between man and man than naked self-interest, than callous "cash payment." It has drowned the most heavenly ecstasies of religious fervor, of chivalrous enthusiasm, of philistine sentimental-

ism, in the icy water of egotistical calculation. It has resolved personal worth into exchange value, and in place of the numberless indefeasible chartered freedoms, has set up that single, unconscionable freedom—Free Trade.[11]

Despite his evident nostalgia for the *Gemeinschaft*-world we have lost, Marx understands that the travail of the present age of Ishmael is not only inevitable, it is an opportunity; it is the fulcrum of history. At one point in his writings, Marx refers to the crisis of modernity as "the Golgatha" of the present. The hell into which we have descended therefore paves the way for a total reversal. The bourgeois *Gesellschaft* "is, in short, a *total loss* of humanity which can only redeem itself by a *total redemption of humanity*."[12] In keeping with the redemption metaphor, Marx even refers to the final revolution, the insurrection, as a "resurrection."[13]

So, although things are inevitably getting to be as bad as they can possibly be, salvation is also present within the very crisis itself. Marx sketches the general lines of the salvation he expects—it will be "scientific socialism," that is, the combination of the rationality of the scientific-industrial *Gesellschaft* with the wholeness of the *Gemeinschaft*. It is the solution to the problem of society, the problem of the one and the many, the individual and the community. It will end the alienation of the division of labor:

> [T]he division of labour implies the contradiction between the interest of the separate individual or the individual family and the communal interest of all individuals . . .[,] while in a communist society, where nobody has one exclusive sphere of activity but each can become accomplished in any branch he wishes, society regulates the general production and thus makes it possible for me to do one thing today and another tomorrow, to hunt in the morning, fish in the afternoon, rear cattle in the evening, criticize after dinner, just as I have a mind, without ever becoming hunter, fisherman, shepherd, or critic.[14]

In fact, the salvation with which the present age is in labor is the very end and consummation of human history itself. We are in the crisis through which the human race will come of age and enter into its inheritance as an adult.

> *Communism* as the *positive* transcendence of *private property*, or *human self-estrangement*, and therefore as the real *appropriation of the human* essence by and for man; communism therefore as the complete return of man to himself as a *social* (i.e., human) being—a return become conscious, and accomplished within the entire wealth of previous development. This communism, as fully-developed naturalism, equals humanism, and as fully-developed humanism equals naturalism; it is the *genuine* resolution of the conflict between man and nature and between man and man. . . .

Communism is the riddle of history solved, and it knows itself to be this solution.[15]

KIERKEGAARD: INTRODUCTORY

Like Marx, Søren Kierkegaard sees the present age as an age of Ishmael, characterized—in economics, in politics, in public opinion—by the silent, relentless leveling forces of the marketplace. Like Marx, Kierkegaard plainly finds these modern developments deplorable. Similarly, both thinkers briefly direct some attention to lamenting what has been lost, the world of "natural" relations between inferior and superior, the entire world of *Gemeinschaft*. But, again like Marx, Kierkegaard recognizes that the process is inevitable; it cannot be stopped, so we must instead see our possibilities within the crisis of the present. We must see the crisis not simply as a disaster but as an opportunity, a coming of age.

For Kierkegaard, unlike Marx, while we are indeed faced with a crisis of coming of age, our historical future does not appear to hold a renewed community, a new *Gemeinschaft*. We must not seek our salvation in some new and perfected set of political constellations or social relations. Rather, we must clarify what is and is not the proper sphere for social and political endeavor. We must accept the *Gesellschaft* for what it is worth, and compel politics to be honest about its limitations. Politics must be limited to the daily world of practical utility, of approximations, and it must be prevented from making ultimate or transcendent claims.[16] The seductions of a renewed *Gemeinschaft* are precisely what must be guarded against. If we are honest with ourselves, Kierkegaard argues, we will see that it is in the individual relation to God that true ultimacy and transcendence are to be found, and it was Kierkegaard's self-appointed function to help keep us honest. Let us examine Kierkegaard's treatment of modern bourgeois society in more detail, focusing particular attention on the so-called second authorship (the post-*Postscript* writings), which are the works most immediately relevant to understanding Kierkegaard's diagnosis and prescription for modern society.

PAST AND PRESENT

With Marx and Tönnies, Kierkegaard assumed a radical division between modern times and previous ages, an assumption he exposes in an offhand way in his discussion of "the present age" as an age of irony, when he remarks that "the true ironist [is] the hidden enthusiast in a negative time (just as the hero is the manifest enthusiast in a positive time)."[17] Thus, we are now in a "negative time," as contrasted with the "positive time" of past ages. Similarly, modernity's absolute difference from antiquity is that the whole is not the concretion which supports and educates the individual, . . . but is an abstraction, which, in its abstract equality, repels him and helps him to be educated in the absolute sense—if he does not perish.[18]

The past, then, was supportive and educative in a "positive" and "concrete" fashion, while the present is "negative," "abstract," and "repellent," and is thus both supremely dangerous and potentially educative.

THE PRESENT AGE: ENVY, LEVELING, ISHMAEL, AND THE "FEAR OF MAN"

Modern times are a period of abstraction and negation, characterized by "reflective envy" and "leveling" (*Nivellering*), which does not represent true equality but is a mere "mathematical equality," the "negative unity of the negative reciprocity of individuals."[19] The present is under the tyranny of anonymous public opinion, of "town gossip and rumors."[20] Kierkegaard clearly has in mind his own victimization at the hands of his anonymous opponents in the *Corsair*, the aptly named piratic journal that brazenly displayed the Ishmaelic inscription (Genesis 16:12) on its masthead. The importance Kierkegaard attributed to opposing the sort of modern *Gesellschaft*-individualism represented by Goldschmidt and his journal is made conveniently explicit for us at one point in his discourse, "Purity of Heart is to Will One Thing," in which he asks his reader: Are you in "unity" [*Samdrægtighed*] with all and "in family with divinity" by "willing One Thing"—that is, willing "the Good in Truth"? Or "Is your hand raised against all and all against you?"[21] This is Kierkegaard's only explicit use of the Ishmael passage, but it is clear that he, too, sees Ishmael as emblematic of the anonymous, self-interested individualism of modern times. Another phrase Kierkegaard repeatedly uses to characterize this side of modernity is "the tyranny of the fear of man" (*Menneske-Frygtens Tyrannie*). "To equality corresponds a form of tyranny: fear of man."[22] "Gradually, as a certain superficial culture spreads," he writes, we become fearful of our fellow man, who becomes our anonymous oppressor;[23] this, once again, is clearly the same tyranny. Similarly, "when the public, the highly-honored, cultivated public, or the People" commits a crime in collectivity, it is no longer a crime but "God's will"[24] (*vox populi vox dei*); this, too, is the tyranny of the fear of man.

BOURGEOIS-PHILISTINE CHRISTENDOM: SHREWDNESS AND SPIRITLESSNESS

Kierkegaard defines the present age more precisely as the age of bourgeois-philistine Christendom, of "spiritlessness" (*Aandløshed*), "shrewdness" (*Klogskab*), and calculation. "So-called Christendom is not Christian at all . . .

[L]ike 'spiritlessness,' [it] is much more heathen than heathendom was."[25] Indeed, "the heathens who are found in Christendom are those who have sunk the deepest."[26] Kierkegaard compares the state of Danish Christianity to the mediocrity and foolishness of "the parlor of a bourgeois philistine."[27] Again and again in Kierkegaard's writings, we are told explicitly that the commonest form of despair is "spiritlessness,"[28] which is typical of the "bourgeois philistine," the well-integrated, self-satisfied, and respectable type, who is "a man who has learned what life's seriousness is . . . a husband, citizen, and father," a heathen of Christendom, who "lives in the world without God."[29] "Most people's lives are, Christianly understood, too spiritless even to be called sin in the strict sense."[30]

No one is so shrewd as the bourgeois gentleman of modern times, but Kierkegaard warns us that "in God's eyes there is nothing so disgusting as the sin of shrewdness."[31] We must "beware of cowardly shrewdness and spineless cleverness . . . which is, from the Christian point of view, perhaps the most dangerous plague."[32] The motto of the shrewd, Ishmaelite-individualist businessman, Kierkegaard tells us, is "everyone is a thief in his own profession"—and then this philistine adopts the Christianity of Christendom![33] "It is bourgeois philistinism to situate oneself like this in supposed Christianity so that one actually abolishes Christianity."[34] Indeed, "bourgeois philistinism is spiritlessness."[35]

THE PRESENT CRISIS: TRIAL AND OPPORTUNITY

But for all their appalling qualities, the egoistic shrewdness, the calculation and reflection of the present age are not merely a catastrophe. They are at once a trial and an opportunity. In 1846 Kierkegaard refers to the modern age as an "*examen rigorosum*";[36] the reflectiveness of the modern age is "a snare, in which the situation is transformed—then the snare becomes something which catapults one into the embrace of the Eternal."[37] By late 1848 Kierkegaard is able to use a very similar phrase in stressing the enormous historical significance of the revolution of that year: "Not even the dissolution of ancient civilization was as great as the world-historical catastrophe which has loomed up, and which is the absolute *tentamen rigorosum* for everyone who *was* an author."[38]

WORKING THROUGH THE PRESENT

The reason why we must see the terribleness of the modern age as an opportunity, Kierkegaard explains, is that "there is no *immediate* form of spiritual health";[39] that "in order to reach the Truth one must go through every negativity";[40] because "the prize of infinity is never won except *through* despair."[41] It is true that the present age is an age of reflection, but "reflection is not corrupting in and of itself . . . [O]n the contrary, working one's way through reflection is the precondition for being able to act more intensively."[42] Similarly, Kierkegaard insists that "knowledge does not contaminate a person; it is mistrustfulness which contaminates a person's knowledge, just as Love purifies it."[43] As becomes clear in Kierkegaard's ethical works, reflection and rationality underlie law and the demand for justice. These same principles also underlie the modern *Gesellschaft*, based as it is upon the "rational will," upon equality and "measure for measure." We must not repudiate them, but go through and beyond them to find Love, which is the fulfillment (and the abolition) of the Law.

"The Principle of Association": The Proper Limits of Politics

One of the primary escapes that people attempt is politics, cohering in groups, "the idea of sociality," which, Kierkegaard insists, is "in our time" "an escape" and "a diversion," and "is at most valid with respect to material interests."[44] Kierkegaard allows that politics ("the principle of association") and majoritarianism have their proper (if limited) sphere: "Indeed, I have never denied that with respect to all temporal, earthly, worldly purposes, the mass [i.e., the power of the majority] can have its validity, even decisive validity."[45] But there is a boundary that must be rigorously drawn:

> I can understand that a politician would believe that free institutions are beneficial to the state, because politics is an external thing which, by its very nature, not having any life in itself, must take its life from forms . . . [but Christianity is completely different, precisely because it] has its life in itself.[46]

> That which is at times partially and at other times completely valid in politics and similar fields becomes Untruth when it is transferred to the areas of mind, spirit, religiosity. . . . By "Truth" I always mean "eternal Truth," but politics and the like do not have to do with "eternal Truth."[47]

Thus, the politics and majoritarianism of the modern *Gesellschaft* have their proper sphere of activity, but "from an ethical-religious point of view, the mass is Untruth when it is supposed to be the court of appeal as to what 'the Truth' is."[48] The difference, the boundary, is very clear to Kierkegaard: "*Essentially*, Christianity is inwardness" and is unconcerned with outward forms, while "politics is this external thing, this tantalizing busyness with changing externalities."[49]

The proper sphere of politics, of "the public," is clear. It is the task of the state to see to it that various things that people need are available to them reliably and at reasonable cost. This is the case with roads and highways, street illumination, public water supply, and public safety. So, society argues, why not also purchase "eternal blessedness" in bulk and distribute it at lowest cost?[50] But Kierkegaard objects that there is a radical difference between such properly social-political concerns of material prudence as piped water and one's relation to the Eternal, which must be obtained individually and not "comfortably."[51] Therefore, Kierkegaard writes in the strongest possible terms that *"there is nothing which makes me so uneasy as anything which tastes of even the merest trace of this disastrous confounding of politics and Christianity."*[52] In the context of the modern bourgeois *Gesellschaft*, Kierkegaard does not claim to be a reformer, a seer, or a deep thinker and even disclaims being a Christian. No, he insists, he is just "an unusually-talented police detective,"[53] with an agenda of honesty, whose task it is to clear up this case: Precisely "because Christianity is Spirit . . . nothing is more suspicious to its police officer's gaze than all these fantastical entities—Christian states, Christian nations, a Christian people, and, wonder of wonders, a Christian world!"[54]

THE DEIFICATION OF THE ESTABLISHED ORDER

We must discriminate clearly between what is permissible and what is impermissible in the modern world. For example, "paying taxes to Caesar [is] the most indifferent thing of all, i.e., something one must do without wasting one word or one moment in talking about it, in order to have all the more time in which to render unto God what is God's."[55] Again, "because paying taxes is an indifferent externality, Christ submits and avoids giving offense. *It would be otherwise in relation to an externality which impudently claimed to be piety."*[56] In other words, for Kierkegaard, the greatest danger is that the modern *Gesellschaft*, compounded as it is of millions of anonymous individuals, will wish to *deify* itself:

> The deification of the Established Order makes everything worldly. The Established Order can be completely right in asserting that, with respect to worldly matters, one must adhere to the Established Order, that one must be satisfied with what is relative, etc. But they finally come to make the God-relation worldly as well, wishing to make it conform to a certain relativity, in order that it not be essentially different from one's station in life, etc., instead of willing that *this* [the relation to God] *must be the Absolute for every person, must be precisely that which makes every Established Order tentative.*[57]

But, no matter how much modern society tries to deify itself and to repress "the Eternal," the repressed will return:

> Well-meaningly or in rage, our times even want to make the Eternal completely superfluous by means of a conjured-up imitation, which can never succeed in all Eternity, because the more one thinks one can harden

oneself to be able to dispense with the Eternal, the more one needs it deep down.⁵⁸

We must beware of these conjured-up imitations, these relentless, anonymous abstractions—"public opinion," "the public," "popular sovereignty," and so on—which have resulted from the modern triumph of a "pantheism [which] is an acoustic illusion which confuses *vox populi* and *vox dei*, an optical illusion which forms a cloud-image from the fogs of temporality, a mirage, cast by its own reflection, which claims to be Eternal."⁵⁹

Childhood's End

The present crisis is a crisis of coming of age, Kierkegaard writes. The Revolution of 1848 is a sign that we have come of age, with all the dangers and responsibilities of maturity. "The threads of intelligence snapped in '48; the whine which heralds chaos was heard."⁶⁰ Because they were able to overthrow the unconditional authority of the antiquated, hierarchical *ancien regime*, people now think that they can do without "the Unconditioned" (i.e., the absolute authority of God) altogether:

> If (to stay with my theme, the religious) if the human race, or a large number of individuals in the race, have outgrown the childlike stage in which another person can represent the Unconditioned for them—well, even so, for this very reason the Unconditioned cannot be dispensed with; indeed, it is all the less possible to dispense with it.⁶¹

We have come of age, and the popular-sovereignty *Gesellschaft* is both appropriate and inevitable, but this only makes it all the more necessary that each person relate individually to God.

As he approaches his attack on Christendom, Kierkegaard seems to see an increasingly apt and powerful image in the idea of coming of age, of childhood's end. The common people have become "knowing" about the worldly purposes to which Christianity has been put in Christendom, and "in our time" (that is, in the time of popular sovereignty and "The People's Church") it is dangerous to maintain any longer the pretense of their ignorance. ⁶²

> There have been times when this way of proclaiming Christianity was less offensive—even if it were not praiseworthy, which it never is—times, namely, when the congregation was less knowing, less aware of the relationship between a striving for that which is infinite and that which is finite. . . . As things now are, a preacher of Christianity cannot come to any openness or good conscience vis-à-vis *the all-too-knowing congregation* without making it apparent which is which, whether it is the finite or the infinite which he wills.⁶³

The coming of age of the common people in this time of popular government makes it mandatory to sort out and disentangle the proper spheres of what is relative and what is absolute, of the political and the religious. Continuing the metaphor about the end of childhood, Kierkegaard tells us that the situation in post-absolutist Denmark is similar to the problem of talking to a now-grown-up child about sexuality. The kind of circumlocution and picturesque language that was "modesty" for an adult to use when the child was young and innocent is now no longer modesty, but is "the most corrupt and corrupting sort of immorality":

> The dangerous situation is, when the congregation is knowing, and when the preacher is knowing, and when each knows that the other knows—then, not to say it, to wish to keep things in a higher, more ceremonious tone, the truth of which is a shared secret—this is what is dangerous and demoralizing.[64]

The human race has "grown up" in modern times, and it is essential that we take our maturity seriously and take it all the way. This means realizing that true Christianity is not for children: "The truth is that one cannot become a Christian as a child. . . . According to the New Testament, becoming a Christian presupposes a completely human existence, presupposes what, in the natural sense, one might call man's *maturity*."[65] Thus, as mentioned earlier, for Kierkegaard, as for Marx, the present, terrible as it appears, is the human race's breakthrough into the challenge of maturity.

"I AM HUMAN HONESTY"

The human race, Kierkegaard tells us, is now lost in confusion. We have jumbled together the finite and the infinite, the temporal and the eternal, so that "the situation is an impenetrable ambiguity."[66] In our confusion we have built a sort of modern Tower of Babel, a popular-sovereignty *Gesellschaft* that is stabilized and legitimized by its amalgamation with the watered-down Christianity of the People's Church. We are intoxicated, "drunk in the sensory illusion that this mild doctrine, that this, is true Christianity."[67] Therefore, we must become "sober," and the way to sobriety is "honesty," that is, the "humbling admission" that the mild religiosity by which we have tranquilized our society and ourselves is not the Christianity of the New Testament.[68]

"What do I want?" Kierkegaard asks. "Very simply, I want honesty. . . . I am neither mildness nor strictness. I am human honesty."[69] Kierkegaard's task is to reveal, honestly and "recklessly" [*hensynsløst*], what the real Christian requirement is and what the actual situation is in Danish society.[70] Kierkegaard stresses repeatedly that he wants neither "mildness" nor "pietistic strictness," but rather "human honesty" and the "confession" of our shortcomings, in order "to bring, if possible, some more truth into these . . . imperfect existences such as we lead; and this is something, anyway, and is in any case the first condition for coming to exist as more capable beings."⁷¹ Thus, "honesty" and "an admission" that Christianity is "the Ideal" are what we need now, when "being a Christian has become a nothing, a joke, something which everyone automatically is, something one attains more easily than the most insignificant skill. Truly, it is high time that the requirements of the Ideal were heard."⁷² "Thus, one or the other: *Either* there must be a real renunciation . . . or [there must be] a confession that this sort of preaching is not really Christianity."⁷³

The point of Kierkegaard's repeated insistence upon "honesty" and "human honesty" is that it enables him to take a stance that is not peculiarly Christian; Kierkegaard's call for "honesty" is easily defended, because it is on the shared ground of secularism, the terrain appropriate to the modern, liberal *Gesellschaft*. We do not have the right to demand true Christianity, with its renunciation and sacrifice, of one another, Kierkegaard writes, but we do have the right to demand honesty of one another, and no "honest" person can object that Kierkegaard is being too strict.⁷⁴

Indeed, so serious and consistent is Kierkegaard about the matter of honesty that he repeatedly insists that honest atheism is to be preferred to the "official Christianity" of modern Denmark. If "the times wish, honestly, genuinely, unreservedly, openly to make a straightforward revolt against Christianity," Kierkegaard says, "I can go along with it," but he cannot go along with the charade of "official Christianity," with its dishonest claim of being "the Christianity of the New Testament."⁷⁵ At least the free thinker is an honest man—even God thinks so: "It is infinitely dearer to God in Heaven that you honestly admit that you are not and do not wish to be a Christian, than this loathsome situation, in which to worship God is to make a fool of Him."⁷⁶

"My Task Has a Double Direction"

Because the drunkenness and confusion of the present day are rooted not merely in the individual but in the peculiarly powerful social institutions of the modern *Gesellschaft*, Kierkegaard explains, "[my] task has a double direction": (1) to help dispel the "sensory illusion" within the individual as to what Christianity is; (2) and to attack the governmental and social apparatus that perpetuates these illusions.⁷⁷ Thus we have an outer task (politics) as well as an inner one, or, as Kierkegaard puts it, while we work on the problem "psychically," we must also work on it "physically."⁷⁸ This is why—in a move that otherwise would be uncharacteristic of him—Kierkegaard enters the political arena during the attack on Christendom that marked the final phase of his career. The emergence of the modern *Gesellschaft* left him no choice.

Taking Secularism Seriously: "Fresh Air" Instead of "Christendom"

The purpose of Kierkegaard's foray into the political arena was to drive home to post-1848 society a very simple message: the market-based, liberal-individualistic, popular sovereignty state must take seriously the secularism of its own foundations. "Official Christianity" is out of place in a liberal-democratic society. "The People's Church" is an abomination and a contradiction in terms.

Kierkegaard calls unambiguously for the complete and final separation of church and state, a position much more radical than most 1848 liberals had been able to countenance, even those on the left.[79] They had been afraid of the 1848 slogan, "A free Church in a free State," and had colluded with the old establishment conservatives to contrive the continuation of the old, composite Christendom under the guise of "the People's Church." It is clear that this fear of genuine secularization derived from the parallel fear—shared by liberals and conservatives alike—of the post-1848 ascendancy of "the common man" (*den menige Mand*), whose turn to rule had arrived. In its attempt to evade the full cultural and political consequences of the post-1848 era by retaining Christendom as a guarantor of social solidarity and cultural continuity, liberalism had been dishonest with itself.

This was where Kierkegaard found his *entré*, insisting that "the official worship of God" is "a falsity, a fake"—and that therefore we must boycott it, and at the least put a stop to "making a fool of God."[80] "Whoever you are, consider this: Flee the guidance of the priests at all costs. . . . Flee them, they are fooling you out of Eternity."[81] Therefore, we must turn the preaching of Christianity into a voluntary, private matter—"this is the only true Christian requirement, and also the only reasonable thing."[82] We try all kinds of superficial remedies for the Church, Kierkegaard tells us. We try new hymnals, altar rituals, and so on, when the sickness is in the structure itself, as in a cholera-ridden hospital building, and the only solution is to tear the structure down.[83] Christianity needs "a divorce": "What Christianity needs is not the smothering protection of the State. No, it needs fresh air."[84] This, in short, is Kierkegaard's political argument: The liberal-individualist *Gesellschaft* must live by "fresh air." It must embrace the secularism, the voluntarism, and "the individual" that constitute its foundation.[85]

"The Individual"

Thus, if the modern liberal era is to be honest with itself, its category is, and must be, "the individual." "If order is to be maintained in existence . . . attention must be given first and foremost to the fact that every person is an individual person, and becomes aware of himself as an individual person."[86] Things may have been different in the past. However, "the situation of these times" makes it clear that we have to combat

> an immoral confusion which wishes, with the assistance of "humankind" or fantastical social categories [i.e., the various "conjured-up imitations of the Eternal" that our anonymous society provides], to demoralize the individual philosophically and socially; it is a confusion which wishes to teach ungodly disdain for that which is the first condition for all religiosity, namely, being an individual person.[87]

Individuation is the diametric opposite of the deification of the Established Order; "the [human] race" subtly abolishes God as ruler, while the person who insists on referring to people as "individuals" (*Enkelte*) is a rebel in God's name against this usurpation.[88] The leveling of the present age is not the work of any individual. It is an abstraction, and "it can only be stopped if the individual, in individual differentiation, wins the fearlessness of the religious."[89] Radical individualism is the only suitable posture for the present age. It is not permissible, in Kierkegaard's view, to employ groups or leaders even to combat these same social constellations, such as "Christendom" and so on. This is the age of the *Gesellschaft*; it is the great test, which will make or break the individual.

> [I]t must not be as in the past, when individuals, as soon as things began to become dizzying to them, could look to the nearest great man in order to orient themselves. This is past; they must either become lost in the dizziness of abstract infinity, or be saved infinitely in the essentiality of the religious. . . . This development is, however, progress, because all the individuals who are saved win the specific gravity of the religious, win its essentiality first-hand from God. Then the word will be: "See, everything is ready. See the terribleness of abstraction which makes finitude reveal itself, disappointingly, as itself. See the chasm of the infinite open up. See the sharp scythe of leveling forcing everyone to jump over the blade. See, the God waits! So leap, then, into the embrace of divinity!"[90]

This is Kierkegaard's venture into politics, but that is not to say that "the individual" is itself a political category. No, "'the individual' is the category of spirit, of the awakening of spirit, as opposite to politics as is indeed possible."[91] (As we have seen, the category of politics, of "the principle of association," is the group, and it is valid only for the attainment of relative ends, for such purposes of material prudence as street lighting, public water supply, and so on, and must not aim at any absolute purpose or lay claim to any ultimate meaning.) In conformity with the new liberal *Gesellschaft*, Kierkegaard agrees that the fundamental unit of society is indeed "the individual," but first of all and most fundamentally this individual exists "before God": "[T]hose who confess are not together in a society; each is as an individual before God."[92] Therefore, Kierkegaard explains, it has been the goal of his entire authorship "to *come to* simplicity. The movement is *from* the Public *to* 'the individual.' *Religiously understood*, there is indeed no Public, but only individuals."[93]

THE DISCOVERY OF ONE'S "NEIGHBOR"

But Kierkegaard's insistence upon "the individual" as the appropriate unit for the modern age does not mean that he promotes solipsistic self-absorption, for it is only as an "individual" before God that we first experience our "Neighbor."[94] In the self-interested individualism of Ishmael in the market-based *Gesellschaft*, the other person is an object to be manipulated for one's private gain. At best, the other person is perhaps a friend or the object of romantic love (*Elskov*), who is cherished for the special qualities he or she possesses as "the only one" in relation to the lover; the other person is not seen or loved in his/her own right, but only egoistically, as "the second I." It is only when one has become "an individual before God" that one is capable of seeing the other person as one's Neighbor, as "the first person you see," as "the first Thou" rather than the "second I." [95]

Kierkegaard deliberately develops the category of "the Neighbor" as a foil to Ishmael-style worldly relationships, which have never been more crass than they have become in the present. Modern society claims to establish equality, Kierkegaard notes, but "'the Neighbor' is the absolutely true expression for human equality" (*Menneske-Lighed*, which also means "humanity").[96] The Neighbor is the category of true Christianity, which is the only representative of "the universally human" (*det Almene-Menneskelige*); all groups within society represent something less, because they "deny one's kinship to all people, to every person unconditionally," and therefore such groups cannot participate in "the Good."[97] The Neighbor is thus the category of genuine Love (*Kjerlighed*), and the loving individual, of course, behaves in a manner diametrically opposed to the selfish mistrustfulness and misanthropy of the modern Ishmael: "Love believes all, and yet is never deceived."[98] "Love builds up" by seeing Love beneath the uncongenial appearance of one's Neighbor, by building up the presence of Love in the Neighbor—which can be done because Love is really there in every Neighbor, "like the sprout within the seed"—because God put it there.[99]

Thus the individualism that Kierkegaard finds so absolutely necessary in the modern age is not an exclusive, self-interested individualism at all. The highest Good—loving one's Neighbor in one's equality with one's Neighbor before God—differs from the worldly goods of the market society in that the latter can only be enjoyed exclusively, while the Good "is the greatest thing. You can have it in common with all."[100] Kierkegaard's individualism is tailored to modern individualistic society, but it is anything but asocial. Under all its fine talk of "society" and "the people," it is the self-interested individualism of the modern *Gesellschaft* that is truly asocial.

Living in the World: "Contemporaneity" and the "Traveler"

The way out of the modern age is not to flee it, but to go through it, to live as "a traveler,"[101] to be *in* the present age but not *of* it, to exist "before God" as "an individual" who is historically in the present but who is also "contemporaneous" with Christ. The most anyone can do for another person is to point out the necessity of living in this fashion. No one—and certainly not the keepers of Christendom—can live for anyone else: "Every generation has to begin from scratch with Christ. . . . And therefore being a Christian in Christendom is as different from being a Christian in contemporaneity with Christ as heathendom is from Christianity."[102]

Kierkegaard as "Gadfly": "Fear and Trembling"

Kierkegaard writes that the world needs "a smart aleck" (*Peer Næsviis*), whose task it is to remind the Established Order of its own limited competence. Such a person

> may well be the "gadfly" which the Establishment needed in order not to fall asleep, or to fall into self-deification, which is worse. Every person must live in fear and trembling, and therefore no Established Order may be free of fear and trembling. Fear and trembling means that everyone is becoming, and every individual, also including the race, is and must be conscious of being in becoming. And fear and trembling means that there is a God, which no individual and no Established Order dare forget for an instant.[103]

This "smart aleck" and "gadfly" role is, concretely, *Søren Kierkegaard's* way of being a Neighbor in the post-1848 world, and his repeated invocation of "fear and trembling" is certainly calculated to call into mind his earlier depiction of Abraham as the archetypical "individual" who exists "before God." For the purposes of this chapter, Abraham also forms the perfect counterpart to Ishmael, who is the miserable symbol of the present age.

To return, in closing, to our title, Melville ends *Moby Dick* with "Ishmael," our narrator, as the solitary survivor, struggling amid the wreckage of the *Pequod*:

> [G]aining that vital centre, the black bubble upward burst; and now, liberated by reason of its cunning spring, and, owing to its great buoyancy, rising with great force, the coffin life-buoy shot lengthwise from

the sea, fell over, and floated by my side. Buoyed up by that coffin, for almost one whole day and night, I floated on a soft and dirge-like main. The unharming sharks, they glided by as if with padlocks on their mouths; the savage sea-hawks sailed with sheathed beaks. On the second day, a sail drew near, nearer, and picked me up at last. It was the devious-cruising *Rachel*, that in her retracing search after her missing children, only found another orphan.

It is of course Kierkegaard's principal disagreement with Melville that, although we are individuals in the modern world, we need be neither Ishmaels nor orphans.

Notes

1. Adam Smith, *The Wealth of Nations*, ed. Edwin Cannan (New York: Random House, 1937), p. 14
2. John Locke, *The Second Treatise of Government*, ed. Thomas P. Peardon (Indianapolis, IN: Bobbs-Merrill, 1952), pp. 53–54.
3. Ferdinand Tönnies, *Community and Society (Gemeinschaft und Gesellschaft)*, trans. and ed. Charles P. Loomis (East Lansing, MI: Michigan State University Press, 1957), pp. 64–65.
4. Tönnies, p. 234. Emphasis added.
5. Karl Marx, *The Marx-Engels Reader*, 2nd ed., ed. Robert C. Tucker (New York: W. W. Norton, 1978), p. 213.
6. Ibid., p. 476.
7. Ibid., p. 488.
8. Ibid., p. 777.
9. Ibid., p. 476.
10. Ibid., p. 482.
11. Ibid., p. 475.
12. Ibid., p. 65.
13. Ibid.
14. Ibid., p. 160.
15. Ibid., p. 84.
16. See Michele Nicoletti's chapter in this volume for a clear account of Kierkegaard's claims about the limitations of the political sphere. [This and all other cross references to articles in the present volume, as well as some other references, have been added by the editors.]
17. *Søren Kierkegaards Samlede Værker* (The Collected Works of Søren Kierkegaard), 14 vols., 1st ed., ed. A.B. Drachmann, J. L. Heiberg, and H. O. Lange, (Copenhagen: Gyldendal, 1901–6). Volume VIII, p. 76. All further quotations from Kierkegaard except for those from the *Papirer* will be from this edition, and volume and page number will be cited. All translations are by the present author.
18. Kierkegaard, VIII, p. 86.
19. Ibid., p. 79.
20. Ibid., p. 60.
21. Ibid., p. 233.

22. *Søren Kierkegaards Papirer* (The Papers of Søren Kierkegaard), 13 vols. in 22 tomes, ed. P. A. Heiberg, V. Kuhr, and E. Torsting, 2nd augmented edition by N. Thulstrup, index by N. J. Cappelørn (Copenhagen: Gyldendal, 1968–78), VIII, 1 A 598, p. 276. All *Papirer* translations are by the present author.
23. Kierkegaard, VIII, pp. 402–3.
24. Ibid., XI, p. 232.
25. Ibid., p. 89.
26. Ibid., X, p. 18.
27. Ibid., XIV, p. 36.
28. Ibid., XI, p. 157.
29. Ibid., X, pp. 24–25.
30. Ibid., XI, p. 214.
31. Ibid., X, p. 183.
32. Ibid., XII, p. 385. That such shrewdness was equated with rationality casts important light on Kierkegaard's supposed irrationalism. Compare on this point the chapters in this volume by Westphal and Ziolkowski.
33. Kierkegaard, XIV, p. 246.
34. Ibid., XII, p. 467.
35. Ibid., XI, p. 153.
36. Ibid., VIII, p. 82.
37. Ibid., p. 83.
38. Ibid., XIII, p. 555.
39. Ibid., XI, p. 139.
40. Ibid., p. 156.
41. Ibid., p. 140. Emphasis added.
42. Ibid., VIII, p. 103.
43. Ibid., IX, p. 223.
44. Ibid., VIII, p. 99.
45. Ibid., XIII, p. 592n.
46. Ibid., pp. 439–40.
47. Ibid., pp. 595–96.
48. Ibid., p. 592n.
49. Ibid., p. 439.
50. Ibid., XIV, pp. 121–22 (paraphrase).
51. Ibid., p. 122.
52. Ibid., XIII, p. 438. Emphasis added. However, to say that politics and Christianity shouldn't be confounded with each other is not to say they have nothing to do with each other. See, for example, *Papirer* X 3 A 679. The implication is that the state is only able to be truly a state (i.e., a useful but limited, relative institution) when its members are aware that they exist before the Absolute (God) and so refuse to absolutize/deify the state. Westphal expands on this point in his chapter in this volume, as does Nicoletti.
53. Kierkegaard, XIV, p. 46.
54. Ibid., p. 43.
55. Ibid., XII, p. 159.
56. Ibid., p. 88. Emphasis added.
57. Ibid., p. 86. Emphasis added.
58. Ibid., XIII, p. 590.
59. Ibid., p. 609. Note how Westphal, in this volume, argues that religion can itself be one of these conjured-up imitations.

60. Kierkegaard, XIII, p. 508. For further discussions of the political, social, and economic situation in Denmark in Kierkegaard's time, see Bruce Kirmmse, *Kierkegaard in Golden Age Denmark* (Bloomington, IN: Indiana University Press, 1990).
61. Kierkegaard, XIII, p. 509.
62. Ibid., XII, p. 404.
63. Ibid., pp. 410–11. Emphasis added.
64. Ibid., p. 411.
65. Ibid., XIV, p. 253. Emphasis added.
66. Ibid., XII, p. 402.
67. Ibid., p. 418.
68. Ibid., p. 320.
69. Ibid., XIV, p. 52.
70. Ibid., p. 53.
71. Ibid., XIII, p. 506.
72. Ibid., XII, p. 64.
73. Ibid., p. 412.
74. Ibid., p. 418.
75. Ibid., XIV, pp. 54–55.
76. Ibid., p. 111.
77. Ibid., p. 119.
78. Ibid., p. 120.
79. This point introduces an important qualification to Michael Plekon's argument that Kierkegaard is a theologian of the Church. While Plekon is right to see Kierkegaard as speaking from a position of orthodoxy, one that is in spiritual affinity with the true church, this must not be taken as an endorsement of an official, established church. To use the sociologist's language of church and sect, while Kierkegaard is no sectarian, he is no friend of an established church that identifies itself with the temporal status quo. On this point Kierkegaard's motivations are recognizably similar to some of the radical Protestant reformers. (Editors' note.)
80. Kierkegaard, XIV, p. 86.
81. Ibid., p. 310.
82. Ibid., p. 161.
83. Ibid., p. 170.
84. Ibid.
85. Compare with Dietrich Bonhoeffer's thoughts on coming of age in his *Letters and Papers from Prison* (New York: Macmillan, 1972), pp. 327, 329, 361.
86. Kierkegaard, XI, p. 227.
87. Ibid., XIII, p. 603.
88. Ibid., X, p. 213.
89. Ibid., VIII, p. 81.
90. Ibid., pp. 100–01.
91. Ibid., XIII, p. 607.
92. Ibid., VIII, p. 239.
93. Ibid., XIII, p. 499.
94. See on this point the chapters by Louise Carroll Keeley and Wanda Warren Berry in this volume.
95. Kierkegaard, IX, pp. 47–62.
96. Ibid., XIII, p. 597.
97. Ibid., IX, pp. 74–75.

98. Ibid., pp. 216–34.
99. Ibid., pp. 201–15, especially p. 210.
100. Ibid., p. 31.
101. Ibid., X, p. 35.
102. Ibid., XII, p. 102. Also see Stephen Dunning, this volume, on the concept of contemporaneity.
103. Kierkegaard, XII, p. 84.

11 Politics and Religion in Kierkegaard's Thought: Secularization and the Martyr

MICHELE NICOLETTI

TOWARD A HERMENEUTICS OF KIERKEGAARD'S THOUGHT ON POLITICS

It is not easy to approach the social and political dimension of Kierkegaard's thought. There are two risks involved in the operation, as some of the best-known critics have shown.

One risk is to situate Kierkegaard at all costs within the political sphere and either refer to the rare passages in which he expresses his social and political evaluations with a political or ideological bias, or try to draw from his work his personal political position *vis-à-vis* the events of his time. In so doing, it is too easy to dismiss Kierkegaard's position as conservative—a position basically incapable of grasping the positive meaning of nineteenth century liberalism and democracy.

One may recall, in this regard, Lukács's opinions on the Kierkegaardian "single individual" as a supporter of conservatism and reaction.[1] Alternatively, yet differently and less ideologically, one may recall Adorno on the dissolution of history, exteriority, and objectivity attained by Kierkegaard's incapacity to free himself from the bourgeois *interieur*.[2]

The second possible risk is to evaluate Kierkegaard's thought by comparing its social and political aspects with other nineteenth century philosophical trends that were critical of contemporary society and culture. Such parallels, imposed from the outside, may lead us to miss the specificity of Kierkegaard's thought and force it into a deterministic derivation from the historical condition of his time.

One instance of this faulty approach is given by Löwith's classic interpretation. Löwith establishes a parallelism between Marx's critique of bourgeois society and Kierkegaard's critique of bourgeois Christianity.[3]

The only hermeneutical approach to Kierkegaard's thought that can truly appreciate his contribution to reflection on society and politics is one that places itself inside Kierkegaard's own thinking, taking into account the peculiar "point of view" of his activity as a writer—a point of view he explicitly acknowledged as "religious."[4] Hence, what is interesting in Kierkegaard is not a political stand or a philosophy of politics but only a consideration of politics—through fragments and intuitions—from a religious point of view, with a specific reference to the relationships between politics and religion.[5] In Kierkegaard's thought it is not really possible to find a true philosophy of politics. Politics itself is considered as something outside his interests, as he ironically underlines: "Politics is too much for me. I love to focus my attention on lesser things, in which one may sometimes encounter exactly the same."[6]

THE DEPOLITICIZATION OF RELIGION

Kierkegaard's first concern with regard to the relation between politics and religion is to state the existence of a qualitative difference between these two realities. He appears at first to separate them completely. Generally speaking, this is the same difference he vigorously asserts between the finite and the infinite, which—on an actual historical level—reflects the difference between the state and Christianity. Such a difference becomes apparent when the various relationships these two realities establish within human existence are examined.

On the one hand, the state considers humans only quantitatively, with respect to their pure force and power. From a political point of view people are important since they can "count"; hence politics makes the greatest effort to acquire the consent of the greatest number of individuals. On the other hand, religion considers the single individual, aside from his or her force and power, as a unique entity. The aim of religion is the salvation of the soul, and from this perspective the only significant power is God's power. Humans are powerless; rather, before God, every person must recognize his or her impotence. Politics and religion therefore follow inverse logics. Kierkegaard writes in this regard:

> Political and religious actions have an inverse relation. Political action is preoccupied with having the masses on its side; religious action attempts to have God on its side and therefore it can disregard the force of the number. . . . From a religious perspective, I have to serve a religious cause, and, above all, to keep myself away from politics and from political considerations.[7]

The difference between politics and religion consists in their different relations to the world. Politics wants to triumph in temporality, because time is its proper dimension. Politics plans, regulates, and governs human life in and for temporality. On this level, which is the level of finitude, the realization of an idea is so important that the means and the instruments to be used become indifferent; the form of the realization is not so important. From a political perspective the result is the main thing; therefore the criterion is efficacy. To succeed is more important than "how" one succeeds.

Such logic can by no means apply to religion. When the criterion of success—of quantitative results, of power—is applied to religion, its essence becomes empty and worldly. Kierkegaard's thought is very clear on this point. Religion cannot serve its cause, the salvation of souls, following a secular logic, that is, the logic of power, the logic of triumphing in temporality. The conversion of man cannot be realized by political majorities or by governments.

Kierkegaard's condemnation of any mingling of politics and religion is derived from these premises. For example, he sharply opposed a state church during the last years of his life.[8] His rejection of any political contamination of religion—that is, of any "ecclesiastical politics"—was so radical that his critique involved not only the traditional state church of Bishop Mynster, but also those reformists who fought for reconciling Christianity with national spirit, Grundtvig being the most notable example. Although Grundtvig was different from Mynster, his position was still characterized by an attachment to earthly things and as such can be characterized as a worldly religion.[9]

According to Kierkegaard, then, the logic of religion is opposed to that of politics, as Christ's behavior shows.[10] For religious existence to be authentic it must "repeat" the logic of the Cross. Authentic religion operates in the world in the form of the sacrifice of the self and is preoccupied with repeating the teaching and the example of Christ, who has saved the world through his personal sacrifice. On the contrary, the dimension of "success," so important for political action, has no value within the religious sphere. With regard to faith, success depends on God; in order to succeed, God does not compromise. God wants to sacrifice neither a single person nor a single part of the truth. Since success transcends human capability, the most important thing becomes how to achieve one's purpose. The essence of authentic religion lies in every person living his or her actions authentically.[11]

Even the respective virtues of politics and religion are different. In political affairs, in order to achieve a successful result, calculation of probabilities and prudence have predominant importance; in religion, however, it is most important to be able to risk everything with no calculation of the odds.[12]

With these considerations, Kierkegaard presents politics and religion as two separate realms in mutual opposition. Between them there seems to be and must be no point of contact, because every connection between politics and religion creates confusion. Kierkegaard has severe things to say on this issue. With regard to Jesus' maxim, "Render therefore unto Caesar the things which are Caesar's and unto God the things which are God's" (Matthew 22:15–22), his comment is: "Christ clearly means this: 'If you want to be a Christian, then snap your fingers first and foremost and above all at politics.'"[13]

The authentic religious attitude seems to be the complete separation of politics from Christianity in order to "purify" faith of earthly incrustations as much as possible. This is why, at a time when the motto "politics is everything" was becoming popular, Kierkegaard wanted to reestablish the difference between the two dimensions:

> In these times politics is everything. Between this and the religious view the difference is heaven-wide (*toto caelo*), as also the point of departure and the ultimate aim differ from it *toto caelo*, since politics begins on earth and remains on earth, whereas religion, deriving its beginning from above, seeks to explain and transfigure and thereby exalt the earthly to heaven.[14]

THE THEOLOGICAL CLAIM OF POLITICS

Such a sharp separation between politics and religion, however, does not exhaust the relation between the two spheres for Kierkegaard. As Gregor Malantschuk wrote:

> Kierkegaard asserts the unconditioned dissimilarity between the political and the religious. The political—and the same holds for the social—has its goal within finitude. The religious points toward an eternal reality. These two spheres must never be confused. But the fact that they are completely dissimilar and must not be confused does not mean that they are not to interact.[15]

Actually, the relation between politics and religion is very similar to that between reason and faith, since politics is nothing else but the practical application of reason to social life. Hence, by analogy, from the relationship between faith and reason we can derive some indications as to the relationship between faith and politics.

Kierkegaard's fight against reason is not against reason as such but rather against the absolute claims of reason, a reason that poses itself as a supreme power, capable of explaining everything and solving all contradictions within its own dialectics.[16] Thus the first task of faith is that of unmasking the totalizing claims of reason.

Like reason, which wants to have unlimited power, politics wants to achieve human happiness and even human salvation. By a close examination of this issue, we can determine the ground of Kierkegaard's opinion about politics: the society of his time wanted to solve by itself the question of the meaning of existence and refused to accept any limits. This was a eudaimonistic and rationalistic dream; politics governed by reason wished not only to solve the problems of finitude but also to guarantee human beatitude. Kierkegaard does not condemn politics as such, only its absoluteness—the extension of politics beyond its limits.

The modern age, which Kierkegaard saw as culminating in the social and political movements of 1848, eliminated the difference between politics and religion and lived under the illusion that it was possible to anticipate eternity in time and to realize heaven on earth. Kierkegaard recognized in politics the new religion of his time: "the whole modern mentality can be reduced to that damned caricature of religion, which is represented by politics."[17] In other words, politics is a masked religion.

By this judgment Kierkegaard shows himself once again to be an acute observer of his time. In fact, it was typical of nineteenth century European thought to coat political reality with religious characteristics; suffice it to mention the sacred aura that surrounded the century's political myth *par excellence*—the nation. All over Europe the nation is sacred and those who die for it are called martyrs of the fatherland. As we can see, this is religious language applied to political reality, an apparent sign that the secularization process that followed the French Revolution cannot be solely interpreted as the separation of the political from the religious; it is also an attempt by political action to co-opt those characteristics that previously were exclusively religious. The secularization of nineteenth century politics tendentially implicates also the sacralization of politics itself. In these years various authors showed an awareness of this theological kernel of politics, particularly socialists and anarchists such as Proudhon and Bakunin, as well as counter-revolutionaries such as Donoso Cortés.[18] This issue becomes evident, for example, in relation to the problem of social equality. Considering everything from a religious point of view, Kierkegaard believes that ideal human equality is not realizable in time, because temporality is dominated by the interaction between human freedom and historical necessity. Therefore, temporality is the dimension within which diversity is dominant. As Kierkegaard says, human equality is realizable only before God, in the sense that every person has the same possibility to save his or her soul.

> Throughout Europe people have *in a worldly way*, with ever-increasing velocity of passion, lost themselves in problems which can be solved *only in a godly way*, which only Christianity can solve, and *has* solved long ago. . . . All men (wish) to solve the problem *of likeness and equality* between man and man in the medium of worldliness, i.e. in the medium the nature of which is difference and inequality.[19]

In his struggle against the confusion between politics and religion, Kierkegaard himself does not distinguish the different levels of the problem of equality and confuses ideal equality with social equality. He condemns the struggle for equality (i.e., the communist movement) and exposes himself to the charge of legitimating the social discriminations of his time. This position can certainly be influenced by his fear of losing his own property rights,[20] but it cannot be explained by such fear; it is more deeply rooted, once again, in religion. What Kierkegaard fears most is the emergence of a mass society that abolishes every qualitative criterion and allows the force of numbers to prevail:

> The idea of equality will be regarded as up for debate; equality has now become a question discussed throughout Europe. Consequently every one of the older forms of tyranny will now be powerless (emperor, kin, nobility, clergy, even money-tyranny). But another form of tyranny is a corollary of equality—fear of men. . . . Of all the tyrannies, it is the most dangerous, in part because it is not directly obvious and attention must be called to it.[21]

According to Kierkegaard the roots of this totalizing claim of politics, which has eventually determined the predominance of the logic of numbers—the power of crowds—dwell in distant times. They do not simply derive either from the French Revolution or from the leveling effects of the emerging capitalist society. More deeply, Kierkegaard traces them to Luther and the role Luther ascribed to the principle in his reform.[22] Once political power is given the role of custodian of authentic religion, the shift to a political power that considers itself as representative of such reality is easy.

Besides discussing the deep origins of the totalizing claim of politics, Kierkegaard directs his critique against the new divinity of his time—the "crowd," the "public," the omnivorous and greedy monster that swallows and destroys everything. What matters is simply numbers, the majority complying with "public opinion." Any personal choice, any individual responsibility are dissolved. However, another clarification is due in this regard. If it is true that Kierkegaard may end up condemning democracy by condemning the principle of the number—popular sovereignty and election by majority—it is also true that his rejection is mostly related to his fear that such a principle will be extended to the ethical and religious as well. He is afraid one might end up deciding by vote what is the truth or whether God exists.[23] In fact, in other instances (that is to say, in the purely mundane sphere), Kierkegaard is ready to acknowledge the crowd's competency, "even decisive competency as a court of last resort."[24]

In any case, even if he assumes a conservative political position in face of the liberal, democratic, and socialist movements, Kierkegaard does not defend the existing privileges, unlike the aristocrats of his time. He acknowledges that these social movements would also produce positive effects on Christianity:

The conflict about Christianity will no longer be a doctrinal conflict (this is the conflict between orthodoxy and heterodoxy). The conflict (occasioned also by the social and communistic movements), will be about Christianity as an existence. The problem will become that of loving the "neighbor."[25]

The Contradictions of Modern Politics

Kierkegaard's hermeneutics is not exhausted by the mere identification of a theological kernel or by emphasizing the totalizing claim of modern politics. One of the most significant aspects of Kierkegaard's thought about politics is to be found in his forecast about the final development of the political movement of his age. He foresaw that the absoluteness of politics would produce a dissolution of politics itself, just as the absoluteness of finitude was to cause the dissolution of finitude itself. The illusion of a human, self-sufficient self-government, which is concealed in modern politics, will eventually show its contradictions. Those are rooted in modernity itself.[26]

The illusion of human self-sufficiency is based on a vision of the person as capable of infinity. The contradiction lies in posing such a self's opening to infinity as a political reality without taking into account the finitude of politics. Therefore, as soon as such a self appears on the political stage, it is condemned to failure; the political sphere cannot satisfy the needs of a being capable of infinity. As a consequence, the movement born on a political level must seek a response to its demands on other levels:

> The new development in our time cannot be political, because politics through the *representing* individual is dialectical in the relation between the generation and the individual, but in our time each individual is already on the way to being too reflective to be able to be content with merely being *represented*.[27]

Here we find another of Kierkegaard's profound intuitions concerning the political changes of the time. He was perfectly aware of the fact that, after the French Revolution, a shift from a political system in which the political unity of the people was "represented" by a sovereign (monarchy) to a system in which the people refuse to be represented and advocate a relation of "identity" with political unity (popular sovereignty) had taken place.[28] The people's refusal to be represented was soon to be extended, as 1848 showed, not only to monarchy but also to the earliest forms of representative democracy.

With the modern intensification of reflectivity, people have become so conscious of their eternal value that they refuse to be completely objectified and dissolved in another person—the representative. But as soon as one tries to assert directly and personally in history and in the world such eternal value, one does not find an adequate realization and either remains melancholic or rebels. In political reality this anxiety becomes frustrated and this subjectivity becomes ungovernable:

> For tyrants (in the form of emperors, kings, popes, Jesuits, generals, diplomats) have hitherto in a decisive moment been able to rule and direct the world . . . but from the moment the fourth estate came into the picture, it will be seen—even when the crisis has been overcome—that it is not possible to govern in a *worldly* way.[29]

What does Kierkegaard mean by this statement? Certainly he does not mean that a new sacralization of political power is necessary, or that a new theological legitimation of the social order is required. The process of secularization, which involves the worldliness of politics, is considered irreversible and to a certain extent even positive for the purification of Christianity. What Kierkegaard means is that the claim of sovereignty on the part of subjectivity involves demands that transcend politics itself. The process of secularization will create a new demand for religiosity: "the movement of our time, which appears to be purely political, will turn out suddenly to be religious or the need for religiosity."[30]

The problem of modernity is hidden within this process; modernity has recognized more completely than previous epochs that humans are capable of infinity, but modernity has at the same time rejected every type of infinity and has denied every infinity external to itself. Kierkegaard's answer to this problem is not a refusal of modernity. He does not take refuge in the past, at a time when the subject was not yet born and the sacred order was still the dominant one. He seeks an answer in the present, but he seeks one that follows a logic that is different from the dominant one. How is it possible to guarantee the government of the world, if a worldly government is necessarily going to fail and if a religious government is impractical in modern time? The only way to restore government in modernity is to give a place to "the single individual." Politics, but also religion on its part, has forgotten that the real existing subject is the single individual, and that this individual is the interlocutor as much of infinity as of finitude. This subjectivity cannot be canceled; the way out of the crisis is to make it deeper. First of all it is the single individual that has to be reformed: "Every reform which does not realize that the real problem is to reform every single individual, is *eo ipso* an illusion."[31]

It is interesting to note that Kierkegaard emphasizes the importance of the single individual for the world, not just for religious life. In the face of the process of secularization, of the domination of quantity, number, and crowd (nowadays we would say of technology) Kierkegaard's proposal is to reform the single individual rather than to escape from the world and to consign history to damnation. Only the single individual who lives in the world without confiding in it is able to govern the world at the decisive moment.

The necessary condition for such government is maximum detachment from the world. The political order needs someone who can detach himself from it and who has the courage to take responsibility for government. Precisely here lies the bourgeoisie's fault, in not having had the moral courage to use political power, believing that the "public" criteria were sufficient for government, in other words, by relying on market criteria. In so doing it has brought the state to its dissolution. What is politically needed, on the other hand, is precisely government.[32]

However, at this point a worldly government is no longer sufficient. What is necessary is an interior government, that of the single individual. This government is, of course, different from the government of worldly powers; the single individual governs not through force or through worldly success but through suffering. Here we have an instance of an inverse relationship between politics and religion that is treated dialectically. As politics relates itself inversely to religion, so religion must relate itself inversely to politics, not through a direct superiority but through a "suffering superiority."

THE MARTYR

The theme of "suffering superiority" leads us to the theme of the martyr. When it appears evident that a worldly government is impossible, "it will be seen that in the decisive moment only martyrs are able to rule the world."[33] The real government of reality is the one that respects the internal structure of reality. This means that the dialectical conflict between infinitude and finitude must not be solved through the elimination of one of the two poles. Mysticism wants to remove both finitude and politics; mundanity wants to remove infinity. To realize a real government it is necessary to retain the specificities of the two poles and their dialectical relation. The martyr is that person who is able to exist in her life with these differences, even when they are expressed in their extremities; she is prepared to die, rather than to betray not only the truth but also finitude. The martyr dies in the world, because she wants to "bear witness" to the truth *in* the world. The martyr maintains not only the importance of the truth but also the relevance of the world as the only place where a person has to live and can realize the truth.

This is the meaning of the phrase "only martyrs are able to rule the world." Martyrs are not those who are defeated by history but those who express authentic sovereignty over history—by refusing every form of absolutization of the political, they restore the world to itself. Kierkegaard recalls the example of Socrates:

The martyr's superiority consists in laying down his life. He conquers as the dead man who returns. The dead Socrates stopped the vortex, something the living Socrates was unable to do. But the living Socrates understood intellectually that only a dead man could conquer, as a sacrifice—and he understood ethically how to direct his whole life to becoming just that.[34]

It is quite interesting to see that in the 1930s many Lutheran and Catholic theologians, especially in Germany, found the inspiration for their opposition to the Nazi regime in Kierkegaard's thought. I want to recall the name of Erik Peterson, who wrote in 1937 a book with a Kierkegaardian title, *Zeuge der Wahrheit* (Witnesses to Truth),[35] devoted to the martyrs of the first centuries of Christianity. It is also significant to find the Kierkegaardian quotation of the "martyr's government" in the pages of the jurist, Carl Schmitt, where he revised his political choice after World War II and his support of Hitler in the 1930s.[36]

With reference to the "martyr's government" my thesis is that the qualitative dialectic that is peculiar to Kierkegaard's thought[37] can be applied even to the relation between politics and religion. In this dialectic finitude is not definitely annihilated but is restored within a new context. Abraham has his son Isaac back; in the same way, the single individual can have finitude restored.[38] This means that the single individual, while renouncing all power, can have a restoration of reality.[39] In this new reality the individual has been liberated from the absolutist pretensions of the world, even as the world has been liberated from the human will to domination. However, the destruction of the absolutist pretensions of politics, which is what religion does, does not mean the elimination of politics but rather its purification. After this event we can have politics back.

In this new stage of the dialectic there is no total reconciliation between politics and religion. Their difference is maintained, and with it the possibility of conflict. But a new sort of relation presents itself, which recalls an ancient analogy that was only partially lost. In this analogy politics is liberated from the condemnation that put it into the realm of pure force and power, and it can give space to love. Religion reveals itself not only as the negation of politics but also as a "transfiguration" of it:

> . . . the religious is the transfigured rendering of that which the politician has thought in his happiest moment, if so be that he truly loves what it is to be a man, and loves people really, although he is inclined to regard religion as too lofty and ideal to be practical. . . . But "unpractical" as he is, the religious man is nevertheless the transfigured rendering of the politician's fairest dream. No politics ever has, no politics ever can,

no worldliness ever can, think through or realize to its last consequence the thought of human equality.[40]

Notes

1. See the pages Lukács devotes to Kierkegaard in his chapter on the foundation of irrationalism in Georg Lukács, *Die Zerstörung der Vernunft* (Berlin: Aufbau Verlag, 1954). (English translation by Peter Palmer, *The Destruction of Reason*, London: Merlin Press, 1981.)
2. See T. W. Adorno, *Kierkegaard*, (Tübingen: Suhrkamp, 1933). (English translation by Robert Hullot-Kentor, *Construction of the Aesthetic*, Minneapolis: University of Minnesota Press, 1989.) It is necessary, however, to say that Adorno has also acknowledged Kierkegaard's great capacity—which puts him in the company of a few other thinkers of his time like Poe, Tocqueville, and Baudelaire—to foresee the radical changes capitalist society was to bring to human behavior.
3. See K. Löwith, *Von Hegel zu Nietzsche* (Zürich: Kohllammer, 1941). (English translation by David E. Green, *From Hegel to Nietzsche*, New York: Holt, Rinehart & Winston, 1964.)
4. See Søren Kierkegaard, *The Point of View for My Work as an Author* (New York: Harper and Row, 1962).
5. Significant contributions to this issue are A. Hügli, "Kierkegaard und der Kommunismus," in *Kierkegaardiana* 9(1974): 220–47; G. Malantschuk, *Den kontroversielle Kierkegaard* (Copenhagen: Vinten, 1976) (translated as *The Controversial Kierkegaard*, H. V. - E. H. Hong (Waterloo, Ontario: Wilfrid Laurier University Press, 1980); S. Spera, *Introduzione a Kierkegaard* (Bari: Editori Laterza, 1983); K. M. Kodalle, *Die Eroberung des Nutzenlose* (Paderborn: F. Schöningh, 1988).
6. Søren Kierkegaard, *Breve og Akstykker vedrørende Sören Kierkegaard*, ed. N. H. Thulstrup (Copenhagen: Munksgaard, 1953–1954); *Letters and Documents*, trans. H. Rosenmeier (Princeton, NJ: Princeton University Press, 1978), no. 184 (August 1848), p. 253.
7. *Søren Kierkegaards Papirer*, 13 vols. in 22 tomes, ed. P. A. Heiberg, V. Kuhr, and E. Torsting, 2nd augmented ed. by N. Thulstrup (Copenhagen: Gyldendal, 1968–1978), XI 2 A 413.
8. See Søren Kierkegaard, *Attack on Christendom*, trans. Walter Lowrie (Princeton, NJ: Princeton University Press, 1968).
9. See S. Holm, *Grundtvig und Kierkegaard. Parallelen und Kontrasten* (Copenhagen: Nyt Nordisk Forlag, 1956). Kierkegaard states very clearly that the religious renovation he advocated is by no means an outer renovation to be realized through political or institutional transformations; rather, it is solely and uniquely an interior renovation (see, among other passages, Kierkegaard's answer to Rudelbach published in *Faedrelandet*, no. 26 [January 31, 1851]).
10. See Søren Kierkegaard, *Training in Christianity*, trans. Walter Lowrie (Princeton, NJ: Princeton University Press, 1941). Interesting for this argument, is the passage in which Kierkegaard describes the reaction of the "careful statesman" to Christ's message.
11. See *Papirer*, X 3 A 696.

12. On this point Kierkegaard writes: "Politics is: never venturing more than is possible at any moment, never beyond human probability. Christianity is: wherever there is no venturing beyond the probable, God is unconditionally not along; this of course, does not mean that he is along—wherever there is a venturing beyond the probable" (*Papirer*, XI 1 A 502).
13. *Papirer*, IX A 353.
14. Søren Kierkegaard, "The Individual," in *The Point of View for My Work as an Author*, p. 107.
15. G. Malantschuk, *The Controversial Kierkegaard*, p. 16.
16. See *Papirer*, X 4 A 581.
17. Ibid., X 4 A 84. See also *Papirer*, I A 285:

    Since every development, in my opinion, is finished only with its own parody, it will soon become apparent that politics is the parody in the development of the world—first of all, genuine mythology (God's side), next, human mythology (man's side), and then a realization of the world's aim in the world (as the highest), as a sort of Chiliasm, which meanwhile brings the individual politicians, carried away by abstract ideas, into contradiction with themselves.

18. See Pierre J. Proudhon, *Confessions d'un revolutionnaire* (Paris: Garnier Freres, 1851); M. Bakunin, *Dieu et l'Elat* (Geneva, 1902) (English translation by Carlos Cafiero and Elisee Reclus, *God and the State*, Freeport, NY: Books for Libraries Press, 1971); J. Donoso Cortés, *Ensajo sobre el catolicismo, el liberalismo y el socialismo* (Madrid: Librería Católica Internacional, 1880). On the process of secularization as sacralization see also K. Löwith, *Meaning in History: The Theological Implications of the Philosophy of History* (Chicago, IL: University of Chicago Press, 1949); and E. Voegelin, *The New Science of Politics* (Chicago, IL: University of Chicago Press, 1952). See also Merold Westphal's chapter in this volume.
19. Søren Kierkegaard, *On Authority and Revelation. The Book on Adler, or a Circle of Ethico-religious Essays*, trans. Walter Lowrie (Princeton, NJ: Princeton University Press, 1955), p. xxi.
20. See *Papirer*, VIII 1 A 531.
21. Ibid., VIII 1 A 598.
22. Ibid., IX A 96, IX A 145, X 2 A 559, XI 1 A 108, X 3 A 696, X 5 A 115.
23. Ibid., X 2 A 413, X 2 A 664, X 4 A 35, X 4 A 43, X 4 A 47.
24. Søren Kierkegaard, *The Point of View*, p. 110. So Malantschuk comments: "In other words, Kierkegaard concedes the legitimacy of majority decisions when they pertain to relative, practical matters—but not when they concern ethical and religious decisions," *The Controversial Kierkegaard*, p. 7.
25. *Papirer*, X 3 A 346.
26. The analysis of modernity that follows parallels very nicely that offered by Bruce Kirmmse in his chapter in this volume.
27. *Papirer*, VII 1 A 17. See also *Papirer*, X 3 a 690:

    Total publicity makes it absolutely impossible to "govern." For all "government" is grounded on the idea that there are a few individuals who are more insightful than others and for that very reason are able to see so much farther that they are able to pilot: but total publicity is grounded on the idea that everybody should govern.

28. For a clarification of the concepts of identity and representation in constitutional

theories, see C. Schmitt, *Verfassungslehre* (Munich: Duncker and Humblot, 1928).
29. Søren Kierkegaard, *On Authority and Revelation*, p. xxiv. Emphasis by translator.
30. Søren Kierkegaard, *Letters and Documents*, no. 186 (August 1848), p. 262.
31. Søren Kierkegaard, *On Authority and Revelation*, p. xxiv.
32. See *Papirer*, X 6 B 39. On the bourgeoisie's refusal to use power, see also R. Guardini, *Die Macht* (Munich: Piper, 1950).
33. Søren Kierkegaard, *On Authority and Revelation*, p. xxiv. In his answer to Kolderup-Rosenvinge, who was convinced that in 1848 a tyrant was necessary to restore order, Kierkegaard insisted that a martyr was required. *Letters and Documents*, no. 188 (August 1848), p. 270. On the "martyr's government" see also A. Hügli, "Kierkegaard und der Kommunismus," in *Materialien zur Philosophie Søren Kierkegaards*, ed. M. Theunissen (Frankfurt a. M.: Suhrkamp, 1979), p. 530.
34. Søren Kierkegaard, *Letters and Documents*, no. 186 (August 1848), p. 263.
35. See E. Peterson, *Zeuge der Wahrheit* (Leipzig: Hegner,1937). On the meaning of this book see F. Scholz, *Zeuge der Wahrheit—ein anderer Kierkegaard*, in *Monotheismus als politisches Problem? Erik Peterson und die Kritik der politischen Theologie*, ed. A. Schindler (Gütersloh: Gunterslohe Verlagshaus Mohn, 1978).
36. See C. Schmitt, *Ex Captivitate Salus. Erfahrungen aus der Zeit 1945–1947* (Cologne: Greven Verlag, 1950), pp. 107–8. On the relationship between Kierkegaard and Schmitt, see K. M. Kodalle, *Politik als Macht und Mythos. Carl Schmitts "Politische Theologie"* (Stuttgart: Kohlhammer, 1973); K. M. Kodalle, *Der non-konforme Einzelne: Kierkegaards Existenztheologie*, in *Der Fürst dieser Welt. Carl Schmitt und die Folgen*, ed. J. Taubes (Munich: Schöningh, 1983), pp. 198–223; M. Nicoletti, *Trascendenza e potere. La teologia politica di Carl Schmitt* (Brescia: Morcelliana, 1990).
37. See Gregor Malantschuk, *Kierkegaard's Thought*; Michele Nicoletti, *La dialettica dell'Incarnazione. Soggettività e storia in S. Kierkegaard* (Bologna: EDB, 1983).
38. On this point see Edward Mooney's essay above, "On Getting Isaac Back." The same theme emerges in the chapters in this volume by George Connell and Mark Lloyd Taylor.
39. "In Kierkegaard's words, man must try to 'translate himself' from the one sphere to the other, that is, from the religious to the political and social sphere." G. Malantschuk, *The Controversial Kierkegaard*, p. 16.
40. Søren Kierkegaard, "The Individual," in *The Point of View*, p. 107.

12 Finally Forgiveness: Kierkegaard as a "Springboard" for a Feminist Theology of Reform

WANDA WARREN BERRY

Introduction: The Title's Temporality

Kierkegaard as "Springboard"

Day before yesterday the notion of feminist theology was inconceivable. This was true even for those few women who, in "fear and trembling," teleologically suspended the regnant "feminine mystique" to study theology. When this now aged century was still in its midlife crisis, some of us met Kierkegaard through the neo-orthodox great ones who then prevailed in the few seminaries that admitted women. For at least some of us, long before we learned to pay careful attention to what such theologians said or failed to say about women, they initiated us into the powerful maieutic of Kierkegaard's authorship. Now, inasmuch as we were not "born yesterday" like some of our students who have never known a world without the women's movement, we must reassess the consequences of such nonfeminist midwifery for the frameworks of our thought. To the complicated hermeneutical tasks of reading Kierkegaard we must add strategies to deal with the questions now rendered unavoidable by the topical organization of the new English edition of the *Journals*, which forced us to face point-blank what those papers say about "Woman."[1] A glance at that section of the *Journals* is enough to encourage the "Qualitative Leap Beyond Patriarchal Religion" for which revolutionary feminists call.[2] Nevertheless, this paper is a piece of an effort at "reform," rather than "revolution," being built upon the conviction that Kierkegaard's primary impact on my being has been liberating and that I cannot benefit as much from an attempt to leap completely away from him as from working through my transference-relation with him. One way to picture the goal of such work, of which I think Kierkegaard himself would approve, is found in Mary Daly's image of a "springboard."

In *Gyn/Ecology*, Daly demotes male-authored texts to the status of secondary sources, at the same time as she promotes women's experiences into priority.[3] Those who would encourage concrete becoming in all humans can hardly object to this strategy for those whose femaleness has proved to be an important factor of existence. At the same time, in this book and increasingly in the more recent *Pure Lust*, Daly allows for a constructive use even of texts that were written "at the expense of women," so long as they are used as "springboards," rather than as authorities. The function of a springboard is to provide an optimal starting point, one with propulsive power, for one to jump off into one's own movement. As historical beings, each of us finds her/his mind furnished with certain possible starting points. The task is to assess each for its ability to propel us powerfully into authentic existence. Thus Daly again and again uses certain aspects of Aquinas (or Tillich or Buber or Whitehead) as "springboards" that provide helpful starting points for her analyses. Self-consciously resisting using non-woman-identified materials as authoritative, she nevertheless proceeds in terms of the historically developed dialogue to which intellectual disciplines are accustomed. For example, in *Pure Lust* she builds her analysis of the passions in terms of Aquinas, saying

> I have chosen medieval naming of the passions as a springboard for Elemental Naming of them, for there is a refreshing vigor, clarity, bluntness, and complex simplicity in that analysis that is lacking in contemporary psychobabble.[4]

That one starts with a particular thinker as one's springboard (e.g., Kierkegaard) rather than another (e.g., Aquinas) manifests with special power the concrete synthesis of the temporal/historical and the eternal/absolute that one is. Thus Kierkegaard might well approve of being treated as a springboard both because such imagery recognizes the fact that we are concrete and need to recognize our starting points, and because it forbids us to use him slavishly as an authority rather than as a midwife.

The overall approach of my work with Kierkegaard at this point is to argue that being historically conditioned in terms of a dialogue with Kierkegaard (rather than, e.g., Aquinas) can provide a constructive starting point for one's feminism in spite of Kierkegaard's own conflicting statements about women.[5]

The Title as a Clue to the Conclusion

The foregoing reflections on the approach of this paper were developed in terms of constant attention to historicity. It may help to reflect at this time that temporality as a fundamental category of human existence is presupposed by all of the key terms in the title. "Finally," "forgiveness," and "reform" are quickly recognized as premised in their meanings upon the importance of prior developments of human reality for present meanings. Arguments for such recognition of the importance of history will be central to this paper. In addition, in my usage, both "feminist" and "theology" are comparably temporal. "Feminism" is belief and action that affirm women's equal access to fully human possibilities; the premise of its meaningfulness is the reality of historical systems that block women's existence. One hopes that eventually feminism will itself be only a matter of *past* history, because those oppressive systems will have been transformed worldwide. "Theology" in this paper also functions in historical context as an interpretation of the meaning of God for humanity developed in terms of the symbols of a particular religious tradition and/or particular human situations (e.g., those of women).

Kierkegaard and Metaphorical Theology

There is space for only a brief *nota bene* concerning another aspect of my approach: I understand all of Kierkegaard's expressions of religious meaning metaphorically, rather than literally. Too often interpreters who recognize the poetic medium of Kierkegaard's message put that perspective aside when they treat the Christian works. They interpret Kierkegaard as if his use of Christian-talk was intended in an almost fundamentalist mode, losing the context of religious existentialism he had painstakingly developed for all of his assertions. I want to insist that this is to misunderstand the authorship. Throughout my discussion I will presuppose the orientation to religious language found in the opening of Part II of *Works of Love*: "All human language about the spiritual, yes, even the divine language of Holy Scriptures, is essentially transferred or metaphorical language."[6] Since Kierkegaard's talk of forgiveness of sins often has been connected to "atonement-talk" in ways that tend to ignore this theopoetic orientation of his theological expressions, my concerns will be misunderstood if this caution is not kept in mind.

KIERKEGAARD AND THE FINALITY OF FORGIVENESS

There is no controversy about the finality of the appropriation of the forgiveness of sins within Kierkegaard's existential dialectic. It is clear in the autobiographical materials that forgiveness was a central element in Kierkegaard's culminating religious experience.[7] In addition, virtually all of those who trace the temporal becoming of the self as analyzed in Kierkegaard's pseudonymous and Christian works agree that in his view the last step in becoming oneself requires the profound willingness to be oneself before God that is realized in reliance on forgiveness.[8] However, there *are* issues about the meaning and value of this emphasis on the finality of forgiveness in the influential interpreters of Kierkegaard.[9] And while Kierkegaard himself anticipated some kinds of "offended" responses to the emphasis on forgiveness,[10] his own historicity blocked anticipation of the intensification of such offense within twentieth century liberation movements, such as that among women. Emphasis on forgiveness often has been associated with what Daly has called "the scapegoat syndrome."[11] Therefore, many of those whose historical powerlessness (e.g., women) allowed them to be used as scapegoats bearing the "guilt" of the powerful are negatively affected by "forgiveness-talk." Nevertheless, this paper argues that even in this "offensive" emphasis on forgiveness, Kierkegaard can provide a springboard for the movement needed at this time not only by feminists, but by all liberation theologies.

Forgiveness as the Final Work of Love

The meaning of forgiveness for Kierkegaard is best discovered in *Works of Love*, where it is identified toward the end of that book's analysis of "love in its outgoing movement"[12] as an action by which "love hides the multiplicity of sins." All works of love are modes of action (not just feeling) in relation to the other/the neighbor.[13] Kierkegaard identifies three ways in which such action hides sin: (1) love does not discover sin, does not seek out or "place a premium" on knowing "how envious, how selfish, how unreliable" human beings are;[14] (2) love "hides in silence" or in a "mitigating explanation" the human evil it cannot avoid knowing.[15] While Kierkegaard, at first, connects this second way of hiding human sin with forgiveness, later he distinguishes (3) love as forgiveness, the "most significant way" of dealing with the other's sin. The meaning of forgiveness is established, then, by contrast with the other ways of hiding sin, as a way that neither denies its reality nor tries to explain it away. Forgiveness is analyzed as a form of faith which like all faith "relates itself to what is not seen."[16]

> The lover sees the sin which he forgives, but he believes that forgiveness takes it away. . . . Just as one by faith *believes the unseen* in the seen, so the lover by forgiveness *believes* the seen away. Both are faith.[17]

The "miracle" of forgiveness-faith is: "that which is seen nevertheless by being forgiven is not seen." Forgiveness is like "blotting out," like "forgetting," like the biblical picture of God "hiding sins behind his back"—all actions that recognize the reality of the sin that is now refused attention.

> What is hidden from my eyes I have never seen, but what is hidden behind my back I have seen. And this is the very way in which the lover forgives: he forgives, he forgets, he blots out sin; in love he turns to the one he forgives, but when he turns toward him he simply cannot see what lies behind his [own] back.[18]

The full import of forgiveness then is this turning toward the other in full knowledge of the other's sins but in a way that does not focus upon those egregious wrongs. The significance of this work of love is reenforced by remembering Kierkegaard's discussion earlier in *Works of Love* of Christ's relationship to Peter. In order to exemplify "our duty to love those we see," the neighbor who is there, rather than the ideal neighbor for whom we would wish, Kierkegaard considers the work of love revealed in Christ's forgiving Peter who has betrayed him. Here the point is that love does not demand that the other become what he/she ought to be in order that friendship be renewed. Instead Kierkegaard interprets Jesus as saying: "Peter is Peter, and I love him; love, if anything, will help him to become another man." The meaning of love is clarified as Kierkegaard goes on to say that Christ "did not break off the friendship in order perhaps to renew it again when Peter had become another man. No, he preserved the friendship unchanged and in this very way helped Peter to become another man."[19]

Kierkegaard offers Christ's "faithful friendship" as the paradigm of love in action. This outward work of love, rather than some inner feeling only, is the meaning of forgiveness. Forgiveness is faithfulness to a relationship, not "in spite of" the other's sins against the relationship, but because "Peter is Peter," because the concrete other, the neighbor who "is seen," is loved.

> For to be able to love a man in spite of his weaknesses and errors and imperfections is not perfect love; it is rather to be able to find him lovable in spite of and together with his weakness and errors and imperfections. . . . It is a sad upside-downness . . . to talk on and on about how the object of love should be in order to be lovable enough, instead of talking about how love should be in order that it can love.[20]

Those whose consciousness resonates with biblical associations will here recognize *chesed*, covenant love. As its meaning is developed in *Works of Love*, forgiveness means action that preserves the bond of relation in full knowledge of the other party's sin against that bond. Insofar as Kierkegaard's own culminating religious experience centered in forgiveness, it should be seen as an experience in which the God-relation was confirmed as such a "faithful friendship." Taking seriously the meaning of forgiveness-love as it is developed in *Works of Love* enables one to appreciate his religious experience as much more than deliverance from neurotic guilt.[21]

The meaning of forgiveness is further delineated in *Works of Love* when Kierkegaard distinguishes the meaning of "reconciliation in love" from that of forgiveness *per se*.[22] During most of the section on reconciliation, Kierkegaard is seeking to draw out the meaning of reconciliation-love by contrast with forgiveness-love. Whereas forgiveness is the loving response to one who "has done you wrong" and "comes to you and seeks restoration,"[23] reconciliation seeks "to forgive beforehand long before the other person is perhaps thinking of seeking forgiveness."[24] At one point in the discussion forgiveness is clearly identified as restoration of relationship in full knowledge of the other's having wronged the relationship, whereas reconciliation encompasses any unsolicited initiative to restore relationship. Nevertheless, Kierkegaard speaks of such initiative as "battling in love so that the other will accept forgiveness,"[25] so that the awareness of the other's sin would seem to be present even in reconciliation.

The most important part of this discussion for our purposes is Kierkegaard's raising the question of whether both parties, both the wronged and the wronger, in any sense need forgiveness. Here it becomes clear how very relational his view of existential being is:

> Who is it, then, who needs forgiveness, the one who did wrong or the one who suffered wrong? Certainly he who did wrong is the one who needs forgiveness. But, O, the lover who suffered wrong needs to forgive or needs restoration, reconciliation, words which do not like *forgiveness* make a distinction by remembering right or wrong but in love note that both stand in need.[26]

Both forgiveness and reconciliation are actions by which concrete bonds or relationships are restored; that is, they are "works of love." The religious significance of such action is invoked again and again, not only as Kierkegaard develops his discussion by talking both of the love of God and of human persons, but as he repeatedly reminds us that "God is Love."[27]

Forgiveness as the Teleological Suspension of the Ethical

In *Works of Love* Kierkegaard is particularly concerned that forgiveness-love not be apprehended as a weak, sentimentalized "coddling love." To take the strenuousness and offense of forgiving love away for the sake of a "pleasant" and "delightful" or "enervated form" of sentimentality makes both love and (thus) God "fanciful and childish."[28] Indeed, much of Kierkegaard's corpus was shaped by this very concern to delineate faith as a courageous and mature strength. Both in *Fear and Trembling*, with its delineation of "the teleological suspension of the ethical," and in *Sickness unto Death*, with its emphasis on the "offense" of Christianity, this effort to rescue faith from the realm of comfortable affect is determinative. The meaning of forgiveness in Kierkegaard, then, can be further clarified by attention to its significance in those texts.

While both Malantschuk and Mackey have drawn attention to the presence of forgiveness as the final issue in *Fear and Trembling* through the pseudonym's analyses of the story of the merman,[29] I want to go further to argue that the deepest irony of the text is in Johannes' failure to see that forgiveness manifests a "teleological suspension of the ethical." The pseudonymous author of *Fear and Trembling* knows much that is religious truth, but he has not subjectively appropriated Christianity. His struggles with the controversial idea of the teleological suspension of the ethical help us to see much that Kierkegaard considers important. For example, they help us to understand that the ethic of rational principles is not the same as the ethic of love. In addition, his reflections highlight for us the unique and personal character of the God-relation, in which one "speaks *Du* to God in heaven."[30] He also presents truly the dynamics of faith, as it embraces existence with ultimate caring at the same time as it is fully aware of the finitude both of all that we want and all that we "ought."

In addition, beyond all these matters that we can begin to understand existentially if not logically, we learn with Johannes the truth that we, the offenders, cannot will to sacrifice our Isaacs, since they represent not just our loves but our communal obligations. From the point of view of the offender, the suspension of the ethical obligation to parent Isaac rather than kill him cannot be willed. It is clear that the ethic of caring for one's neighbor cannot be suspended, although particular moral norms can be for the sake of the unique, concrete existence that is truth. Those who want to appreciate the special place of *Fear and Trembling* in the authorship need to place it always in dialogue with *Works of Love*, where Kierkegaard paraphrases the Johannine counsel, "let us love one another," as meaning to say

> to love human beings is still the only thing worth living for; without this love you really do not live; to love human beings is also the only salutary consolation for both time and eternity, and to love human beings is the only true sign that you are a Christian.[31]

All this and much more of religious truth can be apprehended by Kierkegaard's "reader" in *Fear and Trembling*. But the final step in this text's powerful religious maieutic lies beyond it, although it is indicated within it. This development can be grasped through the ironic tension between, on the one hand, Christendom's/Johannes' offense at the idea of "the teleological suspension of the ethical" and, on the other, "the good news of the forgiveness of sins" that initiated Christianity. Forgiveness is the suspension of the ethical for the sake of one's bond with the offender. Suspension of the commandment to love others cannot be willfully enacted without sin. But our lives are finally sustained by the reality of forgiveness, which involves the suspension of required obedience to this commandment by action of the one who has been wronged, rather than by the offender.

The question of whether such forgiveness is possible is introduced early in *Fear and Trembling*:

> It was a quiet evening when Abraham rode out alone . . . he threw himself down on his face, he prayed to God to forgive him his sin, that he had been willing to sacrifice Isaac, that the father had forgotten his duty

to his son. He often rode his lonesome road, but he found no peace. He could not comprehend that it was a sin that he had been willing to sacrifice to God the best that he had, the possession for which he himself would have gladly died many times; and if it was a sin, if he had not loved Isaac in this manner, he could not understand that it could be forgiven, for what more terrible sin was there?[32]

In spite of this early clue to the importance of forgiveness, it cannot be directly present in the text as the climactic issue because of the viewpoint of the pseudonym. The text must make its point ironically, needling us through the idea of "the teleological suspension of the ethical" to appropriate many aspects of our existence, including, finally, forgiveness. This existential appropriation is accomplished through two realizations: (1) that the *offender*, the one who contemplates doing a wrong, cannot justify the suspension of human obligation; and (2) that, nevertheless, there is a "teleological suspension of the ethical" that sustains existence, since we must rely upon the wronged/the *offended* to put ethical guilt "behind her/his back" through forgiveness. Thus in faithful friendship, for the sake of the *telos* of his personal bond with Peter, Christ "hides the multiplicity of sins" without denying their reality. In the light of this "root experience" of Christianity, it is the triumph of irony that Christendom has been so exercised over "the teleological suspension of the ethical."

Forgiveness and Faith in Sickness unto Death

Kierkegaard, of course, intends the triumph of faith rather than the triumph of irony. The exposition of forgiveness as a form of faith in *Works of Love* can illumine the definition of faith in *Sickness unto Death*.

> The opposite to being in despair is to have faith. Therefore, the formula . . . which describes a state in which there is no despair at all, is entirely correct, and this formula is also the formula for faith: in relating itself to itself and in willing to be itself, the self rests transparently in the power that established it.[33]

In the penultimate step[34] of the "algebraic" desentimentalization of faith that Kierkegaard accomplishes in this text, he considers "the sin of despairing of the forgiveness of sins" by attending to the "offense" of Christianity. The section begins by reviewing the picture of human becoming that has been drawn: starting from aesthetical denial of ultimate concern ("ignorance of having an eternal self"), the move is to ethical affirmation of our responsibility to choose the good ("knowledge of having a self in which there is something eternal"), and then to a position "before God," before the Absolute, which transcends one's power to choose and identifies one's existence as sin. On the basis of this whole religious development, finally "a self comes directly before Christ, a self that in despair still does not will to be itself or in despair wills to be itself."[35] Now before Christ, despair/sin is rejection of resting without self-deception on the power of forgiveness, which is the only power that can reconstitute the self that has rejected the tasks of selfhood before God. Here despair can take either the form of willing not to be the sinner that one is (the new form of weakness) or of willing to be a sinner "in such a way that there is no forgiveness" (the new form of defiance). In either case, denial of God is denial of the possibility of forgiveness.

As he works through what it means to despair of forgiveness, Anti-Climacus reenforces the concerns we have noted in the discussions of forgiveness in *Works of Love* and *Fear and Trembling*. Especially important is the discussion of the serious misunderstanding of forgiveness that results from modern abolition of the sense of an absolute ethical demand. Kierkegaard maintains that forgiveness, as well as religiousness itself, is "conceived erroneously" if "thou shalt" is "abolished as the sole regulative aspect of man's relationship to God. This 'thou shalt' must be present in any determination of the religious."[36] Thus the ethical-religious, as the obligation to become oneself authentically before God, is not abolished. Indeed, "before Christ," there is even a "thou shalt" that makes one responsible for believing in the good news of forgiveness of sins. Forgiveness-faith is no denial of ethical stringency in existence. To understand oneself as finally reliant upon another's forgiveness is to take very seriously the tasks at which one has failed. Far easier is modern relativism, which removes "the earnestness of existence"[37] and, thus, the need for forgiveness.

The final form of despair in *Sickness unto Death*, the highest intensification of sin, actually is that of dismissing Christianity, of declaring it untrue.[38] But this does not contradict the "finality" of forgiveness, since it involves certain more or less credal manifestations of the existential situation of being unable to appropriate the forgiveness manifested in Christ. To appropriate God/Possibility as forgiveness-love preserves "the kinship" between God and the self, but in terms of an awareness of sin that causes Kierkegaard to speak of "an infinite qualitative difference" between God and the human being.[39] The "offense" is that in the renewal of the God-relation in terms of a particular human life, Jesus Christ/the God-Human, "infinite love" affirms the ultimate significance of individual human life, but this affirmation comes through an experience of forgiveness-love, rather than simple elevation of humanity.[40]

> As sinner, man is separated from God by the most chasmal qualitative abyss. In turn, of course, God is separated from man by the same chasmal qualitative abyss when he forgives sins. If by some kind of reverse adjustment the divine could be shifted over to the human, there is one

way in which man could never in all eternity come to be like God: in forgiving sins.[41]

Christianity, in affirming the reality of forgiveness, both "makes too much of what it is to be a human being" and, at the same time, makes too little. The experience of forgiveness is the root of Kierkegaard's characteristic interpretations of divine immanence/transcendence as well as of the incarnation.

Forgiveness as Existential Truth: Theological/Ontological Significance

Moreover, it is in discussing the authenticity of forgiveness in *Works of Love* that Kierkegaard's religious existentialism is more powerfully invoked than in some of the algebraic and doctrinal formulations of other works and/or passages. In the context of positing that faith in the power of forgiveness is "so small and rare" because there is no sense of its "power to help," Kierkegaard addresses the reader: "Yet, if you yourself have ever needed forgiveness, then you know what forgiveness accomplishes."[42] Such a challenge to self-reflection as a test of the existential validity of forgiveness is characteristic of the Christian discourses. But more theologically significant is the emphasis in the "Conclusion" of *Works of Love* on the "like-for-like of the eternal."[43] While the emphasis on the finality of the forgiveness of sins as it is usually developed out of the autobiographical *Journal* entries encourages some to see the culmination of Kierkegaard's existential dialectic as a privatistic and moralistic matter, here we encounter a basis for a communal existential ontology/theology. As it is developed through discussion of "the Christian like-for-like," the theological significance of the concept of reduplication is exposed. Reduplication formulates for the sphere of religiousness B the import of subjective appropriation as the criterion of truth. It involves living the truth one teaches or proclaims.[44]

Early in the conclusion to *Works of Love* Kierkegaard interprets "the eternal like-for-like" of Christianity as directing attention toward inward appropriation of the God-relation as the motive for all action. This "makes your every relationship to other human beings into a God-relationship."[45] The ontological significance of this like-for-like is clearest when he considers forgiveness. Kierkegaard aims to correct any notion that one can rely on forgiveness if one does not forgive others, saying

> Christianity's view is: forgiveness *is* forgiveness; your forgiveness is your forgiveness; your forgiveness of another is your own forgiveness; the forgiveness which you give you receive, not contrariwise that you give the forgiveness you receive. . . . It is also conceit to believe in one's own forgiveness when one will not forgive, for how in truth should one

believe in forgiveness if his own life is a refutation of the existence of forgiveness.[46]

Remembering his earlier claim that the "like-for-like of the eternal" is "such an important and decisively Christian category" that he wished he could end every book with it,[47] one is convinced of the thoroughness of his theological existentialism.

> For God is himself really the pure like-for-like, the pure rendition of how you yourself are. If there is wrath in you, then God is wrath in you; if there is mildness and mercifulness in you, then God is mercifulness in you. Infinite love is this, that above all he wills to have to do with you and that no one, no one, so lovingly discovers the slightest love in you as God does. God's relationship to a human being is the infinitising at every moment of that which at every moment is in a man.[48]

It is not inappropriate to speak of the ontological significance of forgiveness in the light of such passages, as well as of an earlier discussion of the "like-for-like" of reduplication that culminates:

> You have to do only with what you do unto others or with the way you receive what others do unto you; the direction is inwards; essentially you have only to do with yourself before God. This world of inwardness, the new version of what other men call reality, this is reality.[49]

Forgiveness is truth when it is lived and because it can be lived transparently, without self-deception. Lived meanings are truth for the existing individual.

Throughout *Works of Love* Kierkegaard aims to correct the modern loss of authenticity due to collectivized "crowd" existence, but so as to create a communal existential ontology through which one learns "all over again the most important thing, to understand oneself in one's longing for community."[50]

> . . . God is love, and when a human being because of love forgets himself, how then should God forget him. . . . But the lover who forgets himself, is remembered by love. There is a One who thinks of him, and in this way it comes about that the lover gets what he gives.
>
> Note the reduplication here: what the lover does, he is or he becomes; . . .[51]

This is the "like-for-like" that Kierkegaard believes can be realized in his "present age" only on the basis of the birth of individual freedom and responsibility for which he aims to provide a maieutic in the authorship. For the mature individual who can develop from that birth, the Christian authorship presents the challenge of the New Testament's many "like-for-like" sayings in order to encourage subjective appropriation of one's communal being. Finally, forgiveness is preached because it is the ground of one's being; it is the ground of one's being because it is the only reality that can be lived authentically. Only forgiveness-love synthesizes both the self's infinitude (freedom/responsibility) and its finitude (sin/rejection of love) in such a way as to re-create community.

Summary: Kierkegaard's Desentimentalized Forgiveness

To summarize, to choose as one's springboard Kierkegaard's view of forgiveness would be to choose a view of human existence that would emphasize:

1. *Temporality.* Forgiveness deals with the past, rather than seeing the self in discrete moments only.
2. *The eternal dimension of human existence.* Forgiveness sees the self as free and, thus, responsible for past violations of the good, rather than seeing it as simply a function of relative, changing conditions.
3. *Action.* Forgiveness is a "work of love," a way of acting, rather than simply an inner feeling or emotion.
4. *Relationships/community.* Forgiveness is "faithful friendship" in which the wronged party preserves the bond of relation in full knowledge of the other party's violation of the bond.
5. *The distinction between viewpoints.* Forgiveness may have somewhat different significance for the wronged party, who needs to forgive, than for the offender, who needs forgiveness; but both parties have in common a need for restored relation.

FORGIVENESS AND OUR PRESENT AGE

Questioning for Forgiveness in the Present Age

Can Kierkegaard's analysis of forgiveness provide a springboard for authentic existence in these last years of the twentieth century? Today a person who is preoccupied with the question "Am I forgiven?" seems weird to our children and our students, the barometers of contemporary culture in our lives. Indeed, not just the young but other creatures of the day find it odd when someone needs to deal with the past in terms of a sense of guilt and of responsibility rather than simply by ignoring it for the sake of the plethora of momentary diversions that can fill life in the modern world.

Kierkegaard's concern to highlight both the temporal/historical and the eternal/absolute in human life is alien to our late twentieth century consciousness. Modern systems of transportation, fluid societies, and ever-new technologies of entertainment encourage most to move away from the past and toward new places, new relationships, new diversions. For most people, only relations to parents, children, and siblings raise any need to transform the past, rather than leave it behind. There seem to be easy replacements for all but certain birth-determined relationships, and even these are easily eclipsed by what Buber has called "the progressive augmentation of the world of *It*."⁵² There are many strategies for living toward transient stimuli rather than through old bonds. Any residual conscientiousness about past wrongs is referred away from our sanctioned spaces to seek psychotherapeutic treatment for "neurotic" guilt and/or "paranoiac" hurt. The drug culture epitomizes our entrenched aestheticism; we rely for meaning upon external sources of altered consciousness, expecting "better living through chemistry." Gone is the inner sense of obligation to meaningful development of selfhood through willed actions, the consequent experiences of at least occasional failure, and the need for forgiveness. The cultural pluralism and relativism characteristic of our present age have dissolved for many the premise of ethico-religious development in Kierkegaard, that is, that of ultimate responsibility to a good that is not to be identified with our conditioned desires. The rare person who asks "Am I forgiven?," thus demonstrating commitment to standards that are not simply functions of historical conditions or fluctuating desires, is in tension with the dominant orientations.

There are two ways of asking about forgiveness that do seem characteristic of "the present age." These questions, however, are posed in the first person plural; they ask either "Are *we* forgiven?" or "Can *we* forgive?" rather than "Am I forgiven?" Indeed the viability of forgiveness as a mode of action in relations between communities, traditions, and institutions can be seen as a basic issue for twentieth century theology. Modern recognition of the systemic nature of much that destroys human beings has brought to some a sense of solidarity in responsibility. For example, at least some Christians ask whether they can be forgiven for the religious imperialism of their tradition, which they now see as a root of anti-Semitism, as well as of colonial subjugation and enslavement of peoples. More often than the question for forgiveness surfaces among such members of communities who have wronged others, the other question, "Can we forgive?," is formulated by those who have been wronged.⁵³

We now associate such questions with liberation theology. However, an intense sense of forgiveness as an issue for communities, and not just for individuals, was powerfully developed earlier in this century as theology focused upon certain historical atrocities against peoples. "Can we forgive?" has been the twentieth century issue for the Jew who understands the importance of remembering the Holocaust. Whether forgiveness is possible has been a crucial issue for the Jew, not only in relation to Christians, whose civilization allowed Nazi anti-Semitism to find soil for growth, but also for some Jews in relation to their own God and tradition. This same question continues for Christians, as they remember the Holocaust in the framework of a recovery of the corporate sense of responsibility characteristic of the Bible.

Theology done out of the African American and Native American experiences in the United States also has raised first-person plural questions about forgiveness. Such questions epitomize the pain of conscientious persons in the United States who see how some Americans continue to suffer the heritage of earlier enslavement, injustice, and hatred. Both African Americans and Native Americans cannot help but wonder about the obscenity of forgiving those who inherit the fruits of the virtual genocides committed by Eurocentric white communities. As such heirs, others of us wonder, "Can we be forgiven?," asking a basic question for any theology for the oppressors.

On the other hand, the question "Can we forgive?" formulates the critical issue for the oppressed, especially for women. Insofar as women have been and are a subordinated caste within virtually all cultures and religious traditions, those who identify with this sisterhood of the oppressed must formulate the question of forgiveness in the first-person plural. The dynamics of individual women forgiving individual men (e.g., their fathers, brothers, husbands, lovers, friends, etc.) can be compared to those of any other human relations up to the point where one profoundly knows that the wrongs involved were done to one as a woman. At that point the question should emerge: "Can *we* forgive?"

Forgiveness has become the definitive issue for the rapidly developing feminist theologies. One's attitude toward preserving one's relationships to traditional communities, in full cognizance of their past and present wrongs to women, determines whether one's religious feminism is called "reforming" or "revolutionary."[54] While both reformers and revolutionaries recognize the wrongs done to women in the past, "reformers" preserve their relations to the religious traditions, not in terms of forgetting the wrongs done, but in terms of a complex recognition of their own historicity as the source of both their liberation and their oppression. The term "revolutionary" in feminist religious thought is applied to those who, like Mary Daly, choose a complete separation from traditional religious institutions.[55]

Feminist reformers have often justified their continued relation to the traditions existentially, on the basis of the truths of their lived experience.[56] Others like Rosemary Radford Ruether have begun to develop what I am calling a theology of reform, wherein they justify their stance not simply on the basis of individual experience but of systematically explicated orientations to human existence.[57] When such arguments for reform are developed by those who have been wronged by beloved traditions they know to be sources of strength as well as sources of oppression, they tend to develop in terms compatible with the five elements of Kierkegaard's view of forgiveness.

Allow me to briefly justify this claim, using Ruether as our example and encouraging review of the five elements of Kierkegaard's orientation summarized above. In an important section of *Sexism and God-Talk*, (1) Ruether recognizes the importance of preserving awareness of human temporality, arguing that it is both "self-deluding and unsatisfactory" to try "to express contemporary experience in a cultural and historical vacuum."[58] She notes that such an effort is delusive, since one cannot communicate with either oneself or others except by use of thought forms and language "that have a history." (2) At the same time, even Ruether, with her profoundly historical methodology, recognizes the function of seeing oneself before "some original base of meaning and truth." Here and throughout her authorship Ruether acknowledges what Kierkegaard calls the "eternal" dimension of authentic existence. Those familiar with her extensive body of works know as well the recurrence of (3) an emphasis on organic wholeness in which feelings are not dualistically separated into an inner realm divorced from action, (4) insistence upon recognition of past wrongs in order to restore relations between women and men in the tradition, (5) analysis of the distinct viewpoints of the wronged and the wronger, and recognition of the common need for self-criticism and restored relations.[59]

Jumping Off the Springboard

This level of compatibility with Kierkegaard suggests that feminist reformers might well use Kierkegaard's in-depth analyses of human selfhood as a springboard. Nevertheless, before we go further in indicating those aspects of Kierkegaard that can provide feminism with propulsive power, we must take care to notice how our emphasis has changed from his by virtue of the first-person plural pronouns of our existential questions. With that usage we may already have jumped off the springboard. We have been developing the meaning of forgiveness in terms of a more thoroughly assimilated communal and historical viewpoint than his. Many feminist theorists have commented on the critical role of the community of women in enabling their new visions. Ruether says:

> The woman who experiences dissenting thoughts alone, without any network of communication to support her, can hardly bring her own dissent to articulation. Without a social matrix, she will simply be terrorized into submission by the authorities that surround her or acquiesce in their judgment that she is a "witch" or a "madwoman."[60]

This emphasis on the social matrix that supports liberation has caused many feminists to be antithetical toward existentialism, since they perceive it as isolating women in their subjectivity. One can hope that our earlier treatments of *Works of Love* have balanced that perspective with Kierkegaard's affirmation of our communal fulfillment.

While I agree with emphasis on the need for "base communities" to support liberation of the oppressed, I also believe that feminist theologies need to preserve the dialectic between the individual and the social if they are to be truly liberating. In order to challenge the heteronomous determinism that was described above as characteristic of contemporary consciousness, a Kierkegaardian maieutic for "the single one" is needed. Persons need to be challenged by questions of meaning that are existential. Such questions ask for the meaning of a lifetime, rather than only of present moments, hours, and ages. When individuals each appropriate individual freedom and responsibility, a community can be brought together around a common commitment to truth and justice. Without affirmation of the possibility of individual agency, the recognition of collective systems simply brings the hopelessness of determinism, and no question for forgiveness emerges. However, a community of free individuals can ask "Are *we* forgiven?" with regard to their collective actions and/or the benefits certain groups enjoy as classes or nations; it also can project new policies for the future. This does not deny the continuing relevance for individuals of the questions "Am I forgiven?" and "Can I forgive?"

Jumping off the springboard, then, contemporary religious feminists find the urgent meaning of forgiveness to be *action to preserve the bonds of community and between communities by continuing in concrete historical traditions in terms of recognition of past wrongs as well as through the intention to redress those wrongs*. We have been able to see that such forgiveness is a crucial issue for religious traditions in the twentieth century by reversing our usual viewpoint on forgiveness. This reversal is comparable to that required earlier in order to understand how "the teleological suspension of the ethical" is existentially possible, since it starts from the point of view of the offended party who must forgive, rather than that of the offender. Of course, the corollary of such forgiveness is the action of the offending party both to recognize the past wrongs it has perpetrated and to receive the forgiveness-love that renews relations. If Kierkegaard's analysis of reconciliation is right, however, special opportunities to transcend the destructive past are in the hands of the offended one who must teleologically suspend the ethical requirement for the sake of love.

This cannot be said without the desentimentalization of forgiveness that was developed through Kierkegaard. Theologies of reform cannot be liberating if they require complete transcendence of the negative feelings derived from past injustice. Like other peoples who now see the dynamics of their historic dehumanization, women cannot be asked up front to have positive feelings toward those who have perpetrated that oppression. Nevertheless, such women can be encouraged to choose actions that preserve bonds and enable transformation, without expecting themselves, at least initially, to feel differently either about the injustices that have been received or even the perpetrators of those wrongs.

Why, Finally, Forgiveness?

Why should one make that choice? Once consciousness has been raised and the effects of devastating injustices and atrocities have been recognized in one's own self and in one's people, why should one forgive? Why should one choose the stance of reform rather than revolution? Why, finally, forgiveness?

If subjective appropriation is one's criterion for truth, one finally chooses to restore relations with others who have betrayed those bonds because that action can be lived without self-deception and with passionate commitment. This is true with regard to institutions and/or traditions as well as individuals. Feminist reformers employ certain specific applications of this existential principle. First, as has been noted above, they argue for reform because they have known the tradition in their own lives and in historical studies as a source of liberation as well as oppression. In an early article Elizabeth Schussler Fiorenza reveals both the personal and the historical claims for liberating power in her tradition that account for her identity as a feminist reformer:

> Despite all masculine terminology of prayers, catechism, and liturgy, despite blatant patriarchal male spiritual guidance, my commitment to Christian faith and love first led me to question the feminine cultural role which parents, school and church had taught me to accept and internalize.[61]

> To affirm that Christian faith and theology are not inherently patriarchal and sexist and, at the same time, to maintain that Christian theology and Christian churches are guilty of the sin of sexism is the task of feminist theology.[62]

In all religious traditions, the feminist reformers make such claims, whereas the revolutionaries find the tradition "inherently patriarchal" and, finally, personally oppressive. Rosemary Radford Ruether joins Elizabeth Schussler Fiorenza in rejecting the revolutionary simplification of what she calls the "ambiguous" heritage of Roman Catholic tradition. Ruether's pattern is to insist upon recognition both of the Church's participation in and sponsorship of oppressive structures and of its role as a source for positive identity, both in its originating events and in present movements of the oppressed. I would want to add, on behalf of the possibility of feminist reform in religious traditions other than Christianity, that a religious sense of connection to sources of meaning beyond both the self and society, that is, recognition of transcendence, is a positive basis for human liberation whenever it allows criticism of present systems in the light of the transcendent. In Kierkegaardian terms, to see the self as finally "before God" is to see the self as able to criticize culture in terms of one's own responsibility, rather than only one's victimization. Kierkegaard's emphasis on freedom is the anthropological corollary of his emphasis on God as "Possibility," and is fundamental to any theology of liberation.

A second specific argument for reform or forgiveness-love that has been expressed by religious feminists is more pragmatic than directly existential, although it can be expressive of a choice of self-orientation. Once one decides that an institution/tradition is not inherently oppressive, but that it represents in its original intent a liberating power, one can choose reform rather than revolution as the most effective way of working in the light of historico-political realities. Thus Ruether points out the folly of ignoring the value of the international network available to Roman Catholic women who preserve their relations with that tradition; such connections can be used to further worldwide improvement in the lot of women and other oppressed peoples.[63] Just as the preceding point caused us to recall Kierkegaard's emphasis on human infinitude or freedom, so this recalls his stress on the finite/temporal/historical dimensions of selfhood. Kierkegaard's view of the self is pragmatically liberating in that it avoids "the fantastic"[64] and supports a freedom/liberation that is concretely realizable. His complex view of the self takes seriously both genetic and historical determinants at the same time as it calls for choices that are synthesized with those factors of finitude. Such a psychology sets the stage for concretely effective reforming action that supports historically realized liberation. For example, Episcopalians, who were able to use a polity that allowed more rapid change than some other communions toward the ordination of women to priesthood, have initiated not only precedent-setting ecclesiastical changes but deep "sea changes" in social-psychic symbolic structures, having positive impact even for women who have no connection to religious institutions.

Beyond these existential and pragmatic reasons for choosing reform, there is a third that Kierkegaard expressed for us when he said, "if you yourself have ever needed forgiveness, then you know what forgiveness accomplishes."[65] Those who cannot without self-deception deny their own sin, those who know that they, too, "have done what they ought not to have done and left undone what they ought to have done," can choose forgiveness because they know that all humans "fall short of the glory of God." Those who have looked hard at human irrationality and human egoism as well as at human potential for justice-making and love are unable without self-deception to separate from the former oppressors in some expectation of an ideal community elsewhere. Starting from acceptance of sin, one is engaged always in self-criticism, which, if correlated with faith in Possibility, preserves human community. For those who, like women within patriarchy, are conditioned to weakness (i.e., the inability to will to be themselves before God), the self-criticism encouraged by Kierkegaard's twofold doctrine of sin can open an experience of empowerment.[66] For those who like men in patriarchal culture are conditioned to defiance, self-criticism is essential to restoring relation and renouncing habits of exercising "power-over."[67] In both cases the principles involved should be applied to communities as well as individuals.

In the fourth place, one chooses reform rather than separation because one *loves* particular others, both individuals and communities. By seeking to reform our traditional communities rather than separate from them, we preserve the possibility of living in all those richly concrete ways in which we grew. The music, stories, architecture, liturgies, and celebrations that provide the deep rhythms and resonances of our psyches can be reformed and renewed rather than erased. More importantly, we thus preserve connections that cross generations, keeping children and grandchildren under a canopy of meaning that through reforming action embraces growth and change as well as continuities. We also in this way can be loyal to some people who made life-saving differences in our lives through our religious communities in spite of institutionalized sexism. All of this is to say that one chooses forgiveness because one loves, is bonded and covenanted to, particular persons and communities, and does not exist in abstraction. For example, Roman Catholic women who are acting to reform the Church want to insist that it is, after all, their church as much as it is the patriarchs'. Indeed, they can say with deep irony, "Peter is Peter and I love him."

This forgiveness-love toward particular communities is possible for feminists only with the premise of the first reason for reform discussed above: that the root experiences definitive of the tradition enable liberation. For Jews the primacy of the Exodus provides the premise for reform. Christian feminist reformers discover in Jesus as well a moment in history from which they trace their own possibilities for freedom. They can affirm in this person the historical beginnings of their own concrete synthesizing of freedom and finitude.[68] Nevertheless, if one is a woman, to seek restoration of covenants with these communities requires, finally, forgiveness.

A cautionary word may be in order to guard against any chance that advocacy of forgiveness-love might be misunderstood as requiring a reduction in the level of feminist criticism of the traditions. To the contrary, I want to suggest that Kierkegaard's uncompromising polemical writings might be seen as manifestations of a desentimentalized forgiveness. Living the vocation of authorship, such writings were his action in the world to express his criticism of Christendom for the sake of the authentic originating tradition. One can question Kierkegaard's own denial that he was a "reformer,"[69] since he continued to address Christendom rather than completely separating from it. Today's polemical feminist reformers, such as Rosemary Radford Ruether, are comparably relentless in creating authorships that criticize Christian institutions for their failure to be Christian. Finally, such address manifests forgiveness in action insofar as it aims to preserve historical bonds by encouraging the kinds of mutual agreements between the wronged and the wronging communities that will manifest new life. For "how in truth should [we] believe in forgiveness if [our] own life is a refutation of the existence of forgiveness."[70]

Ah, "Søren is Søren, and I love him"! This is not to deny Kierkegaard's participation in the collective sin of patriarchy, but it is to restore my relation with him.

Notes

1. *Søren Kierkegaard's Journals and Papers*, Vol. 4, ed. and trans. Howard and Edna Hong (Bloomington, IN: Indiana University Press, 1975), pp. 572–85.
2. Mary Daly, "The Qualitative Leap Beyond Patriarchal Religion," *Quest* 1, no. 4 (Spring 1975): 20–40. Reprinted in *Women and Values*, ed. Marilyn Pearsall (Belmont, CA: Wadsworth, 1986), pp. 198–210.
3. Mary Daly, *Gyn/Ecology: The Metaethics of Radical Feminism* (Boston, MA: Beacon, 1978), p. 27.
4. Mary Daly, *Pure Lust: Elemental Feminist Philosophy* (Boston, MA: Beacon, 1984), p. 198.
5. In another place and time I would want to call attention to aspects of Kierkegaard (such as much of his imagery) that prophetically affirm women's experience. I would argue as well that Kierkegaard himself is a key source of the catalytic vision expressed in Daly's early works, which themselves are the "springboards" of virtually all of the rich varieties of contemporary religious feminism in the United States. While Daly herself uses Kierkegaard only as a negative foil for the development of her thought, Tillich and Buber were constructively used in the early works in which she challenged women to have existential "courage to see" their nonbeing within patriarchy and to begin the task of becoming themselves through the choice of freedom, thus refusing to be sheer objects within male-defined processes.
6. Søren Kierkegaard, *Works of Love*, trans. Howard Hong and Edna Hong (New York: Harper & Row, 1962), p. 199 (hereafter abbreviated WOL).
7. *Journals and Papers*, Vol. 5, especially numbers 6131 (VIII A 640), 6133 (VIII A 645), 6135 (VIII A 650), pp. 443–447.
8. See, for example, Louis Mackey, *Kierkegaard: A Kind of Poet* (Philadelphia, PA: University of Pennsylvania Press, 1971), pp. 203, 225, 235ff; Gregor Malantschuk, *Kierkegaard's Thought*, ed. and trans. Howard V. Hong and Edna H. Hong (Princeton, NJ: Princeton University Press, 1971), pp. 303ff; Mark C. Taylor, Kierkegaard's *Pseudonymous Authorship* (Princeton, NJ: Princeton University Press, 1975), p. 325; *Journeys to Selfhood: Hegel & Kierkegaard* (Berkeley, CA: University of California, 1980), p. 257; and Reidar Thomte, *Kierkegaard's Philosophy of Religion* (Princeton, NJ: Princeton University Press, 1948), p. 182. My article, "Kierkegaard's Existential Dialectic: The Temporal Becoming of the Self," *Journal of Religious Thought* 38, no. 1 (Spring-Summer 1981): 20–41, was developed some years before its publication, prior to my knowledge of all of these concurring interpretations except that by Thomte.
9. See, for example, Mackey, *Kierkegaard*, p. 243; and Taylor, *Journeys to Selfhood*, p. 257 (including footnote).

10. Søren Kierkegaard, *The Sickness unto Death*, ed. and trans. Howard V. Hong and Edna H. Hong (Princeton, NJ: Princeton University Press, 1980), pp. 113*ff* (hereafter abbreviated SUD).
11. Mary Daly, *Beyond God the Father* (Boston, MA: Beacon, 1973), p. 60*ff*.
12. WOL, p. 263.
13. See the conclusion to Louise Carroll Keeley's article in this volume, in which she emphasizes the outward thrust of genuine love as a "Reduplication."
14. WOL, p. 264.
15. Ibid., p. 268.
16. Ibid., p. 273.
17. Ibid., p. 274.
18. Ibid., p. 275.
19. Ibid., p. 168. Note that Carol Gilligan claims in *In A Different Voice* (Cambridge, MA: Harvard University Press, 1982) that the characteristic mark of female ethical thinking found in her research is a preeminent interest in preserving human connectedness.
20. WOL, p. 156.
21. See, for example, Henning Fenger, *Kierkegaard, The Myths and Their Origins* (New Haven, CT: Yale University Press, 1980), especially pp. 62–80, for a summary of various views of Kierkegaard as pathological.
22. WOL, pp. 308ff.
23. Ibid., p. 309.
24. Ibid., p. 310.
25. Ibid.
26. Ibid.
27. For example, WOL, pp. 310 and 262.
28. WOL, p. 345.
29. Mackey, *Kierkegaard*, pp. 223–25; and Malantschuk, *Kierkegaard's Thought*, pp. 242*ff*.
30. Søren Kierkegaard, *Fear and Trembling* in *Kierkegaard's Writings*, vol. 6, ed. and trans. Howard V. Hong and Edna H. Hong (Princeton, NJ: Princeton University Press, 1983), p. 77.
31. WOL, p. 344.
32. *Fear and Trembling*, p. 13
33. SUD, p. 49.
34. Ibid., pp. 113–24.
35. Ibid., p. 113.
36. Ibid., p. 115.
37. Ibid., p. 130.
38. Ibid., p. 125.
39. Ibid., pp. 125, 127.
40. Ibid., pp. 126, 122.
41. Ibid., p. 122.
42. WOL, p. 274.
43. Ibid., p. 345.
44. Once more here we encounter the emphasis on "outwardness" that Merold Westphal sees as characteristic of what he calls religiousness C. See p. 123, this volume.
45. WOL, p. 345.
46. Ibid., pp. 348–49.

47. Ibid., p. 345.
48. Ibid., p. 352.
49. Ibid., p. 351.
50. Ibid., p. 153.
51. Ibid., pp. 261, 262.
52. Martin Buber, *I and Thou* (New York: Scribner's, 1958), p. 35.
53. To exemplify both of these questions for forgiveness see, for example, The Amanecida Collective, *Revolutionary Forgiveness: Feminist Reflections on Nicaragua* (Maryknoll, NY: Orbis, 1987). Compiled for the collective by Carter Heyward and Anne Gilson, this book came to my attention after this paper had taken shape. It was gratifying to find confirmation of my focus upon forgiveness in these feminists. Very significant is the fact that this focus in their case derived from direct experience of enacted forgiveness on the part of the Nicaraguan people as well as in the policies of the Sandinista government. The book's analysis offers many parallels to what I am calling desentimentalized forgiveness.
54. Carol P. Christ and Judith Plaskow, *Womanspirit Rising: A Feminist Reader in Religion* (San Francisco, CA: Harper and Row, 1979), p. 10.
55. It may be that feminist theology is more explicitly divided over the possibility of forgiveness than other liberation theologies because most heterosexual women cannot subjectively appropriate the possibility of separatism rather than restored relations. In addition, while separation from the oppressors through identification with the heritage of one's ethnically defined culture is a possible ideal for many African Americans and Native Americans, an isolatable women's culture lacks a heritage and seems utopian.
56. See Elizabeth Schussler Fiorenza, "Feminist Spirituality, Christian Identity, and Catholic Vision," in Christ and Plaskow, *Womanspirit Rising*, pp. 136–48.
57. Rosemary Radford Ruether has authored about 23 books. On this point see, for example, *Sexism and God-Talk* (Boston, MA: Beacon, 1983).
58. Ruether, *Sexism and God-Talk*, p. 18.
59. Ibid., pp. 183–92.
60. Ibid., p. 184.
61. Schussler Fiorenza, "Feminist Spirituality," p. 137.
62. Ibid., p. 145.
63. Rosemary Radford Ruether, "Contemporary Catholicism: Crisis and Challenges," *Conscience* 8 (January/February 1987): 7–9.
64. SUD, p. 30.
65. See above, note 42.
66. See my use of Kierkegaard in Wanda Warren Berry, "Images of Sin and Salvation in Feminist Theology," *Anglican Theological Review* 60 (1978):25–54.
67. This kind of distinction between "power-from-within" and "power-over" has become common in feminist religious thought. See, for example, Starhawk, *Dreaming the Dark* (Boston, MA: Beacon, 1982).
68. This does not require that they assert that revelatory moment imperialistically for all. See, for example, Rosemary Radford Ruether, *To Change the World* (New York: Crossroad, 1981), p. 43.
69. Søren Kierkegaard, *Attack upon "Christendom,"* trans. Walter Lowrie (Princeton, NJ: Princeton University Press, 1968), pp. 32–33.
70. See above, note 46, and WOL, p. 349.

13 Toward a Kierkegaardian Understanding of Hitler, Stalin, and the Cold War

CHARLES BELLINGER

> He came to his own home, and his own people received him not.
> John 1:11

Søren Kierkegaard is widely acknowledged today as one of the most insightful philosophical and religious thinkers of western history. Although he was ignored in the nineteenth century, he has become a widely read, if not widely understood, contributor to twentieth century intellectual life. Can he assist us in our ongoing attempt to understand the large-scale political violence of our age—the wars, persecutions, and holocausts that have made the twentieth century the bloodiest in history? I believe that he can, and it is my purpose in this paper to suggest the way in which his thought helps us to understand the basic motives that impel human beings to violence. In this task I will draw on *The Concept of Anxiety [Dread]*, *Philosophical Fragments*, and *The Sickness unto Death*. A brief discussion of these works will lay the groundwork for subsequent comments on Nazism, Stalinism, and the East-West conflict. In the concluding section, the theory of violence implicit in Kierkegaard's thought will be compared with the contributions of Carl Jung, Ernest Becker, Alice Miller, and René Girard. Throughout I will be arguing that Kierkegaard's insights into the roots of violence grow out of his distinctive interpretation of the Christian doctrine of creation.

In the first chapter of *The Concept of Anxiety* Kierkegaard is at pains to make the point that Adam and Eve must not be placed "fantastically on the outside" of human history. That is, there is no essential difference between their spiritual situation and ours. The key to the spiritual situation of Adam and Eve and all their descendants is the concept of anxiety, which Kierkegaard describes as "a sympathetic antipathy and an antipathetic sympathy."[1] The following passage from the *Journals* relates to this expression:

> The nature of original sin has often been explained, and still a primary category has been lacking—it is anxiety; this is the essential determinant.

> Anxiety is a desire for what one fears, a sympathetic antipathy; anxiety is an alien power which grips the individual, and yet one cannot tear himself free from it and does not want to, for one fears, but what he fears he desires.[2]

What is it that we both fear and desire, at the most basic level? It is freedom, possibility, the future.

> I must point out that [anxiety] is altogether different from fear and similar concepts that refer to something definite, whereas anxiety is freedom's actuality as the possibility of possibility. For this reason, anxiety is not found in the beast, precisely because by nature the beast is not qualified as spirit.[3]

That which we simultaneously fear and desire, that which awakens anxiety in us, is not a "thing" in the external world, but—possibility. This possibility that we both fear and desire is the possibility of our own spiritual transformation. That is, the roots of anxiety are to be found in the spiritual relationship between human beings and their Creator, which excludes us from the immediately determined world of nature and throws us into our own world, a world in which our deepest, most primitive relationship is to the possibilities inherent within our own developing beings. Anxiety arises within us when we both fear and desire the spiritual transformation we must undergo as beings who are coming into being. That which we both fear and desire is our own creation.

The subtle but profound change Kierkegaard is accomplishing in *The Concept of Anxiety* is a shift away from thinking of creation in the past tense to thinking of creation in the present tense.[4] Instead of looking backward through human history to find the *origin* of sin in Adam and Eve's disobedience, Kierkegaard is teaching us to look inward (within ourselves) and upward (to God) to find the origin of sin in our own individual flight, in anxiety, away from *our origin*, God the Creator.

Through every man's sin, sin comes into the world; that is, through every individual's failure to respond in faith to the creative Word of God, the sin of Adam and Eve is repeated once again. Kierkegaard defends himself against the apparently Pelagian implications of this thought by stressing that even though each individual sins through his own disobedience (sin is not a category of necessity), nevertheless, in this act of disobedience he reveals his solidarity with Adam and Eve and all other persons in history, who together make up the collective human race which, in Adam, stands guilty before God. Because every individual is at the same time himself and the race, the solidarity of sin is inescapable, even though the leap into sin is made by the individual without external compulsion. For Kierkegaard there is no "solution" to this paradox, other than the greater paradox of the God-man, who, without ever making the leap into sin, became sin for us, that is, accepted his human solidarity with us, so that in him we might be reconciled with God through the Atonement. The underlying theological dynamic here is the sovereign act of creation that brings human beings into being as God's children in spite of their anxiety, disobedience, and guilt.[5]

In *Philosophical Fragments*, which was published in 1844 along with *The Concept of Anxiety*, this same dynamic of creation is presented from a different angle. In *Fragments* the Christian doctrines of sin, the Incarnation, and redemption are contrasted with the Socratic doctrine of recollection. Essentially, this is a clash between a world-view that is grounded in an ongoing gracious act of creation and one that presumes a static order of reality from which the individual has become estranged through ignorance and to which he may return through recollection and self-knowledge. In the Socratic doctrine there is no true sin, there is only the mist of ignorance that is dispelled by the discovery of the truth within oneself; there is no true Savior, because the identity of the midwife is inconsequential; there is no true moment in time, because the moment of self-awareness is swallowed up by the recollection of the eternal truth. In the Christian doctrine, on the other hand, sin is presented in its starkest reality as an act of rebellion against the Creator which throws the individual into a bondage from which he cannot save himself; the only hope for the individual lies in the coming into time of God himself, so that the individual may be given both the truth and the ability to receive it, which he has forfeited through his own fault; thus the moment in time in which God came to us in person acquires an eternal significance, and the moment in time in which the individual is met by this God-man and becomes contemporaneous with him also acquires an eternal significance. This eternal significance, this meaning that transcends all human meanings, is the sovereign act of creation through which God speaks to us and brings us into being, an act which is completely "over our heads," beyond our powers of rational understanding.

> —In *the moment*, a person becomes aware that he was born, for his previous state, to which he is not to appeal, was indeed one of "not to be." In *the moment*, he becomes aware of the rebirth, for his previous state was indeed one of "not to be." If his previous state had been one of "to be," then under no circumstances would the moment have acquired decisive significance for him, as explained above. Whereas the Greek pathos focuses on recollection, the pathos of our project focuses on the moment, and no wonder, for is it not an exceedingly pathos-filled matter to come into existence from the state of "not to be"?[6]

In *The Sickness unto Death* Kierkegaard describes the self that is coming into being as a synthesis of paradoxical elements: the infinite and the finite, the temporal and the eternal, freedom and necessity. The self is constituted by this synthesis, which he calls a "relation that relates itself to itself." But a self is not a static, given entity; a self is a potentiality. There are two sides to this potentiality; on the divine side there is the creative call of God, and on the human side there is the response to this call—either willing to be oneself or not willing to be oneself. Kierkegaard's formula for the state of the self when despair is absent is this: "in relating itself to itself and in willing to be itself, the self rests transparently in the power that established it."[7] This is the formulation of the ideal relationship between the infinite creator and the finite creature.[8]

But as is only too obvious, this ideal relationship is not seen in the life of individuals and the life of the nations they make up.[9] Human beings do not will to be their self before God; they evade the Word of God that is calling them into being and fall into despair. Despair is sin, which is understood by Kierkegaard to be active avoidance of the possibility of being a self constituted by the coming together of the infinite and the finite, the temporal and the eternal, freedom and necessity.

If I may use a simile, responding to the call of God, the call of creation, is like walking up a narrow mountain ridge that drops off steeply on either side. The way of willing to be oneself before God keeps one moving forward on the ridge. Sin, on the other hand, is falling off to one side or the other of the ridge. Kierkegaard spends much of the first half of the book describing the various forms of despair that result from falling off to one side or the other. His section titles are: "Infinitude's Despair Is to Lack Finitude," "Necessity's Despair Is to Lack Possibility," "Despair Over the Earthly or Over Something Earthly," "Despair Over the Eternal or Over Oneself," and so on. For Kierkegaard the self that God is calling into being is a synthesis of these paradoxical elements. The way of faith is the way of allowing these paradoxical elements to come together within one's being. To be in despair is to not allow the synthesis to come together.

As we shift from a focus on Kierkegaard's writings in themselves to their application to contemporary life, we must draw on the concept of the spheres of existence, in connection with the fourth chapter of *The Concept of Anxiety*.[10] In this chapter Kierkegaard speaks of anxiety before the good and anxiety before the evil. Anxiety before the good is the category he uses to interpret the demoniacs in the gospels. While he does not explicitly refer to the Pharisees in this context, it seems clear that the category of anxiety before the evil is an allusion to the particular form of offense the Pharisees manifested. These two character types represent the extreme, pathological forms of the aesthetic and ethical spheres of existence. In this dialectic we see once again what I have described as falling off to one side or the other of the ridge of human existence before God.

The essence of the demoniac mode of existence is anxiety before the good, shrinking back from the redemption that God offers in the person of Jesus Christ. The demoniac is afraid of the future, that is, he is afraid to allow God to transform and re-create him. He tries to hide from God's voice because he is afraid that this voice is out to undo and "destroy" him. He prefers the unfreedom of closed-upness (*Indesluttethed*) to the expansive world of freedom and communication. In this state, the appearance of freedom before the demoniac, that is, the appearance of Christ, can only awaken anxiety once again. The demoniac becomes anxious when he hears the call of creation, spoken to him through the incarnate Word. In Kierkegaard's words:

> The demonic is *closed-upness and the involuntarily revealed*. These two definitions indicate, as they should, the same thing, because closed-upness is precisely the mute, and when it is to express itself, this must take place against its will, as the freedom which is the ground underlying unfreedom revolts upon entering into communication with the freedom without; it now betrays unfreedom, and the individual betrays himself against his will in anxiety. . . . The demonic does not close itself up with something, but closes itself up, and in this lies the profundity of existence, that unfreedom makes a prisoner precisely of itself. Freedom is constantly communicating (even if we consider the religious meaning of the word [i.e., communion], no harm is done), unfreedom becomes more and more closed-up and wants no communication. . . . Closed-upness is precisely the mute; language, the word, is precisely that which saves, that which saves from the closed-upness of empty abstraction. . . . A demoniac in the N.T. says therefore to Christ, when he approaches: τί ἐμοὶ καὶ σοί [What have I to do with you? (Mark 5:7; Luke 8:28)]; he continues that Christ has come to destroy him (anxiety before the good). Or the demoniac begs Christ to go another way.[11]

Adolf Hitler's life reveals anxiety before the good in its ultimate demonic extreme. The demoniac fears above all else the possibility of becoming that self which God is calling him to become. He thus desires above all else to be in complete control of his environment. He must be like God in order to prevent himself from being changed by God. The social form this spiritual panic takes is a deification of the nation-state of which one is a part, creating a sacred "nest" that protects one from the voice of God. The social group that is made up of people who are "in untruth"—who are fleeing from God—aesthetically idolizes itself in its attempt to hide from God. A charismatic leader can exploit this untruth very easily.

The crowd is untruth. Hence none has more contempt for what it is to be a man than they who make it their profession to lead the crowd. . . . For it is not so great a trick to win the crowd. All that is needed is some talent, a certain dose of falsehood, and a little acquaintance with human passions.[12]

The demoniac is afraid of the future and wants to keep it away; the essence of Pharisaism, on the other hand, is a dissociation of oneself from the sinful past in an anxious movement into "repentance." Anxiety before the good switches over to anxiety before the evil as the individual seeks to create his own world of "righteousness," separate from the "lost" world of the "sinners." But he is just as closed-up and unfree as the demoniac because he is still evading the Word of God, which is calling him into being as a synthesis of temporal creatureliness and eternal spirit.

In the century and a half since Kierkegaard's time the world has witnessed the eruption into history of a fervent political form of ethical Pharisaism. I am referring to the appearance of Marxism and the subsequent polarization of the world between the revolutionary impulse and the conservative reaction against it.

In Kierkegaardian terms, Karl Marx is a classic example of the ethical sphere of existence. Marx became profoundly alienated from the "aesthetic" milieu in which he found himself, which was a scene of misery for millions of workers, while a few business owners reaped huge profits. Marx rebelled against this exploitation and began to develop in his mind a vision for an alternative social order in which all exploitation would disappear.

The key to the ethical sphere of existence is confidence in humanity's ability to bring the good into existence in time. The person who has entered into this sphere begins to believe that this good has come into being in his own existence and in the existence of others who have begun to think and act as he does. Those who have not entered into this new sphere of ethical existence, those who continue to be trapped by the past, are seen by the revolutionaries as the enemies of this good that is coming into being in time. A sharp moral dichotomy is drawn between *we* who are for justice, peace, equality, and *they* who are the "capitalists," "reactionaries," "imperialists." *We* are good and *they* are evil.[13] The following quotation from Lenin evokes very clearly this dichotomizing outlook:

> Thousands of practical forms and methods of accounting and controlling the rich, the rogues and the idlers should be devised and put to a practical test by the communes themselves, by small units in town and country. Variety is a guarantee of vitality here, a pledge of success in achieving the single common aim—to cleanse the land of Russia of all sorts of harmful insects, of crook-fleas, of bedbugs—the rich, and so on and so forth. In one place half a score of rich, a dozen crooks, half a dozen workers who shirk their work . . . will be put in prison. In another place they will be put to cleaning latrines. In a third place they will be provided

with "yellow tickets" after they have served their time, so that all the people shall have them under surveillance, as *harmful* persons, until they reform. In a fourth place, one out of every ten idlers will be shot on the spot. In a fifth place mixed methods may be adopted, and by probational release, for example, the rich, the bourgeois intellectuals, the crooks and hooligans who are corrigible will be given an opportunity to reform quickly. The more variety there will be, the better and richer will be our general experience, the more certain and more rapid will be the success of socialism, and the easier will it be for practice to devise—for only practice can devise—the *best* methods and means of struggle.[14]

The revolutionary is one who cuts himself off from the sinful past of the human race in a movement of "repentance" that leads to the setting up of another closed-up, unfree sphere of existence.

Kierkegaard's understanding of personality as a synthesis of opposing elements leads us to understand the concept of scapegoating in dialectical terms, in relation to the spheres of existence into which humanity divides itself.

For those who inhabit the aesthetic sphere of existence, such as the Nazis, the creating Word of God continually brings the possibility of redemption and new life. This possibility is feared and is struggled against (*Mein Kampf*). The demoniac personality attempts to fight off the possibility of its "destruction" by finding scapegoats and destroying *them*. In other words, the scapegoat is an unconscious symbolization of the self the individual is called to become. *For those who live in the aesthetic sphere, the scapegoat is the "shadow" of the future.* The Nazis killed the Jews because they were panic-stricken before the redemptive future into which God was calling them.

The sphere of existence opened up by Marxism is a mirror image of Nazism. Here, the scapegoat that is killed is the symbol of the sinful past that has been left behind in the wake of the righteous revolution. The scapegoat now represents the egocentric, backward, "aesthetic" being who is responsible for the alienated condition of society. The revolutionary has escaped from this "bourgeois" sphere of existence and now turns against it with a vengeance, separating himself from it completely. *For those who inhabit the ethical sphere of existence, the scapegoat is the "shadow" of the past.* In this we can see the "anxiety before the evil" that signifies once again the human avoidance of becoming a self, a paradoxical synthesis. Stalin's purges were a working out of the inner dynamic of this form of flight from God.

There is a sense in which World War II has not yet come to an end.[15] The struggle between Nazism and Stalinism that was set up at that time has continued on in the form of the struggle between the capitalist West and the communist East, the so-called Cold War. In Kierkegaardian terms this is a struggle between the aesthetic and the ethical spheres of existence. In the violent polarity that has developed between the eastern and western blocs we see the way in which people fall off to one side or the other of the dialectic of human existence. Each person is being called by God to become a synthesis of the temporal and the eternal, the finite and the infinite, necessity and freedom, the past and future, and yet it is possible for us to reject this call and prevent the synthesis from coming together within our existence. We thus become estranged from ourselves and enter into a battle with the other side of the dialectic, from which we have alienated ourselves. We battle against the shadow of the future or against the shadow of the past, turning our fellow human beings into the embodiment of that against which we are struggling. We either try to kill the "new Adam" we are called to become or we try to kill the sinful "old Adam" from which we are attempting to escape. In either case, we are preventing the coming together of the synthesis that constitutes true human personality.

From the point of view we have been developing it becomes apparent that the citizens of the United States and the Soviet Union need each other in order to play out their despair; they need to have a scapegoat against which to battle in order to fortify their precarious sphere of existence. This is the central fact that lies at the root of the insanity of nuclear weapons. The magnitude of our weapons is a measure of the magnitude of our fear of being brought into being by God.

It is due chiefly to the influence of Carl Jung that the idea of the "projection of the shadow" has entered into popular consciousness.[16] My use of the world "shadow" in this paper is in a sense an echo of Jung, but unlike him I do not see the shadow as one among various elements which make up the psyche. I see the shadow as a possibility of being that is held at bay by the individual who is trying to avoid becoming the self that God is creating. The shadow is oneself, changed by the hearing of the Word of God. A Jungian reading this paper might say that what I have referred to as recognizing one's own sinfulness is essentially what Jung meant by the "withdrawal of the projection of the shadow." I have no objection to this comparison, but the question that needs to be asked is: "How does this withdrawal come about?" Is it a matter of a person simply deciding to stop hating his enemy? Is it a matter of a psychotherapist meeting with a person once a week for five years? Is it a matter of reading a book by Jung or Neumann and thinking about it? For Kierkegaard the recognition of one's sinfulness is only made possible by the reality of God's judgment; it is not an autonomous human possibility. If Kierkegaard were here today, he might say that instead of speaking of "the unconscious" we should speak of that of which we are not conscious, because of our closed-upness. We are not conscious of the God who brings us into being as he forgives our sins and calls us to enter into the new creation.

In relation to Kierkegaard's thought, Ernest Becker's theory of scapegoating is interesting but seriously flawed. In *The Denial of Death* and *Escape from Evil* Becker tries unsuccessfully to force Kierkegaard's thought into the mold of his own theory.[17] He argues that the "mainspring of human behavior" is the fear of death, and he seeks to explain all human culture on this basis. But his main blind spot in relationship to Kierkegaard was his inability to see that, for Kierkegaard, the individual exists before the living God, who is calling him into fullness of life. Sin, for Kierkegaard, is avoidance of this call; in other words, sin is the denial of life, fear of creation, flight from God. Becker never took this essential theological basis of Kierkegaard's thought seriously, which left him fixated on the individual's relationship with his own physical death.

In *For Your Own Good: Hidden Cruelty in Child-Rearing and the Roots of Violence*, Alice Miller argues that all violent actions of adults, whether self-destructive or destructive of others, are the result of some form of neglect or abuse they suffered as a child. In her words, "every act of cruelty, no matter how brutal and shocking, has traceable antecedents in its perpetrator's past."[18] Instead of looking primarily toward the past, Kierkegaard's thought leads us to find the roots of violence in the violent person's evasion of the call of God, the call of the future. Miller remains limited to the web of human relationships and does not acknowledge the theological dimension of human existence. In the language of *The Concept of Anxiety*, she only sees the "quantitative determinations" of sinfulness in human history, without seeing the "qualitative leap into sin," which is human evasion of God in the present moment in time. She sees victims everywhere, but no sinners, no willful defiance of God. Her thought is analogous to the Marxist mythology that identifies evil with the bourgeoisie, the past, and identifies good with the proletariat, the future; Miller identifies evil with the parents and good with the children. But the human condition cannot be divided up so simply; the buck must stop being passed at some point. The doctrine of sin must be grounded in the real, active sin of each individual, instead of being watered down and lost in a universal haze of repetitious victimage that absolves everyone of responsibility (even Adolf Hitler!).

Among the various attempts to understand political violence of which I am aware, René Girard's is the most impressive and thought-provoking.[19] His writings are justly described as having an epochal place in social science, and in general I find myself in agreement with his theses, to the extent that I can grasp them. My criticism of Girard is, however, that he is stronger in "social psychology" than in "individual psychology"; that is, his sociological edifice seems to lack the understanding of individual motivation I have been attempting to articulate in this paper. Kierkegaard's dictum, "the crowd is untruth," is the perfect epigraph for Girard's work, but an understanding of the "untruthfulness" of the individuals who make up the crowd is only vaguely presented there, in the presupposition of a "desire" that drives the mechanism of mimeticism. In the end it seems that Girard's doctrine of sin is essentially Socratic: sin is ignorance, unconsciousness of the scapegoat mechanism. For a deeper understanding of sin we must turn to Kierkegaard. From him we can learn that the "social crisis" that is resolved through the "scapegoat mechanism" is in reality the crisis of human existence before God, the crisis of creation. Sin is flight from the possibility of new creation.

In fairness to Girard, I must say that he realizes very clearly that the key to the whole problem is found in the Prologue of John, but he writes in the genre of sociological theory rather than the genre of theology, which prevents him from speaking as freely as he might of the Incarnation of the Word of God in human history. The central point of the preceding criticisms of these four thinkers is that it is not possible to understand human violence without acknowledging that human beings are addressed by the Word of God and live their lives in reaction to this Word. I believe that Girard would agree with this statement.

In this chapter I have argued that Kierkegaard's thought helps us to understand the basic motivations that impel human beings to violence. This insight Kierkegaard has into the human condition is not simply a product of his own genius; his source of knowledge is the New Testament. Everything he knows about humanity comes from his lifelong attempt to understand the meaning of Christ's life, teachings, and death.

Christ is the creating Word of God. As such, he speaks the message humanity cannot bear to hear in its attempt to flee from its own creation. This message is a paradoxical call to the individual—a call "forward" into fullness of life as a child of God and a call "backward" into a true awareness of one's sin. The gift of forgiveness brings new life and hope as it opens up the individual to God's future, but at the same time forgiveness brings with it the sorrow of confession and repentance. The person who is brought into being by Christ must live in this tension, without trying to escape from it.

That we do in fact try to escape from this tension is the most obvious fact in the modern world, for those who have eyes to see. Speaking very generally, we can see that the capitalist sphere manifests "anxiety before the good," a rejection of the call to move forward into the kingdom of God, while the communist sphere manifests "anxiety before the evil," a rejection of the call to confess one's own guilty participation in the sinfulness of humanity. In this sense the East-West conflict unwittingly bears witnesses to the world-creating message spoken by Jesus Christ, the Word of God.

AFTERWORD (1990)

The chapter you have just read was presented at a conference in 1988 and revised in the following months. Since that time the remarkable events that have occurred in Eastern Europe and the Soviet Union, which can be called a "thawing" of the Cold War, have made some of the sentences in the paper sound a bit dated. In this connection, I have three brief comments to add: (1) The heart of the paper is an attempt to use Kierkegaard's thought as a help in understanding certain momentous events in twentieth century history —the Holocaust, Stalin's purges, and the nuclear arms race. These events have occurred; they have become a permanent part of human history. If there is any validity in the way in which I have applied Kierkegaard's thought to the task of understanding these events, that validity will not be lost due to the occurrence of any other events later on in history. (2) I did not say, and did not mean to imply, that the Cold War would continue on indefinitely. To the extent that the Cold War has indeed "thawed" (in the Eastern bloc, if not in China), that is a sign that individuals in both the East and the West have become less fearful (less anxiety dominated) and more open to change (more open to the process of creation). Once again, that does not invalidate anything that was said in the chapter, but is in fact the sort of change that was implicitly hoped for in it. Neither the present author nor Kierkegaard is a determinist with regard to the future. (3) I believe that there is a value in allowing this piece of writing to stand intact as an artifact of the year in which it was written. If it so happens that 10 or 20 or 50 years from now all nuclear weapons have been abolished, a few of the persons who grow up in that post-nuclear era may read this essay at some point in their lives and glean from it a feeling for what it was like to live under the threat of global nuclear war. Of course, there is a wealth of other writing they could read to similar effect, but this one is rather unusual in being a piece of Kierkegaard scholarship.

As a final note, even if 50 or a 100 years from now all armies have been abolished (or if they haven't), there will still be an ongoing debate between advocates of differing social philosophies. If this debate is still being carried on by those whose interpretation of human existence is distorted by what I have called falling off to one side or the other of the ridge, this essay will still be as relevant then as it is today, although the tone of urgency in which it was written will indeed be dated. That Kierkegaard's thought is an important contribution to the debates over social and political philosophy is my firm belief, as against those who would dismiss such an idea with a wave of the hand and a chuckle. When social and political thought is distilled to its essence, it always returns to the problem of understanding human nature, human psychology, the human condition. In this realm, those who wave off Kierkegaard do so at the risk of their own intellectual stultification (which is precisely what the Master of Irony expected to happen). It is my hope that at least a few persons will see in Kierkegaard not an impossible "individualist" but a profound visionary of the actualities and potentialities of human community.

Notes

1. *The Concept of Anxiety*, trans. Reidar Thomte (Princeton, NJ: Princeton University Press, 1980), p. 42.
2. *The Journals and Papers of Søren Kierkegaard*, trans. Howard V. Hong and Edna H. Hong (Bloomington, IN: Indiana University Press, 1967–1978), vol. 1, entry 94.
3. *Anxiety*, p. 42.
4. Stephen Crites gives a strikingly similar analysis of divine creation as something to be understood in terms of creative possibilities. See p. 154 in this volume.
5. The theme that the doctrine of creation is fundamental to Kierkegaard's understanding of human life and relationship is also prominent in the chapters by Michael Plekon and George Connell in this volume.
6. *Philosophical Fragments*, trans. Howard V. Hong and Edna H. Hong (Princeton, NJ: Princeton University Press, 1985), p. 21.
7. *The Sickness unto Death*, trans. Howard V. Hong and Edna H. Hong (Princeton, NJ: Princeton University Press, 1983), p. 14.
8. Compare Stephen Crites' account of the self-synthesis on pp. 149–58 in this volume.
9. Notice how naturally this analysis is extended from individuals to nations, confirming Crites' argument on p. 150.
10. For an introduction to the spheres, see Gregor Malantschuk, *Kierkegaard's Way to the Truth*, trans. Mary Michelsen (Minneapolis, MN: Augsburg, 1963).
11. My translation. Cf. *Anxiety*, pp. 123–24.
12. *The Point of View for My Work As an Author*, trans. Walter Lowrie (New York: Harper & Row, 1962), pp. 113, 115. I have found an extraordinary quotation from Franklin Roosevelt that bears directly on the subject of this essay. It is found in a book by Frances Perkins, *The Roosevelt I Knew* (New York: The Viking Press, 1946), p. 148. Perkins describes how during World War II Roosevelt became acquainted with a young Kierkegaard scholar named Howard A. Johnson, who encouraged the President to read some of Kierkegaard's writings. Roosevelt did so (apparently he read at least *The Concept of Dread*), and Perkins recounts a conversation with him that went as follows:

> Some weeks later I happened to be reporting to Roosevelt on problems concerning the War Labor Board. He was looking at me, nodding his head, and, I thought, following my report, but suddenly he interrupted me. "Frances, have you ever read Kierkegaard?"
>
> "Very little—mostly reviews of his writings."
>
> "Well, you ought to read him," he said with enthusiasm. "It will teach you something."
>
> I thought perhaps he meant it would teach me something about the War Labor Board.
>
> "It will teach you about the Nazis," he said. "Kierkegaard explains the

Nazis to me as nothing else ever has. I have never been able to make out why people who are obviously human beings could behave like that. They are human, yet they behave like demons. Kierkegaard gives you an understanding of what it is in man that makes it possible for these Germans to be so evil. This fellow, Johnson, over at St. John's, knows a lot about Kierkegaard and his theories. You'd better read him."

13. Of course Marxists by no means have a monopoly on this kind of dichotomous thinking; all of us tend to think that "God must be on our side."
14. *The Lenin Anthology*, ed. Robert C. Tucker (New York: W. W. Norton, 1975), pp. 431–32.
15. Perhaps the recent events in Eastern Europe mean it has finally ended. See the Afterword to this essay.
16. See "After the Catastrophe," in *The Collected Works of Carl Jung*, vol. 10, *Civilization in Transition*, trans. R. F. C. Hull (London: Routledge and Kegan Paul, 1964); *The Undiscovered Self*, trans. Eugene Rolfe (New York: Mentor Books, 1957); and Erich Neumann, *Depth Psychology and a New Ethic*, trans. Eugene Rolfe (New York: Putnam's Sons, 1969).
17. See *The Denial of Death* (New York: The Free Press, 1973); *Escape from Evil* (New York: The Free Press, 1975); and "Heroics of Everyday Life," in *Voices and Visions*, ed. Sam Keen (New York: Harper and Row, 1974).
18. *For Your Own Good*, trans. Hildegarde and Hunter Hannum (New York: Farrar, Straus, and Giroux, 1984), p. ix.
19. See *Violence and the Sacred*, trans. Patrick Gregory (Baltimore, MD: Johns Hopkins University Press, 1977); *Things Hidden Since the Foundation of the World*, trans. Stephen Bann and Michael Meteer (Stanford, CA: Stanford University Press, 1987); and *The Scapegoat*, trans. Yvonne Freccero (Baltimore, MD: Johns Hopkins University Press, 1986).

Index

A, xv, 60, 62, 134; experiments, 61; and Judge William, 57, 66
Abraham, xiii; absurdity and, 72; as exception, 48; and Isaac, 35, 41, 71–93, 113, 115, 123, 202–3; and Ishmael, 163, 178; and Job, xiii, 34, 35, 37–50; as knight of faith, 34, 114, 131, 133, 135; ordeal of, xiv, 38–40, 45, 49, 52, 71–73; and paradox, 38–39, 41; silence of, 39–40, 44; and sin, 46
absolute: God as, 78; and individual, 79, 86; and relativity, 112, 173; and self, xiv–xv, xvii, 80; and society, xvii; subjectivity as, 97; and universal, 79
absurdity, the absurd, 49; Abraham and, 72; and Christ, 48; double movement by virtue of, 41–42; faith and, 41–42, 83, 84; and rationality, 34; and scripture, 50; and understanding, 42–43
acosmism, viii, xvi, 32, 96–98, 104; ethical, xv
action: and forgiveness, 207, 209–10; and knowledge, 119; and love, 101
actuality: and ethical, 47; and future, 101; and sin, 47
Adler, Adolph, xii, 19, 20, 22, 24–29; as genius or apostle, 26, 27; Hegelianism of, 24–25; inwardness of, 24–25; and revelation, 24
admirer: vs. follower, 114, 121, 124
admission, 173, 174
Adorno, 183
aesthetics, the aesthetic, aesthete, 24, 208, 224; Don Juan, Faust, and, 135; and ethics, 44, 47–48, 58, 62, 112–13, 221–22; Friedrich Schlegel as, 56; and irony, 133; and sin, 47–48; teleological suspension of, 112
Agamemnon: and Iphigenia, 44

Agnes: and the merman, 44
alienation, 166, 225
Ambrose, 3
Anti-Climacus, Johannes, xviii–xix, 28, 144–49, 154, 204; champions individual, 151, 152; and Climacus, 146; as physician, 147; as unique pseudonym, 146–48, 151–52
anti-Semitism, 208
anxiety, 228; before evil, 221; and freedom, 219; before good, 221–22; and original sin, 218–19; and possibility, 219
apostle(s): Adler as, 26, 27; and authority, 28; and eternity, 26; flogging of, xvi, 110, 123–24; and genius, 20, 23, 28, 116; and presence of God, 27
appropriation, 212
Aquinas, St. Thomas, 197
Aristotle: *Poetics*, 44; *Politics*, 44
association: and politics, 170, 176
atheism: honest, 174
atonement, 33
Auden, W. H., 131, 137
Augustine, 112
authenticity: and reduplication, 23
authority, xi, 18–29, 172; and apostle, 28; and authoritarianism, 18; and choice, 63, 65; and Christianity, 21; and doctrine, 22; ecclesiastical, 19; and faith, xii–xiii, 18–19, 27, 29; and false prophets, xii; and freedom, 63; and genius and apostle, 23; and God's presence, xiv, xxii, 27, 29; and God-relationship, 27–28; human vs. divine, 20–23, 29; and obligation, 56, 65, 67; and policeman, 23; and rationality, 20–21; and revelation, 22, 23, 24, 26–29; and scripture, 18, 22; and single individual, 22; and task, 19; and teacher, 23; without, 19, 29

authorship: aesthetic, 132; ethical, 97; first and second, xv, xvii, 19, 29, 34, 67, 167; polemical, 214; pseudonymous, xv, 34, 110–11, 114, 116, 123, 145–46; religious, xv, 97, 110–11, 114, 145–46; as whole, 110
autonomy, 116; and ethics, 62
awakening, 23, 24
Axel: and Valborg, 44

Bakunin, 187
Balle, Bishop, *Lærebog i den Evangeliske-christelige Religion*, xiv, 67
baptism, 7, 8, 13
Barth, Karl, 3, 18
Becker, Ernest, 218; *Denial of Death*, 226; *Escape from Evil*, 226
belief: and knowledge, 118; in nothing or everything, 101
Bellinger, Charles, "Toward a Kierkegaardian Understanding of Hitler, Stalin, and the Cold War," xx, 218–30
Berry, Wanda Warren, xix; "Finally Forgiveness: Kierkegaard as a 'Springboard' for a Feminist Theology of Reform," 196–217
betrothal: and love, 35
Bonhoeffer, Dietrich, 3, 13
bourgeoisie, 165
Buber, Martin, 197; "The Question of the Single One," vii–ix
Bultmann, 18

calculation, 168; and politics, 185
capitalism: and individual, xix
causation: God and, 153–54
Cavell, 74, 76
Cervantes, Miguel de: as humorist and ironist, 133, 134; *Don Quixote*, 130–33
character: and choosing to be ethical, 57–58; and volition, 58–59
choice, choosing: and authority, 63, 65; and character, 57–58; and creation, 64; despair, 60; ethical, 57, 60–62; and existence, 64; free, 58; and inclination, 59; and obedience, 66; and obligation, 61, 64–65; of oneself, 60–61, 64–65, 66; and reason, 59; and resolution, 61, 62; and thanksgiving, 66; and will, 59

Christ: and absurd, 48; authority of, 21, 22; being like, 2; contemporaneity with, 178; crucified and risen, 13; and Don Quixote, xviii, 130, 131–32; as God-man, 12; humanity of, 12; imitating, 4–5, 6, 12, 116–17, 119, 121, 125, 126, 185; and love, 12; as paradox, 115, 117, 119, 125; as pattern, 115, 116; pays taxes, 171, 186; and reason, 87; as redeemer, 9; as way, 13. *See also* Jesus
Christendom, vii, 119, 120, 121, 124, 214; and honest atheism, 174; and Christianity, xviii, 4, 24, 25, 28, 137, 139–40, 171, 172–74, 178, 203; individual in, 137, 140, 176; in present age, 168–69; and Religiousness B, 116
Christian(s), xvi; becoming, 113, 116, 125, 173; being, 146–47; and doubt, 134; religious, xii–xiii; in world, 138, 140
Christianity, xii; and asceticism, 138; and authority, 21; bargain, 122; bourgeois, 183; and Christendom, xviii, 4, 24, 25, 28, 137, 139–40, 168–69, 171, 172–74, 178, 203; and cosmism, 98; dismissing, 204; and doubt, 21; and erotic love, 100; and established order, xvi, 31; and ethics, 98; and friendship, 100; and ideal, 147, 174; as incommensurable with externality, xvi; and individual, 174, 175; inwardness of, 6–7, 170; and irrationality, xviii; and love for God, 11; and maturity, 173; and offense, 23, 203; playing at, 11; and politics, 170–71, 174; and reason, 116; and revelation, 26; and social movements, 188–89; as spirit, 171; as subjective, xvi, 8, 125–26, 190; understanding of, 20; and world, 6–7, 134
Christology, 8
Chrysostom, John, 3
church, xi; attack on, xvii; 3–4, 6, 8, 11, 12, 13–14, 137, 138–39, 172, 174–76, 185; God and, 12; militant, 117; people's, 172, 175; and state, 175, 185; theologian and, 3;

triumphant, 117, 124
clergy, 172–73; attack on, 14; oratory of, 121
Climacus, Johannes, xii, xvi, 4, 46–47, 49, 77–78, 113, 115, 119, 125, 133, 136, 145; and Anti-Climacus, 146
close reserve, ix
closed-upness, 222
Cold War, 218, 224–25, 228
comedy, the comic, 132; and contradiction, 133, 136, 137; and tragic, 136
communalism, ix
communication: direct, 114; on faith, xii; human, xiii; indirect, 29, 35, 44, 47–49, 133
communism, 166–67, 188, 189, 227; as humanism, 166
community, x; and ethics, xiii; and faith, xiii, 154–55; and forgiveness, 208, 211, 213; humans and, 12; and individual, xiii, 14, 104, 154–55, 166, 206, 207, 210–11, 214, 229; and individualism, 11–12; and religious commitment, x. *See also* society; world
comparison: and love, 101
Concept of Anxiety, 46, 49, 152, 218
Concept of Irony, xvii, 133
Concluding Unscientific Postscript, vii, xvi, xvii, 3, 4, 12, 28, 46, 49, 77, 79, 81, 102, 110, 113, 115, 123, 136, 137
confusion: of present day, 173, 174, 176
congregation: knowing, 172–73
Connell, George, xiv, xvi; "Judge William's Theonomous Ethics," 56–70
conscience: and God-relationship, 100; and love, 99–100
consciousness: and self-consciousness, 111
conservatism: and individual, 183
consistency: of ethical action, 59–60, 61
Constantius, Constantin, 33, 35, 36; as silent, 35
consumption: and production, 165
contemporaneity, 178; and offense, 116–18, 122, 124

contradiction, vii; and comic, 133, 136, 137
Corsair, 163, 168
Cortés, Donoso, 187
cosmism: and Christianity, 98
creation, creating: and choosing self, 64; and ethics, 67; God and, 8, 220; goodness of, xi, 6; openness to, 228; and sin, 227; vs. static order of reality, 220; and violence, 218
Crites, Stephen, xviii, xx; "*The Sickness unto Death*: A Social Interpretation," 144–60
Cross, 5, 7, 9, 11, 13, 14, 117, 185
crowd, 152, 188; leaders of, 222–23
culture: and individual, 157

Daly, Mary, 196, 209; *Gyn/Ecology*, 197; *Pure Lust*, 197
death: fear of, 226
debt: and giving, 101
deconstruction, xviii, xx, 144
defiance: men and, 213; and racism, 158; and weakness, 155
democracy, 183, 188, 189; and individual, xix
demoniacs: and anxiety before good, 221–22; fear future, 222; Hitler as, 222
Denmark: modernization of, xix; monarchies in, xvii
despair, xiv, xv, xviii; A, Judge William, and, 60; aesthetic existence and, 60; choosing, 60; collective, and society, 150–51, 152; and doubt, 30; and faith, 145, 146, 152, 153, 154, 203; and finitude, 150, 155; and forgiveness, 203–4; and freedom, 150–51, 152, 153; God and, 153–54, 155; and mass man, 150; and miracles, 158; and necessity, 156–57; and possibility, 153–54, 155, 156–57, 158; and racism, 158; and self, 155; as self-isolation, 155; and sin, 148, 152, 203–4
dialectic, the dialectical, 5, 144, 151; of existence, 29; experiential, 111; Hegelian, 111–13; and immediacy, 111–12
difference: qualitative, xvii, 67, 123, 204–5

Discourses at the Eucharist on Fridays, 6, 8, 13
doctrine: authority and, 22; teleological suspension of, 119
Dominic, 3
Don Juan, 133; and Leporello, 135
Don Quixote: death of, 139–40; female counterpart to, 134; as knight of faith, 131–32, 134–35; and Christ, xviii, 130, 131–32, 136–37; as Christian, 133–34, 136–39; as comic contradiction, xviii, 132, 133, 134, 137, 139, 140; and religious persecution, xviii; and Sancho Panza, 135, 138; and three stages of existence, 135–36
Dostoevsky, Fyodor, 119, 137
doubt: and Christians, 134; and despair, 30; and intelligence, 21
Dulcinea, 132, 135
Dunning, Stephen, "Who Sets the Task? Kierkegaard on Authority," xi, xiv, 18–32

Edifying Discourses, 6, 11
Edifying Discourses in Varying Spirits, 123
Either/Or, xvi, xvii, 35, 112, 134–35; *I*, 33, 56; *II*, xiv, 80
electoral process: and popular sovereignty, 162–63
Elrod, John, *Kierkegaard and Christendom*, ix
Elster, Jon, 84
Emerson, R. W., 76
enthusiasm, enthusiast, 136–37, 139, 165; and ironist, 167
envy: reflective, 168
equality: of individuals, 168, 187–88; and neighbor-love, 98, 192; social, 187–88
Eremita, Victor, 35
erotic love, 98, 113, 177; and Christianity, 100
established order, 90, 110, 114, 117, 125, 171; and Christianity, xvi, 31; individual in, 176, 178
esthetics. *See* aesthetics
eternity, the eternal, 169; apostle and, 26; and external, 171; and

forgiveness, 207, 209–10; modern society and, 171–72; and moment, 220; and self, 105; and temporal, 104–5
ethic(s), the ethical, x, 24, 26, 223–25; as accomplishment, 113; and actuality, 47; and aesthetics, 44, 47–48, 58, 62, 112–13, 221–22; and autonomy, 62; choosing to be, 57, 60–62; and Christianity, 98; and creation, 67; and community, xiii; and consistency, 59–60; and faith, xiii, 82–83; and God-relationship, 39, 40, 66–67; and Hegel, 25; and humor, 133; and individual, 39, 96; and irony, 133; and marriage, 62; and ordeal, 38–40, 48; and religious, xiv, 34, 113, 118, 188; and self, xiv–xv; and sin, xiii, 47–48, 66; and single individual, 39, 82–83; and society, 115; teleological suspension of, xiii, xiv, xv, xix, 38–40, 46, 47, 48, 66, 75, 78–79, 81, 82–83, 86–87, 89, 112–13, 114, 116, 201–3; theonomous, 57, 63–67; and universal, xiii, xiv, 56, 59; and world, xiv–xv, 96
Eucharist, 8, 13
Evagrios, 3; *On Prayer: One Hundred and Fifty-Three Texts*, 2
Evil: and fear, 102; and good, 57
exception: Abraham as, 48; Job as, 48
existence: aesthetic and ethical, 58; and choice, 64; human, and sociality, xviii; stages of, xx, 24, 56, 113–14, 133; as task, 65
expectation: and possibility, 101–2
experience: lived, 209; women's and men's, 197
experimentation: A and, 61, 62; Sancho Panza and, 62
exterior, the external, xvi; and eternal, 171; and internal, xvi, 25, 31, 104–5; and self, xv
faith, xi, 33, 43, 80, 120, 125, 201, 202; Anti-Climacus and, 146–47; Abraham, Job, and, 47–48; and absurd, 41–43, 83, 84; as achievement, 84; and authority, xii–xiii, 18–19, 27, 29; and border

conflicts, 34; and community, xiii, 154–55; compound attitude of, 72–74; and despair, 145, 146, 152, 153, 154, 203; double movement of, 42, 43; and ethics, xiii, 82–83; and finite, 42; and forgiveness, 84, 199, 205; and God, xiv; and God's presence, 28; and imagination, 155–56; and immediacy, 30, 42, 125; incognito of, xvi; and individual, 74, 82–83, 151–52, 154–55; knight of, xiii, xv, xvi, 41–42, 71–72, 74, 81, 82, 85–86, 131–32; and knowledge, 118–19; leap of, xii, 116, 118, 176; and material things, 75; objective expression of, xvi; and offense, 116; and ordeal, 38–40, 41, 44, 71, 75; and paradox, 42; and passion, vii; and possibility, 154, 155–56, 158; potentiated self and, 156; and rationality (reason), 21, 48, 134, 137, 186–87; and receptivity, 80, 83, 86; and repetition, 38–40, 44, 49–50; and resignation, 73, 84, 85; and responsibility, 18–19; and self, 75; and social morality, 82; and sociality, 151; and stories, 49–50; and subjectivity, 74; and suffering, xvi–xvii; as transcendent, 44; and uncertainty, 118; and universal, 75; and value, 76; and virtue, 83; and will, 84; and world, xiv, 72, 78
Fatherland, The, 138
Faust, 44; and Wagner, 135
Fear and Trembling, xiii, xiv, xvii, 3, 33–50, 66, 71–91, 131, 132, 135, 201, 202, 204
feminism: and offense, 199; as temporal, 198
fideism, 19, 21
finitude, the finite, 187, 189; and despair, 150, 155; and faith, 42; and infinite, 101, 155, 172, 176, 184, 191; and repetition, 50; and self, xv, xviii
Fiorenza, Elizabeth Schussler, 212
follower: vs. admirer, 114, 121, 124
For Self-Examination, 3, 114
forgiveness, 103, 227; and action, 207, 209–10; and community, 208, 211, 213; and despair, 203–4; and faith, 84, 199, 205; finality of, 198–99; and finitude and infinitude, 207; as ground of being, 206–7; and guilt, 200, 203; and knowledge of sin, 200–201; and love, 102, 199–201; misunderstanding of, 204; offended, offender, and, 203, 211; and offense, 199; in present age, 207–10; and racism, 209; and reconciliation, 200–201, 211; and reduplication, 205–6, 215; and relation, 200; and restoration, 207, 209–10, 212; and scapegoat, 199; self and, 198; and sentimentality, 201, 207, 209–10, 211, 214; and sin, 203–4; as teleological suspension of ethical, 201–3; as temporal, 197–98, 207, 209–10; who needs, 201; as work of love, 199, 200–201
Francis, 3
Frankfurt, Harry, 80
Frater Taciturnus, 135
freedom, 75, 80, 82; and authority, 63; and despair, 150–51, 152, 153; God and, 154; and guilt, 58; and individual, 97; and necessity, 56; and obedience, 58, 64, 113; and obligation, 65; and possibility, 154; and repetition, 37; and responsibility, 65; self and, 150–51, 152, 153, 154; of will, 59
French Revolution, 188, 189
friendship: and Christianity, 100; faithful, 200
future: and actuality, 101

Gadamer, xx
Gamaliel, 110
Gasset, Ortega y, 137
Gemeinschaft, 164, 165, 166, 167
genius: Adler as, 26, 27; and apostle, 20, 23, 28, 116
Gesellschaft, 164, 166, 167, 168, 170, 171, 172, 174, 176
gift, giving, the given: and indebtedness, 101; and task, 60, 65–66
Girard, René, 218, 226–27
Glenn, John D., Jr., 75, 82

God: as absolute, 78, 113; authority of, 172; being before, xiii, 99, 176–78, 184, 198, 203, 212, 226; being in wrong before, 43; and causation, 153–54; and church, 12; communion with, 3–4; and creation, 8; and despair, 153–54, 155; existence of, 76–78, 188; and faith, xiv, 28; freedom through, 63–64, 154; goodness of, 6–7; and humans, 10–11; icon of, 8; image of, 8–9, 10–11; and love, 2, 6–8, 99, 100, 201; nature of, 7; and obligation, 63; and offense, 115; as other, xiii, 76; and possibility, 153–54, 155, 157–58, 213; presence of, xii–xiii, xiv, xxii, 27, 28, 29; and repetition, 36; self and, 153, 154, 157–58; and society, 115; transcendence and immanence of, xi, xvii; triune character of, xi, 7; unchangingness of, 13; and world, xiv, xvii, 11

God-relationship, viii, x, xii, xiii, 2, 4–5, 6–7, 8–12, 13, 14, 29, 64, 202, 204, 206, 227; as absolute, 171; and conscience, 100; and creation, 220–21; and divine authority, 27–28; and ethical, 39, 40, 66–67; and freedom, 65; as motivation, 205; and ordeal, 40; and self-relation, 155; and single individual, 39, 172; as transcendent, 167

Goldschmidt, Meir Aaron, 163, 168

good and evil, 101–3, 226; choosing, as categories, 57

good: absolute, and individual, 76–78; and evil, 57; and hope, 102

government: by martyrs, 191–92; and single individual, 190-91

grace, 119–20, 121, 152

Gregory of Nyssa, 5

Grundtvig, N. S. F., ix, 185

guilt: and forgiveness, 200, 203; and freedom, 58

H. H., 19
Habermas, xx
Hagar, 163
Hamann, vii
Hannay, 73, 79, 82

Haufniensis, Vigilius, 46, 152
Hegel, G. W. F., ix, xvii, 25, 58, 72, 74, 86, 112, 113; Logic, 111; *Phenomenology*, 111; *Philosophy of Right*, 111
Hegelianism, vii, xvi, 24–25, 36–37, 90, 121
Heidegger, 66, 76
Hitler, Adolph, 192, 226; as demoniac, 222
Holocaust, 208, 228
honesty, 174–75; and sobriety, 173
Hong, Howard and Edna, 145
hope, 36; and love, 101–2
human being(s), humanity: and community, 12; as confused, 173; equality of, 192–93; essential, 79–81; fear of, 168, 188; and God, 10–11; loss of, 166; and nature, 166; and power, 184; redemption of, 166; as synthesis, 197
humility, humbleness, 27, 84–86, 116; and moral objectivity, 73; and value, 80
humor, 131, 133
Hus, 3

ideal(s), ideality, the ideal: and Christianity, 147, 174; and incarnation, 147; and reality, 132; and society, xviii
imagination: and faith, 155–56; and possibility, 155–56
immanence, xiii; God's, xiv; and transcendence, 20
immediacy, 117, 123; and dialectic, 111–12; faith and, 30, 42; and self, xiv; and universal, xiv; Young Man and, 66
incarnation, 6, 8, 33, 116, 147, 205. *See also* Christ; Jesus
inclination: and choice, 59; and reason, 59; and respect, 58–59
incognito, 88–89; of faith, xvi, 87; of integrity, xvi; of love, xvi
independence: and involvement, xv
Indesluttethed, ix
individual, viii; and absolute, 76–78, 79, 86–87; and authority, 22; in

Christendom, 137, 140, 176; and Christianity, 174, 175; and community, xiii, 14, 154–55, 166, 206, 207, 210–11, 214, 229; and culture, 157; and democracy and capitalism, xix; development of, 76, 80–83, 111–12, 208; and equality, 168; and ethical, 39, 96; and faith, 74, 82–83, 151–52, 154–55; and freedom, 97; and God-relationship, 39, 172; and mass man, 150; and original sin, 219; and other, 97, 150; and politics, 189, 190–91; and public, 177; and religious, xix, 184, 190–91; self-interested, 162–65, 166–68; and sin, 45–46, 152; single, xix; and society, viii, ix–x, xviii, xix, xx, 72, 74–75, 83, 113, 115, 130–32, 136–37, 139, 140, 151, 157, 161, 163, 171, 175–79, 226–27; and spirit, viii, 176; and state, xvii; and universal, xiii, 45–46, 74–75, 78, 79, 83; and value, 74–75, 83; and world, 97. *See also* self

individualism, individualist, vii; acosmic, xvi; asocial, ix, xv, xix, xx; and community, 11–12; and religion, 176, 177; self-interested, 168, 177, 178; and sociality, xi, 177–78

infinitude, the infinite, 189, 190; and finite, 101, 155, 172, 176, 184, 191

Instant (The Moment), 13

integrity, 75, 80; incognito of, xvi

intelligence: and doubt, 21

interest: and repetition, 37

interior, the internal: and external, xvi, 25, 31, 104–5

International Kierkegaard Commentary, ix

interpretation, 88

intoxication: and sobriety, 173

involvement: and independence, xv; in objective order, xvi; and separation, xv

inwardness, 97; Christianity and, 170; vs. outwardness, 123–25; and reality, 206; teleological suspension of, 123

irony, 49, 131, 133, 203; in present age, 167

irrationality, vii, ix, xxi, 20–21, 143; and Christianity, xviii; and rationality, xviii, 86

Ishmael, 161; and Abraham, 178; as self-interested individual, 163, 168, 177; and modern society, 163

Jacobi, vii
James, 5, 120
Jesus, 112; life of, xvii, 117; name of, 110. *See also* Christ
Job: and Abraham, xiii, 34, 35, 37–50; as exception, 48; and God's authority, 18; ordeal of, 40–41, 45, 49, 52; paradox and, 43; and repetition, 36, 37
Johannes the Seducer, 61, 136
John, 120
Judge for Yourself!, 3, 114
Judge William, ix, xiv, xv, 80, 133; and A, 57, 66; Kant and, 56–63, 67; and Pascal, 57
Jung, Carl, 218, 225
justice, 170; and love, 102
Juvenal, 62

Kafka, Franz, "Abraham," 131
Kant, Immanuel: as ethicist, 56–63, 67, 113; and Judge William, 56–63, 67; and Kierkegaard, 86–88; *Doctrine of Virtue*, 58; *Groundwork*, 58, 87; *Religion Within the Limits of Reason Alone*, 58
Kaufman, Gordon D., 18, 20
Kavanagh, Aidan, 4
Keeley, Louise Carroll, "Subjectivity and World in *Works of Love*," xv, xvi, 96–108
Kirmmse, Bruce: "Call Me Ishmael— Call Everybody Ishmael: Kierkegaard on the Coming-of-Age Crisis of Modern Times," 161–82; *Kierkegaard in Golden Age Denmark*, ix, xvii, xix
knight: of faith, xiii, xv, xvi, 41–42, 71–72, 74, 79, 81, 82, 85–86, 88–89; of infinite resignation, xiii, 41–42, 71–72, 74
knowledge: and action, 119; and faith, 118–19; and love, 101, 170; and mistrustfulness, 170

labor: division of, 165, 166
law: love and, 99–100; obedience to, is freedom, 58; and rationality, 170
Leibniz, 36
Lenin, 223
Lennox, Charlotte, *The Female Quixote*, 134
leveling, 136, 161, 167, 168, 176
liberalism, 175, 183
life views, 82
Locke, John, 161–64
Lonergan, Bernard, 3
love: and action, 101, 200; and belief, 101; and betrothal, 35; builds up, 101; Christ and, 12; Christianity and, 11, 202; and comparison, 101; conscience and, 99–100; covenant, 200; debt of, 100–101; divine, 9–10; duty to, 100; as eternal, 102, 103, 104–5; and familiarity, 63; and forgiveness, 102, 199–201; God and, 2, 6–8, 11, 99, 100, 201; and hope, 101–2; incognito of, xvi; inwardness of, 100–101, 102, 104; and justice, 102; and knowledge, 101, 170; law and, 99–100; mistrust and, 101; and neighbor, 10, 22, 98, 177, 192, 199; objective expression of, xvi; and other, 100; perseverance of, 100; possessive, 73; praising, 99; and rationality, 202; reduplication of, xv, 104–5; remembers one dead, 103; and self-denial, xv; and sin, 102, 199; subjectivity of works of, xv, 97, 98–104; and Trinity, 7–8; works of, xv, 7, 9–10, 96–106, 199; and world, 97, 104–5, 106
Löwith, 183
Lowrie, Walter, 114, 187
Lukács, 183
Luther, Martin, ix, 3, 5, 119, 120, 188
Lutheran Book of Worship, 4
Lutheranism, 119

Mackey, Louis, 201; "The Loss of the World in Kierkegaard's Ethics," xv, 96
majoritarianism, 170
Malantschuk, Gregor, 186, 201
man, men: and defiance, 213–14

market, 162–63; effects of, on individuals, 164–66, 167; as leveling force, 167, 188
marriage, 65; and ethics, 62
Martensen, Hans Lassen, 5, 121, 126
martyr(s), martyrdom, 12; government by, 191–92; and sacrifice, 192
Marx, Karl, 165–67, 224, 226; and Kierkegaard, 167, 173, 183; as Pharisee, 223–25; *Communist Manifesto*, 161
mass man, 150; politics and, 184
material things: and faith, 75; and politics, 170
maturity: and Christianity, 173
Maximus, 3
mediation, 111–12; and repetition, 36–37
Melanchthon, 3
Melville, Herman, *Moby Dick*, 161, 163, 178–79
mentality: philistine-bourgeois, 152, 169
mercifulness, 104; and world, 102
merman, 66, 201; and Agnes, 44
Merton, Thomas, 3
Michelet, vii
Miller, Alice, 218; *For Your Own Good: Hidden Cruelty in Child-Rearing and the Roots of Violence*, 226
mistrust: compared with love, 101
Mitchell, Basil, 18
modernity, xix
modesty: and immorality, 173
moment: and eternity, 220
monopoly, 163
Mooney, Edward, "Getting Isaac Back: Ordeals and Reconciliations in *Fear and Trembling*," xiv, xv, xvi, xix–xx, 71–95
moral(s), morality: as compromise, 115; conventional, 89–90; exceptions to, 75; knight of faith and, 79; and modesty, 173; and motivation, 86–87; social, 78–79, 82, 113; and uncertainty, 87–88; and will, 86
Moralität, 111
motivation: and morals, 86–87
movement: double, 41–42; and repetition, 36–37

mundanity: and mysticism, 191
Mynster, J. P., 5, 24, 121, 126, 185
mysticism: and mundanity, 191

nation(s): and stages of existence, xx
nationalism, 187; and demonic, 222
Nazi(s), Nazism, 192, 208, 218, 224
necessity: despair and, 156–57; freedom and, 56; and given self, 156–58; and possibility, 155, 156–57
neighbor(s), xix, 177, 178; and love, 10, 22, 98–99, 177, 189, 199–202
Nicoletti, Michele, xviii; "Politics and Religion in Kierkegaard's Thought: Secularization and the Martyr," xix, 183–95
Nordentoft, Kresten, xvi, 9; *Hvad Siger Brand Majoren? Kierkegaard's Opgør med sin Samtid*, ix
novelty: and repetition, 37

obedience: and choice, 66; as liberating, 58, 64, 113
objectivity, the objective, xvi, 119, 121; aesthetic and speculative, 118; moral, and humility, 73; overcoming, 124; and self, xv; and subjectivity, xvi, 25, 101, 118, 122
obligation(s), 61, 62, 208; and authority, 65, 67; and choice, 61, 64–65; communal, 202; and freedom, 65; God and, 63; moral, and authority, 56; and resolution, 61; and self, 66; and task, 66
"Of the Difference between a Genius and an Apostle," xi, 19
offense, 28, 83, 125, 201, 202; of Christianity, 23, 203; and contemporaneity, 116–18, 122, 124; and faith, 116; and feminism, 199; and forgiveness, 199; God and, 115; of loftiness and lowliness, 117; and society, 23
Olsen, Regine, viii, 132; and faith, 91
omnipotence, 66
On Authority and Revelation, xi, 19
optimism, incarnational, xii, 5, 7
ordeal(s): and ethical, 38–40, 48; and faith, 38–40, 41, 44, 71, 75, 84; and God-relationship, 40; and rationality,

40; and repetition, 38–40, 43, 44; and restoration, 72; and sin, 47, 48; stories as, 49; and time, 46, 47; as transcendent, 40; and understanding, 44
other(s): self and, xvii, 150, 153
outcome, 92, 162–63. *See also* result
outwardness: vs. inwardness, 123–25; of religious suffering, xvi

pantheism, 172
Panza, Sancho, 62; and Don Quixote, 135, 138
paradox, the paradoxical, 83; and Abraham, 38–39, 41; and aesthetic, 20; Christ as, 115, 117, 119, 125, 220; and faith, 42; and rationality, vii, xxi; and religious, 21; and revelation, xii, 27
parenthetical, the, 20
particular, the: and universal, 79, 87
Pascal, Blaise, 57
passion, 136–37; and faith, vii
patriarchy, xix
Pentecost, 7
Perkins, Robert, viii
persecution: religious, xviii
Peter, 110, 120, 200, 203
Peterson, Erick, *Zeuge der Wahrheit*, 192
Pharisees: and anxiety before evil, 221–22, 223
Philosophical Fragments, xvii, 3, 12, 49, 113, 218
philosophy: Greek, 36–37, 43; modern, 36–37, 43; speculative, 20, 25
Plato, 115; *Apology*, 121; *Gorgias*, 121
Plekon, Michael, "Kierkegaard the Theologian: The Roots of His Theology in *Works of Love*, x–xi, xii, xiii, xiv, xvi, 2–17
poet, poetry, the poetic: and prose, 132; and religious, 45; and repetition, 45
Point of View for My Work as an Author, viii
policeman: and authority, 23
politics, the political, x, 167; and association, 170, 176; and Christianity, 170–71, 174; as

diversion, 170; as everything, 186; as finite, xix, 189; and individual, 189, 190–91; proper sphere of, 170–71, 176, 186–87, 188; and reason, 186–87; as relative, xix; and religious, 173, 184–85, 186–88, 190–92; and result, 185; sacralization of, 187–89, 191–92; and temporality, 184–85; and truth, 170

popular sovereignty, 172, 189; and electoral process, 162–63

possibility: despair and, 153–54, 155, 158; and expectation, 101–2; and faith, 154, 155–56, 158; and freedom, 154; God and, 153–54, 155, 157–58, 213; and imagination, 155–56; and miracles, 158; and necessity, 155; self and, 155, 157–58

power, 184, 192

prayer, 154; and theologian, 2–3; trinitarian, 7–8

present age: Christendom in, 168–69; confusion of, 174, 176; forgiveness in, 207–10; individual in, 178–79; as negative, 167–68; as trial and opportunity, 169–79. *See also* society

production, 166; and consumption, 165

property, 162, 164, 166, 188

prophet(s): false, xii

prose: and poetry, 132

Proudhon, 187

pseudonyms, pseudonymity, xviii–xix, 145–47, 151–52; as poetic creations, 35–36

public, 168, 172, 188; and individual, 177

public opinion, 188

Purity of Heart Is to Will One Thing, 27, 29, 168

Quidam: as knight of unhappy love, 135–36

racism: and despair, 158; and forgiveness, 209

Rahner, Karl, 3

rationality, 74; and absurdity, 34; and authority, 20–21; and faith, 21, 48; and *Gesellschaft*, 166; and irrationality, xviii, 86; and law, 170; and love, 202; and ordeal, 40; and paradox, vii, xxi; and society, xviii. *See also* reason

reacceptance: and renunciation, xiv–xv

reality, the real: and ideal, 132; and inwardness, 206

reason: as absolute, 86, 186; and choice, 59; Christ and, 87; Christianity and, 116; as devil's work, 134; and enthusiasm, 136–37, 139; and faith, 134, 136–37, 186–87; and inclination, 59; and politics, 186–87; and repetition, 37; and revelation, 25–26. *See also* rationality

receptivity, reception, 76, 84; faith as, 80, 83, 86; and resignation, 74, 88–89

recollection, xii, 115, 116, 118; and recognition, 113; and repetition, 35, 36–37, 44–45

reconciliation: and forgiveness, 200–201, 211; with vanquished one, 103

redemption, 6, 8

reduplication, 24, 28; and authenticity, 23; and forgiveness, 205–6, 215; and love, 104–5

reflection: and representation, 189; working through, 169–70

reform: feminist, vs. revolution, 196, 209, 212–14; and individual, 190; as temporal, 197–98

Reformation, 14

relativity, the relative, 112, 173

religion, the religious, x–xi, 24, 35, 172; as absolute, xix; and ethical, xiv, 34, 113, 118, 188; and "how" of living, 185; and humor, 133; and individual, xix, 176, 177, 184, 190–91; as infinite, xix; and paradox, 21; and poet, 45; and politics, 173, 184–85, 186–88, 190–92; and repetition, 36–37, 45; and sin, 47; and sociality, 186; and state, xix

Religiousness A, 114, 115–19, 121–24; and Religiousness B, 113

Religiousness B, 205; and Religiousness A, 113; and Religiousness C, xvii, 115–26;

teleological suspension of, 114, 125–26
Religiousness C, 114, 142, 216; and Religiousness B, xvii, 116–19, 121–23, 125–26
renunciation: and reacceptance, xiv–xv
repentance: and sin, 45–46
Repetition, xiii, 33–50, 66; and *Either/Or*, 35
repetition, 35; and Christian existence, 33; and faith, 38–40, 44, 49–50; and finite, 50; and freedom, 37; and interest, 37; and Job, 36; meaning of, 45, 51; and mediation, 36–37; and movement, 36–37, and novelty, 37; and ordeal, 38–40, 43, 44; and poet, 45; and reason, 37; and recollection, 35, 36–37, 44–45; and religious, 36–37, 45; and restoration, 43; and sin, 48; stories and, 49–50; and transcendence, 37, 43, 46
requirement, 173, 174, 204
resignation: and faith, 73, 84, 85; knight of infinite, xiii, xv, 41–42, 71–72, 74; and reception, 74, 88–89; and value, 73
resolution(s), 63; and choice, 61, 62; and obligation, 61; and thanksgiving, 65; of will, 58
respect, 63; and inclination, 58–59
responsibility, 82; and faith, 18–19; freedom and, 65; for self, 60–61, 64, 65
restoration(s): of finitude, 192; and forgiveness, 200–201, 207, 209–10, 212, 214; of Isaac to Abraham, 41–43, 192; Job's, 42–43; ordeal and, 72; of reality, 192; and repetition, 43
result(s), xix, 101–2, 104, 185; and moral worth, 56. *See also* outcome
resurrection, 5, 7, 9, 13, 154
revelation(s), xii; and Adler, 24; and authority, 22, 23, 24, 26–29; and Christianity, 26; as paradoxical, xiii, 27; and reason, 25–26; and secrecy, 44
Richard III, 44
Richter, Jean Paul, 131
Romantics: in Germany, 131, 132–33, 139

Rousseau, 113
Ruether, Rosemary Radford, 209, 212, 214; *Sexism and God-Talk*, 210

sacraments, xi, 8
salvation, 166–67, 186–87
sanctification, 8, 9
Sarah, 44, 163
Satan: and ordeals, 52
Savonarola, 3
Scaevola, Mucius, 110
scapegoat, 224, 227; forgiveness and, 199
Schelling, 131
Schillebeeckx, Edward, 3
Schlegel, Friedrich, 131, 133: as aesthete, 56
Schmemann, Alexander, 3, 4, 11
Schmitt, Carl, 192
scholarship: biblical, 120
scripture(s), 8, 122; and absurd, 50; and authority, 18, 22
secrecy: and revelation, 44
secularism, secularization, 174, 175, 189, 190
self, selves: and absolute, xiv–xv, xvii, 80; authentic, viii; becoming, 79, 90, 198, 225; bound and unbound, 63; change in, 81, 228; choosing, 60, 61, 64–65, 66; collective and individual, 157; and community, 206; creation of, 219; and despair, 155; and eternal, 105; and ethics, xiv–xv, 82; and external, xv; and faith, 76; and finitude, xv, xviii, 189; and forgiveness, 198; and freedom, 150–51, 152, 153, 154, 212; as gift or given, 78, 86, 156–58, 156–57; and God, 153, 154, 157–58; and God-relationship, 155; and immediacy, xiv; interdependent, 85; misrelation of, 152, 153; and objective, xv; and obligation, 66; and other, xvii, 150, 153; and possibility, 155, 156–58; potentiated, 156–58; proto-, 80, 83, 90; receiving or receptive, 71, 75, 78, 84; relating to self, 148, 149–50, 152, 153, 220; responsibility for, 60–61, 64, 212; as social, 150; and society, xvii; and

spirit, xviii, 149, 150, 154, 155; as synthesis, xviii, 220–21, 224–25; and temporal, xvi; and universal, xiv; and value, 76; and will, 62; and world, xiv–xv, xx, 85, 90–91. *See also* individual
self-assessment, 88
self-consciousness: consciousness and, 111; critical, 85
self-denial: and love, xv
self-disinterestedness, 99
self-love, 98
self-renunciation, 100; and neighbor-love, 98–99
selfhood, 80, 81, 90, 204; ethical, xvi; and feminist reform, 210
separation: and involvement, xv
sexism: and Christianity, 212; in Kierkegaard, 158–59
shrewdness, 168–69
Sickness unto Death, xviii, xx, 3, 28, 49, 79, 81, 144–58, 201, 203, 218
Silentio, Johannes de, xii, xiii, xiv, xv, xvi, 33, 34, 35, 36, 67, 71–93, 114, 131; and Abraham and Job stories, 37–50
sin, 33, 66, 83, 220, 226; Abraham and, 46; and actuality, 47; and being before God, xiii; and despair, 148, 152, 203–4; and forgiveness, 203–4; knowledge of, 200–201; and love, 199; and ordeal, 47, 48; original, 219; as pride, 115; and religious, 47; and repentance, 45–46; and repetition, 48; and single individual, 45–46, 152; and suspension of ethical, xiii, 47, 48, 66; and universal, 45–46
Sittlichkeit, 111
Sløk, Johannes, xvi, 3; *Da Kierkegaard Tav: Fra Forfatterskab til Kirkestorm*, ix, xvii
Smith, Adam, 161–64, 165
sobriety: and honesty, 173; and intoxication, 173
sociability, human, ix
social pathologies, 150, 151, 157, 158
sociality, the social: Anti-Climacus denies, 152; faith and, 151; and human existence, xviii; and

individualism, xi; and politics, 170, 186
society: and absolute, xvii; amorality of, 162–63; bourgeois, 183; Christianity and, 174; and collective despair, 150–51, 152; and coming of age, 166, 172–73; and culture, 157; economic, 162; and eternal, 171–72; and ethics, 115; and God, 115; and ideals, xviii; and individual, viii, ix–x, xviii, xix, xx, 72, 74–75, 83, 113, 115, 130–32, 136–37, 139, 140, 151, 161, 163, 166–68, 171, 175–79, 226–27; and Ishmael, 163; and law, 165; modern, 161–63; modern vs. traditional, 164, 167–68; and morality, 165; and neighbor, 177; and offense, 23; political, 162; and rationality, xviii; relentlessness of modern, 161, 163, 164–67; and religion, 165, 184; and religious persecution, xviii; and self, xvii; and self-relation, 158. *See also* community; present age; world
sociopolitics, the sociopolitical, xvi
Socrates, 86, 121, 191–92
Solger, K. W. F., 133
spirit: Christianity as, 171; God as, 153; human being as, 149; and individual, viii, 176; and self-relating self, xviii, 149, 150, 154, 155; and spiritlessness, 152
spiritlessness, 168–69; and bourgeois philistinism, 169; and crowd, 152; and spirit, 152
springboard(s): rather than authorities, 197
stage(s): aesthetic, xx; ethical, xx; on life's way, 111–12; of personal development, 81, 82. *See also* existence, stages of; *individual stages*
Stages on Life's Way, 33, 135
Stalin, Stalinism, 218, 224, 228
state, 164; church and, 175, 185; and individual, xvii; political life of, xix; and religion, xix; and secularism, 175; and stages of existence, xx
stories: and faith, 49–50; as ordeals, 49; and repetition, 49–50
subjectivity, the subjective, 86, 116; as

absolute, 97; becoming, 79; Christianity and, xvi, 8, 125–26, 190; faith and, 74; and objectivity, xvi, 25, 101, 118, 122; and works of love, xv, 97, 98–104; and world, xv

success, 185

suffering, 154; apostle and, 28; faith and, xvi–xvii; for Gospel, 12; religious, vs. misfortune, 110, 122–24; outwardness of religious, xvi

synthesis: human as, 197, 220–21, 224, 225

System, vii

task(s), xiv; and authority, 19; existence as, 65; and given, 60, 65–66; of humans, 2, 29, 80, 81, 84, 90, 125; and obligation, 66; of selfhood, 204

Taylor, Charles, *Sources of the Self*, 77

Taylor, Mark C.: *Journeys to Selfhood*, viii–ix; *Kierkegaard's Pseudonymous Authorship*, viii–ix

Taylor, Mark Lloyd, "Ordeal and Repetition in Kierkegaard's Treatment of Abraham and Job," xiii, 33–53

teacher: and authority, 23

teleological suspension(s), 112–13. *See also* aesthetics; ethics; religion

temporality, the temporal: and forgiveness, 207, 209–10; and politics, 184–85, 187; and self, xvi

Tertullian, 18

thanksgiving, 84; choice and, 66; and resolution, 65

theologian: and church, 3, 181; and communion with God, 3–4; definition of, 2–4; negative, 20; and prayer, 2–3

theology(ies): affirmative, 12–13, 14; communal, 10–11; creation, 6–7; feminist, 196, 209; full, 11–13; incarnational, 8–9; liberation, 199, 208–9, 212–13; metaphorical, 198; practical, 9–10; as temporal, 198; trinitarian, 7–8

Thoreau, H. D., 76

Tieck, Ludwig, 131, 133

Tillich, Paul, 197

time, temporality, the temporal: and eternal, 104–5; forgiveness and, 197; and human existence, 197–98; and ordeal, 46; reform and, 197

Tobit, 44

Toftdahl, Hellmut, ix

Tönnies, Ferdinand, 164, 167

tradition: Christian, xi; as idol, token, and icon, 53

tragedy, the tragic; and comic, 136; and contradiction, 136

Training in Christianity (Practice in Christianity), 3, 13, 49, 90, 114, 125, 147

transcendence, xiii, 28, 113, 212; God's, xiv; and immanence, 20; and repetition, 37, 43, 46

trial, xiii; spiritual, 134

Trinity, 6, 11; and love, 7–8

truth, 115, 116, 117, 118; and learner, xii; and martyr, 191; and politics, 170; Socratic vs. Christian, 113

Two Ages: A Literary Review, 136, 161

Two Minor Ethico-Religious Treatises, 19

tyranny, 163; of fear of man, 168

Unamuno, Miguel de, 131, 137

uncertainty: faith and, 118; and morality, 87–88; and virtue, 81

unconditionedness, the unconditional, 139, 172

understanding: and absurd, 42–43; and ordeal, 44. *See also* rationality; reason

universal, the: and absolute, 79; and ethical, xiii, xiv, 56, 59; faith and, 75; immediacy and, xiv; and individual, xiii, 45–46, 74–75, 78, 79, 83; and particular, 79, 87; and self, xiv; and sin, 45–46; suspending and receiving, 76; and value, 74–75, 83

value(s), the valuable: and faith, 76; gift of, 76, 90; humility and, 80; and individual, 74–75, 83; and resignation, 73; and self, 76; and universal, 74–75, 83

violence, 226; and creation, 218; motivations to, 227

virtue(s): faith and, 83; personal, 75, 80–82, 84–85, 87; and uncertainty, 81
volition: character and, 58–59; ethical, 56; and moral worth, 56. *See also* will

weakness: and defiance, 155; women and, 213
Weil, Simone, 85
Wesley, 3
Westphal, Merold, xvi, xviii, xx; *Kierkegaard's Critique of Reason and Society*, ix, xvii; "Kierkegaard's Teleological Suspension of Religiousness B," 110–29
Whitehead, 197
will: choice and, 59; faith and, 84; freedom of, 59; and morality, 86; natural and rational, 164; as practical reason, 58; resolutions of, 58; and self, 62. *See also* volition
Wisdo, David, 85
woman (women): Kierkegaard on, 196, 197; as offended by Kierkegaard, xix; as oppressed, 209
Word of God: doers of, 121; as mirror, 120
Works of Love, xi, xiv, 2–17, 63, 96–106, 198–206
world: Christian in, 138; Christianity and, 6–7, 134; dying from, 12; dying to, 11; and ethics, xiv–xv, 96; and faith, xiv, 72, 78, 85–86, 88–89; and God, xiv, xvii, 11; and individual, 97, 190–91; and love, 97, 104–6; and mercifulness, 102; and self, xiv–xv, xx, 85, 90–91, and subjective, xv. *See also* community; society

Young Man, 34, 35, 36, 37, 66; and Abraham and Job stories, 37–50

Ziolkowski, Eric, xvi; "Don Quixote and Kierkegaard's Understanding of the Single Individual in Society," xviii, 130–43

About the Authors

THE EDITORS

George B. Connell teaches philosophy at Concordia College (Moorhead, Minnesota).

C. Stephen Evans teaches philosophy and directs the Hong Kierkegaard Library at St. Olaf College (Northfield, Minnesota).

OTHER CONTRIBUTING AUTHORS

Michael Plekon teaches sociology at Baruch College of the City University of New York, and is an ordained Lutheran minister.

Stephen N. Dunning teaches religion at the University of Pennsylvania (Philadelphia).

Mark Lloyd Taylor teaches religion at Seattle Pacific University (Seattle, Washington).

Edward Mooney teaches philosophy at Sonoma State University (Sonoma, California).

Louise Carroll Keeley teaches philosophy at Assumption College (Worcester, Massachusetts).

Merold Westphal teaches philosophy at Fordham University (New York).

Eric J. Ziolkowski teaches religion at Lafayette College (Easton, Pennsylvania).

Stephen Crites teaches religion at Wesleyan University (Middletown, Connecticut).

Bruce Kirmmse teaches history at Connecticut College (New London, Connecticut).

Michele Nicoletti has a position in the philosophy department at the University of Padua (Italy).

Wanda Warren Berry teaches in the department of philosophy and religion at Colgate University (Hamilton, New York).

Charles Bellinger is a graduate student in the department of religion at the University of Virginia (Charlottesville).